RENEWALS 458-4574
DATE DUE

GAYLORD

EXPLAINING GROWTH IN THE MIDDLE EAST

CONTRIBUTIONS TO ECONOMIC ANALYSIS

278

Honorary Editors:
D.W. JORGENSON
J. TINBERGEN[†]

Editors:
B. BALTAGI
E. SADKA
D. WILDASIN

ELSEVIER

Amsterdam – Boston – Heidelberg – London – New York – Oxford – Paris
San Diego – San Francisco – Singapore – Sydney – Tokyo

EXPLAINING GROWTH IN THE MIDDLE EAST

Edited by

Jeffrey B. Nugent
University of Southern California, USA

M. Hashem Pesaran
University of Cambridge, UK

ELSEVIER

Amsterdam – Boston – Heidelberg – London – New York – Oxford – Paris
San Diego – San Francisco – Singapore – Sydney – Tokyo

Elsevier
Radarweg 29, PO Box 211, 1000 AE Amsterdam, The Netherlands
The Boulevard, Langford Lane, Kidlington, Oxford OX5 1GB, UK

First edition 2007

Library of Congress Cataloguing-in-Publication Data
A catalog record for this book is available from the Library of Congress

British Library Cataloguing in Publication Data
A catalogue record for this book is available from the British Library

ISBN-13: 978-0-444-52240-5
ISBN-10: 0-444-52240-9
ISSN: 0573-8555

For information on all Elsevier publications
visit our website at books.elsevier.com

Printed and bound in The Netherlands

07 08 09 10 11   10 9 8 7 6 5 4 3 2 1

Working together to grow
libraries in developing countries

www.elsevier.com | www.bookaid.org | www.sabre.org

ELSEVIER   BOOK AID
            International   Sabre Foundation

INTRODUCTION TO THE SERIES

This series consists of a number of hitherto unpublished studies, which are introduced by the editors in the belief that they represent fresh contributions to economic science.

The term 'economic analysis' as used in the title of the series has been adopted because it covers both the activities of the theoretical economist and the research worker.

Although the analytical method used by the various contributors are not the same, they are nevertheless conditioned by the common origin of their studies, namely theoretical problems encountered in practical research. Since for this reason, business cycle research and national accounting, research work on behalf of economic policy, and problems of planning are the main sources of the subjects dealt with, they necessarily determine the manner of approach adopted by the authors. Their methods tend to be 'practical' in the sense of not being too far remote from application to actual economic conditions. In addition, they are quantitative.

It is the hope of the editors that the publication of these studies will help to stimulate the exchange of scientific information and to reinforce international cooperation in the field of economics.

The Editors

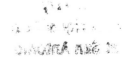

PREFACE

This book is about the Middle East and North Africa (MENA) region. This region is generally perceived as having experienced the most disappointing growth performance over the last couple of decades among all regions in the world with the possible exception of Sub-Sahara, Africa. Despite the region's immense endowment of natural resources, its *per capita* income is often viewed as having stagnated. At the same time, most economies of the region have been characterized by extremely high volatility, a condition only partly attributable to the fluctuating price of oil.

Another motive for writing about the MENA region is that it has been far less studied and researched than the other regions of developing countries such as Latin America, East Asia, South Asia, and Sub-Sahara, Africa. Much of what has been written about the region is confined to the country level or to a specific aspect of the economy such as agriculture, finance, trade, or poverty. Moreover, seldom has any of these themes or aspects of the economy been treated comprehensively.

A third motive, and one closely related to the other two, is the prominence of the MENA region in the global energy markets and the world political system. Countries in the MENA region are in the international headlines virtually on a daily basis. The topics of interest are wide ranging and diverse, ranging from dictatorships, civil wars, terrorism, and water shortages, to more economic problems arising from volatile oil prices, barriers to trade and foreign investment, dominance of public enterprises, and low-skill work forces. Many of these are interdependent and are collectively worthy of explanation.

For all these reasons, we feel that a comprehensive treatment of the factors responsible for the relatively poor performance of the countries in the MENA region would be needed. This is especially true at this critical juncture of the economic and political development of the region and the important implications thereof for growth and growth policies in other parts of the world. A comprehensive treatment should combine micro-level as well as macro-level analyses. It should also make ample use of comparisons between MENA and the other regions, within the MENA region itself, and the two comparisons over time, especially in cases where policy and institutional orientations have changed over time.

Since the MENA region is subject to a rather unique and volatile combination of common factors such as oil, religion, poor governance, and substantial migration flows, the volume provides the reader with a better understanding of how these factors have interacted with initial conditions and with each other to explain variations in growth and development patterns across the MENA countries and over time. Quite naturally, there is greater focus on these rather unique factors than might appear in similar studies of the other regions.

The book is meant for a wide readership and to the extent possible technical details have been deliberately kept to the bare minimum. It ought to be of interest to economists of all persuasions, and for the most part should be accessible to non-economists with special interest in the economics of the MENA region. In virtually every chapter of the book there is considerable emphasis on policies and institutions, and it is, therefore, also hoped that the book will be of interest to policy makers in the MENA and other regions.

The raw material and idea for the book originated in a very ambitious project compiled by the Economic Research Forum (ERF), a network of scholars, practitioners, and policy makers interested in the MENA region. ERF has counterparts in other regions, for example, LACEA in Latin America and the Caribbean and AERC in Africa. As with the other networks, the ERF has been supported by numerous agencies, bilateral donors, regional financial institutions, and international institutions such as the UNDP and the World Bank.

The specific ERF project, which made this book possible was sponsored by the Global Development Network (GDN) which links the various regional networks mentioned above. Various researchers (both individuals and teams) were selected by the ERF specifically for the GDN-sponsored project. Different researchers were commissioned to write papers on various aspects of the development process in the region, both country-specific as well as thematic contributions relevant to the region as a whole. Each of the resulting papers was presented and discussed formally at a conference organized by the ERF. All these papers, with a few exceptions, were submitted to us to be considered for publication. In addition to these papers, we also commissioned a paper on Turkey which was not covered by the ERF–GDN initiative.

All the submitted papers were then reviewed again by at least two referees and subsequently assessed by us. The authors of those papers considered for publication in this volume were then requested to revise their papers in line with the comments of the referees and editors. The resulting re-submissions were eventually refereed again and in most cases a third time. Inevitably, this meant that some papers could not be included in the volume and that the review and revision process for those included has been rather long and protracted.

We wish to express our deep appreciation to all the referees, internal to the group (i.e., authors of the contributed papers) as well as external to it. The external referees included Agnes Benassy, Mongi Boughzala, Nauro Campos, Merih Celasun, Mine Cinar, Christopher Clague, Ali Darrat, Panicos Demetriades, Matthias Doepke, Alpay Filiztekin, Dipak Gupta, Hassan Hakimian, Andrew Horowitz, Hyeok Jeong, Magda Kandil, Taher Kanaan, Massoud Karshenas, Andrew Mason, Hamid Mohtadi, Mokhtar Metwally, Jennifer

Olmsted, Serdar Sayan, Edward Sayre, Paul Schultz, Ajit Singh, John Strauss, T.G. Srinivasan, Erol Taymaz, Jonathan Temple, Insan Tunali, and Tarik Yousef. We are grateful to all the referees for their help on each draft, in many cases having to operate under very severe time constraints. Their comments have contributed substantially to the final form and character of the volume. Above all, we wish to thank the authors for their patience and willingness to revise and re-submit their papers despite their own hectic schedules. We also appreciate the authors' willingness to modify their papers so that they would fit together in a more coherent whole. Finally, we would not have been able to communicate with the authors and referees and keep track of the status of each paper, without the help of the ERF Secretariat, its Directors (first, Heba Handoussa and more recently, Samir Radwan), and our assistant Julia Murkin in Cambridge.

Jeffrey Nugent and Hashem Pesaran
May 2006

CONTENTS

CHAPTER 10   THE POLITICAL ECONOMY OF
            DEVELOPMENT POLICY IN TUNISIA   307
            Mohamed Z. Bechri and Sonia Naccache

List of Contributors

Ragui Assaad

Population Council, West Asia and North Africa Office, Cairo, Egypt, and Humphrey Institute of Public Affairs, University of Minnesota, USA

Mohamed Z. Bechri

Professor of Economics, Faculty of Law and Economics, Sousse, Tunisia

Mohamed Abdelbasset Chemingui

United Nations Economic Commission for Africa Trade, Finances and Economic Development Division, P.O. Box 3001, Addis Ababa, Ethiopia

Adam B. Elhiraika

Economic and Social Policy Division, United Nations Economic Commission for Africa, POB 3005 Addis Ababa, Ethiopia

Moataz Mostafa El-Said

Fiscal Affairs Department, International Monetary Fund, 700 19th Street, N.W. Washington, DC 20431, USA

Hasan Ersel

Faculty Arts and Social Sciences, Sabanci University, Orhanli, 81474, Tuzla, Istanbul, Turkey

Hadi Salehi Esfahani

210 David Kinely Hall, 1407 W. Gregory Dr. Urbana, IL 61801, USA

Zeki Fattah

UN ESCWA, Beirut, Lebanon, Riad El Solh SQ., Beirut, Lebanon

Annas H. Hamed

Abu Dhabi Fund for Development, Abu Dhabi, UAE

Ahmad R. Jalali-Naini

The Institute for Management and Planning Studies, Tehran, Iran

Magda Kandil

International Monetary Fund, IMF Institute, HQ2, 4-899, 700 Nineteenth St., Washington, DC 20431, USA

Hanaa Kheir-El-Din	Department of Economics, Faculty of Economics and Political Science, Giza, Egypt
Imed Limam	The Arab Fund for Economic and Social Development, P.O. Box 21923, Safat 13080, Kuwait
Samir Makdisi	American University of Beirut, Nicely 316, Bliss Street, Beirut 1107 2020, Lebanon
Tarek Abdelfattah Moursi	Department of Economics, Faculty of Economics and Political Science, Giza, Egypt
Sonia Naccache	Faculty of Economics and Management, Tunis, Tunisia
Jeffrey B. Nugent	USC Department of Economics, University Park Campus, University of Southern California, Los Angeles, CA 90089-0253, USA
Kıvılcım Metin Özcan	Department of Economics, Bilkent University, Bilkent 06800, Ankara, Turkey
Ümit Özlale	TOBB University of Economics and Technology, Department of Economics, Söğütözü 06560, Ankara, Turkey
M. Hashem Pesaran	Faculty of Economics, Sidgwick Avanue, Cambridge CB3 9DD, UK
Christopher A. Pissarides	Department of Economics, London School of Economics, Houghton Street, London WC2A 2AE, UK
Djavad Salehi-Isfahani	Department of Economics, Virginia Polytechnic Institute and State University, Blaksburg, VA 24061, USA
Çağrı Sarıkaya	The Central Bank of The Republic of Turkey, Research and Monetary Policy Department, Istiklal Caddesi No 10, Ulus 06100, Ankara, Turkey
Marie Ange Véganzonès-Varoudakis	CERDI, CNRS, Université d'Auvergne, 65 Boulevard Francois Mitterand, 63 000 Clermont Ferrand, France

CHAPTER 1

Introduction: Explaining Growth in the Middle East

Jeffrey B. Nugent* and M. Hashem Pesaran

Keywords: Middle East, North Africa, economic growth, oil, institutions, policy choices

JEL classifications: O1, O4, O53, E00

1. Coverage of the book

The Middle East and North Africa (MENA) region, in its broadest sense, is defined as the 21 Arabic-speaking countries of the League of Arab States[1] plus Iran and Turkey. Despite its geographical location, Israel is normally not included in the region on the grounds that it is a highly developed country and as such is usually included by the World Bank and other international agencies in Europe (along with Cyprus and Malta).

While the MENA region has been the subject of a large literature on terrorism, religion, oil, governance, international political relations and economic history, compared to other regions, comprehensive studies of economic growth in the MENA region are very few and tend to focus on individual

---

*Corresponding author.

[1] The 22 Arabic-speaking members of the League of Arab States are Algeria, Bahrain, Comoros, Djibouti, Egypt, Iraq, Jordan, Kuwait, Lebanon, Libya, Mauritania, Morocco, Oman, Qatar, Palestinian Territories, Saudi Arabia, Somalia, Sudan, Syria, Tunisia, UAE and Yemen. Eritrea is an observer in the organization and hence is often included in the definition of the region. Because they are extremely small in size, have little reliable statistics, and in some cases have been subject to so much fighting as to make it hard to describe them as nation states, Comoros, Djibouti, Eritrea, Somalia and to a lesser extent Mauritania are often excluded (as they are for the most part in this volume). Another reason for their exclusion is that most of these countries are often classified as being in Sub-Sahara Africa.

CONTRIBUTIONS TO ECONOMIC ANALYSIS
VOLUME 278   ISSN: 0573-8555
DOI:10.1016/S0573-8555(06)78001-4

countries rather the region as a whole. The purpose of this book is to fill this gap by providing a relatively comprehensive overview of the growth experience of the MENA region as a whole as well as that of important individual countries in the region. It covers different aspects of the growth process, such as growth of different sectors, population growth and patterns of demographic change, integration of the MENA countries within the global economy and it addresses the different sources of growth, i.e., the accumulation of factors (labor and capital), technological change and institutional factors. Particular attention will also be paid to the cross-country comparisons of growth rates and their volatilities and the various factors that might be responsible for their evolution.

The countries in the MENA region share a number of common features, but also differ in a number of important respects. They vary in geographic size, population density, endowment of cultivable land, access to international markets, oil and other natural resources, income and wealth, ethnic, religious and language diversity, vulnerability to civil and international wars and other conflicts, governance types and qualities and policy orientations. Despite these differences, the MENA countries, with varying degrees, have been subject to common effects of the Arab–Israeli conflicts, the Iran–Iraq war, the Gulf war, the recent invasion of Iraq, the volatility of oil prices, the rise of Islamic fundamentalism and the geopolitical considerations that are largely governed by the desire of the industrialized countries (and more recently, the emerging market economies) to have access to the Middle East oil and gas resources. Many of these factors are addressed in this volume, with different authors discussing the subset of factors deemed to be the most relevant to the economies or issues that they investigate.

In addition to the traditional proximate drivers of economic growth, namely accumulation of factor input and technological progress, the papers in this volume also emphasize some of the fundamental determinants of growth such as geography, institutions, ethnicity and cultural heritage as important primary factors in the growth process. The importance of geography, institutions and ethnicity as root causes of observed persistent differences in per capita output across countries have been recently emphasized in the work of Gallup and Saks (2000), Acemoglu et al. (2001), Easterly and Levine (2002) and many others. The individual country studies conducted in this volume complement well the recent evidence on the fundamental determinants of cross-country differences in log per capita output obtained using static cross-section regressions. Such regression results, even if estimated by instrumental variables can be subject to endogeneity problems and conclusions based on them should be treated with care.

In studying the MENA countries a number of features specific to the region need to be borne in mind. Here we focus on three of them: oil, demography and institutions.

At the end of 2004, it was estimated that 61.7% of the world's proven oil reserves and 40.6% of world natural gas reserves were located in the Middle East region.[2] In the same year the Middle East accounted for 30.7% of world oil production and only 6.7% of world oil consumption. The production share of the Middle East area would have been even much higher if it were not for the conflicts and political instabilities that have beset the region over the past century. The large reserves of the Middle East oil combined with the fact that they are relatively cheap to produce means that in a politically neutral world the exploitation of Middle East oil and gas fields would have been given priority over the less-productive oil and gas fields elsewhere.[3] The relatively large investments committed to the exploitation of oil and gas fields outside the MENA region largely reflect the understandable desire by oil-consuming countries to diversify the sources of their energy supplies in the face of mounting uncertainties in the region. However, the relatively cheap and abundant oil and gas reserves of the region will continue to be a source of disequilibrium and induce economic and political intervention by major oil-consuming countries in the region. This in turn could lead to further conflicts and political uncertainties, setting in motion a vicious circle of conflicts and uncertainties from which neither side (producers and consumers) could benefit.

On the domestic front, revenues from oil and gas exports account for a large part of government revenues and a substantial part of foreign exchange earnings in some of the major MENA countries, notably, Saudi Arabia, Iran and Iraq. Since these revenues accrue wholly to the government, there are domestic political ramifications emanating from rent seeking, non-accountability of government agencies and sluggish policy responses to a volatile and fast-changing international oil prices.[4] These factors tend to create further impediments to the development of competitive market-oriented institutions.

Another acute and pervasive problem in the MENA region is the extremely rapid growth of its labor force. This is often referred to as a "demographic gift", made possible by a fairly lengthy period of very high fertility rates combined with declining mortality rates, followed by sharply declining fertility rates. Like oil, this demographic gift can be a blessing as well as a curse. As with oil, rather than benefiting from this situation, the MENA countries have instead been struggling with how to provide their rapidly growing labor forces with productive employment. Institutional factors and policy mismanagement seem to have been the root cause of the problem. The economic incentives in many of the countries in the region have tended to accentuate labor market rigidities, with

---

[2] Source: British Petroleum Statistical Review of World Energy, June 2005.
[3] The theory of exhaustible resource extraction, pioneered by Hotelling (1931), is concerned with the intertemporal optimization of the rate of resource extraction and does not address the issue of relative production rates of oil fields with different reserve endowments and different marginal extraction costs that is of concern here.
[4] See Pesaran (1982) for a discussion of the interaction between oil revenues, dictatorship and dependent capitalism in the case of Iran under the Shah.

government and state enterprises often providing remuneration and benefits that are high relative to those employed in the private sector.

Institutional problems have also hampered the development of capital and financial markets, and are most likely partly responsible for the low labor force participation rate of women in the region. Once again, these problems are confounded by cultural and institutional factors.

While these institutional problems are by no means unique to the MENA region, they tend to be more formidable and persistent in this region than elsewhere. Several of the authors of this volume delve into political economy to explain why countries of the MENA region have tended to lag behind other regions in carrying out the kinds of policy and institutional reforms that are generally believed to mitigate these problems. This is done for the region as a whole, for oil and non-oil countries and for several individual countries (in particular, Tunisia, Turkey, Algeria and Egypt).

2. Limitations and omissions

Despite its wide coverage, largely owing to data limitations, the present volume focuses on the development experience of some of the main countries in the region post 1950s.[5] The book, being primarily an overview of growth at the macroeconomic level, does not go into individual sectors nor does it attempt to provide a multisectoral account of the calibrated computable general equilibrium (CGE) variety.[6] For the same reason, neither does it go into detail about non-oil minerals, agriculture or animal husbandry, even though some agricultural crops such as cotton, tomatoes, qat and fruits or phosphates in the case of minerals are important to some individual countries of the region.[7] The related issues of property rights in land and water resources are also largely left out.[8] Trade and foreign direct investments are covered, but only in relation to the macroeconomic developments of the region and the individual countries.[9]

There are also some gaps in terms of the geographic coverage of the book. As noted earlier, the MENA region consists of 21 Arabic-speaking countries of the MENA as well as Iran and Turkey. But for several of the 21 Arabic-speaking countries, the necessary statistical information is largely lacking. Table 1

---

[5] For excellent historical accounts of important parts of the MENA region, the reader is referred to Owen (1981), Issawi (1982) and Owen and Pamuk (1999).

[6] For some examples of multisectoral CGE models of the MENA countries see Maskus and Konan (1997) and Konan (2003).

[7] For agriculture in general and specific crops of the region in particular see Lofgren (2003).

[8] For some interesting accounts of property rights issues in the MENA region see de Soto (2000); Nugent and Sanchez (1999) for Sudan and Nugent and Sanchez (1993, 1998) for much of the rest of the MENA region.

[9] For studies on trade, trade issues and trade policies in the MENA region, see Galal and Hoekman (2003); Hoekman and Zarrouk (2000); Miniesy, *et al.* (2004).

Table 1. *Selected statistics for the countries in the MENA region*

Country	Population (millions)	Share of Population in MENA (%)	GDP 2004 (Current US Million Dollars)	Share of GDP in MENA (%)	GDP per Capita 2004 (Current US Dollars)
Algeria	32.4	7.22	80,783.09	6.20	2497
Bahrain	0.725	0.16	10,975.12	0.84	15,332
Djibouti	0.716	0.16	663.80	0.05	852
Egypt	68.7	15.30	88,783.56	6.81	1222
Eritrea	4.5	1.00	793.21	0.06	187
Iran	66.9	14.90	165,200.80	12.68	2401
Iraq	25.3	5.64	26724.14	2.05	952
Israel	6.8		123,109.11		18,651
Jordan	5.4	1.20	10813.60	0.83	1945
Kuwait	2.5	0.56	51,805.23	3.98	19,876
Lebanon	4.6	1.02	19,946.00	1.53	5634
Libya	5.7	1.27	19,535.86	1.50	3403
Mauritania	2.9	0.65	1238.95	0.10	416
Morocco	30.6	6.82	49,814.13	3.82	1589
Oman	2.7	0.60	24,465.55	1.88	9656
Palestinian Territories	3.5	0.78	5600.00	0.43	1600
Qatar	0.637	0.14	28,451.37	2.18	36,620
Saudi Arabia	23.2	5.17	24,4339.41	18.75	10,202
Somalia	9.9	2.21	2088.01	0.16	262
Sudan	34.4	7.66	19,948.94	1.53	562
Syria	17.8	3.96	23,440.20	1.80	1261
Tunisia	10	2.23	28,134.48	2.16	2815
Turkey	71.7	15.97	301,999.46	23.18	4182
UAE	4.4	0.98	84,226.68	6.46	19,659
Yemen	19.8	4.41	13,079.57	1.00	643
MENA	448.978	100.00	1,302,851.15	100.00	143,768

Source: World Bank, *World Development Indicators* (2005) CDROM.

provides some basic data on all the 23 countries, plus Israel for the purpose of comparison. But, because of data limitations, several of these countries, Comoros, Djibouti, Eritrea, Iraq, Palestinian territories, Somalia and sometimes even Libya and Yemen, will seldom be treated in the rest of the volume. Given their small sizes and peripheral locations, for the most part these omissions are not serious. For the Palestinian territories, even though central to the region and the political conflicts within the region, since they are of course not yet a country and hence not generally covered in international data sources, their omission is perhaps understandable.

The omission of Iraq, however, throughout much of the analysis presented in this volume is a more serious shortcoming, especially since it is the fourth largest economy of the region (in population). Were it not for the three wars that it has fought (and lost) in the last 20 years, Iraq would most likely have been among the top two or three MENA countries in aggregate GDP in 2004.[10] Since virtually all estimates of the trajectory of Iraq's GDP over time (even if primitive and therefore not usually included by the more reliable sources) indicate that its income per capita has declined quite substantially over time, its exclusion from MENA aggregates probably understates MENA's growth prior to 1975 (when Iraq was growing rapidly) but overstates MENA's growth since then. The omission of Iraq also deprives us from taking advantage of some of the political economy lessons of its experience.

3. Cross-country heterogeneity in the MENA region

As Table 1 shows there are important differences across the countries in the MENA region. While Turkey, Egypt and Iran all had populations of at least 66 million in 2004, four MENA countries (Bahrain, Comoros, Djibouti, and Qatar) had populations under 1 million. Similarly, Gross National Income (GNI) per capita at dollar purchasing power parity (PPP) prices of 2004 varied widely from a low of $820 for Yemen to about $22,000 for Qatar. It is important to point out to the reader various other ways in which these countries differ. For example, many of these countries are in Africa (including Comoros which is in the Indian Ocean far south of other countries of the region), but others are in Western Asia. Some (Bahrain, Comoros, Djibouti, Qatar and even Lebanon and the Palestinian territories) are geographically rather tiny whereas Saudi Arabia covers a sizable portion of Western Asia and Algeria and Sudan are the largest countries in Africa. Comoros and Bahrain are islands whereas Jordan (except for its port of Aqaba on the Red Sea) is virtually landlocked. While manufacturing is well developed in Algeria (especially heavy industry), Egypt, Iran, Morocco, Tunisia and Turkey, there is very little manufacturing in Comoros, Djibouti, Eritrea, Jordan, Libya, Mauritania, Sudan and Yemen. Agriculture is relatively important in Algeria, Egypt, Iran, Iraq, Lebanon, Morocco, Sudan, Syria, Turkey and Yemen, while it hardly exists in many of the other countries. In several countries of the region, such as Algeria, Eritrea, Iran, Jordan, Mauritania, Morocco, Somalia, Sudan and Yemen, animal husbandry is relatively important.

Jordan, Mauritania, Morocco, Oman, Saudi Arabia, Tunisia and Turkey have important mineral deposits that are exploited and exported whereas mining is relatively unimportant in most of the other countries of the region. Algeria, Bahrain (until recently), Egypt, Iran, Iraq, Kuwait, Libya, Qatar, Saudi Arabia, Syria, the United Arab Emirates (UAE) and more recently, Sudan and Yemen are exporters of oil and in many cases also of natural gas. Virtually, all the other countries of the region, however, do not possess such resources and are importers of oil and natural gas.

---

[10] For historical as well as contemporary analyses of Iraq, see Issawi (1992) and Alnasrawi (1994).

In terms of governmental types, many of the countries are or were until recently monarchies. The ones which are still monarchies are Bahrain, Jordan, Kuwait, Morocco, Oman, Qatar, Saudi Arabia and the UAE. Several of these (Bahrain, Jordan, Kuwait and Morocco) have legislatures that are rather democratically elected. Iran is an Islamic state (with some democratic trimmings). Saudi Arabia is also an Islamic kingdom, but without democratic trimmings. Algeria, Libya, Sudan, Syria, Yemen and, until the overthrow of Saddam Hussein, also Iraq were classified by Henry and Springborg (2001) as "bunker states" ruled by single dictators backed by the military. Fairly close to these are countries such as Egypt, Tunisia and until recently, the Palestinian territories labeled by Henry and Springborg as "bully praetorian states", in which the leadership was again largely dictatorial. Their distinction between bunker and bully praetorian states is that in the latter type the private sector is allowed to have a larger role in the economy than in the bunker states. At the other end of the spectrum are Lebanon and Turkey that are classified as secular and "fragmented democracies". While secular and having many characteristics of true democracies, these countries have state institutions that show them fragmented along ethnic, religious and regional lines.

The countries in the region also differ by their respective degrees of centralization (vis-à-vis decentralization). Not surprisingly, the small states tend to have a highly centralized governmental system, while the large ones are somewhat decentralized. But even among the large ones, Algeria, Egypt, Saudi Arabia and Turkey are all quite centralized, whereas Sudan is not. Among the small states, the UAE has a relatively decentralized governmental structure in the sense that it is a federation of seven emirates (Abu Dhabi, Ajman, Al Fujayrah, Dubai, Ra's-al Khaymeh, Sharjah and Umm al Quwayn) with many of the functions of the government reserved for decision-making at the individual emirate level.

The MENA countries differ considerably in their degree of openness to trade, as well. Algeria, Egypt, Lebanon, Morocco, Sudan, Syria and Tunisia all had tariff rates (on a trade-weighted basis) averaging over 13% in 1997, with Syria's being almost 30%. In several of the Gulf States, however, tariff rates are very low and there are virtually no other barriers to trade (other than on goods from Israel). MENA countries have also differed in their proclivity for establishing free trade arrangements with other countries. Tunisia was the first MENA country (in 1996) to sign a free trade agreement (FTA) with the European Union, to be followed by Morocco, Jordan, Egypt, Turkey and Lebanon. Jordan and Morocco have also signed FTAs with the United States, and Turkey is moving toward becoming a full-fledged member of the European Union. But other countries like Algeria, Iran, Libya, Syria and Yemen have signed no such agreements.

With respect to intra-MENA trade arrangements, several MENA countries have signed agreements for partial free trade among themselves in the past. Notable examples were Turkey and Iran (with Pakistan as well) as part of the

Table 3. Inward and outward flows of remittances across the MENA countries

Part A: inward remittances as percentage of GDP[a]

Country	1970 s	1980 s	1990–1994	1995–1999	2000–2003
Algeria	3.1	1.1	2.2	2.3	1.6
Djibouti	–	–	3.5	2.0	–
Egypt	6.9	9.9	11.0	4.6	3.2
Iran	–	–	2.1	0.7	0.3
Jordan	12.8	19.3	15.0	22.8	22.4
Lebanon	–	–	38.6	9.7	12.7
Morocco	6.1	7.0	7.2	6.0	8.1
Oman	1.0	0.8	0.3	0.2	0.1
Palestinian Territories	–	–	24.4	19.8	13.6
Syria	–	–	6.9	6.1	3.6
Tunisia	3.5	4.2	3.8	4.1	4.8
Turkey	3.1	2.8	2.0	2.3	1.7
Yemen	–	–	26.2	19.7	13.8

Part B: outward remittances as percentage of total imports[b]

Country	1975	1990	1997	2000	2001
Bahrain	6.4	21.6	7.7	15.4	8.9
Kuwait	11.6	19.7	17.1	26.8	35.1*
Oman	27.2	30.5	12.0	14.5	16.7
Qatar		66.8	15.2	18.8	20.0
Saudi Arabia	13.2	46.9	53.0	51.2	50.3*
UAE	26.4	21.9	10.2	10.3	8.3

[a]Source: World Bank, *World Development Indicators*, 2005, CDROM.
[b]Askari, Nowshirvani and Jaber (1997, p. 67). The 1997–2001 figures are calculated from remittance data of Gulf News Online quoted in Alexander's Gas & Oil Connections and The GCC Economic Bulletin, 2002. Figures for 2001 are calculated from World Development Indicators and Gulf Research Center, 2004. The percentages calculated using remittance figures from the Gulf Research Center for Saudi Arabia (39.7) and Kuwait (27.0) differ rather significantly from those calculated using Gulf News Online and The GCC Economic Bulletin, 2002.
*For the year 2002.

especially considering the aforementioned low female labor force participation rates in these countries. To the extent that Arabic language or common cultural values were of special use for employment in the labor-scarce countries of the region, this made it possible for workers from the labor-surplus countries of the region to find employment in the labor-scarce countries of the region. From these labor flows come remittances back to the countries of origin of these workers.

Table 3 provides data on both inward and outward flows of remittances as shares of the GDP and imports, respectively. Although the availability of such data is limited across countries and time, it is clear that virtually all countries in the region are quite important either as sources or recipients of migrant labor. Although, the data are insufficient to show this in these tables, it is well recognized that because of differences in the quality or skills of labor supplied and demanded, the same country (in some cases) can be both an important source country and an important destination country at the same time. For example, Lebanon and Jordan import low-cost unskilled labor from Syria and Egypt, but export skilled labor to the Gulf countries.

Note from Panel A of Table 3 that inward remittances have constituted over 20% of the GDP in some years for Jordan, Lebanon, the Palestinian territories and Yemen. Similarly, on the outflow side (Part B of the Table), even for the few selected years shown, there has been at least one year for which the remittance outflows were at least 20% of the total import bill in each of the six GCC countries. In the case of Saudi Arabia, in all three of the most recent years shown, then were over 50%. Especially, in the earlier years sizable portions of these remittances from GCC countries were from workers from other MENA countries back to their countries of origin (especially, Egypt, Lebanon, Syria and Yemen). The same would have been true for Libya in the past decades, in this case, the workers would have been largely from Egypt.

In the case of the Maghreb countries (Algeria, Morocco and Tunisia) and also Iran and Turkey, the remittances received were largely from Europe, especially France and Germany. In each case, the magnitude of these remittances relative to the GDP of the recipient country tended to induce a positive association between the incomes of the source and destination countries. Adams and Page (2003) showed that both the stock of migrants abroad (measured as the percentage of the population of the country of origin living abroad) and remittances received as a share of the GDP have the effect of significantly reducing the poverty rates (irrespective of how it is measured) in the country of origin. Hence, this would suggest that these migration flows have been beneficial to the source as well as the destination countries. The size of remittances in the MENA region tended to be larger than those in many other regions with similar migration patterns as in Latin America, particularly Mexico.

There are, however, three possibly important qualifications to the alleged highly beneficial effects of the sizable migration flows in the MENA region. First, to the extent that the out-migrants represent "brain drain", i.e. the loss of skilled workers and entrepreneurial talent to the country of origin, this could represent a social loss to the countries of origin. This would be especially true where the country of origin has invested in nourishing, educating and training the workers, the productive use of whose skills will therefore be lost to the economy.[11] Second, it is frequently suggested that the remittances are mainly used for consumption purposes and therefore do not do much for the

---

[11] While this condition would seem to be generally satisfied, the out-migration of skilled workers may raise the wage rates of such workers in the country of origin and hence stimulate investments in human capital by numerous others. The migrants may also learn skills in the destination countries that they might subsequently bring back with them to their countries of origin.

development of the country.[12] Third, there is a possible political economy effect wherein the remittance income can help balance the current account and keep income at tolerable levels so as to weaken the pressure for welfare and growth-increasing reforms.

Another important characteristic of Table 3 is that the entries in some cases reflect distinct trends over time as well as considerable variability from one period to another. Remittances and out-migration seem to be declining over time in the case of Iran (where much of the out-migration has been of highly skilled people to Europe and North America) and Turkey. Foreign labour force as the share of total labour supply seems to be declining in several of the GCC countries, and as a result there have been associated declines in outward remittances and employment opportunities for workers in the other MENA countries. The share of Arab workers in the foreign labor force of Kuwait and probably all GCC countries has declined substantially over time (Adams and Page, 2003).

Given also the increasing resistance in Europe to migrants from the Maghreb, it is clear that out-migration is less and less reliable and feasible as a means of alleviating high unemployment rates and low remuneration at home. The volatility in the inward remittances relative to GDP is also quite significant indicating that remittance income can serve as an important source of income volatility in the recipient country. Particularly vulnerable in this respect have been Palestinian workers to variations in the incidence of "border and crossing closures" by Israel and the changing political relations between Palestinian and host-country governments on the other hand. Some of these fluctuations can also be attributed to the changing demands and requirements of the recipients. Witness the very high percentages of inward remittances during difficult times, e.g. in Algeria in the early 1970s and much of the 1990s, and Lebanon as well as Yemen during their civil wars.

The third and considerably less well-known means of linking countries of the MENA region is the capital flows, especially in the form of Foreign Direct Investment (FDI). The extent of FDI is typically measured by the Inward FDI Performance Index (IFPI) defined as the share of a country's inward FDI flow in its GDP relative to world FDI as a proportion of world GDP.[13] Table 4 presents estimates of IFPI. If this ratio is 1 it indicates that it receives a share of FDI exactly in proportion to its share in world GDP. A figure below 1 indicates that the country is relatively an underachiever in attracting FDI whereas one above 1 may be interpreted as indicating overachievement in the same sense. Unfortunately, while such measures of FDI inflows can be obtained from individual OECD countries in many cases, information on flows from other MENA

---

[12] Such effects, however, should be balanced by the fact that the very act of migration represents saving and investment, so that the remittances, even if taking the form of consumption, represent the return on these prior investments.

[13] IFPI is reported by UNCTAD in its *World Investment Reports*.

Table 4. Inward FDI performance index (1988–2004)

Country	Average 1988–1996	Average 1997–2004
Algeria	0.11	0.45
Bahrain	8.02	2.74
Djibouti	n/a	n/a
Egypt	1.82	0.43
Eritrea		
Iran	−0.01	0.05
Iraq		
Israel	0.74	1.01
Jordan	0.34	1.51
Kuwait	0.14	0.05
Lebanon	0.25	0.57
Libya	0.16	−0.07
Mauritania		
Morocco	1.36	1.10
Oman	1.05	0.19
Palestinian Territories	n/a	n/a
Qatar	1.05	1.06
Saudi Arabia	0.25	0.26
Somalia		
Sudan	0.18	1.57
Syria	0.82	0.68
Tunisia	2.48	1.09
Turkey	0.51	0.26
UAE	0.40	0.12
Yemen	4.63	−0.52
MENA	1.28	0.66

Note: Inward FDI Performance Index is calculated as (FDI inflows in the country/world FDI) divided by (country's GDP/world GDP). The index is calculated as the moving average over a 3 year-period to overcome high fluctuations.
Source: World Investment Report Series, UNCTAD.

countries are unfortunately not available.[14] Since such data are quite volatile from year to year, meaningful comparisons must be based on averages for several years. While the overall MENA average reported for 1997–2004 is below 1, it is above 1 if one considers the sample period 1988–1996. But since it is the small countries like Bahrain, Jordan, Qatar and Tunisia that have the larger IFPI measures, and the large countries like Turkey, Egypt (in the second period at least) and Algeria that have the smaller measures, weighted averages of the index for MENA as a whole would be below 1 in both periods. Egypt in the first period in which most of its privatization and other reforms were concentrated

[14] In part, this is because such investments are smaller and less subject to formal regulation than in the cases of investments from outside the region.

was an exception. The periods in which Sudan and Yemen had IFPI measures > 1 were those in which these countries were opening up their oil sectors to foreign companies.

Anecdotal and incomplete information is available on FDI flows into MENA countries from the other FDI countries, most often from the GCC countries. Virtually, all the periods of high and rising oil prices (1973–1974, 1979–1981 and 2002–2006) have witnessed surging flows of FDI from oil-exporting countries of the region to the other countries (including the MENA countries). While much of the earlier FDI flows were by official organizations and joint ventures with a large public sector component, increasingly, the sources of these flows are private. Indeed, political trends in the region have tended to favor this as MENA tourists as well as foreign investors feel more comfortable and secure in investing in the other MENA countries. Morocco, Lebanon, Jordan and Tunisia, for example, have long been popular destinations for investments from the GCC countries. Some stock markets in the region, while closed to other foreign investors, are open to investors from the other MENA countries.

The fourth type of interlinkages across the MENA countries is through political relations, bilateral as well as multilateral. Among these are organizations, such as the Arab League, the Organization of Islamic States, the regional bodies of the United Nations such as Economic and Social Commission for Western Asia (ESCWA) and the United Nations Economic Commission for Africa, GCC, Maghreb and other subregional groupings as well as through various specialized agencies. When political relations are good between any two or more countries, one or more of these linking mechanisms is likely to be in place and working quite well. When economic complementarity makes such flows desirable, trade, labor and /or capital flows are all likely to be apparent. Yet when political relations deteriorate, any and all of these flows may be vulnerable to abrupt political interference. Examples have included border closures (as between Syria and Jordan, Algeria and Morocco, Jordan and the Palestinian territories, Kuwait and Iraq), abandoning of trade or investment treaties and expulsions of foreign workers by the host country (e.g. of Egyptian workers by Libya, or Palestinians by Kuwait, Yemenis by Saudi Arabia). These sudden changes in political relationships can therefore become an important source of income volatility in the region.

5. Growth and volatility in MENA compared to other regions

While it is generally conceded that the MENA region enjoyed relatively rapid growth over the period 1950–1980, a period in which massive pools of oil were being found and exploited in the region, even then it was hardly a match for the East Asia region. Over the last two decades, however, especially during 1980–1994, it is generally believed that the MENA region experienced relative stagnation. For example, Elbadawi (2005) reported MENA's per capita GDP growth rate to have been about 1% per annum over this period compared to a

important change in the sources of economic growth in the Turkish economy. While the output growth was largely driven by the increases in factor inputs (labor and physical capital) between 1960 and 1990, the growth since then has been primarily due to increases in TFP.

The last phase covers the financial crisis of February 2001 and the subsequent stabilization attempts. By utilizing an output gap measure, the authors find that short-term capital flows are likely to be the main driving force in generating excessive output fluctuations in Turkey. Based on these findings, it is argued that the high economic growth rate that the Turkish economy has achieved over the recent years owes much to massive short-term capital inflows. Given the long history of volatile economic performance in Turkey, the authors conclude that it is too early to evaluate the effects of recent structural reforms on the long-term output dynamics.

Chapter 9 by Ahmad Jalali-Naini provides an analysis of trends and developments of the Iranian economy over the period 1950–2003. The author argues that the Iranian experience reveals, in a number of ways, the potentials, problems and challenges that have been confronted by the other populated oil-exporting countries – a tale of high expectations turning into mediocre performance. From the 1960s up to the first oil boom (1973–1974) the economy exhibited high GDP growth and low inflation rates. The oil boom brought in large financial resources, but also induced soft-budget constraints and expanded the public sector. The huge increase in oil-financed government spending raised growth temporarily above its trend; however, by creating inflation and opportunities for rent seeking, it resulted in economic and social instability. The positive wealth and saving effects of the oil boom did not have a long-lasting effect on either economic growth rates or per capita income levels. Since 1974 economic growth has been volatile and factor-intensive and TFP did not make a significant contribution to the economic growth. The evidence also does not support that human capital accumulation has strongly contributed to economic growth. While fixed investment/GDP ratios in Iran compare favorably with high-growth economies, the growth performance does not; too many resources have been spent to produce only an average growth performance. It is argued that Iran's relatively rich resources, high rates of accumulation of physical and human capital, but a mundane growth performance and continued dependence on oil reflect inadequate economic institutions, price/incentive distortions, policy coordination and rent-seeking problems and the effect of the Iran–Iraq war.

Chapter 10 by Mohamed Bechri and Sonia Naccache discusses the political economy of Tunisia. The chapter examines the development of the economy over the past five decades and identifies the following main features: (1) an early and sustained focus on social modernization and population control, (2) a heavy involvement of the State in the economy, even after the abandonment of collectivism in 1969 and (3) a robust long-run GDP growth of about 5% per year, against only 3.5% for the MENA region as a whole. The chapter adopts a political economy approach to explain independent Tunisia's development policy choices. Since the country's independence from France in 1956, these policies shifted from State intervention (1956–1960) to socialism (1961–1969), to export promotion (1970–1985). Finally, following a severe balance of payment crisis in 1986, Tunisia adopted a structural adjustment program under IMF guidance. The liberal policies implemented under this framework were further boosted with the signing of an FTA with the European Union in 1995. In conclusion, the chapter draws on some lessons from Tunisia for the other MENA countries. It stresses the importance of women rights, population control and modern education, and refers to recent examples of Morocco and Kuwait regarding women status reform to argue that action is still possible.

Chapter 11 by Mohamed Abdelbasset Chemingui and Moataz Mostafa El-Said reviews the macroeconomic performance of Algeria over the period 1962–2000. The chapter considers prevailing economic policies and changes introduced into the economic environment over this period. It also conducts a growth accounting exercise to disaggregate output growth in Algeria into growth in capital, labor and TFP. Over the past four decades, Algeria's growth performance has been characterized by high fluctuations and generally slower growth than in the neighboring developing countries. The poor economic growth performance that Algeria has experienced is shown to be the result of a slow growth in TFP which can be attributed to the following factors: (i) the inefficient management of the country's natural resources; (ii) inappropriate use of macroeconomic policies, specifically price deregulation and economic reforms aimed at increasing investment; (iii) structural impediments limiting the private sector's contribution to the country's economic activities and (iv) an overall economic environment dominated by the public sector, a weak financial sector and a slow and non-transparent privatization process. The authors argue in favor of policy measures that focus on boosting the economy's potential growth capacity. These include measures to improve the competitiveness of existing activities, to attract investment in sectors other than the energy-related ones so as to diversify the economy, to accelerate the trade liberalization process, to encourage domestic and foreign investment in export-oriented industries, and to adopt complementary supply-side policies such as promoting education and training and increasing spending in the health sector. In addition, Algeria should aggressively focus its efforts on the improvement of its investment climate.

Chapter 12 by Adam B. Elhiraika and Annas H. Hamed explores the economic performance of the UAE as an example of an oil-dependent economy. It attempts to explain the determinants of economic growth in the UAE using growth-accounting as well as regression techniques. The chapter shows that overall the performance of the economy fluctuated widely over the period 1975–2002 under the influence of volatile oil prices. The period up to the early 1980s saw sustained high real growth rates owing to rising oil prices and huge government investment in physical and social infrastructure. As from around the mid-1980s, GDP growth decelerated sharply with generally declining oil prices. Subsequent government austerity measures were directed largely toward capital expenditure since most of the basic infrastructure projects had been completed by then, while most current expenditure categories have become long-term commitments. The chapter also makes a number of recommendations. To reduce exposure to exogenous shocks (in particular the oil price shocks), the economy needs to be diversified by encouraging private sector participation in production of goods and by expanding markets for the UAE's products regionally as well as internationally. The authors also argue for a more developed financial sector, with a well-functioning equity market, expansion of non-oil government revenues through privatization of public enterprises, rationalization of government expenditures and a reassessment of subsidies and incentive programs.

Chapter 13 ends the volume with an essay by Ragui Assaad on the importance of institutions and households' decisions for the growth process in Egypt. The chapter begins with the observation that macroeconomic analyses of growth in Egypt indicate that labor contributes very little to growth, and that human capital, and in particular female human capital, contributes little to increases in TFP (see, for example, Chapter 7 by Kheir-Eldon and Morsi in this volume). These puzzling results come at a time when the role of human capital in generating growth is being increasingly stressed in the international literature and when investment in female human capital, internationally, is deemed to be one of the activities with the highest social returns. One of the main objectives of this chapter is to shed light on these seemingly puzzling results by analyzing the microeconomics of the production and deployment of human capital in the Egyptian economy, with a particular emphasis on the institutional contexts in which these decisions are made. The chapter argues that the long-standing policy of the Egyptian government to guarantee employment in the government sector for upper secondary and university graduates has distorted household decisions as to the level and type of human capital to acquire and has resulted in the entrapment of significant portions of the human capital in unproductive government employment. With the distorted signals they receive from the labor market, the educational decisions of households are strongly shaped by the desire to ensure access to lifetime employment in the government, an objective that might well be at odds with realizing the productivity benefits of education for the economy as a whole. In the case of women the situation is further compounded by social norms defining what constitutes appropriate female employment. The author argues that such norms tend to restrict women's employment to a limited range of occupations, types of workplaces and locations, which in turn leads to overcrowding in these segments of the labor market and depressed wages.

The chapters that follow further our understanding of the economies of the MENA countries and highlight the common issues that are important to the region as a whole. It is hoped that a better understanding of the economic issues and problems of the region will help foster a better understanding of the nature of the political conflicts that have afflicted the region for decades. It should be clear that the resolution of economic problems of the region without a proper understanding of the political, sociological, cultural and religious dimensions of the problems is unlikely to be sustainable. This is largely reflected in the multidisciplinary nature of the contributions. It is hoped that this volume encourages further investigation of the problems of the MENA region.

References

Acemoglu, D., S. Johnson and J.A. Robinson (2001), "The colonial origins of comparative development: an empirical investigation", *American Economic Review*, Vol. 91, pp. 1369–1401.

Adams Jr., R.H., and J. Page (2003), "International migration, remittances and poverty in developing countries", Washington, DC, World Bank Policy Research Working Paper 3179.

Alnasrawi, A. (1994), *The Economy of Iraq*, Westport: Greenwood.

Askari, Nowshirvani and Jaber (1997), "Economic Development in the GCC: The Blessing and the curse of oil", Greenwich, CT: JAI Press.

De Soto, H. (2000), *The Mystery of Capital: Why Capitalism Triumphs in the West and Fails Everywhere Else*, New York: Basic Books.

Easterly, W. and R. Levine (2002), "Tropics, germs, and crops: how endowments influence economic development", NBER Working Papers 9106, National Bureau of Economic Research, Inc.

Elbadawi, I.A. (2005), "Reviving growth in the Arab World", *Economic Development and Cultural Change*, Vol. 53, pp. 293–326.

Galal, A. and B. Hoekman (editors) (2003), *Arab Economic Integration: Between Hope and Reality*, Washington, DC: Brookings.

Gallup, J.L. and J.D. Saks (2000), "Agriculture, Climate, and Technology: Why are the Tropics Falling Behind?", *American Journal of Agricultural Economics*, Vol. 82, pp. 731–777.

Henry, C.M. and R. Springborg (2001), *Globalization and the Politics of Development in the Middle East*, Cambridge: Cambridge University Press.

Hoekman, B. and J. Zarrouk (editors) (2000), *Catching up with the competition: trade opportunities and challenges for Arab countries*, Ann Arbor: University of Michigan Press.

Hotelling, H. (1931), "The economics of exhaustible resources", *Journal of Political Economy*, Vol. 39, pp. 137–175.

Issawi, C. (1982), *An Economic History of the Middle East and North Africa*, London: Methuen.

Konan, D.E. (2003), "Alternative paths to prosperity: economic integration among Arab countries", pp. 61–101 in: A. Galal and B. Heokman, editors, *Arab Economic Integration*, Washington, DC: Brookings.

Lofgren, H. (editor) (2003), *Food, Agriculture, and Economic Policy in the Middle East and North Africa*, Amsterdam: JAI Press, Elsevier Science.

Maskus, K.E. and D.E. Konan (1997), "Trade liberalization in Egypt", *Review of Development Economics*, Vol. 1, pp. 275–293.

Miniesy, R., J. Nugent and T. Yousef (2004), "Intra-regional trade integration in the Middle East: past performance and future potential", in: H. Hakimian and J. Nugent, editors, *Trade Policy and Economic Integration in the Middle East and North Africa: Economic Boundaries in Flux*, London: Routledge.

Nugent, J.B. and N. Sanchez (1993), "Tribes, chiefs and transhumance: a comparative institutional analysis", *Economic Development and Cultural Change*, Vol. 42, pp. 87–113.

Nugent, J. B. and N. Sanchez, (1998), "Common property rights as an endogenous response to risk", *American Journal of Agricultural Economics*, Vol. 80, pp. 651–657. (Reprinted in Bruce Larson, editor, *Property Rights and Environmental Problems*, Aldershot: Ashgate Publishing Ltd., 2003.

Nugent, J.B. and N. Sanchez (1999), "The local variability of rainfall and tribal institutions: the case of Sudan", *Journal of Economic Behavior and Organization*, Vol. 39, pp. 263–291.

Owen, R. (1981), *The Middle East in the World Economy, 1800–1914*, London: Methuen.

Owen, R. and S. Pamuk (1999), *A History of the Middle East Economies in the Twentieth Century*, Cambridge: Cambridge University Press.

Pesaran, M.H. (1982), "The system of dependent capitalism in pre- and post-revolutionary Iran", *International Journal of Middle East Studies*, Vol. 14, pp. 501–522.

Pesaran, M.H. (2006), "A pair-wise approach to output and growth convergence", *Journal of Econometrics* (forthcoming).

World Bank (2005), Unlocking the Employment potential in the Middle East and North Africa: Toward a new Social contract. Washington, D.C.

Graph 1. Evaluation of the relative income (PPP) of MENA region countries with respect to US (1980–2002)

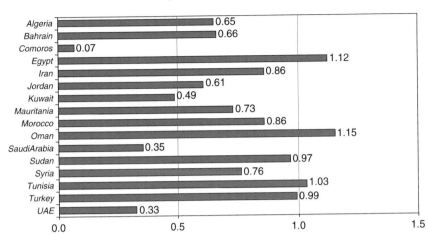

Another salient feature of the recent growth performance of the MENA countries is its high volatility. Table 3 shows that during the period 1970–2000, the average per capita GDP growth rate of the MENA countries has been characterized by a high variability in comparison to the other regions and with the world average. The average growth variability as measured by the standard deviation of the real per capita GDP growth rate for the MENA region is almost four times that of the world and twice that of the low-performing SSA region. Starting from the second half of the 1980s, although the variability of growth rates has declined somewhat for the MENA region as a whole, it remained higher than the world average.

This high variability in the growth performance of the MENA region may be explained by several factors including the lack of economic diversification that increases vulnerability to external shocks. This applies especially to the oil-exporting countries that are frequently subject to the vagaries of the international oil market as well as to countries that rely heavily on agriculture and whose performance is frequently affected by unfavorable weather conditions. Political instability and the perennial regional conflict may further explain the very high variability of the growth performance in a number of countries in the region.

Tables 4 shows that the pattern of investment has also followed the growth pattern described above. Investment has declined sharply during the 1980s and the 1990s. Oil countries have borne the brunt of this adjustment with substantial declines in the investment ratios. Non-oil countries have maintained, over the same period, fairly stable investment rates above the level of their low saving ratios.

Table 3. Average per capita GDP growth rates (1970–2000)

Country	Average Growth	Standard Deviation of Growth
Algeria	1.1	5.7
Bahrain	0.3	6.0
Djibouti	−4.6	3.0
Egypt, Arab Republic	3.2	3.0
Iran, Islamic Republic	−0.3	7.6
Iraq	−5.1	21.3
Jordan	2.0	7.7
Kuwait	−2.6	11.7
Lebanon	3.2	18.4
Libya	−5.4	10.0
Mauritania	0.2	4.0
Morocco	1.7	4.6
Oman	2.7	7.3
Saudi Arabia	0.4	6.5
Sudan	1.5	6.1
Syrian Arab Republic	2.4	7.9
Tunisia	3.1	3.8
Turkey	2.2	3.8
UAE	−3.4	8.7
Yemen, Republic	1.6	4.9
MENA	0.2	4.8
East Asia and Pacific	5.6	2.3
Latin America & Caribbean	1.5	2.5
SSA	−0.1	2.6
World	1.5	1.3

Source: World Bank, *World Development Indicators* (2003).

Table 4. Gross domestic investment (per cent of GDP)

Group	1961–1970	1971–1980	1981–1990	1991–2000
MENA	17.4	26.3	24.1	22.5
MENA oil-producing countries	21.3	29.1	23.6	22.0
MENA non-oil producing countries	14.9	24.1	24.4	22.1
East Asia and Pacific	19.1	28.6	31.8	34.4
Latin America and Caribbean	20.4	23.6	20.3	20.8
SSA	16.9	21.1	17.5	17.1
World	24.3	25.3	23.2	22.6

Source: World Bank, *World Development Indicators* (2003).

Many studies link the performance of the MENA region to the wide fluctuations in its terms of trade. For instance, comparing terms of trade fluctuations across a number of regions for the period 1980–1995, Gamo *et al.* (1997, p. 14) have found that the oil-exporting countries in the region have the highest terms of trade variability. In addition, terms of trade variability of the MENA non-oil exporting countries were also found to be higher than that of the developing countries as a group. This pattern may be attributed to the excessive reliance of the MENA countries on volatile oil receipts that account for a large part of their total export revenues. Even non-oil MENA countries have been subject to fluctuation in their own terms of trade, being exporters of primary products themselves. Oil price fluctuation has also indirectly affected these countries through its impact on the flows of workers' remittances, investment and financial assistance flows from the oil-exporting countries. All these factors combined show *a priori* that the MENA region is remarkably vulnerable to external shocks.

3. MENA economic growth in a global context

In this section we will put MENA's growth performance into an international perspective by: first, using a cross-country regression framework to analyze the main determinants of growth in the MENA region as compared to the rest of the world and second, using an accounting framework to identify the relative contribution of the different factors of production to the growth of the countries of the region in comparison to the other developing countries.

3.1. Cross-country regression

The absence of guidance from the growth theory as to which variables to include, makes the choice among the great number of possible correlates of growth a difficult one. However, our selection will be guided by variables that proved more "robust" than others in recent literature.[5] Therefore, we attempted to identify a small set of regressors that would account for most of the variation in cross-country per capita GDP growth. In addition, we focused on variables of relevance to the MENA region's recent growth performance. With the above strategy in mind, the set of chosen variables included initial conditions, human capital, investment ratio, external shocks, macroeconomic performance, openness, natural resource abundance, and output volatility. We deal with each one of them in detail.

Concerning initial conditions, recent empirical growth literature provides ample evidence about the existence of conditional income convergence across countries. Conditional on the rate of investment and the other relevant variables, a poor country would tend to grow relatively faster because the marginal productivity of capital is relatively higher.

---

[5] There is a lot a spuriousness associated with the Barro-type (Barro, 1991) cross-country regression framework. However, it could be used as a suggestive tool to measure the relative contribution of the many sources of growth across countries and regions.

This convergence is evidenced by the negative relationship between the growth rate of per capita GDP and the initial level of GDP per capita after controlling for other relevant variables such as measures of government policies, institutions, politics and variables related to the character of national population. We will consider the 1960 level of real GDP per capita, Y60, as a measure of initial income.

Countries with higher initial stock of human capital and knowledge have also been found to be able to forge ahead through higher growth rates. The simple inclusion of a measure of human capital in a Barro-type regression equation, however, overlooks the dual role played by the latter. Human capital not only affects growth as an additional factor of production, together with physical capital and labor, but also the efficiency with which these factors are combined.

Benhabib and Spiegel (1994) have found evidence that human capital affected Total Factor Productivity Growth (TFPG) through its impact on the capacity of a country to innovate and the capability of using and adapting foreign technology. Arguably, human capital also encourages the accumulation of other factors of production. In our analysis, a measure of human capital will be used to explain both growth as well as TFPG. As a proxy for the level of human capital, we will take the 1960 primary school enrollment ratio, PESENR60.

The investment ratio, INVY, is included as a regressor since it has been found by many studies, including that of Levine and Renelt (1992), to have a positive and robust correlation with the growth rates. Since it is generally assumed that positive external shocks are associated with higher growth and vice versa, we have included for each country in the sample the GDP per capita growth of its trading partners weighted by trade shares, GPART. Other conventional proxies for external shocks such as the percentage change in the terms of trade and its variability have not resulted in statistically significant impact on growth.

Macroeconomic performance plays an important role for growth sustainability. Fischer (1993) has shown that growth is negatively associated with inflation, large budget deficits and distorted foreign exchange markets. Among the three measures, we favor inflation for several reasons. First, internationally comparable data on budget deficits are scattered and not available for a large number of the MENA countries. In contrast, the widely used black-market premium (BMP) rate as a measure of distortion in foreign exchange market is neither a good proxy for the level of distortions in the economy nor an appropriate measure of the adequacy of macroeconomic policies. For instance, the low BMP rates in Egypt or the Arabian Gulf countries reflect a greater abundance of foreign exchange more than the absence of distortions in the economy or the presence of stable macroeconomic environment. In addition, the high BMP rates in many countries of the MENA region tend to reflect the impact of wars and sociopolitical instability characterizing these countries.

The only exception was inflation whose parameter became less significant, but remained rightly signed even after the elimination of outliers. This confirms the fact that inflation hurts growth especially at unusually high rates.

In an attempt to disentangle the regional from the global growth characteristics, we have allowed for differentiated growth impacts of relevant variables depending on whether the country under study is from the MENA region. These variables pertain to some of the factors that are often presented to explain the lower growth performance of the MENA region: the lack of capital efficiency, lack of integration in the world economy and vulnerability to external shocks. More specifically, the MENA region is allowed to have different slope coefficients from any non-MENA region in the sample with respect to the three variables: INVY, SOPEN and GPART. To do this, we have included interaction terms between these three variables and a dummy variable, MENA, taking a value of 1 if the country is from the MENA region and 0 otherwise. The third column of Table 6 gives the previous OLS results with MENA-specific coefficients. A separate dummy variable for the MENA region was also included in the last regression to see whether the included variables account for a fairly reasonable. Explanation of growth in the region.

In contrast with the previous OLS results related to the whole sample, the MENA-specific interaction terms reported in column 3 of Table 6, seem to suggest that the MENA region differs significantly from the rest of the world in the three variables believed to affect their performance. Interestingly, the MENA region has been found to be more vulnerable to uncertainty caused by changes in trade partners' income. This result notwithstanding, one should bear in mind that the influence of the above sources of uncertainty and the impact of external shocks may vary from one country to another.

To give further evidence on the vulnerability of the MENA region to external shocks, we have tried different measures of terms of trade change. However, all of these measures turned out to be statistically insignificant. The ambiguous impact of terms of trade on long-term growth has been reported in several instances in the literature.[10] There are several plausible explanations for that. The terms of trade variable has been obtained, given the requirements of our cross-country analysis, by computing its average growth over the entire period 1960–1998. Therefore, the impact of terms of trade as an exogenous shock could be diluted owing to the operated smoothing. To take this shortcoming into account, we have used the standard deviation of the terms of trade of each country over the entire period as an alternative. The new variable turned out to be insignificant as well.

---

[10] For instance, Gamo *et al.* (1997, p. 27) reported a similar result for the case of several countries in the region.

The impact of terms of trade on economic growth could be proportional to the dependence of any country on a limited number of exported commodities. In other words, a diversified economy is less likely to be affected by a decline in the terms of trade given that the impact will be limited to a relatively small number of sectors. In contrast, deterioration in the terms of trade will be felt throughout the economy in case of high export concentration or excessive dependence on a limited number of export commodities such as oil.

Finally, the ambiguous effect of terms of trade on growth could be due to the asymmetry of this effect. A persistent improvement in terms of trade might lead to an improvement in income and expenditure, while deterioration does not necessarily lead to a proportional reduction in these variables. The 2000 World Bank report on Global Economic Prospects, reports several cases in point from the MENA region.[11] For instance, following the 1998 slump in oil prices, Bahrain, Oman and Saudi Arabia used foreign reserves and accumulated foreign assets to alleviate the pressure on fiscal deficits and trade balances. In contrast, other oil exporters such as Algeria and Yemen with more binding financial constraints had to adjust through expenditure cuts and exchange rate devaluation. This asymmetry in policy reaction might have affected the growth performance in many MENA countries by increasing uncertainty.

Our results also show that the investment coefficient for the MENA region is statistically different from and much lower than that of the whole sample. This result is *prima facie*, at odds with the fact that the MENA countries have persistently maintained high investment ratios that were for the most part above the world average.[12] The negative MENA-specific investment coefficient is largely attributed to the endemic problem of capital inefficiency in the region.

Many researchers have presented plausible explanations for the low efficiency of capital in the MENA region. Page (1998) suggests that this low efficiency of capital is due to the dominant role of the public sector and the nature of capital inflows in the region destined mainly to finance public investments and low-productivity projects in a non-tradable sector such as housing. He also points out that protectionism and lack of integration in world economy precluded these countries from boosting their efficiency and competitiveness. Others, such as El Badawi (1999), argue that the low efficiency of capital may be attributed to the fact that most of the countries in the region provide an inadequate business environment and institutional support for investment and private sector development.

Openness does not seem to play an important role in the MENA region as for the whole sample. The lower impact of openness on growth in the MENA region may be explained by the prolonged application of high tariffs in support

---

[11] World Bank (2000, pp. 142–143).
[12] Refer to Table 3 in the paper.

of import-substitution strategies in many MENA countries during the 1960s and the 1970s. Excluding the Arab Gulf States that maintain relatively low tariff rates, the average unweighted tariff rate in the MENA countries is high relative to most regions of the world. Protection remains high even in the most advanced reformers in the region including Egypt, Morocco and Tunisia. Indeed, trade protection in the non-oil MENA countries generally remains higher than in the low-income countries (Table 7). In addition, the rate of reduction in trade barriers has been lower compared to the other regions (Srinivasan, 2002).

Finally, lack of statistical significance of the MENA dummy shows that the general factors and the MENA-specific factors mentioned above, provide a fairly good explanation of the region's growth performance.

Table 7. Trade protection indicators for MENA (most recent year in the late 1990s)

Country/Region	NTB Coverage (per cent)	Standard Deviation (per cent)	Weighted Average (per cent)	Simple Average (per cent)
Jordan	0.0	15.8	18.9	21.6
Algeria	15.8	16.7	17.3	24.2
Tunisia	32.8	12.8	28.8	29.9
Morocco	5.5	31.2	25.8	35.7
Egypt	28.8	130.6	13.7	28.1
Oman	13.1	1.2	4.7	4.7
Saudi Arabia	15.6	2.7	10.3	12.0
MENA	15.9	30.1	17.1	22.3
Comparators				
By income group				
Low-income countries	5.5	10.9	12.6	15.5
Lower middle-income countries	13.4	15.0	12.5	15.3
Upper middle-income countries	14.7	12.3	11.6	13.8
High-income countries	15.6	7.0	3.4	4.3
By region				
Europe and Central Asia	10.9	11.0	6.7	9.8
East Asia	9.9	16.8	8.7	13.1
Latin America	17.1	8.5	11.9	13.1
SSA	4.5	13.3	14.2	17.7
South Asia	8.2	11.7	18.8	19.7

Source: Srinivasan (2002).

3.2. Growth accounting in international perspective

To put MENA growth performance in further international perspective, we use the growth accounting framework to see whether factor accumulation or factor productivity has accounted for most of the growth differential between MENA and the other regions in the sample.

Growth can be the result of the growth of inputs such as capital and labor or the increase in the efficiency of these inputs, namely, their productivity. The debate over the share of inputs as compared with that of their total productivity is still very lively. The empirical evidence is mixed. Mankiw *et al.* (1992) and many others argue that the share of physical and human capital together with population growth account for as much as 80 percent of international variation in per capita income. Young (1995), in contrast, argues that what is often labeled as the "Asian miracle," is the outcome of a temporary rapid factor accumulation. Those holding a different view claim that TFP is the key to economic growth and that factor accumulation plays only a less important role.[13]

The share of capital in total income needed in a typical growth accounting exercise could be imposed *a priori*, computed from national income accounts or estimated. Each one of these approaches has its own caveats. Imposing a uniform value, typically between 0.3 and 0.4, is not realistic since this value varies a great deal across a wide spectrum of countries. Computation of this value from national accounts, in contrast, is too data demanding especially in light of the availability of internationally comparable data on capital stock and labor that would readily permit the direct estimation of the capital share. In this paper, we have chosen the estimation approach.

To carry out the accounting exercise, we have used a two-factor, homogeneous of degree one, Cobb–Douglas production function in per capita form. Capital shares required to measure the relative contribution of factor accumulation and productivity were estimated using the following regression equation:

$$\Delta \text{Log}(Y_{it}/L_{it}) = \lambda_i + \alpha_i \Delta \text{Log}(K_{it}/L_{it}) + \varepsilon_{it}$$

The slope coefficient in the above equation represents the capital share in output, Y represents real output, K the capital stock and L the labor. Y is measured by real GDP and is obtained from the World Bank database. The capital stock data are taken from Nehru and Dhareshwar (1994) and L is approximated by total labor force and taken from the World Bank World Development Indicators. Real GDP and capital stock series are based on 1987 constant prices.

The sample we used comprises 92 countries and the data cover the period 1960–1997. The list of countries included in our sample was determined on the basis of the availability of capital stock data in Nehru and Dhareshwar (1994)

---

[13] See for instance, Klenow and Clare (1997).

Table 8. *Regional average capital shares*

Region	Number of Countries	Average Capital Share (Short-term Version)	Average Capital Share (Long-term Version)
Whole sample (world)	92	0.67	0.59
MENA	11	0.61	0.54
East Asia	6	0.48	0.38
SSA	21	0.59	0.48
Latin America	22	0.79	0.78

that used the perpetual inventory method to obtain capital stock series for the period 1950–1990 assuming a fixed annual depreciation rate of 4 percent.[14] In this paper, we have completed the capital series from 1991 until 1997 with fixed investment figures from the World Bank database using the same methodology and assumption.

To account for the possible impact of the noise generated by the high variability of yearly data, we have estimated two versions of the above equation. A short-term version using original data for the output per worker and capital per worker and a long-term version were obtained by smoothing the short-term variation of the same variables using three-year moving averages.

Table 8 provides the regional averages of capital shares using the two specifications indicated above. In this table, several remarks are in order. First, our estimates of the world average capital share were found to be above the commonly assumed values of 0.3 or 0.4. This finding is in line with the estimation results provided, for instance, in Senhadji (1999) and Nehru and Dhareshwar (1994) who have found capital shares above 0.5. Recently, Keller and Nabli (2002) reported an estimated value for the capital share of 0.49 based on a sample of 95 economies. Bisat *et al.* (1997) have previously found that the average capital share in many countries of the MENA region is well above 0.5 and ~0.7 for some oil-producing countries.

Second, high-performing East Asian countries hold the lowest capital shares in the group. Third, Latin American and industrialized countries have the highest capital shares. These findings have an implication for the computation of TFPG. Instead of imposing a uniform value for the share of capital over the entire sample of countries, we have made the less-restrictive hypothesis of assuming region-specific values based on the estimation results.

Table 9 provides estimates of the relative contribution of capital, labor and TFPG to the economic growth of the MENA countries included in the sample in comparison with the other regions.

---

[14] The MENA countries included in the sample are: Algeria, Egypt, Iran, Iraq, Jordan, Kuwait, Libya, Morocco, Sudan, Tunisia and Turkey.

Samir Makdisi, Zeki Fattah and Imed Limam

Table 9. GDP growth rate decomposition (1960–1997)

Country	Growth	Capital	Labor	TFP
Algeria	0.031	0.034	0.006	−0.009
Egypt	0.057	0.035	0.011	0.011
Iran	0.046	0.049	0.010	−0.013
Iraq	0.023	0.020	0.020	−0.016
Jordan	0.052	0.116	−0.013	−0.051
Kuwait	0.022	−0.015	0.056	−0.052
Libya	0.058	0.165	−0.011	−0.095
Morocco	0.049	0.025	0.013	0.011
Sudan	0.030	0.028	0.014	−0.020
Tunisia	0.051	0.028	0.012	0.010
Turkey	0.050	0.040	0.007	0.003
MENA	0.043	0.048	0.011	−0.020
SSA	0.028	0.020	0.011	−0.003
HASIA	0.066	0.044	0.015	0.008
LATIN	0.034	0.035	0.005	−0.006
World	0.037	0.032	0.007	−0.003

Overall, the results show the predominance of capital contribution over that of labor and TFPG in growth performance during the period 1960–1997. The MENA region as a whole, has experienced the lowest contribution of TFP to economic growth in comparison with the rest of the regions. For the 11 MENA countries included in the sample, only the diversified economies of Egypt, Morocco, Tunisia and Turkey managed to have positive TFPG. Out of the seven remaining MENA countries in the sample that had negative TFPG, five were oil-exporting countries. Although, the use of oil GDP in the computation of TFPG may be problematic owing to its large and persistent fluctuation (Bisat *et al.*, 1997, p. 17), lack of ample available data on employment and capital stock in the oil sector did not enable us to compute TFPG after excluding oil.

To assess the relative contribution of the variables accounting for interregional TFPG performance, we have regressed TFPG on relevant variables based on recently established results in the literature.[15] We conducted these regressions using values for capital shares ranging from 0.3 to 0.7. Each hypothetical value for capital share was applied uniformly over the different countries in the sample. This was done to see whether different values of the capital share affect the impact of the regressors on TFPG.

---

[15] Only six MENA countries were included in the analysis given the lack of data. They were: Algeria, Egypt, Jordan, Morocco, Tunisia and Turkey.

Table 10. **Determinants of TFPG at different values of capital share** [a,b] **dependent variable: TFPG**

Variable	$\alpha = 0.3$	$\alpha = 0.4$	$\alpha = 0.5$	$\alpha = 0.6$	$\alpha = 0.7$
ICRG	0.24 (3.00)[**]	0.18 (2.31)[**]	0.13 (1.56)	0.07 (0.83)	0.02 (0.20)
INFL	−0.001 (−2.08)[**]	−0.001 (−1.75)[*]	−0.001 (−1.44)	−0.0005 (−1.17)	−0.0004 (−0.94)
Y60	0.0004 (−6.62)[**]	−0.0003 (−5.37)[**]	−0.0002 (−4.05)[**]	0.0002 (−2.8)[**]	−0.0001 (−1.70)
PRIM60	0.02 (2.75)[**]	0.02 (2.59)[**]	0.02 (2.41)[**]	0.02 (2.21)[**]	0.01 (2.01)[**]
SXP	−1.71 (−2.01)[**]	−1.12 (−1.31)	−0.55 (−0.61)	0.03 (0.04)	0.61 (0.62)
EASIA	−0.19 (−0.51)	−0.49 (−1.42)	−0.79 (−2.38)[**]	−1.09 (−3.30)[**]	−1.39 (−4.07)[**]
SSA	−0.89 (−2.60)[**]	−0.68 (−1.87)[*]	−0.47 (−1.20)	−0.26 (−0.61)	−0.05 (−0.11)
LATIN	−0.67 (−2.27)	−0.61 (−1.99)[**]	−0.56 (−1.71)	−0.50 (−1.43)	−0.45 (−1.19)
Adjusted R^2	0.58	0.45	0.29	0.16	0.09
Number of observations	75	75	75	75	75

[a]Constant terms not included and *t*-ratios in parentheses.
[b]Estimation based on White heteroskedasticity-consistent standard errors.
[**]Significant at the 5 percent level,
[*]Significant at the10 percent level.

The included regressors were the quality of institutions, International Country Risk Guide, ICRG;[16] inflation rate, INFL; the initial income, Y60; the initial enrollment rate in primary school, PESENR60 and the adopted measure of natural resource abundance, SXP. Other conventional variables such as openness, growth in terms of trade and political stability have been tried, but were dropped for lack of statistical significance. Regional dummies were also included to account for interregional differences.

Table 10 reveals that for lower values of the capital share, the parameter estimates tend to be significant and of the expected signs. Institutions and the stock of human capital, as approximated by the initial enrollment rate, positively affect the TFPG. The negative sign attached to the initial income points to the existence of a catching-up effect at the TFPG level. Inflation was also found to affect the TFPG negatively. Finally, the natural resource curse was found to apply at the productivity level, too. In other words, natural resource abundance affects TFPG negatively.

At higher values of the capital share, the explanatory power of the model drops. This is due to the fact that at higher values of the capital shares, capital accounts for a higher portion of the overall economic growth as well as the TFPG. Hence the other variables become less relevant. However, it should be

---

[16]Our measure of institutions, ICRG, is a composite of four indicators: (a) government repudiation of contracts, (b) risk of expropriation, (c) rule of law and (d) bureaucratic quality. This measure is computed for the decade of the 1980s and is borrowed from Easterly and Levine (1997). Knack and Keefer (1995) were the first to introduce these institutional variables into growth empirics.

Table 11.   **Relative contribution of relevant variables to TFP growth differential**[a]

Variable	MENA–World	MENA–SSA	MENA–Hasia	MENA–Latin
ICRG	−0.18	−0.04	−0.48	0.49
INFL	0.03	0.04	0.00	0.05
Y60	0.39	−0.07	0.05	−0.01
PESENR60	−0.31	0.19	−0.54	−0.21
SXP	0.01	0.06	0.09	−0.13

[a]Assumptions: MENA $\alpha = 0.5$; SSA $\alpha = 0.5$; Hasia $\alpha = 0.4$; Latin $\alpha = 0.7$; world $\alpha = 0.5$.

mentioned that the only two variables that remained significant for different values of the capital share were the initial income and human capital. This result is widely in line with the recent empirical findings on the TFPG.[17] While the initial level of income affects the potential of catching up notably through higher productivity, human capital affects the TFP by determining the capacity of a country to innovate and the speed of technological diffusion.

To put the TFPG performance of the MENA countries into global perspective, we have computed the contribution of the relevant variables to TFPG for different values of the capital share. Table 11 reports the results after applying different regional values for the capital share. Based on our estimation, we have applied the value of 0.5 to the MENA, Sub-Saharan regions as well as to the whole sample. The values applied for the other regions were 0.4 for East Asia and 0.7 for Latin America.

Overall, the results exhibited in Table 11, point to the overriding importance of the quality of institutions and the stock of human capital in explaining the lower productivity performance of the MENA countries in comparison with the high-performing East Asian countries and with the rest of the world in general.

More specifically, Table 11 shows that human capital, as approximated by initial enrollment ratios, accounts for the MENA region's TFPG underperformance with respect to East Asia and Latin America. Despite the net improvement in many educational institutions in the MENA countries, illiteracy ratios remain very high and the educational attainment of the labor force very low in comparison with the other regions in the world.

For the year 2000, UNESCO predicted that the illiteracy ratio in the MENA region would be around 31 percent for adults above 15 years compared to 26 percent in the group of developing countries and 13 percent in the East Asia and Pacific region. These statistics are even more alarming given the high gender gap in terms of literacy and in comparison with the other regions in the world. The average illiteracy rate among females in the MENA region for the year 2000 was expected to be around 40 percent; almost double the average

---

[17]See for instance the findings of Senhadji (1999) and Benhabib and Spiegel (1994).

illiteracy rate for males.[18] Illiteracy among women is linked to poor health and low education attainment among children, and hence the low quality of human capital.

The recent statistics published by Barro and Lee (2000) provide further evidence of the relative weaker educational attainment of the labor force in the MENA region in comparison with the other regions in the world. For instance, they estimated that the average years of schooling for the population aged 15 and over, for the year 2000, for the high-performing MENA countries such as Egypt, Jordan, Syria, Tunisia and Turkey will be: 5.51, 6.91, 5.77, 5.02 and 5.29, respectively. These rates do not compare favorably with 8.83 for Argentina, 7.55 for Chile, 10.84 in Korea, 7.05 for Singapore and 8.76 in Taiwan.[19]

Using panel data for six countries in the MENA region, El-Erian *et al.* (1998, p. 11) have found that the rapid expansion in education did not result in higher productivity or more rapid economic growth.[20] They argue that the weak link that they found between education and growth may be due to the low quality of education that focuses more on repetition of definitions, knowledge of facts and concepts and less on developing critical thinking and problem-solving capacity. In addition, the educational system had been focused on preparing students for public sector employment. This outcome is largely attributed to distorted educational choices in these countries caused by the higher wages prevailing in the dominant public sector that are set without consideration for alternative employment opportunities in other sectors.

Economic Research Forum (ERF) for the Arab countries, Iran and Turkey (2000, p. 6) reports that for the early 1990s, the average share of civilian government employment in the MENA region was about 17.5 percent compared with <9 percent for the developing countries as a group. In addition, the share of central government wages in GDP was at 10 percent; almost double that of the world average. As rightly argued by the report, this situation has resulted in the prevalence of acute job redundancies and increasing unemployment rates in the region owing to the glaring mismatch between the outcomes of the educational system and the requirements of the rapidly changing labor market.

To explain the lower quality of education, Ridha (1998) argues that in most countries of the region education systems are overpoliticized to the extent that they deviate from the objectives they are supposed to achieve. The educational tools and practices such as the curriculum, textbooks and teaching methods are often manipulated to reach political ends.

---

[18] These statistics are derived from the UNESCO *Statistical Yearbook* (1999).
[19] These updated statistics are available on the following web site: http://www2.cid.harvard.edu/ciddata/. The data set could also be accessed through the web page of Jong-Wha Lee: web.korea.ac.kr/~jwlee.
[20] The countries included in their studies are: Algeria, Egypt, Jordan, Kuwait, Syria and Tunisia.

Another argument advanced by Pritchett (2001) can possibly explain the weak link between education and productivity growth in the MENA countries. He argues that in a perverse institutional environment such as the one prevailing in many MENA countries, education and accumulated capital could be used in wasteful and counterproductive activities. In addition, the fact that most of these countries are natural resource-abundant, provides further incentives for the proliferation of rent-seeking activities.

The second important factor explaining the underperformance of the MENA region in terms of the TFPG is the quality of its institutions. Institutions can be defined as the regular and patterned forms of social behavior and interaction among human beings established by formal and informal rules.[21] Institutions matter for growth and productivity because they affect incentives of actors. For they affect the behavior of people in a society and very often lock their behavior within a regularized pattern, institutions may produce path dependence that could explain prolonged periods of poor economic performance and hence the inability of the poor countries to catch up.

Many published indicators for the quality of institutions show that the MENA region lags behind most of the regions in the world. The average value of the variable used in our paper to depict the overall quality of institutions, ICRG, for MENA countries was 4.31. This score is below that of the world average, 5.59, and the high-performing East Asian countries, 6.37. A recent report by the World Bank (2002) using a composite index of governance that includes several relevant indicators of the quality of institutions such as the quality of administration and accountability shows that the MENA region ranks at the bottom when compared with countries with the same level of income.

A similar conclusion can be reached based on the results of a study by Kaufman *et al.* (2002) to estimate six dimensions of governance that represent reasonable indicators for the quality of institutions. In comparing the score of the different regions in the world for the year 2000, we have found that MENA lags behind most of the regions in terms of voice and accountability, that is, the ability of citizens to participate in decision making and hold accountable public officials and regulatory quality that has to do with regulations governing the business sector, government intervention, quality of legislation, investment environment and tax effectiveness.

Table 12 shows the average scores for five institutional indicators published by the Political Risk Services: government stability, investment profile, corruption in government, rule of law and quality of bureaucracy. Despite the fact that the MENA countries have better scores than the world averages for three out of the five reported indicators, the indicators of corruption and bureaucracy

---

[21] North (1990).

Table 12.   Institutional indicators of the MENA region[a]

Group	MENA (1995)	East Asia[b] (1995)	World (1995)	MENA (2000)	East Asia (2000)	World (2000)
Government stability	6.9	7.1	6.2	7.5	10.3	7.4
Investment profile	5.7	6.5	5.5	10.2	8.0	9.9
Corruption in government	3.1	3.9	3.5	2.5	2.8	3.0
Rule of law	4.4	5.1	4.3	4.1	4.1	4.0
Quality of bureaucracy	2.0	2.8	2.3	1.7	3.0	2.2

Source: PRS Group (2002), *International Country Risk Guide.*
[a]Higher scores mean better institutions and vice versa.
[b]Includes only the eight best-performing East Asian countries.

remain, however, below world averages and much lower than those of the high-performing East Asian countries.

Empirical work has shown that governance and institutions affect the quality of policy which has a direct bearing on investment and business climate (Knack and Keefer, 1995, 1997). As regards the MENA countries, reducing bureaucratic ineffectiveness, red tape, corruption, excessive government intrusion and improving the deplorable state of government services remain, in this regard, major challenging tasks for the MENA region.

4. Explaining intraregional MENA growth performance

In the previous section, the growth performance of MENA countries was compared with the other reference regions. In this section, we will dwell on the relative performance of individual MENA countries with respect to the region's average performance.

As shown previously in Table 3, there is a considerable variation in the growth performance of MENA countries during 1970–2000. It was also shown that growth in the oil-exporting countries was subject to a higher variability than that of the non-oil exporting countries. In addition, the average growth performance of the oil-exporting countries has been below that of the non-oil exporting countries. The MENA countries that were able to achieve an average real per capita GDP growth rate over 2 percent a year during the period 1960–1998 were the non-oil exporting countries, except, Oman. The best growth performers were Egypt, Jordan, Morocco, Oman, Syria, Tunisia and Turkey. Oman's average growth rate was the highest followed by that of Egypt and Tunisia.

Interestingly enough, only countries with relatively high growth rates have managed to achieve positive TFPG over the last three decades or so. Oil-exporting countries have, in general, had negative TFPG. These facts are corroborated by our own estimates and those of the few studies such as, Keller and Nabli (2002), Bisat *et al.* (1997) and Nehru and Dhareshwar (1994) that have provided estimates for TFP growth rates for countries in the MENA region.

In addition, MENA growth overachievers had in general the lowest growth variability among the sample group except, Oman. The higher variability of the latter can be attributed to the fact that it is an oil-exporter and therefore subject to the effect of oil price fluctuation.

Available data and the scope of this study do not permit the establishment of systematic links between growth performance and the country-specific character-istics (structural, policy, initial conditions, institutional, political and other internal and external factors). Preliminary analysis indicates, however, that the better achievers tend to have above-average indicators for integration in the world eco-nomy; be it through the crude measure of openness, share of FDI in GDP or share of manufactured exports in total exported commodity. They also tend to be more diversified and have initiated economic reform earlier than the other countries.

To account for the relative growth performance within the MENA region, we have used a cross-country regression framework applied to a panel of data comprising 13 MENA countries and spanning the period 1970–1998. For the sake of increasing sample variation, we have used for each country six 5-year period averages for all variables and for the periods 1970–1974, 1975–1979, 1980–1984, 1985–1989, 1990–1994 and 1995–1998. The last period is one year shorter than the previous periods for lack of relevant data.

We have adopted the same cross-country regression framework used previ-ously. However, some of the variables were discarded for lack of statistical sig-nificance. Other variables were appended to reflect either specific characteristics of the region or cross-country differences in terms of factors affecting growth. For instance, we have included government consumption as a ratio to GDP, GCY, to reflect the predominant role of the state in the region and the impact of govern-ment-induced distortions. We have also included the share of manufactures in total merchandise exports, MANUF, to reflect the impact of economic diversi-fication (or the lack of it) on growth as well as the extent of competitiveness in international markets. The debt-service ratio, DEBTS, was included to reflect the impact of debt overhang on the growth of many countries in the region.

The other variables we have used are: the share of investment in GDP, INVY; the GDP per capita growth of each country's trading partners weighted by trade shares, GPART and the level of income per capita in the beginning of each period, YINI.

The model was estimated using the random-effect panel regression method.[22] Although the estimation results of this dynamic panel may have been plagued by

---

[22] Hausman's specification statistic for the test of fixed versus random-effect model was (1.23 at 6 degrees of freedom) in favor of the latter with a *p*- value of 0.98.

Table 13. **Panel data estimation of growth determinants in the MENA region dependent variable: per capita GDP growth rate**

Variable	Coefficient	T-Ratio
INVY	0.15	2.46**
DEBTS	−0.10	−2.91**
GPART	0.91	2.48**
MANUF	0.03	1.72*
YINI	−0.0004	−4.48**
GCY	−0.16	−2.33**

Number of countries = 15; number of observations used = 61; adjusted R^2 = 0.51; country intercepts not reported.
**Significant at the 5 percent level.
*Significant at the 10 percent level.

Table 14. **Relative contribution of relevant variables to growth differential in selected MENA countries**

Country	Predicted Growth	INVY	DEBTS	GPART	MANUF	YINI	GCY	Individual Effect
Algeria	0.36	4.88	−4.38	1.65	0.07	−0.98	−2.44	1.54
Bahrain	−1.21	3.94	0.00	0.36	0.27	−3.74	−3.41	1.36
Egypt	2.93	3.27	−1.76	1.90	0.91	−0.60	−2.60	1.81
Iran	−0.03	3.72	−0.27	1.50	0.08	−1.69	−3.13	−0.23
Jordan	2.19	4.52	−1.56	1.52	1.40	−1.10	−4.23	1.64
Morocco	1.66	3.56	−3.02	1.45	1.34	−0.71	−2.72	1.76
Oman	3.15	4.16	−0.35	2.64	0.55	−2.46	−4.23	2.85
Saudi Arabia	0.02	3.18	0.00	2.37	1.15	−3.37	−4.09	1.77
Sudan	0.45	1.96	−1.75	1.35	0.04	−0.30	−1.93	1.09
Syria	1.67	3.47	−1.36	1.52	0.67	−1.58	−2.60	1.54
Tunisia	3.09	4.11	−1.91	1.55	1.85	−0.98	−2.45	0.92
Turkey	2.33	2.95	−2.58	1.39	1.58	−1.13	−1.65	1.78
UAE	−3.09	4.23	0.00	2.28	0.99	−9.25	−2.55	1.22

the inconsistency of the estimates owing to short sample size, we use these results to convey some of the views presented above and to single out country-specific factors that have shaped growth in certain MENA countries.[23] The estimation results reported in Table 13 show that the parameters of all the variables considered were statistically significant and of the expected sign.

Based on the data available for 15 countries, Table 14 shows that high investment ratios have contributed significantly to the relatively better growth performance of countries such as Oman and Tunisia. In contrast, export

---

[23] We owe this argument to an anonymous referee.

diversification and international competitiveness explain the relatively better performance of countries such as Tunisia, Turkey, Jordan and Morocco. Debt overhang has negatively impacted growth in Algeria, Morocco and Turkey. Large government size has had a detrimental effect on growth in Jordan, Oman and Saudi Arabia. Variation in trading partner growth has had a notable impact on the growth of oil-exporting countries such as Oman, Saudi Arabia and the UAE. Finally, the high variation in individual country's intercepts in Table 14, points to the fact that the country-specific growth determinants or the unexplained growth, remain relatively high. These individual factors should be tackled at a more disaggregated country-specific level.

5. Concluding remarks

The overall growth performance of the MENA region has been mixed as well as characterized by a higher degree of volatility in comparison with the other regions of the world. Several sources of uncertainty in the region can explain this volatility. These include, among others, fluctuations in world oil prices, weather conditions, workers' remittances, capital flows, not to mention factors contributing to sociopolitical instability in the region such as civil wars and regional conflicts.

In analyzing the growth pattern of the MENA region within an international perspective, we have found that: capital is less efficient; trade openness less beneficial to growth and the impact of adverse external shocks more pronounced. In addition and in comparison with the other regions, TFPG was the least important source of growth in MENA.

Among the MENA countries included in the sample, only Egypt, Morocco, Tunisia and Turkey had positive TFPG. The quality of institutions and human capital accounted for the lower performance of the MENA countries in terms of TFPG and in comparison with the other regions of the world. MENA still lags behind the rest of the world in terms of the quality of its bureaucracy and a business environment that provides weak incentives for investment and depresses its return.

Human capital was also found to contribute to the relative underperformance of the MENA region. Educational attainment of the labor force remains relatively low in comparison with the other regions and illiteracy rates, especially among women, continue to be relatively high. The dominance of the public sector in the economy together with guaranteed employment of university graduates in most of the MENA countries may have had a negative impact on productivity.

The degree of exposure to internal and external shocks, the extent of economic diversification and international competitiveness were also found to be relevant factors in explaining variations in growth performance within the MENA region.

In view of the aggregate nature of our study and in light of the above findings, several relevant issues deserve further analysis within a country-specific context. Future research on the region needs to shed important additional lights on the determinants of growth in each of the countries concerned. Among the areas that deserve further investigation are the within-regional variation in the role of human and physical capital, the influence of the State, institutions and the relative impact of external and internal shocks as they relate to economic growth. This analysis would contribute to our understanding of the growth process in the MENA countries. It is equally useful to show, for instance, how economic policy, institutions, politics and other country characteristics affect the way factors of productions are used and combined.

It would also be desirable to analyze the impact of the sectoral decomposition of growth in the MENA countries. Such a decomposition is useful for identifying the sectors that have been successful in achieving better growth performance, expanding investment and employment and raising productivity and earnings. This decomposition should also help explain why certain sectors have been more successful than the others.

Last but not the least is the urgent need for policy makers and researchers alike to find ways to deal with the major challenges in the region, namely, improving resilience to external and internal shocks, diversifying economic activity and reducing excessive reliance on natural resources, improving the business environment and the quality of institutions for higher and more productive investment in physical and human capital and devising an adequate incentive structure for a more job-creating growth.

Acknowledgements

The authors would like to thank Bill Easterly, Dani Rodrik, Jong-Wha Lee, Seppo Honkapohja, two anonymous referees and others for their comments on the earlier drafts of the paper including those present during the World Bank-sponsored workshop on the Global Development Network held in Prague during the period June 9–11, 2000.

References

Barro, R. (1991), "Economic growth in a cross-section of countries", *Quarterly Journal of Economics*, Vol. 104, pp. 407–433.

Barro, R. and J.W. Lee (2000), "International data on educational attainment: updates and implications", *Working Paper No. 42*, Center for International Development at Harvard University, April.

Benhabib, J. and M. Spiegel (1994), "The role of human capital in economic development: evidence from aggregate cross-country data", *Journal of Monetary Economics*, Vol. 34, pp. 143–173.

Binder, M. and M.H. Pesaran (1999), "Stochastic growth models and their econometric implications", *Journal of Economic Growth*, Vol. 4, pp. 139–183.

Bisat, A., M.A. El-Erian and T. Helbling (1997), "Growth investment, and saving in the Arab economies", IMF Working Paper WP/97/85.

Easterly, W. and R. Levine (1997), "Africa's growth tragedy: policies and ethnic divisions", *Quarterly Journal of Economics*, Vol. 112(4), pp. 1203–1250.

Economic Research Forum (ERF) for the Arab Countries, Iran and Turkey (2000), *Economic Trends in the MENA Region*, Cairo.

El Badawi, I. (1999), "Can reforming countries perform an Asian miracle?: role of institutions and governance on private investment", in: I. Limam, editor, *Institutional Reform and Development in the MENA Region*, Arab Planning Institute and Economic Research Forum for the Arab Countries, Iran and Turkey.

El-Erian, M., T. Helbling and J. Page (1998), "Education, human capital development and growth in the Arab economies", Paper presented in the Joint Arab Monetary Fund, Arab Fund for Economic and Social Development Seminar on "Human Resource Development and Economic Growth", May 17–18, 1998, Abu Dhabi, UAE.

Fischer, S. (1993), "The role of macroeconomic factors in growth", *Journal of Monetary Economics*, Vol. 32(3), pp. 485–512.

Gamo, P.A., A. Fedelino and S.P. Horvitz (1997), "Globalization and growth prospects in Arab countries", IMF Working Paper WP/79/127.

Gourieroux, C. and A. Monfort (1996), Statistique et Modèles Econométriques, Vol. 2, *Economica*, 2d edition, Paris.

Kaufman, D., A. Kraay and P. Zoido-Lobaton (2002), "Governance matters II: updated Indicators for 2000/2001", available through internet at: http://www.worldbank.org.

Keller, J. and M.K. Nabli (2002), "The macroeconomics of labor markets outcomes in MENA over the 1990s: how growth has failed to keep pace with a burgeoning labor market", World Bank, available through internet at http://www.worldbank.org/mdf/mdf4/papers/keller-nabli.pdf.

Klenow, P.J. and A.R. Clare (1997), "The neoclassical revival in growth economics: has it gone too far?" in: NBER, *Macroeconomics Annual 1997*, Cambridge, MA: MIT Press.

Knack, S. and P. Keefer (1995), "Institutions and economic performance: cross-country test using alternative institutional measures", *Economies and Politics*, Vol. 7(3), pp. 207–227.

Knack, S. and P. Keefer (1997), "Does social capital have an economic payoff: a cross country investigation", *Quarterly Journal of Economics*, Vol. 112(4), pp. 1251–1288.

Levine, R. and D. Renelt (1992), "A sensitivity analysis of cross-country growth regressions", *American Economic Review*, Vol. 82(4), pp. 942–963.

Mankiw, N.G., D. Romer and D.N. Weil (1992), "A contribution to the empirics of economic growth", *Quarterly Journal of Economics*, Vol. 107(2), pp. 407–437.

Nehru, V. and Dhareshwar A. (1994), "New estimates of total factor productivity growth for developing and industrial countries", Policy Research Working Paper # 1313, World Bank.

North, D.C. (1990), *Institutions, Institutional Change and Economic Performance*, Cambridge: Cambridge University Press, Cambridge.

Nunnenkamp, P. (2004), "Why economic growth has been weak in Arab countries: the role of exogenous shocks, economic policy failure and institutional deficiencies", *Journal of Development and Economic Policy*, Vol. 7(2), pp. 1–18.

Page, J. (1998), "From Boom to Bust- and Back? The Crisis of Growth in the Middle East and North Africa", in: N. Shafik, editor, *Prospects for Middle Eastern and North African Economies: From Boom to Bust and Back?*, Economic Research Forum for Arab Countries, Iran and Turkey, Cairo.

Political Risk Services (PRS) Group (2002), *International Country Risk Guide*, New York.

Pritchett, L. (2001), "Where has all the education gone?", *World Bank Economic Review*, Vol. 15(3), pp. 367–391.

Radelet, S., J. Sachs and J.W. Lee (1997), *Economic Growth in Asia*, Boston: Harvard Institute for International Development, Boston.

Ramey, G. and V. Ramey (1995), "Cross-country evidence on the link between volatility and growth", *American Economic Review*, Vol. 85, pp. 1138–1151.

Ridha, M.J. (1998), "Charting the future education and change in the Arab countries: a platform for the 21st century", Paper presented in the Joint Arab Monetary Fund, Arab Fund for Economic and Social Development Seminar on "Human Resource Development and Economic Growth," May 17–18, 1998, Abu Dhabi, UAE.

Sachs, J.D. and A.M. Warner (1995), "Economic reform and the process of global integration", *Brookings Papers on Economic Activity*, Vol. 10(1), pp. 118, Washington DC.

Sachs, J.D. and A.M. Warner (1997a), "Natural resource abundance and economic growth", Center for International Development and Harvard Institute for International Development, Boston.

Sachs, J.D. and A.M. Warner (1997b), "Sources of slow growth in african economies", *Journal of African Economies*, Vol. 6(3), pp. 335–376, Oxford.

Senhadji, A. (1999), "Sources of economic growth: an extensive growth accounting exercise", IMF Working Paper WP/99/77.

Srinivasan, T.G. (2002), "Globalization in MENA: a long term perspective", Paper presented at the fourth Mediterranean Development Forum, October 6–9, 2002, Amman, Jordan.

UNESCO (1999), *Statistical Yearbook*, several issues, Paris.

United Nations (1999), Human Development Report 1999, New York.

World Bank (2000), *Global Economic Prospects and the Developing Countries 2000*, : World Bank Publication.

World Bank (2002), "Better governance for development in the Middle East and North Africa," available through internet at http://www.worldbank.org.

World Bank, *World Development Indicators* CD-ROM, several issues Washington DC.

World Bank, Global Research Project (GRP) Database Washington DC.

Young, A. (1995), "The tyranny of numbers: confronting the statistical realities of the East Asian growth experience", *Quarterly Journal of Economics*, Vol. 110(3), pp. 641–680.

CHAPTER 3

A Reexamination of the Political Economy of Growth in the MENA Countries

Hadi Salehi Esfahani[*]

Abstract

Since the 1980s, economic growth in the Middle East and North African (MENA) region has been low and volatile. The problem has been attributed to bad economic policies such as excessive government interventions, large public sectors, restrictive trade policies, inefficient mass subsidies, and badly managed fiscal policies. This paper examines the political economy factors that have shaped those policies and their outcomes. It offers a framework based on the recent political economy literature to explore the deeper forces behind the puzzles of growth variations in the region, going beyond the claims that powerful interest groups have been blocking reform. It focuses on the reasons why interest groups and politicians may not have been able to adopt better policies and generate larger surpluses for them to reap. The usefulness of the framework is illustrated by applications to key political economy issues in MENA. The paper examines the mechanisms through which resource rents have affected government policies and economic growth in the region and argues that the impact has varied depending on other factors. The analysis includes the roles of authoritarianism, social heterogeneity, geopolitical rents and threats, human capital, and administrative and judicial institutions. It shows how resource rents and other factors have shaped government interventions and economic growth prior to the 1980s and how they made adjustment and growth costly later on to varying degrees.

Keywords: political economy, growth, Middle East, North Africa

JEL classifications: O1, O4, O5, O53, P16

*Corresponding author.

CONTRIBUTIONS TO ECONOMIC ANALYSIS
VOLUME 278   ISSN: 0573-8555
DOI:10.1016/S0573-8555(06)78003-8

1. Introduction

Over the past two decades, economic growth in the Middle East and North African (MENA) countries has been generally low and relatively volatile (see Figure 1 and Table 1). This has been the case compared to the rest of the developing world as well as MENA's own prior experience. A widely held view among the economists studying the region links the problem to bad economic policies adopted by the MENA governments. The view suggests that those policies can typically be characterized by extensive government intervention, large public sectors, restrictive trade policies, inefficient mass subsidies (especially for energy and food), and precarious fiscal conditions (Henry and Springborg, 2001; Abed and Davoodi, 2003; Sala-i-Martín and Artadi, 2003; Yousef, 2004). However, if such policies can indeed be held responsible for low growth, one has to wonder why many governments have opted for them. Moreover, to the extent that actual policies have been different from this description, there is still a question why those policies were selected and why they did not work in many cases.

Figure 1.   Weighted average PPP GDP per worker in MENA and non-MENA developing countries

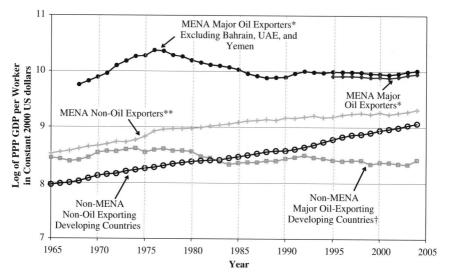

Note: The weights for averaging are countries' PPP GDP.
*Algeria, Bahrain, Iran, Kuwait, Oman, Saudi Arabia, the United Arab Emirates (UAE), and Yemen.
**Egypt, Jordan, Morocco, Sudan, Syria, Tunisia, and Turkey. Other countries are excluded owing to lack of sufficient data. There is data for Lebanon after 1988, but adding it to the chart does not change the picture much for those years.
†Angola, the Republic of Congo, Gabon, Nigeria, Trinidad and Tobago, and Venezuela.
Source: Calculated based on World Bank's *World Development Indicators* (2006).

Table 1. Per worker GDP growth and volatility in MENA countries

Country[a]	Average Per Worker GDP Growth Rate					Standard Deviation for the Years Available
	Period					
	1955–1964	1965–1974	1975–1984	1985–1994	1995–2004	
Oil exporting						
Algeria	1.52	4.71	2.20	−3.16	0.00	8.51
Bahrain	n.a.	n.a.	−6.30	1.01	1.36	6.67
Iran	6.95	9.87	−1.66	−0.26	0.89	7.50
Kuwait	n.a.	−4.17	−8.81	−1.12	−2.95	10.57
Oman	4.30	16.83	4.48	1.72	0.44	16.27
Saudi Arabia	n.a.	13.52	−4.37	−0.32	−0.41	8.69
UAE	n.a.	−6.64	−4.66	−4.58	−0.39	8.60
Yemen	n.a.	n.a.	n.a.	1.90	1.80	4.46
Non-oil exporting						
Egypt	3.42	1.35	6.49	0.78	1.42	3.56
Jordan	6.86	−0.62	8.24	−3.13	−0.72	8.99
Lebanon	n.a.	n.a.	n.a.	8.08	0.59	18.55
Morocco	0.67	2.58	1.95	1.60	0.36	4.43
Sudan	−1.28	−0.11	1.28	1.80	2.90	5.71
Syria	6.78	4.44	3.01	1.35	0.26	8.01
Tunisia	6.05	4.07	1.94	1.14	1.87	3.52
Turkey	4.69	3.74	2.17	1.53	1.86	4.74
Non-MENA oil exporters[b]	5.32	1.94	−2.84	1.08	0.08	6.79
Non-MENA non-oil exporters[b]	4.43	2.98	2.14	2.89	3.18	4.61

n.a., not available.
Source: Calculated based on World Bank's *World Development Indicators* (2006), Augmented for years before 1965 by growth rate data from *Penn World Tables, http://pwt.econ.upenn.edu/*.
[a]Djibouti, Iraq, Libya, Oman, Qatar, and West Bank and Gaza are not included owing to lack of sufficient data.
[b]Weighted averages, with each country's PPP GDP serving as its weight. Oil exporters consist of Angola, the Republic of Congo, Gabon, Nigeria, Trinidad and Tobago, and Venezuela.

A number of political economy studies of the MENA countries have sought to answer the above question by searching for politically organized groups that find growth-enhancing policies inimical to their interests and, thus, try to block the adoption of such policies (see, e.g., Richards, 1991; Sadowski, 1991; Waterbury, 1993; Henry and Springborg, 2001). However, the answers proposed in these studies are often incomplete because they do not explain why in the slow-growing countries the interest groups and politicians cannot find ways to adopt better policies that generate larger surpluses for them to reap.

Another popular explanation of bad policies and growth failures is based on the so-called "natural resource curse" hypothesis. The argument is that large oil rents can induce a voracious rent seeking that erodes institutional development through effects such as massive corruption, patronage, etc. (Leite and Weidmann, 1999). This effect is believed to undermine growth because it hampers the government's ability to implement efficient policies. The problem is further compounded by the oil-rich countries' need to manage the revenue volatility and the real exchange appreciation that oil rents entail (Ersel and Kandil, 2007; Makdisi, et al., 2007). While these effects have often been detected empirically in the data, their theoretical foundations have not been clear. In particular, when one observes countries such as Norway manage their oil rents well without institutional deterioration, it becomes clear that there is a need to explore the conditions under which the explanation applies (Sala-i-Martin and Subramanian, 2003).

A third interpretation of MENA's growth pattern combines the interest group and resource curse explanations into a more structured perspective. This approach argues that the rising natural resource rents prior to 1980 allowed high investment and high growth while strengthening redistributive policies in the form of implicit "social contracts" between the rulers, the public, and various interest groups in MENA societies. Later, those social contracts came to haunt MENA economies when resource rents declined. The reason was that the region's politicians were still expected to deliver on their distributive promises in exchange for public acquiescence to their rule. This may have severely constrained the room for the reorientation of policies toward higher efficiency and growth (Yousef, 2004). However, this view still leaves the details regarding the nature of social contracts and the sources of their variation across countries and over time unspecified. This is important because the view does not show why MENA polities did not continue to demand growth in the past quarter century and often settled with inefficient redistributive deals. Even if the initial contracts had a redistributive character, one wonders why their bases did not shift toward growth, especially when resource rents diminished. This is particularly puzzling because social contracts were also common among East Asian countries, which succeeded with little natural resources by emphasizing shared growth rather than pure redistribution (Campos and Root, 1996).

Another factor often mentioned as a cause of slow economic growth in MENA is the large amounts of labor and public funds devoted to military (Lebovic and Ishaq, 1987; United Nations Development Programme (UNDP), 2002; Abu-Bader and Abu-Qarn, 2003). Indeed, as Figure 2 shows, the MENA countries stand out among developing countries in terms of the military's share in employment and GDP. This is often attributed to the presence of domestic and international conflicts, especially the Arab–Israeli confrontations. Such conflicts and their associated military expenditures are believed to have contributed to economic risks and shortage of funds in the region, thus reducing the incentives and the ability to invest and enhance productivity. They may also have hindered the institutional developments needed for improved policymaking and economic performance. However, some have argued that given the presence

Figure 2. **Military expenditure, military personnel, and GDP growth in developing countries (1985–2004 averages)**

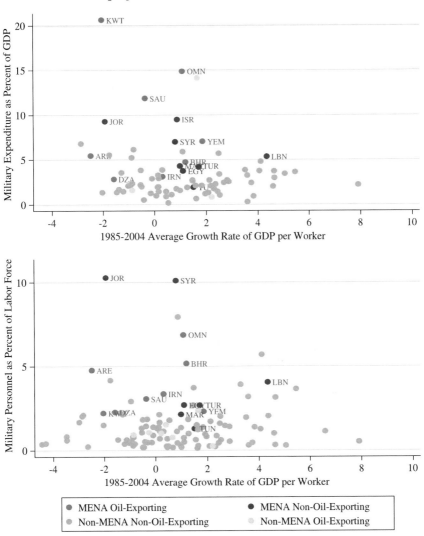

Source: World Bank, *World Development Indicators* (2006).

of conflicts, military expenditure may have played a positive role by bringing about stability and order (see especially the recent panel data analysis by Yildirim, *et al.*, 2005). Again, it is clear that there is a need to further explore the political economy factors that give rise to conflicts in the MENA region and shape their impacts on economic growth.

This paper proposes a framework based on the recent political economy literature that offers ways of finding deeper answers for the puzzles of growth variation and slowdown in the MENA region. The approach presented here is part of a growing number of perspectives on the political economy of growth that seek to explain differences in growth-related policies and institutions across countries. Recent examples of such work that also provide surveys of the literature are Castanheira and Esfahani (2003), Rodrik (2003, 2005) and Acemoglu *et al.* (2005a). Of course, the political economy literature is vast and the references given here are meant to be representative rather than exhaustive. The present paper refines the existing studies by integrating their findings around a key theme – namely, *incomplete contracting* – and by incorporating additional effects implied by that theme into the framework. The value of the framework is highlighted by applying it to some of the major growth issues of the MENA countries. The purpose of this application is not to find a definitive explanation for MENA's growth puzzle. Rather, the aim is to suggest that the proposed political economy framework is a promising approach for further case study and cross-country research on the subject. Some results of such case studies are synthesized in Esfahani (2006).

Section 2 discusses the analytical framework. Section 3 examines a number of policies and institutions in the MENA countries to show how the framework can shed light on the forces that may cause inefficiency in the interactions among the politicians, interest groups, and the public. Section 4 concludes.

2. A framework for analyzing the political economy of growth

The political economy literature studies the role of collective action processes (i.e., interest group activity, policymaking institutions, and the like) in resource allocation and rent distribution. One part of that literature focuses on economic growth and examines the impact of the collective action processes on the incentives of economic agents to invest and to improve productivity. That is, the key question in the *political economy of growth* is how much of an economy's potential surplus (i.e., *rents* and *quasi-rents* or the value produced in excess of the recurrent costs of production) is realized and guided toward growth-enhancing activities. While political economy in general is concerned with growth as well as distribution of the society's surplus, from a growth standpoint, distribution matters only to the extent that it affects the surplus being channeled toward productivity-enhancing investments.

To keep things simple, I identify three main categories of agents in the political economy systems: *the public* (or the population at large who act as *voters* when there are elections or other opportunities to show public approval or disapproval of policies or policymakers), *interest groups* (organized groups that influence policy decisions on a systematic basis but do not control it directly), and *political elites* (or, for short, *politicians*: elected or self-proclaimed policymakers, administrators, and political parties).[1] Politicians are interested in expanding their control over the government apparatus, which requires public and/or interest group support. Each member of the public and each *interest group* wants to maximize its net benefits from the economy and can offer its support to politicians in exchange for receiving the benefits induced by the policy. This implies that in choosing economic policies, politicians are largely motivated by the relative ability of interest groups and various segments of voters to support them. Struggles to capture a larger share of the economic surplus can arise both *within* and *across* interest groups and voter segments, and the eventual allocation is determined by the rules of the political game.

The main premise of the approach developed here is that *contracting problems are the key impediments to economic growth*. The argument is that it is the *incompleteness of contracts*, rather than the presence of social contracts, that has hindered MENA's growth. Contracting problems include asymmetric information and moral hazard as well as the difficulties and costs of writing complete contracts owing to complexities in foreseeing and specifying all possible contingencies in dynamic human transactions. As is well known from the Coase Theorem, in the absence of contracting problems, members of a society should be able to motivate each other and remove all inefficiencies in investment and production. This should render the largest social surplus that is technologically possible, and especially provide opportunities for rapid growth and catch-up when the country is not already at the production possibility frontier. Thus, when growth remains low in a developing country, there must be contracting problems that prevent the realization or proper allocation of the maximum surplus. The claim is that the more serious the contracting problems are, the lower the growth rate is likely to be.

The extent of contracting problems in a country depends on the characteristics of its *resources, politics,* and *institutions.* Here I define these concepts and discuss their relevant characteristics.

2.1. Resources

The available resources – including natural and human resources, physical capital, and technology – matter because they shape the possibilities for production and the nature of contracting and incentives required to reach efficiency. In

---

[1] One can further subdivide these categories to account for the relative powers or the ranks of the officials (e.g., ministers vs. civil servants, the dominant party vs. the others), or the real power of different interest groups (e.g., unions vs. the army or other groups present in the country). These divisions will be discussed below where needed. The main categories highlighted here capture the *functional* differences in their access to power: voters have power at election times, and much less power when elections are away. Instead, interest groups can maintain their influence (sometimes by monetary means, sometimes by demonstrations and strikes) on a more regular basis. Political elites, on their side, directly control the policy levers, favoring one or another group.

political economy studies, the nature of available resources normally receives attention only when natural resources play a major role in the economy. This aspect, of course, is particularly important for the MENA countries that are endowed with oil as well as the others that are indirectly affected through their exchanges with oil-exporting countries (e.g., via foreign aid, capital flows, and labor migration). However, this often overshadows the fact that human resources are also important because they help bring together other resources and make them productive by applying technology. Moreover, human capital can facilitate the identification of growth problems and the design and implementation of effective solutions for them. Most MENA countries face shortages of human capital in a variety of areas. Although there have been major efforts to expand education in the region, the achievements have been uneven partly because the policy circles themselves are often short of the expertise necessary to design and implement productive policies.

The key resource characteristics that need to be recognized and examined for understanding growth are those that determine how much rent and quasi-rent can be generated by the available resources, how elastic their supplies are, and how difficult it is to contract over the process by which they become available for production. For example, natural resources tend to have inelastic supplies and often generate large surpluses relative to costs of production, but the degree of contracting difficulty varies across different types of resources. For example, forests can be quickly cut, but oil requires long-term investment in exploration and extraction (Deacon and Bohn, 2000). The supply of human capital, in contrast, may be relatively more elastic and contracting over its delivery often faces major imperfections, especially in activities that require creativity and innovation (Hart, Shleifer, & Vishny, 1997). For physical capital, the supply is often elastic and contracting problems exist *ex ante*, but those elements diminish *ex post* once capital is in place.

2.2. Politics

Politics shapes the nature of group conflicts that need to be resolved in the collective action process. The diversity of preferences and fragmentation of the society (e.g., differences in language, religion, ethnicity, resource endowments, and others that lead to cleavages among groups) raise the likelihood of difficulties in making deals both at the micro and macro levels. A more contentious set of interest groups may exert greater effort to keep each other at bay and, as a result, may raise bigger obstacles for the adoption of collectively beneficial policies by the government. In particular, such demands can obstruct appropriate regulations (or give rise to excessive and inappropriate regulations) in the economy and, thus, result in significant inefficiency and slow growth (Alesina and Drazen, 1991; Alesina, *et al.*, 2003). In contrast, when there is harmony of interests or when the dominant groups have sufficiently encompassing interests, selected policies are more likely to be efficient (McGuire and Oslon, 1996).

It should be noted that although the boundaries of interest groups and the extent of their heterogeneity may be given in the short and medium runs, they do not necessarily remain fixed factors over decades, even when groups are formed based on language, religion, or ethnicity. In fact, many interest groups form around organizations, where the members develop common interests and specific capital associated with their organizations, as in industry-specific lobbies, the government bureaucracies, or the military. The dynamics of such groups and their interactions can be quite rich and complex, particularly because they strive to influence government policies and expenditures that may in turn affect their own position and strength (see Acemoglu and Robinson, 2001, and references therein).

Analyzing the role of heterogeneity in political and economic performance raises a number of key issues: which dimensions of diversity matter, in which ways, and how those dimensions must be measured. Until recently, the common practice was to use Herfindahl indices of fractionalization for ethnic, linguistic, and religious aspects of heterogeneity, which are more observable and stable over time (see Alesina *et al.*, 2003). This index is often found to be negatively and significantly related to GDP growth. However, it does not appear to be well correlated with most aspects of social and political conflict that are often claimed to be the links between fractionalization and growth. For this reason, to shed light on the underlying connections between heterogeneity and political economy outcomes, a number of studies have offered new measures that focus on other aspects of heterogeneity. In particular, the polarization indices developed by Esteban and Ray (1994) and Montalvo and Reynal-Querol (2005) try to capture the fact that when fractionalization is very high, in a way the society may look relatively homogeneous since the differences among groups may become smaller or their conflicts may be more localized and less consequential for the system as a whole. (It should be pointed out that these polarization indices focus on the probability of intergroup alienation and within-group identity, not on the actual intensity of differences and loyalties.) Montalvo and Reynal-Querol (2005) show that their index explains within-society conflict much better than fractionalization, though it is not well correlated with cross-country growth. The upper panel of Figure 3 compares two indices for fractionalization and polarization for 134 countries and highlights the non-linear relationship between the two.

Heterogeneity factors are not confined to ethno-linguistic and religious polarization. Other notable sources of diversity are ideological and cultural orientation (e.g., modernist vs. traditional), asset ownership, location (region, urban vs. rural), industry, and organizational affiliation (e.g., the military or political parties and cliques). Each of these factors, which are at least partially endogenous, may have rich interactions with other elements of heterogeneity. For example, political parties may add fuel to the fire of intergroup rivalry or may help enhance national identity and, thereby, reduce ethno-linguistic and religious alienation, class conflict, etc. Naturally, the manner in which the economy's resources are applied and the institutional mechanisms needed to achieve good performance are different in those varying political conditions.

Hadi Salehi Esfahani

Figure 3. **Fractionalization, polarization, and GDP growth in developing countries fractional index is the average of ethnic, linguistic, and religious Herfindahl indices for the three dimensions of heterogeneity; polarization index is the average of polarity of ethnic and religious distributions according to the measure proposed by Montalvo and Reynal-Querol, 2005; averaging is done as a rough aggregation method to save space; similar relations emerge when individual components are used.**

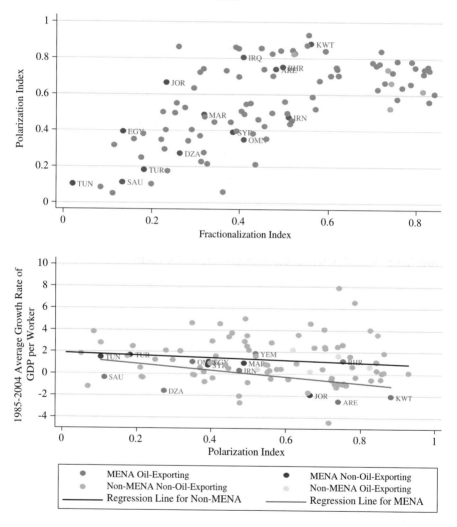

Source: Alesina *et al.* (2003), Montalvo and Reynal-Querol (2005), and *World Development Indicators* (2006).

In the MENA region, the extent of preference diversity and potential conflicts vary greatly. However, by the fractionalization measure of ethno-linguistic and religious diversity, the MENA countries generally do not rank very high. So, to the extent that this factor matters for growth, they should fare well. But, by the polarization index, parts of the MENA region lie in the upper half of the sample, and even that may understate the actual intergroup tensions in some countries where societies are divided into contending groups with distinct fault lines, as in Algeria, Iraq, and Lebanon.

Concentration of land and capital ownership has also served as a source of conflict, resulting in many confiscation and redistribution episodes by national leaders who sought to broaden their public support or dispossess their political rivals, or both. The cases in point are the land reforms and nationalizations in Egypt during 1952–1963, in Iraq, Syria, and Tunisia in the late 1950s, in Algeria after independence in 1962 and again in the early 1970s, and in Iran in 1963 and again after the 1979 Revolution.

Of course, the intensity and role of group interactions depend on prevailing ideologies at the group and national levels. In particular, as North (2005) points out, nationalist ideologies can play important roles in mitigating potential conflicts arising from polarization. In MENA, at many points in time, political leaders have managed to use nationalist ideologies to overcome or suppress major internal conflicts and, thereby, facilitate mobilization of economic resources. These efforts seem to have been most successful in situations when new regimes have come to power following long wars or crises, where the need for establishing order has provided potent arguments and drives for muffling internal conflicts, at least for a while. Although order in these cases has typically come about through dictatorship, sometimes they have been able to strengthen national identities and to dilute religious or ethnic conflicts on a long-term basis (e.g., Turkey under Ataturk and Iran under Reza Shah). In the case of Arab countries, similar ideological tools have also been used for forming cross-country movements. However, these movements have rarely gained strength (with the exceptions of Baath and Nasserist movements) and even when they have gained some force they have intensified conflict at other fault lines and have ultimately disintegrated.

2.3. Institutions

Institutions are the rules that assign roles to individuals in the society and structure their interactions. These rules range from informal cultural norms to formal legal and political procedures governing the country. The allocation of decision-making powers and the constraints that institutions place on individual behavior can help or hinder the potential for resolving conflicts and reaching efficient and enforceable deals. Institutions have many aspects and dimensions. To make the analysis manageable, I focus on governance institutions because they play fundamental roles in alleviating or exacerbating deficiencies in other rules. Furthermore, I concentrate on institutional aspects that affect *representation, commitment*, and *coordination* in the interactions of various groups through the government. These three dimensions of governance institutions are crucial for the extent to which the government can overcome contracting problems and help various groups strike efficient deals that take the economy closer to its production possibility frontier. The following discussion expounds this point.

2.3.1. Representation

For efficient collective decision making in a heterogeneous society, various segments of the population must be somehow represented in the government; otherwise important information about the preferences of some groups may not be incorporated in government decisions. This can lead to distortions in the production incentives, both among those groups as well as others that interact with them. For example, when the government ignores the educational needs of one part of the population, they may be discouraged from engaging in productive activities and may become foot soldiers in rivalries among more powerful groups. Representation can be viewed as the set of political or social institutions that enable various groups to conclude effective contracts with the politicians, offering support or acquiescence to political power in exchange for policies that address those groups' concerns. Effectiveness of such institutions depends on the capability of various parts of the population to ensure that their demands are given due consideration and weight by the policymakers. In the economic growth literature, representation is often identified with electoral democracy, which does not seem to have a direct relationship with growth (Barro, 1996; Acemoglu *et al.*, 2005b). Although democracy certainly enhances representation, it also entails many other institutional aspects with additional multifaceted effects, as we will see below. Besides, having a chance to vote for politicians is only one, often imperfect, mechanism for the population to influence policymakers. In fact, in addition to the opportunity to react to policy outcomes, thorough representation requires channels that connect the public to the process of policymaking through political, professional, and social organizations. These latter channels – whether trade unions, business associations, religious organizations, or tribal structures – may also exist and provide some representation even in the absence of elections and other formal democratic institutions.

In the MENA countries, representation mechanisms are often believed to be weak. This is particularly an issue in the region's larger, more diversified countries that lack democratic institutions. There also seem to be differences in representation across monarchies and republics in the region. In monarchies, the rulers depend more on traditional and family relations to connect with broader segments of the population. In contrast, in countries where republics have been established through military coups, revolutions, or national liberation movements, preexisting power relations have crumbled and the political elite have had to rely more on new forms of political and administrative organization to manage their relations with the population at large (Owen, 2004). However, since these organizations have been initiated from above, they have typically served more as means of political control by the elite rather than representation (Ayubi, 1995).

2.3.2. Commitment

Commitment consists of any cost that policymakers must bear if they decide to reverse an adopted policy in ways that take away the returns to investments made in response to that policy (Levy and Spiller, 1996; Esfahani, 2000). The presence of such costs is crucial for economic growth because otherwise, important investments might be deterred. The reason is that most investments become largely sunk once they are in place, so their quasi-rents can be easily taxed without much economic consequence in the short run. If the politicians can change policies with no cost (or some net benefit) to themselves, they may find it convenient to ignore the losses of the producers. However, this possibility discourages entrepreneurs from investment in the first place. To ensure commitment, a country needs systematic checks and balances and separation of powers so that the decision makers can turn their policies into enforceable contracts (North and Weingast, 1989). However, a dictator with a secure, long-term position may also be able to offer some commitment to efficient policies based on his incentive to maintain a reputation for future dealings.

In recent years, most of the research on the role of institutions in economic growth has focused on the commitment issue – often under the rubrics of property rights' security and constraints on governments – as the key determinant of long-run income levels. (See, in particular, the large volume of work spun by Acemoglu and his associates; e.g., Acemoglu *et al.*, 2001, 2005a, and b and Acemoglu and Robinson, 2005. See also Rodrik, *et al.*, 2002, among others.) As in the case of representation, some authors associate commitment capability with democratic rule. However, the more recent contributions to this literature show that in underdeveloped economies, limitations on democracy may enable the elite to protect their investments against the taxation power of the poor majority, thus ensuring the incentives needed to initiate investment and growth (Acemoglu, 2005). Of course, once the economy develops to some extent, further growth is likely to require transition to democracy.

Commitment through non-democratic mechanisms (reputation of the autocrat and rent sharing with the elite) has been prevalent among the MENA countries, though it has not always worked well, especially in the cases of detailed policy matters. Examples of such cases will be discussed in Section 3.

2.3.3. Coordination

Coordination is another crucial institutional feature needed for minimizing resource waste because distributive struggles typically create a "tragedy of the commons" problem where the parties involved tend to overexploit the rent source over which they compete or overuse their own resource to secure a larger share

(Persson and Svensson, 1989; Alesina and Tabellini, 1990). For example, when government budgets are made in parliaments where the lawmakers can independently and freely propose amendments, total expenditure and the deficit tend to be inefficiently large (von Hagen, 1992; Alesina and Perotti, 1995; Velasco, 2000). The reason is that in such a situation, the cost of an additional dollar spent on the favorite project of each policymaker is shared by the population at large and, as a result, is not fully internalized. Similar problems exist in trade policy formation and many other public policies. Coordination across policy areas (e.g., coordinating trade, labor, and fiscal policies) tends to pose even harder problems and could be the source of major inefficiency in the economy if the country lacks appropriate institutional mechanisms. Of course, coordination would not arise as a problem to the extent that decision making on public policy could be decentralized without external effects – e.g., in a market-like fashion. However, this is not possible in many areas of public policy; hence the need for other institutional mechanisms to bring about coordination. One mechanism is *ex ante* constraints (e.g., balanced-budget laws) that force everyone to act within limits, though such constraints are typically too inflexible and inefficient because specifying *ex ante* rules that anticipate all possible future situations is very rarely practical. A more flexible mechanism is "delegation," where one or a few individuals make the aggregate decisions that bring everyone into line. This obviously implies some centralization and, to be effective, requires proper incentives for those in charge of the aggregate decisions. An intermediate mechanism is *ex ante* limits that are renegotiated on a regular basis and only delegate the task of enforcing the agreed limits. Of course, the effectiveness of all these arrangements varies depending on the nature of other political institutions such as political parties. For example, coordination is much easier when a few parties are in a position to aggregate the population's interests in a decentralized way and negotiate them with each other.

In the MENA countries, high degrees of power concentration have often facilitated coordination over major policies. But, those institutional arrangements have not been suitable for more detailed actions of government agencies because processing the details of minor policy matters quickly becomes overwhelming for the center. More on this will follow.

In making governance work effectively, capabilities in all three institutional dimensions discussed above – *representation, coordination*, and *commitment* – are needed. Indeed, there are complementarities among the three dimensions. In particular, higher commitment capability tends to be complementary with strength in both representation and coordination because it allows the government and interest groups to coordinate their actions over time as well as across policy areas. In addition, it enhances the opportunities for the politicians to assure their constituencies that their interests will continue to be represented in the policymaking process. Conversely, better representation and coordination help ensure that the adopted policies enjoy broader support and greater efficiency and, therefore, are less likely to be reversed in arbitrary manner and without due process. Broader representation of the population in the policymaking process can also help coordination to be achieved with more information and over larger sets of policy issues.

However, there are some tradeoffs among the three institutional dimensions as well, especially between representation and coordination. Better representation can make coordination more difficult because it requires the decision-making process to take account of more political demands. Conversely, coordination mechanisms may constrain the possibilities for broad representation. Of course, such tradeoffs and complementarities vary across countries depending on their economic and institutional conditions. For example, in a country facing chaos, establishing some mechanism for coordination is likely to be crucial and sacrificing it to ensure better representation may come at a huge cost in terms of economic growth. In contrast, when the basic coordination problems have been solved, weak representation can become a key source of instability and inefficiency. Another example is the increased value of commitment capability when the government does not have access to cheap resource rents and cannot create employment and promote growth through subsidized private or public investment (Esfahani and Toossi-Ardakani, 2002). Some countries (e.g., those with less political polarization and better rule-of-law tradition) are able to resolve the tension among the institutional functions relatively well and reach high levels of capability in all dimensions. In other countries, long-term growth performance is constrained by the fact that some institutional capabilities are missing and trying to build them comes at a high cost in terms of other capabilities (e.g., forcing coordination at the cost of representation or vice versa).

2.4. Dynamics in the political economy of growth

The above discussion offers a framework for understanding what the growth potentials of a country are at a point in time given its resources, politics, and institutions. However, the latter factors are by no means static or exogenous. Changes in demographics and resource characteristics, partly as a result of the growth process itself, influence the relative powers and interests of various groups, which lead to changes in politics. Those forces in turn may make the existing institutions obsolete and prompt interest groups to seek changes in rules. In analyzing this process, it is important to note that the existing power structure at each time has important implications for the set of likely institutions that emerge subsequently. As Acemoglu *et al.* (2005a) have emphasized, the desire of dominant groups to maintain their powers plays an important role in enhancing or hindering institutional change. Of course, this effect should be weighed against the shifts in potential balance of power brought about by developments in resources. Moreover, there are important institutional and political changes that come about not through the desire of politically active groups, but rather as byproducts of unintended socioeconomic developments. For example, the turn to religion as a political tool in recent decades could not have happened without deep socioeconomic developments that made such a trend feasible, in some instances in clear opposition to the desire of the ruling elite.

Another important issue in the analysis of growth dynamics is that institutions are by definition costly to change. Indeed, rules that are easy to change cannot become institutions that constrain the behavior of actors in an economy. In other words, the institutions that matter must be rules that are difficult to change either because they are self-enforcing or because they are supported by other institutions that require substantial effort and coordination to change. A key implication of this observation is that institutional change comes about only when shifts in resources and politics have raised the cost–benefit ratio of the *status quo* for a sufficiently large group of actors.

A further consideration in growth dynamics is the fact that the onset of economic growth does not require deep and extensive institutional reform, as Rodrik (2005) and Glaeser (2004) have noted. In many instances, small and limited policy changes have been observed to initiate remarkable growth episodes. One crucial factor that may have been at work in such cases is innovation in business–government and intragovernment relations in ways that made contracting among them more complete via performance indicators that were more easily observable to both businesses and policymakers. For example, a key reason for the success of export promotion policies of Korea and Taiwan in the 1960s and 1970s may have been the use of *net foreign exchange earnings* as an indicator of performance. These policies offered rewards to domestic entrepreneurs based on a criterion that was far more observable than the deals given under import substitution policies (which at least in theory were based on their contribution to production capacity and *foreign exchange savings*). Although both types of policy offered rents to domestic producers and could help mitigate their investment constraints (especially finance and foreign exchange problems) relative to their foreign competitors, export promotion policies proved more successful because they offered more complete "policy contracts." The latter policies were also more effective in enabling the entrepreneurs search for their sources of comparative advantage and break into international markets. Of course, this was not possible in all industries because not all industries could be expected to become exporters and, besides, government subsidy funds were limited. As a result, policymakers maintained import restrictions for quite some time on a wide range of products to protect many industries and collect public funds for subsidizing the rest. Interestingly, the innovation in trade policies seems to have helped address some governance problems as well. By observing export performance and collecting feedback from exporters on their experiences with public services, policymakers could assess the performance of various bureaucracies better and motivate the administrators more effectively (Amsden, 1989; Wade, 1990). Similar effects may help explain the success of Turkey and Tunisia after their moves toward export promotion in the 1980s.

Another mechanism through which a move toward export promotion may induce more extensive change is the incentives it creates for producers to develop export interests and reduce their stakes in import substitution. This can shift the political calculus of trade policy in favor of more liberal trade, especially when the rising export revenues make it easier to import and starving the domestic demand for imports becomes increasingly unattractive (Esfahani and Squire, forthcoming). The import liberalization trends in Turkey and Tunisia during the 1990s following their shift toward export promotion seem to fit this pattern well.

A more general version of the above process is the so-called "dual-track" reform strategy, whereby some marginal areas in a controlled economy are first liberalized and allowed to expand without generating much risk in the rest of the economy. The success of the liberalized part then generates new resources and stronger incentives for reform in the remaining parts, eventually improving the entire economy in a politically palatable and low-risk manner. China has come to represent a highly successful case of this strategy (Lau *et al.*, 2000), though the MENA countries were indeed pioneers in adopting this approach, starting with Tunisia in 1969 followed by Egypt and Syria in 1974, and Algeria in 1978–1979 (Owen, 2004, pp. 115–119). However, unlike China, lack of emphasis on export promotion in MENA limited the benefits of the approach and turned into a very gradual process of change. Tunisia later shifted to export promotion later on in the mid-1980s and reaped more benefits, probably because of its lack of resource and geopolitical rents.[2]

While policy innovations can initiate strong growth episodes, sustaining high growth in the face of changes in circumstances ultimately requires good institutions. Such institutions may, of course, be built as part of a burgeoning growth process (Rodrik, 2005). But, this point raises another question that has not received much attention in the literature. The circumstances under which small policy changes trigger a virtuous circle of growth and institution building seem to depend largely on informal institutions (e.g., social and political culture). Indeed, it is the informal rules and norms imbedded in culture, religion, etc., that ultimately help formal institutions to function and evolve. In particular, without informal institutions that keep the fabric of society together, it is unlikely that reforms in formal institutions can come about. Some research along these lines has started under the rubric of social capital, though further insights from that field await theoretical development and more detailed characterization and quantification of informal institutions. However, it is important to remain aware of the critical roles that such institutions play in the growth process.

Finally, it should be noted that the multifaceted interactions of resources, politics, and institutions imply that the key factors constraining economic growth may vary greatly according to place and time. To identify the cause of stagnation and appropriate solutions to a country's growth problems at a particular time, one needs to focus on specific circumstances, although it is crucial

---

[2] The small size of its domestic market may have also rendered inward-looking policy less practical, though this effect does not seem to have been important for Syria. Also, China's large domestic market does not seem to have deterred its commitment to export promotion.

to work within a theoretically consistent framework that can inform the choice of relevant factors and suggest hypotheses to be examined. Such studies can help improve the growth process by providing better information to the political and economic actors in each country and, thereby, reducing their contracting problems. This observation also suggests a solution to the dilemma noted by Pritchett (2003) regarding the existing political economy models. He points out that those models are incapable of generating useful policy implications because they assume that everyone is already optimizing subject to the constraints of the system. In other words, any proposed policy improvement must be ignoring or violating some constraint. However, in a world with a myriad of dimensions, even optimizing agents may leave many alternatives unexplored, especially when it comes to the options that require collective action. Just the perception that some forms of coordination are costly may give the players sufficient reason to ignore a host of possibilities, some of which may be potentially productive. The players in such complex games may not know exactly what it is that they must strive to know. Systematic research and lessons from experience can lower the cost of considering such alternatives and render them feasible; hence a role for political economy research to contribute to economic and institutional reform.

The approach outlined above suggests that to understand the determinants of growth, one has to identify the political, institutional, and economic characteristics that are most relevant for growth-related contracting in a country. Then, the task is to analyze such characteristics and to show how their evolution has given rise to the country's pattern of economic growth. Below, I provide an overview for the application of this approach to the MENA countries.

3. MENA's growth experience: the roles of resources, politics, and institutions

This section applies the above political economy framework to examine the growth consequences of a number of economic, political, and institutional characteristics that are of broad concern across the MENA countries. I start with a discussion of the role of natural resource rents and then examine the geopolitical factors, domestic political divisions, and governance institutions and human resources. The stylized facts used here regarding the nature of the economic situations and policy responses are largely drawn from the other chapters in this volume. In particular, the empirical connections between those conditions and economic growth are based on Ersel and Kandil (2007); Makdisi *et al.* (2007); and Salehi-Isfahani (2007).

3.1. Natural resource rents

One of the most notable features common to many MENA countries since the mid-20th century is the richness of its natural resource endowments, specially oil and natural gas. Even countries that lack such resources benefit from the region's endowments indirectly through aid from richer countries or remittances from their migrant workers. While there are interesting issues concerning how oil resources are developed and exploited in the MENA countries, they are far outweighed by another question: Why have MENA countries not always used their natural resource rents to help their economies grow faster systematically compared to their less-endowed counterparts in the developing world? Here, I explore the possible answers to this question as an illustration of how the incomplete contracting framework may be shedding light on the subject.

To understand why faster growth is not a systematic consequence of natural resource endowments in MENA, we need to first understand what the MENA countries do with the rents. The first notable pattern in this regard is the relatively low rates of taxation of non-oil income in oil-rich countries. Since natural resources in these countries are generally under public ownership, abundance of the related rents has reduced the need for taxation. Although statutory tax rates are in some cases rather high, especially for the high-income brackets, the typical direct and indirect taxes actually paid remain generally low and finance a relatively small share of the government budget. Interestingly, the low tax rates have not translated into encouragement for investment and growth in many MENA countries. This seems to be partly because of uncertainty in the net returns to production, which could be related to fluctuations in oil revenues. We will explore the reasons for this below.

Another important part of oil rents is spent on large government bureaucracies as well as financing infrastructure and production projects. The latter part could, in principle, be a growth stimulant. However, that role is often undermined owing to the inefficiencies in investment and operation of public enterprises (PEs) and infrastructure.

Finally, the bulk of the remaining revenues are used in the form of transfers and mass subsidies. As Esfahani (2003) shows, in oil-rich countries of MENA the subsidy on gasoline consumption alone ranges between 1 and 5 percent of the GDP. Subsidies are also offered for a variety of other items, especially other forms of energy, staple foods, and credit. This use of resource rents has had limited potential for generating economic growth.

So, why do MENA countries often use their resource rents in these ways rather than channeling them more effectively toward growth? From a contracting perspective, inefficiency arises when the politicians who need to elicit support from the public or politically influential interest groups cannot make them the residual beneficiaries of efficient uses of public funds. For example, the funds subsidizing redundant workers in PEs could be used for creating more productive jobs, but the workers may not consent to such reallocation if they believe that they may not be the beneficiaries of those jobs, or if they suspect that the funds may simply be diverted to other inefficient uses. Similarly, the public may understand that mass subsidies on fuel are inefficient, but if it cannot trust that the politicians will use the saved subsidies to produce a better outcome, broad support for the subsidies may remain strong (Esfahani, 2003). This may not be a concern for democratic regimes that are under close public scrutiny. It may also not matter for authoritarian regimes that can rule with narrow support, at least for a while, as in the case of the Shah's government in the 1960s, which raised the price of fuel and generated substantial funds for its projects. However, most MENA governments rely on some form of public support or acquiescence, without being fully trusted. As a result, when they have access to rents, they feel the need to offer subsidies because the public does not have high hopes of seeing those funds applied toward more efficient alternatives of broad interest. Even if the government intends to make good use of the funds, specifying the details of what must be done and assessing the outcome are often extremely difficult because the factors involved and the possible states of the world are rarely practical. As long as there are opportunities for misallocation or embezzlement of rents, the public is likely to prefer upfront transfers through inefficient subsidies or expenditures, rather than allowing the funds to remain in the hands of the politicians and waiting for possible efficient uses. Upfront subsidies offered in the form of low food and energy prices also act as effective coordination mechanisms for the public to react collectively to policy changes. This may explain why the removal of subsidies has often triggered widespread riots, forcing governments to rescind price hikes at least partially in many cases, as in Iran in 1969, Egypt in 1977, Morocco and Tunisia in 1984, Jordan in 1989 and 1996, and Yemen in 1998 and 2005. It is also notable that the expanded role elections in Iran after the 1979 Revolution has been associated with increased mass subsidies.

The above discussion suggests an important reason why resource rents may not have been channeled toward growth. It can also shed light on the slowdown of growth in MENA economies in the 1980s and the 1990s and their vulnerability to the decline in oil prices in those years. Note that the optimal policy for spending oil revenues would have entailed saving part of the funds during resource booms and to create a stabilization fund to be spent during bust years (or paying back during booms the loans accumulated during troughs). However, this type of policy would have faced the same difficulty as the attempt to put them into more productive uses: The public and most interest groups would have been skeptical about ever benefiting from the saved funds and would not have easily consented to moving them out of current consumption. Indeed, few oil-exporting developing countries other than Kuwait have reached sufficient coordination in their fiscal policies to restrain their expenditures in major ways during boom times. Many MENA countries have done the exact opposite, borrowing during booms when their creditworthiness has risen and paying back with difficulty during busts when foreign lending has dried up. In some cases, this pattern has further forced the government to inflationary financing, as in the cases of Algeria, Egypt, Iran, and Syria during many years in the 1980s and 1990s (see Table 2).[3] For some countries without oil revenues the inflation

---

[3] Note that the overall record of inflation in MENA is much better than that of most of the developing world, as Table 2 shows. The point here concerns the rise and decline of inflation in some countries during some periods.

Table 2. Price volatility in the MENA countries

Country[a]	Average CPI Inflation Rate Period								Standard deviation of CPI for the Years Available
	1965–1970	1970–1974	1975–1979	1980–1984	1985–1989	1990–1994	1995–1999	2000–2004	
Oil exporting									
Algeria	n.a.	4.75	11.70	8.96	9.10	24.75	12.36	2.43	8.38
Bahrain	2.36	10.25	14.88	5.48	−0.98	0.98	0.61	0.25	6.99
Iran	1.53	7.27	14.73	19.16	20.48	20.64	26.78	14.26	10.31
Kuwait	0.00	10.63	1.78	5.60	1.58	4.25	2.01	1.40	5.79
Libya	8.23	1.36	8.40	11.39	4.88	9.18	4.23	−7.17	7.30
Oman	n.a.	n.a.	n.a.	n.a.	n.a.	1.42	0.49	−0.58	1.56
Qatar	n.a.	n.a.	n.a.	4.97	2.82	2.19	3.58	2.48	2.31
Saudi Arabia	1.82	9.39	15.41	1.32	−1.17	1.70	0.89	−0.21	8.32
Yemen	n.a.	n.a.	n.a.	n.a.	n.a.	37.64	20.53	9.89	17.82
Non-oil exporting									
Egypt	5.26	4.83	10.74	15.82	18.92	14.08	6.90	4.69	6.58
Jordan	n.a.	9.79	11.84	7.02	7.02	7.04	3.12	1.85	5.89
Morocco	1.02	6.17	9.41	10.22	4.93	6.19	2.72	1.62	4.24
Syria	1.45	9.65	8.84	13.47	31.75	13.59	2.72	0.04	12.23
Tunisia	n.a.	n.a.	n.a.	8.90	7.32	5.85	3.89	2.78	2.21
Turkey	5.06	13.12	33.52	51.47	51.07	73.74	80.74	37.63	30.01
Non-MENA oil exporters[b]	2.41	6.64	13.78	13.77	27.56	39.32	38.78	23.72	19.63
Non-MENA non-oil exporters[b]	20.71	16.69	33.66	43.24	130.55	68.83	12.50	8.23	121.62

n.a., not available.

Source: Calculated based on World Bank's *World Development Indicators* (2006).

[a]Djibouti, Iraq, Lebanon, UAE, and West Bank and Gaza are not included owing to lack of sufficient data.

[b]Weighted averages, with each country's PPP GDP serving as its weight. Oil exporters consist of Angola, the Republic of Congo, Gabon, Nigeria, Trinidad and Tobago, and Venezuela.

problem has been more chronic, as in Turkey. In either case, the consequence in most countries has been economic slowdown and macroeconomic instability.

The above discussion points to some specific ways in which politics and institutions have interacted with resource rents, shaping the pattern of economic performance in the region. Further causes and consequences of contracting problems, especially the coordination failures that have contributed to the outcome, will be discussed below.

In the absence of well-developed credit and insurance markets (Ersel and Kandil, 2007), the considerable terms of trade fluctuations, the consequent instability, and the availability of public resources during booms must have jointly contributed to the rise and maintenance of extensive PE sectors and large general public employment as social insurance substitute in the MENA countries. (For the available public employment data, see Table 3. A similar conclusion can be drawn, particularly in the case of MENA's oil exporting countries, from the subjective indicators of government intervention and ownership shown in the first column of Table 4 based on the rankings carried out by the Heritage Foundation).[4] In addition, many MENA governments, especially non-oil exporters, have tried to address the demands for the economic security among private sector low-income workers by restricting layoffs. This can be seen in the last column of Table 4, which shows the employment rigidity rankings developed by the World Bank. Of course, such policies provide job security only for the employed workers at the cost of employers and potential entrants into the job market.

The need to manage economic risk through the next best government-controlled mechanisms may have also strengthened protectionist incentives during the 1990s (Esfahani and Squire, forthcoming). However, the recovery of oil prices in recent years seems to have changed this trend and has enabled MENA's major oil exporters to ease trade restrictions (see the middle columns of Table 4). For the rest, except for a few countries, liberalization has not proceeded as fast after the 1990s. Interestingly, the overall rates of protection in the MENA countries before the 1990s used to be below those in most other developing regions (Esfahani and Squire, forthcoming). Indeed, the presence of PEs and other redistribution mechanisms helped MENA governments reduce the impact of openness on parts of population that could potentially lose as a result of foreign competition. That situation, however, changed when per capita oil revenues declined in the 1990s and the MENA countries began to look more inward while most of the developing world raced toward greater economic integration.

Besides their impacts on policy outcomes, natural resource rents have influenced the evolution of political institutions in the MENA countries. Because the

---

[4]Objective and accurate data on public enterprises is limited, especially for the MENA countries. Despite those imperfections, the picture constructed by Tables 3 and 4 is suggestive about the extensive nature of public employment and ownership in MENA, especially in the case of oil-exporting countries.

Table 3. Public employment in MENA countries compared to the weighted average of non-MENA developing countries[a]

Country	Total Public Employment as Percent of Labor Force		Public Enterprise Employment as Percent of Labor Force	
	1991–1995	1996–2000	1991–1995	1996–2000
Oil exporting				
Algeria	n.a.	19.5	7.0	3.5
Bahrain	26.9	n.a.	n.a.	n.a.
Iran	26.3	21.9	n.a.	4.2
Kuwait	n.a.	40.0	n.a.	3.7
Libya	44.9	n.a.	1.41	n.a.
Oman	21.5	16.4	n.a.	7.9
Qatar	n.a.	29.4	n.a.	0.8
UAE	n.a.	n.a.	1.98	n.a.
Yemen	n.a.	14.5	n.a.	1.66
Non-oil exporting				
Egypt	23.8	25.8	13.3	5.0
Jordan	17.1	16.9	n.a.	1.4
Lebanon	8.3	8.1	0.6	0.3
Morocco	n.a.	7.2	n.a.	0.7
Syria	n.a.	n.a.	n.a.	10.0
Tunisia	n.a.	n.a.	5.1	n.a.
Turkey	10.2	9.6	3.0	2.3
Weighted average of developing non-MENA countries[a]	13.8	11.4	4.0	2.7

n.a., not available.
Sources: ILO, Public Sector Employment Database, the website for the *International Labor Statistics*; World Bank, *Public Sector Employment Database, 2002*, and World Bank, *World Development Indicators 2000*.
[a]The developing countries included in the average are those with data for both subperiods. For China, public employment data excludes those in town and village enterprises. Labor force is used as weights across countries.

ruling elites did not have to rely much on taxation, they have found it easier to continue their rule without much representation (Mahdavi, 1970; Elbadawi and Makdisi, forthcoming). The rents have allowed the ruling politicians to buy support from interest groups, rather than being responsible to the tax-paying public. In this way, abundance of natural resources may have contributed to the survival of authoritarian regimes in the region. More on this is discussed in Section 3.4.

3.2. Heterogeneity and polarization

As we have seen in Section 2, MENA societies are not particularly fractionalized, but several of them are quite polarized (Figure 3). The latter pattern has

Table 4.   Government intervention, trade restrictions, and employment rigidity in the MENA countries compared to the weighted average of non-MENA developing countries^a

Country	Government Intervention and Public Ownership		Trade Restrictions		World Bank's Index of Labor Market Rigidity
	1995–2000	2001–2005	1995–2000	2001–2005	2004
Oil exporting	4.3	4.6	4.7	3.8	38.7
Algeria	3.7	4.1	5.0	4.6	55.0
Bahrain	4.2	4.3	2.0	3.0	n.a.
Iran	4.4	4.9	5.0	3.4	40.0
Iraq	5.0	5.0	5.0	5.0	n.a.
Kuwait	4.7	4.5	2.0	2.2	20.0
Libya	5.0	4.6	5.0	5.0	n.a.
Oman	4.4	4.5	2.6	3.0	35.0
Qatar	3.5	4.6	2.5	2.8	n.a.
Saudi Arabia	4.4	4.7	4.2	4.0	13.0
UAE	4.0	4.0	2.0	2.0	33.0
Yemen	4.0	4.1	4.8	3.4	37.0
Non-oil exporting (excluding Turkey)	3.1	3.3	4.7	4.5	54.2
Egypt	3.0	3.4	5.0	4.4	53.0
Jordan	3.7	3.5	4.0	4.2	34.0
Lebanon	2.5	3.0	3.8	3.8	28.0
Morocco	3.1	2.7	4.5	4.8	70.0
Syria	3.8	4.3	4.4	4.6	37.0
Tunisia	3.5	3.1	5.0	5.0	54.0
Turkey	2.0	2.5	1.8	2.6	55.0
Non-MENA oil exporters^a	3.1	4.0	4.8	4.7	47.5
Non-MENA non-oil exporters^a	3.3	3.2	4.2	4.1	41.4

n.a., not available.

Sources: The Heritage Foundation, *Index of Economic Freedom*, and the World Bank, *World Development Indicators* (2006).

^{a}World Bank's rigidity of employment index ranges from 0 (= least rigid) to 100 (= most rigid). Other indices range from 1–5, with higher numbers representing less market-friendly policies. For variable definitions, see Appendix Table A.1. The developing countries included in the average are those with available data for both subperiods. Labor force is used as weights across countries. Non-MENA oil exporters are Angola, the Republic of Congo, Gabon, Nigeria, Trinidad and Tobago, and Venezuela.

been a major source of internal conflicts in the region. In particular, Kurdish minorities and other ethnic groups in Iran, Iraq, and Turkey have at times engaged in political and even armed conflict with their respective governments. In addition, Lebanon, Yemen, and Oman have been the scenes of destructive

Figure 5.   *Central government debt as percentage of GDP across regions*

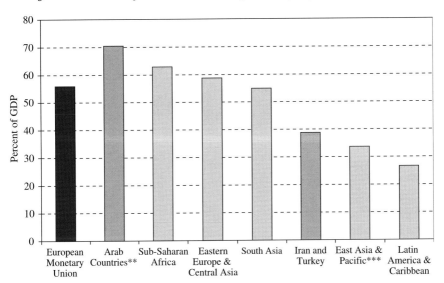

Regional Weighted Averages over 1997–1999 (averaged using GDP weights over countries for which data are available)
Sources: World Bank, *World Development Indicators* (2004), and Joint BIS-IMF-OECD-WB
** Algeria, Bahrain, Jordan, Lebanon, Morocco, Oman, and Tunisia.
*** Excluding China. Central government of China has a low debt and, if included, dominates the region, lowering the average public debt down to 16.7 percent of GDP.
Statistics on External Debt, http://www.oecd.org/site/0,2865,en_21571361_31596493_1_1_1_1_1,00.html.

and poor-quality policymaking at the micro level. Figure 6 depicts a way by which this tradeoff manifests itself. It shows that across countries, accountability is inversely related to the difficulty of doing business (measured by rank in terms of a survey-based index developed by the World Bank). Specifically, MENA countries mostly fall on the upper left part of the chart, reflecting a situation where businesses that are independent of the government and ruling politicians have little say in policy and face difficulties starting up, growing, and adjusting to economic conditions. Similar problems can be observed in terms of poor quality of services with public good components such as education and health-care (World Bank, 2003). Such effects mute the dynamism of the economy at the micro level and counteract with the gains from coordination at the macro level.

Another way of viewing the cost of doing business under centralized MENA regimes is the weaknesses of policy commitment at the micro level. Indeed, changing policies without due process has been a major complaint of domestic and foreign businesses in the MENA countries. Esfahani (1997) offers a host of examples. For instance, in Egypt, following the rise in foreign investments in 1981, the Minister of Energy decided to raise the price of energy and petroleum

Figure 6. **Democratic accountability and ease of doing business**

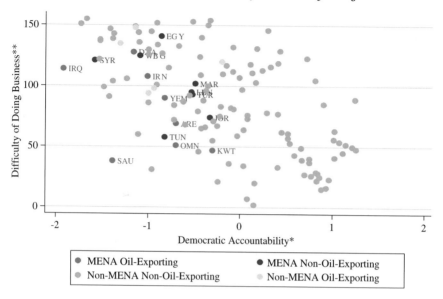

Sources: D. Kaufmann, A. Kraay, and M. Mastruzzi, 2005. "Governance Matters IV: Governance Indicators for 1996-2004", World Bank Website, http://www.worldbank.org/wbi/governance/govdata/; World Bank, "Doing business: economy rankings", http://www.doingbusiness.org/Economy-Rankings/.

* Combined index of voice and accountability calculated by Kaufmann *et al.* Units are standard deviations of rankings around zero.

** Based on rank calculated by the World Bank in terms of ease of doing business. Higher numbers indicate greater difficulty of doing business.

products for FDI (foreign direct investment) projects by a factor of 3, bringing it to the world market level. He argued that the substantially subsidized domestic price was for users who did not enjoy the privileges of the foreign investment code (Middle East News Agency, *Economic Weekly*, 1989, May 19, p. 13). Given that the privileges were supposed to be incentives for foreign investors and those who had invested in Egypt had assumed a uniform price of energy, the policy change placed FDI projects at a disadvantage vis-à-vis their Egyptian competitors. Some investors were so disappointed that they ceased their operations (Sadowski, 1991, p. 115).[6] There are also many other examples where

---

[6] Another relevant example from Egypt is the cancellation of a US firm's contract for the management of duty-free shops at the Cairo airport. The contract was subsequently awarded to Egypt's major public sector airline, EgyptAir, which has been benefiting from the support of airline industry regulators in many other respects, e.g., the limitation of charter flights to Cairo (*Business Middle East*, The Economist Intelligence Unit, 1995, November 16–30, p. 10).

governments simply cancel contracts granted to foreign investors. Just recently, the government of Iran helped a local mobile phone company, Irancell, to cancel its \$3 billion contract with a Turkish company, Turkcell (Turkish Industrialists' and Businessmen's Association (TUSIAD), *Turkey News*, September 6–18, 2005). Another contract with the Turkish operator of Khomeini International Airport was repealed last year owing to pressure from Iran's Revolutionary Guards, claiming security concerns (TUSIAD, *Turkey News*, January 25– February 1, 2005).

The impact of authoritarianism on economic activity has not been uniform across the MENA countries. In particular, the extent and form of government involvement in the economy seems to have systematically varied between monarchies and republics. In monarchies, the survival of the traditional relations of power and the established elite has ensured support for private property, whereas in republics, state ownership has often been used as a means of dispossessing old propertied classes and establishing new orders by subordinating production to the political imperatives of new regimes (Owen, 2004, pp. 45–53). Indeed, the extension of government controls over the economy has been quite visible after the formation of republics in Algeria, Egypt, Iran, Syria, and Tunisia. There are, of course, other forces at work that explain the public sector growth in monarchies or in the case of less authoritarian republics (Turkey in the 1960s) as well – e.g., partial solutions to market failures and the connection between resource rents and public ownership discussed earlier. Many details of such effects and their interactions (e.g., the interaction of authoritarianism and polarization) in shaping economic policy await careful scrutiny.

Although the survival of authoritarianism in MENA has been facilitated by natural resource rents and internal and external conflicts, the institution has deeper social and cultural roots as well. These roots have long been debated in the political economy literature, going at least as far back as Marx's idea of "Asiatic Mode of Production." Whether the root causes will continue to exert their influence in the coming decades or not is an important question. However, it appears that the changing composition of endowments in the region is counteracting with the old causes and is bringing about institutional change. In recent years, there have been persistent efforts to bring about democracy in a number of countries, as in the case of Iran. Many observers have attributed these efforts to the gradual rise of human capital relative to the natural resource rents as a source of income. The more educated labor forces of the MENA countries demand greater participation, organize and articulate their positions better, and when governments ignore them, their increased mobility imposes larger costs on local economies and ultimately on governments.

While democratization is desirable for a variety of reasons, from an economic policy perspective it also poses major challenges. The improved representation under democratic conditions makes coordination more difficult. For example, there is a great deal of historical and cross-country evidence that the expansion of franchise increases demands on public expenditures (Shelton, 2005). Also, compared to stable autocracies, democracy tends to increase the turnover in the leadership. This shortens the horizons of policymakers in office and can weaken their incentives to coordinate or even represent the polity's interests. In MENA countries, where tax administration is underdeveloped and resource rents are declining, these demands may lead to unsustainable budget deficits, a problem that Turkey has experienced for a few decades as it has moved toward a more established democracy. Countering these effects requires a great deal of institution building to enable competing interest groups coordinate their actions in the macroeconomic policy area. Similarly, without enhancing the coordination mechanisms, democratization may increase the demand for protection and undermine the prospects of trade liberalization.

Another implication of democratization in a world of imperfect contracts is the particular difficulties that countries with large resource rents tend to face. As discussed in Section 3.1, when the public knows that the government has access to large rents that may be diverted to particular interests, the voters become keen to capture their shares through the imperfect means that a nascent democracy provides. As a result, mass subsidies and various forms of protectionism may expand in the early stages of democratization process, giving rise to greater distortions in the economy (Esfahani, 2003). This implies that the democratic transition may be particularly difficult times for MENA economies with well-endowed resources.

The impact of democratization on policy commitment is also complicated and depends on the details of the institutions that structure the government's decision-making process. On the one hand, the democratic process is going to make policy change more difficult because a larger number of interest groups become involved and their conflicting preferences may preserve existing policies. On the other hand, the shorter time horizon of policymakers may induce them to choose lower quality policies and refuse to honor promises made by their predecessors. Moreover, unstable coalitions may emerge and undermine the credibility of long-term policies. Again, there are complementary institutions that can mitigate this problem (e.g., an independent and competent judiciary, a strong party system, a capable and meritocratic bureaucracy, etc.). But, MENA nations are not particularly well endowed with such institutions and need to build them as democratization proceeds.

Along with democratization, a process of decentralization is likely to start in some MENA countries. This is a natural development and may contribute to the quality of public services at the local level. However, like democratization, its success is contingent on a set of complementary institutions that ensure coordination at the macro level. The unfortunate experiences of Brazil and Argentina with decentralization in the 1980s and their contrast with the operation of decentralized systems in China and India, among many others, contain important lessons for arrangements that must accompany decentralization to ensure success. (For important lessons from the case of China, see Qian, 2003).

Table 6.   *Average years of schooling in MENA countries, 1970–2000[a]*

Country	1970	1980	1990	2000
Oil exporting	0.97	1.91	3.34	4.69
Algeria	0.82	1.56	3.01	4.72
Bahrain	1.82	3.12	4.87	6.09
Iran	1.01	1.93	3.36	4.66
Iraq	0.76	1.83	3.20	4.34
Kuwait	2.88	4.29	5.99	7.05
Libya	1.38	2.22	3.37	4.67
Non-oil exporting	1.53	2.24	3.40	4.51
Egypt	1.25	2.21	3.57	5.05
Jordan	2.29	2.93	5.39	7.37
Syria	1.67	2.86	4.35	5.74
Tunisia	0.91	1.92	3.02	4.20
Turkey	2.16	2.80	3.95	4.80
Non-MENA oil exporters[b]	1.20	1.91	2.54	3.52
Non-MENA non-oil exporters[b]	2.94	3.77	4.80	5.37

Sources: Barro-Lee education data available from the NBER website, http://www.nber.org. Labor force data extracted from the World Bank, *World Development Indicators* website.
[a]MENA countries shown in the table are only those for which data are available.
[b]The developing countries included in the average are those with available data for both subperiods. Labor force is used as weights across countries. Non-MENA oil exporters are Angola, the Republic of Congo, Gabon, Nigeria, Trinidad and Tobago, and Venezuela.

3.5. Human capital

Until about 1980, educational attainments in MENA were quite low compared with the other developing countries (Table 6).[7] This was largely the legacy of the region's traditional and tribal social structures, though in some areas it has been reinforced by colonial policies (Ayubi, 1995). However, over the past few decades, most MENA countries have been quickly catching up with their peers in terms of schooling quantity, though the achievement is less solid on the quality dimension (Salehi-Isfahani, 2007).

The attention given by MENA governments to education in recent decades started with the post-WWII social contracts promising improvement in the living conditions for broad segments of the population. Expansion of education also served as part of the state's effort to extend its control and shape the development process. Like other dimensions of government controls, the extension of education came easier in quantitative terms and was to some extent complementary to those dimensions (e.g., educating the workforce that was to fill the newly created government jobs). However, extensive government controls

---

[7]This is based on years of schooling. Data on literacy rates reveal similar patterns.

of overeconomic activity seem to have generated negative interactions with education quality. Government jobs focused the goals of the educational system on minimum skills and degrees, rather than entrepreneurship and creativity (Salehi-Isfahani, 2007). The widespread interventions also diverted the government's attention and resources away from more fundamental improvements in educational quality.[8] Weakness of administrative institutions discussed below has further contributed to the problem, and may at the same time have been partly caused by educational deficiencies. In any event, a manifestation of the phenomenon seems to be the apparent puzzle of low economic growth in the face of rapidly expanding education in MENA (Pritchett, 1999). If this conjecture is correct, we should before long observe much higher social returns to education in countries that manage to expand the role of private markets.

3.6. Administrative and judicial institutions

Administrative and judicial institutions are not particularly effective in the MENA region. (Figure 7 shows two indicators in these respects, though the numbers are subjective and subject to the usual caveats.) Typically, court cases take long time to settle and there is considerable concern among the public that judgment may not be competent and impartial. Moreover, in most MENA countries, bureaucrats are viewed as lacking sufficient competence and impartiality (World Bank, 2003).

Effectiveness in judicial and administrative services is highly desirable because these are valuable and crucial public goods particularly for improving contracting conditions in both private and public arenas. However, building a strong bureaucracy and judiciary has posed a number of dilemmas for developing countries. One fundamental problem is that reforming these institutions requires some capability to design and to carry out policies (or deals and contracts) that in turn depend on having capable administrators and state organizations in the first place. Although there are strategies of starting from some parts of these institutions and gradually rebuilding the system, implementing these strategies often faces a number of problems. In authoritarian countries, it is usually difficult for the rulers to grant sufficient autonomy and power to bureaucrats and judges to enable them to move forward with the necessary reforms. This is particularly the case because some partiality in those organizations is needed for maintaining the structure of power. In new democracies, in contrast, the difficult task is to coordinate a multitude of players and convince each that all the others will be cooperating to ensure a desirable long-term outcome for the reforms.

Currently, there is limited knowledge concerning the requirements of reform and the details of judicial and administrative institutions that match each

---

[8] Financial resources, of course, were less of a constraint for oil-exporting MENA countries, which have managed to achieve substantial improvement in schooling since the 1970s (see Table 6).

Figure 7.   Court independence and bureaucratic quality across developing countries

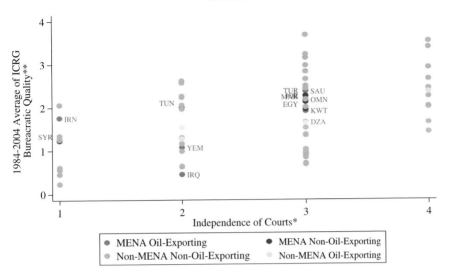

Sources: Charles Humana, *World Human Rights Guide* (1992) and Political Risk Services, Inc. Knack and Keefer (1995).
Court independence is a subjective ranking of autonomy of courts for the early 1990s. The range is 0–4 and higher scores indicate greater independence.
**Bureaucratic quality* is a survey-based subjective measure of autonomy from political pressure and strength and expertise to govern as well as the existence of an established mechanism for recruiting and training. The range is 0–4 and higher scores indicate higher quality.

country's conditions. Despite voluminous literature on these subjects, careful analytical work on them remains inadequate. Recently, some systematic research on these subjects has started (see, for example, La Porta *et al.*, 2004). More work along these lines and applications to the MENA countries should be an important part of further research on the political economy of growth in the region.

4. Conclusion

The factors shaping economic growth are truly numerous and vary greatly across countries and over time. Moreover, these factors interact with each other in multifaceted ways, making every country's situation at each point in time by and large specific. This fact has very important implications for the ways in which research on growth needs to be conducted and for the policy implications for each case. Most importantly, it implies that the causes of stagnation and growth are ultimately situation-specific and must be understood locally. Furthermore, the actions needed to enhance growth must also be assessed and applied at the local level by policymakers who are intimately familiar with the situation.

The situation-specificity discussed above does not mean that no generalizations can be made and there is no role for general frameworks for understanding growth. Indeed, the framework proposed in this paper and the illustration of its use for analyzing major issues of growth in MENA suggest that there are flexible perspectives that can help organize thinking about economic development at general levels. Moreover, such approaches can shed light on why conditions become specific and which lessons from other cases can be transferred to others and which ones are not applicable elsewhere.

The proposed framework and its emphasis on incomplete contracting owing to complexity also highlight the importance of carrying out in-depth case studies for understanding growth in specific context while keeping in mind the lessons of the underlying economic theory. Another important general implication is that solutions to growth problems need to be eventually formulated and implemented at the local level by people who are intimately familiar with the situation at hand and, at the same time, have a good grasp of the available theoretical frameworks and empirical results.

While the incomplete contracting framework proposed here is fairly general, it has basic differences from the earlier approaches to the political economy of growth. Perhaps the most important feature of the framework is that it goes beyond the simple claims that powerful interest groups have been blocking reform. Furthermore, it offers ideas about why interest groups and politicians may not find ways to adopt more efficient policies that yield larger surpluses for themselves. In particular, in the case of MENA, the framework shows that the interactions among the politicians, different interest groups, and the public are far more intricate than the image of authoritarian governments forcing self-serving bad policies on the society. Rather, it may be the need for maintaining public support in the absence of a complete social contract that leads politicians to opt for inefficient policies. This further implies that although some of the institutions or policies one finds in the region may not be desirable from a long-run perspective, under the circumstances of the short and medium run they may be better than feasible alternatives. However, change will be necessary as the underlying problems are better understood and addressed. In fact, there are already some institutions and policies that have better substitutes if the existing political economy knowledge is better disseminated among the politicians and the public.

Future research on the political economy of growth must proceed in a number of directions. To begin with, there is a need for more detailed case studies to explore the roots of failures to improve policies in specific circumstances. Second, among political actors there are many details of interactions that need to be explored theoretically and empirically, especially in the context of non-democratic political systems. This should particularly include studies of how the political structure shapes economic policies and how in turn economic outcomes affect the contracting capability of the political economy actors. Finally, there is a great need for documenting and quantifying institutional details and their dynamics in MENA, especially in ways that would be comparable across countries. This would provide better opportunities for testing hypotheses and digging deeper into the causes of growth and stagnation.

Acknowledgments

I would like to thank Maria Augusztinovics, Micael Castanheira, Shanta Devarajan, Heba Handoussa, Gary McMahon, Jeff Nugent, Lyn Squire, and two anonymous referees for their helpful comments on the earlier drafts of this paper. I am also indebted to the participants in the GDN conferences in Prague and Cairo and the economics workshops at the American University in Washington, American University in Beirut, and the University of Maryland for helpful discussions.

References

Abed, G.T. and H.R. Davoodi (2003), *Challenges of Growth and Globalization in the Middle East and North Africa*, Washington, DC: International Monetary Fund.

Abu-Bader, S. and A.S. Abu-Qarn (2003), "Government expenditures, military spending and economic growth: causality evidence from Egypt, Israel and Syria", *Journal of Policy Modelling*, Vol. 25, pp. 567–583.

Acemoglu, D. (2005), "The form of property rights: oligarchic vs. democratic societies", Manuscript, MIT.

Acemoglu, D., S. Johnson and J. Robinson (2001), "The colonial origins of comparative development: an empirical investigation", *American Economic Review*, Vol. 91(5), pp. 1369–1401.

Acemoglu, D., S. Johnson, and J. Robinson (2005a), "Institutions as the fundamental cause of long-run growth", in: P. Aghion and S. Durlauf, editors, *Handbook of Economic Growth*, Amsterdam: Elsevier.

Acemoglu, D., S. Johnson, J.A. Robinson, and P. Yared (2005b), "Income and democracy", Manuscript, MIT.

Acemoglu, D. and J.A. Robinson (2001), "Inefficient redistribution", *American Political Science Review*, Vol. 95, pp. 649–661.

Acemoglu, D. and J. Robinson (2005), *Economic Origins of Dictatorship and Democracy*, Cambridge, UK: Cambridge University Press.

Alesina, A., A. Devleeschauwer, W. Easterly, S. Kurlat, and R. Wacziarg (2003), "*Fractionalization, Journal of Economic Growth"*, Vol. 8, pp. 155-194.

Alesina, A. and A. Drazen (1991), "Why are stabilizations delayed?", *American Economic Review*, Vol. 81, pp. 1170–1188.

Alesina, A. and R. Perotti (1995), "The political economy of budget deficits", *International Monetary Fund Staff Papers*, Vol. 42(1), pp. 1–31.

Alesina, A. and G. Tabellini (1990), "Voting on the budget deficit", *American Economic Review*, Vol. 80(1), pp. 37–49.

Amsden, A. (1989), *Asia's Next Giant: South Korea and Late Industrialization*, New York: Oxford University Press.

Ayubi, N.N. (1995), *Over-stating the Arab State: Politics and Society in the Middle East*, London: I.B. Tauris Publishers.

Barro, R.J. (1996), "Democracy and growth", *Journal of Economic Growth*, Vol. 1(1), pp. 1–27.

Bates, R.H. (1999). "Ethnicity, capital formation, and conflict", CID Working Paper No. 27, Harvard University.

Campos, J.E. and H.L. Root (1996), *The Key to the Asian Miracle: Making Shared Growth Credible*, Washington, DC: Brookings Institution Press.

Castanheira, M. and H.S. Esfahani (2003), "Political economy of growth: lessons learned and challenges ahead", pp. 159–212 in: G. McMahon and L. Squire, editors, *Explaining Growth: A Global Research Project*, New York, NY: Palgrave Macmillan.

Deacon, R.T. and H. Bohn (2000), "Ownership risk, investment, and the use of natural resources", *American Economic Review*, Vol. 90(3), pp. 526–550.

Elbadawi, I.A. and S. Makdisi (2006), "Democracy and development in the Arab world", *Quarterly Review of Economics and Finance*, Vol. 46(5), .

Ersel, H. and M. Kandil (2007), "Financial development and economic growth in the MENA countries", in: J. Nugent and H. Pesaran, editors, *Explaining Growth in the Middle East, Contributions to Economic Analysis*, Amsterdam: Elsevier.

Esfahani, H.S. (2000), "Institutions and government controls", *Journal of Development Economics, University of Illinois at Urbana-Champaign*, Vol. 63, pp. 197–229.

Esfahani, H.S. and A. Toossi-Ardakani (2002), "What determines the extent of public ownership?", Manuscript, University of Illinois.

Esfahani, H.S. (2003), "A political economy model of resource pricing with evidence from the fuel market", Manuscript.

Esfahani, H.S. (2005), "Institutions and fiscal discipline in MENA region", Manuscript, University of Illinois at Urbana-Champaign.

Esfahani, H.S. (2006), "Understanding common trends and variations in the growth experience of MENA countries", Manuscript, University of Illinois at Urbana-Champaign.

Esfahani, H.S. and L. Squire (2006), "explaining trade policy in the Middle East and North Africa", *Quarterly Review of Economics and Finance,* Vol. 46(5).

Esteban, J. and D. Ray (1994), "On the measurement of polarization", *Econometrica*, Vol. 62(4), pp. 819–851.

Glaeser, E.L., R. La Porta, F. Lopez-de-Silanes and A. Shleifer (2004), "Do institutions cause growth?", *Journal of Economic Growth*, Vol. 9, pp. 271–303.

Hart, O., A. Shleifer and R.W. Vishny (1997), "The proper scope of government: theory and an application to prisons", *Quarterly Journal of Economics*, Vol. 112, pp. 1127–1161.

Henry, C.M. and R. Springborg (2001), *Globalization and the Politics of Development in the Middle East*, Cambridge, UK: Cambridge University Press.

Knack, S. and P. Keefer (1995), "Institutions and economic performance: cross-country tests using alternative institutional measures", *Economics and Politics*, Vol. 7(3), pp. 207–227.

La Porta, R., F. López-de-Silanes, C. Pop-Eleches and A. Shleifer (2004), "Judicial checks and balances", *Journal of Political Economy*, Vol. 112(2), pp. 445–470.

Lau, L., Y. Qian and G. Roland (2000), "Reform without losers: an interpretation of China's dual-track approach to transition", *Journal of Political Economy*, Vol. 108(1), pp. 120–143.

Lebovic, J.H. and A. Ishaq (1987), "Military burden security needs and economic growth in the Middle East", *Journal of Conflict Resolution*, Vol. 31(1), pp. 106–138.

Leite, C. and M. Weidmann (1999). "Does mother nature corrupt? Natural resources, corruption and economic growth", IMF Working Paper WP/99/85, Washington, DC.

Levy, B. and P. Spiller (editors) (1996), *Regulations, Institutions and Commitment: The Case of Telecommunications*, Cambridge, UK: Cambridge University Press.

Löfgren, H. (1993), "Economic policy in Egypt: a breakdown in reform resistance?", *International Journal of Middle Eastern Studies*, Vol. 25(3), pp. 407–421.

Mahdavi, H. (1970), "The patterns and problems of economic development in rentier states: the case of Iran", in: M.A. Cook, editor, *Studies in the Economic History of the Middle East*, London, UK: Oxford University Press.

Makdisi, S., Z. Fattah and I. Limam (2007), "Determinants of growth in the MENA countries", in: J. Nugent and H. Pesaran, editors, *Explaining Growth in the Middle East, Contributions to Economic Analysis*, Amsterdam: Elsevier.

Montalvo, J.G. and M. Reynal-Querol (2005), "Ethnic polarization, potential conflict, and civil wars", *American Economic Review*, Vol. 95(3), pp. 796–816.

McGuire, M.C. and J.M. Olson (1996), "The economics of autocracy and majority rule: the invisible hand and the use of force", *Journal of Economic Literature*, Vol. 34(1), pp. 72–96.

North, D.C. (2005), *Understanding the process of economic change*, Princeton, NJ: Princenton University Press.

North, D.C. and B. Weingast (1989), "Constitutions and commitment: the evolution of institutions governing public choice in seventeenth-century England", *The Journal of Economic History*, Vol. 49(4), pp. 803–831.

Owen, E.R. (2004), *State, Power and Politics in the Making of the Modern Middle East*, London: Routledge.

Persson, T. and L.E.O. Svensson (1989), "Why a stubborn conservative would run a deficit: policy with time-inconsistent preferences", *The Quarterly Journal of Economics*, Vol. 104(2), pp. 325–345.

Political Risk Services, Inc. (1995), *International Country Risk Guide Data, 1982–95*, Computer file, Syracuse, NY: Compiled by IRIS Center, University of Maryland, College Park, MD.

Pritchett, L. (1999), "Has education had a growth payoff in the MENA region?", MENA Working Paper Series No. 18, Washington, DC: The World Bank.

Pritchett, L. (2003), "A conclusion to cross national growth research: a foreword 'to the countries themselves", in: G. McMahon and L. Squire, editors, *Explaining Growth: A Global Research Project*, New York, NY: Palgrave Macmillan.

Qian, Y. (2003), "How reform worked in China?", pp. 297–333 in: D. Rodrik, editor, *In Search of Prosperity: Analytic Narratives on Economic Growth*, Princeton: Princeton University Press.

Richards, A. (1991), "The political economy of dilatory reform: Egypt in the 1980's", *World Development*, Vol. 19(12), pp. 1721–1730.

Richards, A. and J. Waterbury (1990), *A Political Economy of the Middle East*, Boulder, CO: Westview Press.

Rodrik, D. (editor) (2003), *In Search of Prosperity: Analytic Narratives on Economic Growth*, Princeton: University Press Princeton.

Rodrik, D. (2005), "Growth strategies", in: P. Aghion and S. Durlauf, *Handbook of Economic Growth*.

Rodrik, D., A. Subramanian and F. Trebbi (2002), "Institutions rule: the primacy of institutions over geography and integration in economic development", Manuscript, Harvard University.

Sadowski, Y. (1991), *Political Vegetables? Businessman & Bureaucrat in the Development of Egyptian Agriculture*, Washington, DC: Brookings Institution Press.

Sala-i-Martín, X., and E.V. Artadi (2003), "Economic growth and investment in the Arab world", Economics Working Paper 683, Department of Economics and Business, Universitat Pompeu Fabra.

Sala-i-Martín, X. and A. Subramanian (2003), Addressing the natural resource curse: an illustration from Nigeria", NBER Working Paper No. 9804.

Salehi-Isfahani, D. (2007), "Microeconomics of Growth in MENA: the Role of households", in: J. Nugent and H. Pesaran, editors, *Explaining Growth in the Middle East, Contributions to Economic Analysis*, Amsterdam: Elsevier.

Shelton, C. (2005), "The Size and Composition of Government Expenditure", Manuscript, Stanford University.

United Nations Development Programme (UNDP) (2002), *Arab Human Development Report 2002*, New York: United Nations.

Velasco, A. (2000), "Debts and Deficits with Fragmented Fiscal Policymaking", *Journal of Public Economics*, Vol. 76(1), pp. 105–125.

von Hagen, J. (1992). "Budgeting procedures and fiscal performance in the European communities", Economic Papers No. 96, Brussels: Commission of the European Communities Directorate General for Economic and Financial Affairs.

Wade, R. (1990), *Governing the Market: Economic Theory and the Role of Government in East Asian Industrialization*, Princeton: Princeton University Press.

Waterbury, J. (1993), *Exposed to Innumerable Delusions: Public Enterprise and State Power in Egypt, India, Mexico, and Turkey*, Cambridge, UK: Cambridge University Press.

World Bank (2003), *Better Governance for Development in the Middle East and North Africa*, Washington, DC: The World Bank.

Yildirim, J., S. Sezgin and N. Öcal (2005), "Military expenditure and economic growth in Middle Eastern countries: a dynamic panel data analysis", *Defence and Peace Economics*, Vol. 16(4), pp. 283–295.

Yousef, T.M. (2004), "Development, growth and policy reform in the Middle East and North Africa since 1950", *Journal of Economic Perspectives*, Vol. 18(3), pp. 91–116.

Appendix:

The variables are defined and measured according to the following criteria (See Table A.1).

Table A.1.   Variable definitions for Table 4

Score	Government Intervention and Public Ownership	Trade Policy	
	Level of Government Intervention in the Economy	Average Tariff Rate (percent)	Non-Tariff Barriers
1	*Very low*: < 10 percent of GDP; virtually no government-owned enterprises	< 4	Very low
2	*Low*: 11 – 25 percent of GDP; a few government-owned enterprises, like the postal service; aggressive privatization program in place	5–9	Low
3	*Moderate*: 26 – 35 percent of GDP; several government-owned enterprises like telecommunications, some banks, and energy production; stalled or limited privatization program	10–14	Moderate

Hadi Salehi Esfahani

Table A.1. Continued

Score	Government Intervention and Public Ownership	Trade Policy	
	Level of Government Intervention in the Economy	Average Tariff Rate (percent)	Non-Tariff Barriers
4	*High*: 36 – 45 percent of GDP; many government-owned enterprises like transportation, goods distributors, and manufacturing companies	15–19	High
5	*Very high*: 46 percent or more of GDP; mostly government-owned industries; few private companies	> 20	Very high

Source: The Heritage Foundation website, *Index of Economic Freedom* (2006).

CHAPTER 4

Financial Development and Economic Growth in the MENA Countries

Hasan Ersel* and Magda Kandil**

Abstract

Financial development contributes to economic growth through two channels. The direct channel is through mobilizing and allocating financial resources. The indirect channel is through creating the appropriate environment for monetary policy to be effective. The paper analyzes the performance of the MENA countries in mobilizing and allocating financial resources using aggregative indicators. The findings indicate that the MENA countries were quite successful in mobilizing financial resources, but relatively less efficient in allocating these resources. However, on average, the direct contribution of financial development to economic growth in the MENA countries is not significantly different from the other developing economies. Further, the paper analyzes the effect of financial development on the effectiveness of monetary policy in a subset of MENA countries. The findings indicate that monetary policy in these countries is capable of inducing long-lasting non-neutral effects that differentiate trend output growth across countries over time. Monetary policy appears, therefore, to be an important determinant of economic growth in the MENA countries. The paper concludes by pointing out directions to improve financial development in the MENA countries by promoting competition in the financial sector, strengthening supervision, and increasing the independence of central banks. On the other hand, taking further steps to create an appropriate legal environment (e.g., improve the quality of legislation and the judiciary system,

---

*Corresponding author.
**The views in the paper are those of the authors and do not necessarily represent those of the IMF or IMF policy.

CONTRIBUTIONS TO ECONOMIC ANALYSIS
VOLUME 278   ISSN: 0573-5555
DOI:10.1016/S0573-5555(06)78004-X

etc.) may further help the MENA countries to reap the utmost benefits by maximizing the potential of a healthy financial system.

Keywords: monetary policy, financial intermediation, economic growth, price inflation, MENA countries, resource allocation, regulations

JEL Classifications: G20, E50, 011

1. Introduction

A financial system provides means of payment and enables the economic decision makers to establish links between current and future economic activities. In that sense, the necessity of financial development for economic growth is self-evident. However, the existence of an association between these two variables is not sufficient to draw conclusions concerning the role of finance in the growth process. A well-performing financial system is expected to promote growth by influencing positively the rate of accumulation and efficiency of capital by enabling decision makers to take advantage of existing (or potential) financing opportunities. In an imperfect world, a financial system is expected to play an important role in making the decision makers aware of such opportunities and the risks associated with them. Toward achieving such a goal, a financial system is expected to facilitate the mobilization of capital as well as its efficient allocation among different users. To serve this end, a financial system is expected to fulfill the following objectives:

(1) Increase the amount of financial savings (resource mobilization function).
(2) Allocate financial savings to those projects with the highest return and, therefore, help economic agents to realize the value of their decisions in the best possible way. (resource allocation function).
   A financial system, in contrast, has its own operating costs. Therefore, a desirable property of the financial system should be to achieve the aforementioned objectives in a cost-efficient manner. In other words, a well-designed financial system should
(3) Enable financial intermediaries to operate at the lowest cost (operational efficiency).

In such a setting, a financial system can be considered as a resource allocation mechanism designed to achieve the two objectives within a given environment (i.e., institutions and information transmission facilities). The success of the financial system in achieving these objectives provides its *direct contribution* to economic growth.

While the role of financial development is crucial to mobilize and allocate private resources, financial deepening is equally important to enhance the efficacy of the monetary policy. In a market economy, where economic decisions are taken in a decentralized way by numerous and heterogeneous decision-making units, monetary policy is conducted by sending signals to affect their behavior. Therefore, the success of the monetary policy depends not only on the appropriateness of the decisions taken by the monetary authority, but also on the financial system's capability of transmitting policy signals to economic decision-making units as well as on the nature of their responses.

Conceptually, one can distinguish two phases in the implementation of a monetary policy decision. In the first stage, the central bank (the authority responsible for conducting monetary policy) sends its signals through (open market operations, the discount rate, and the required reserve ratio) to financial institutions. In the second phase, financial institutions, primarily banks, serve as financial intermediaries in transmitting central banks' signals to non-financial decision makers. More specifically, banks translate policy signals into actions that eventually affect the volume and allocation of funds that are being transferred. The financial system, therefore, by enhancing the efficiency of monetary policy, can *indirectly contribute* to economic growth.

The purpose of this paper is to examine the relation between financial development and economic growth in a sample of Middle East and North Africa (MENA) countries for which data are available.[1] Section 2 analyzes the direct contribution of financial development to economic growth. Section 3 is devoted to monetary policy to understand the role of the financial system in the transmission mechanism of policy signals. Section 4 provides the conclusions and a summary of policy issues that are relevant to the MENA countries.

2. Financial development and economic growth: direct contribution

Financial development refers to a rather complex and multidimensional process that involves deepening and broadening of the financial markets via changes in the institutions and the regulatory environment as well as the introduction of new financial instruments. Therefore, one can approach the problem of describing financial development by listing all the relevant variables and introducing proxy measures to represent them. That was the approach followed in Creane *et al.* (2003), namely collecting and analyzing information for 100 quantitative and qualitative variables under six themes to describe financial development in the MENA countries. An alternative approach is to reduce the informational requirements of describing the financial development by treating the process in an aggregative framework. In this paper, we follow the aggregative approach to analyze the relation between financial development and growth. Namely, we focus on the two main functions of a financial system in the growth

---

[1] Data problems prevented coverage of all MENA countries.

process (i.e., resource mobilization and allocation functions) and evaluate the efficiency of the financial system in achieving these functions.

The framework incorporates available data for the MENA countries to evaluate the performance of the financial system in achieving resource mobilization, resource allocation, and operational efficiency.

2.1. Resource mobilization function

A financial system intermediates between savings-surplus and savings-deficit agents in channeling funds provided by the former group to the latter. Financial systems offer different types of instruments to make such transfers suitable to the needs and tastes of the parties involved. One major distinction is between "direct" and "indirect" financing. In direct financing, the securities markets play a fundamental role. In indirect financing, intermediaries, i.e., banks, assume the risk of making transformations to satisfy the interests of agents on the two sides of the fund transfer.

In the MENA countries, indirect financing is the dominant form of finance. Therefore, in the rest of the paper, the focus will be on banking. Since markets for financial securities are also developing in these countries, we expect that the role of banks in resource mobilization will gradually decrease over time.[2]

One can follow two different approaches to measure the resource mobilization performance of a financial system. The first approach is to use the volume of funds controlled by the financial system, proxied by Broad Money (currency

---

[2] To quantify the importance of the securities markets in allocating financial resources, two measures are frequently used. These are market capitalization and turnover ratios. In the former ratio, market capitalization is measured by share prices times the number of shares outstanding. The second ratio is defined as total value of shares traded during the period divided by the average market capitalization for the period. The following table indicates that the markets for securities, even under the most generous assumptions, are evident to play a marginal role in allocating financial resources in developing countries.

YEAR 2001	Market Capitalization/ GDP (%)	Turnover Ratio (%)
MENA countries[a]	34.6	6.2
11 Middle-income countries[a]	48.5	7.7
EMU countries	89.9	90.6

Source: The World Bank: *World Development Indicators (WDI)*, Washington, DC, The World Bank, 2002.
[a]Refers to the corresponding sets of countries that are listed in Table 1.

plus demand and time deposits), as a performance indicator for the domestic financial system. The second approach is to evaluate the performance of a financial system by looking at the difference between its "intermediation potential" and its realization.

In Table 1 Broad Money/GDP for nine MENA countries and a set of emerging market economies are given.

As can be seen from the figures in Table 1, the ratio of Broad Money to GDP varies considerably among countries. This may be due to other factors that are independent from the quality of their financial systems (such as accustomed transaction practices, the level of inflation, excess liquidity, migrants' flows, the interest rate, the exchange rate, and supply-side constraints). However, the figures in Table 1 do not indicate a significant difference between the resource mobilization capabilities of the financial systems of the MENA countries and emerging countries in other parts of the world.

It is clear that the domestic financial systems of countries cannot be considered as the only channels that transfer financial resources. One can think of two competing forms of finance that compete with the domestic financial system.

Table 1. Broad Money/GDP Ratio (%) (1997–2001 Averages)

MENA Countries	%
Algeria	44.34
Egypt	75.87
Iran	38.85
Jordan	116.35
Kuwait	85.76
Lebanon	170.62
Morocco	78.34
Saudi Arabia	47.54
Tunisia	51.71
Average	78.82
Middle-income Countries	
Argentina	29.11
Brazil	29.76
Chile	41.81
India	59.37
Korea	173.43
Malaysia	139.72
Mexico	24.89
Phillipines	60.71
Thailand	100.70
Turkey	46.77
Venezuela	18.40
Average	69.56

Source: International Institute of Finance, Data Base.

The first is the traditional finance. It may take various forms ranging from usury to the trade finance among corporations.[3] The effectiveness of the traditional finance depends on many diverse factors, ranging from the development level of the financial system to the size of the underground economy. Although, there are insurmountable difficulties in collecting data for the volume of traditional finance, it is reasonable to assume that its importance declines as the financial system develops.

The second major competitor is the international financial system, whose importance significantly increased for the developing countries during the era of financial globalization. One way of demonstrating its importance for developing countries may be as follows:

Consider the case of a frictionless global financial system where financial institutions are able to offer their services to any customer, irrespective of its location. Then each economic decision-making unit will be in a position to choose to operate with the financial institution that serves its needs best. In today's imperfectly competitive environment, however, national financial systems are protected (both *de jure* and *de facto*) against foreign competition in mobilizing residents' financial resources. But, however perfect (and/or protected) it may be, no country's financial system can be the only intermediary for its residents in a global financial environment. Therefore, major differences between the potential of a financial system and its actual performance in mobilizing financial resources can be considered as an indicator of its effectiveness.[4]

The Institute of International Finance releases data on deposits held abroad by residents[5] of countries in commercial banks that report to the Bank of International Settlements (BIS). Since these deposits belong to those residents that reveal their identity it is highly unlikely that their existence is the result of some illegal operations. Therefore, they can be considered leakage of resources that could have been mobilized by the domestic financial system instead.

In Table 2, the amount of deposits held abroad is measured as ratios to Broad Money and GDP for seven MENA countries and eleven middle-income countries from other regions of the world. From the figures given in the table it is clear that neither these MENA countries nor those from other regions, are homogeneous with respect to their financial system's ability in mobilizing financial resources. The data also reveal that in terms of absolute levels, even after the exceptionally high figure for Jordan is excluded, the leakage is quite

---

[3] In many countries, trade credit among non-financial companies in various forms is used rather widely. In fact, it may even be the major external source for working capital needs of companies. Since standard financial statistics do not cover such trade credits, for the countries where such practice is widely used, the credit to GNP ratio stays at a rather low level.

[4] It should also be pointed out that the reasons behind these divergences may range from mistrust of the economic policies followed in that country, or, in an open-economy context, to the effectiveness of external competition.

[5] These figures exclude assets held abroad by resident deposit money banks, which are given separately.

Table 2. *Deposits held abroad by residents in commericial banks that report to the BIS (1997–2001 Averages)*

Country	As % of Broad money	As % of GDP
MENA countries		
Algeria	27.26	11.69
Egypt	32.20	24.93
Iran	21.67	9.33
Jordan	94.01	109.40
Kuwait	64.25	54.91
Lebanon	57.66	98.32
Morocco	23.59	18.21
Saudi Arabia[a]	82.83	39.21
Tunisia[a]	28.77	13.82
Average (except Saudi Arabia and Tunisia)	45.80	46.68
Middle-income countries		
Argentina	42.16	12.30
Brazil	28.29	8.25
Chile	50.48	20.25
India	9.11	5.23
Korea	5.37	7.94
Malaysia	11.74	15.49
Mexico	41.58	10.09
Phillipines	29.06	16.38
Thailand	10.79	10.32
Turkey	28.41	10.72
Venezuela	145.15	25.61
Average	36.55	12.96

Source: International Institute of Finance, Data Base. For Saudi Arabia and Tunisia: *Comparative Statistics for Emerging Market Economies*, International Institute of Finance, April 2000, pp. 132.
[a]Time series data are not available for these countries. The figures are the averages of 1997 and 1998.

high for the MENA countries. This indicates that the financial systems in these countries have scope to enhance their performance in mobilizing financial resources. Nonetheless, a thorough evaluation of the difference would require analysis of factors (such as the legal environment, uncertainty, agents' confidence, economic policies, etc.) that affect residents' decisions in evaluating the quality of domestic and foreign financial institutions.

2.2. Resource allocation function

A financial system is said to fulfill its resource allocation function if it allocates the resources it mobilized to the most profitable and productive users. A financial system should be in a position of delineating the most profitable users of the funds that it transfers and it can, therefore, be considered relatively more *efficient* if it achieves a better use of financial resources. A financial system may allocate resources based on market information, where competitive forces play more role, or on non-market information, where the weight of other factors (social, political, administrative, etc.) is more prevalent. In repressed/protected economies, a financial system allocates financial resources, but these decisions are based on non-market criteria. In contrast, in many of the developing countries, even after implementing liberalization programs, non-market allocation schemes remain in activities such as financing of state-owned companies and agricultural support programs.

One way of approaching the problem of allocation efficiency is to assume that a financial system has a higher chance in identifying better customers, if its decisions are market based.[6] To approximate the market-based portion of the funds allocated to the domestic economy, the share of claims on the private sector[7] to total domestic credits is used. This choice is based on the assumption that the financial system allocates resources to the private sector according to market criteria. Evidently, such an assumption may not correspond to reality for various reasons. For emerging countries, the most important violation is the "related party lending" practice of private banks. In many countries private banks are affiliated with industrial groups and may frequently extend loans to the group companies based on non-market criteria. In contrast, state-supported programs to the private sector, although included in credits to the private sector, can hardly fulfill the profitability criteria in the usual sense.

In Table 3, claims on the private sector as a percentage of domestic credits is given for 9 countries from the MENA region and for 12 major emerging countries from other regions of the world.

The figures in the table indicate that the MENA countries are far from being homogeneous with respect to the role of their financial systems.[8] The share of private claims in total credits also exhibits a wide variation, ranging between 28.87 (Syria) and 92.49% (Tunisia). However, as the figures for other emerging economies indicate, heterogeneity is not peculiar to the MENA countries. Emerging countries from the other regions of the world also exhibit considerable differences. The figures also reveal that the ratio of the claims on the private

---

[6] Basing decisions on non-market criteria does not necessarily imply an irrational behavior. Many developing countries, which followed planned development strategies to promote industrialization through import substitution policy, created protective environments to allocate their resources. In such environments, the priority was given to financing activities or projects in industries or in regions, which were considered socially important in development plans. Therefore, financial profitability was left out partly (or completely) as a criterion for allocation in such decisions and was replaced by the social benefit. Such a system inevitably generated the concept of "duty loss" even for private companies, including private banks. The implied incentive structure was based on the principle of *"profits are private and losses are social,"* which created the well-known moral hazard problems.

[7] Line 32d in the International Financial Statistics (IFS) data.

[8] See Creane *et al.* (2003) for a supporting argument.

Table 3.   Claims on privatge sector as % of domestic credits (1997–2001 average)

Country	%
MENA Countries	
Algeria	14.62
Egypt	55.53
Iran	49.79
Jordan	83.07
Kuwait	55.91
Lebanon	52.26
Morocco	61.70
Saudi Arabia	69.38
Syria	28.87
Tunisia	92.49
Average	55.77
Middle-income Countries	
Argentina	67.86
Brazil	60.23
Chile	90.62
India	56.62
Korea	89.71
Malaysia[a]	103.42
Mexico	69.62
Phillipines	73.03
Thailand[a]	100.06
Turkey	51.28
Venezuela	79.69
Average	76.56

Source: International Institute of Finance, Data Base.
[a] A larger than 100% ratio in the second column for Malaysia and Thailand indicate, that the public sector is supplying credit in these countries.

sector to total domestic credits is significantly low for the MENA countries compared to other emerging countries. In fact only the ratios for Jordan and Tunisia, exceeds the average of the other emerging countries in Table 3.

2.3. Operational efficiency

Operational efficiency of a financial system refers to its ability to provide finance at the lowest possible cost. The cost of providing finance consists of two components. First, is the interest paid to the ultimate lender and second is the intermediation cost. The operational efficiency of the financial system refers to the latter, since the former is determined by factors that are beyond the control of financial institutions (such as macroeconomic conditions, the depth of the financial system, etc.).

Table 4. *Indicators of operational efficiency*

Country	Real Interest Rate on Deposits (%) (1997–2001 Average)	Cost of Intermediation Ratio (Lending Rate/ Deposit Rate) (1997–2001 Average)	Lending Rate/T-Bill Rate
MENA countries			
Algeria	2.98	1.35	1.26
Egypt	5.50	1.40	1.55
Jordan	5.06	1.59	n.a.
Kuwait	4.04	1.53	n.a.
Lebanon	n.a.	1.26	1.56
Morocco	4.47	1.84	n.a.
Syria	3.05	2.25	n.a.
Middle-income countries			
Argentina	9.8	1.43	n.a.
Brazil	17.1	3.15	3.04
Chile	5.8	1.53	n.a.
Korea	5.3	1.17	n.a.
Mexico	−3.99	2.46	1.2
Phillipines	2.98	1.43	1.8
Thailand	2.91	1.96	n.a.
Venezuela	−7.1	1.49	n.a.

Source: IFS Data Base; n.a., not available

Unfortunately, data concerning operational efficiency indicators are either not available or not reliable for many countries. Therefore, the rather incomplete information given in Table 4 should be treated cautiously. In the first column of Table 4, real interest rates on deposits for the MENA countries are given as averages for the 1997–2001 period. The average value of this ratio for the MENA countries is 4.37%. The London Interbank Offered Rate (LIBOR) rate for US dollar deposits, after adjusting for US inflation, is 3.14% for the same period. As one expects, the cost of resource mobilization is higher for the MENA countries, but not excessively higher than the LIBOR rate.[9]

In the second column of Table 4, the average ratio of lending rate/deposit rate (cost of intermediation ratio) is given for the 1997–2001 period. This ratio, under quite strict assumptions, can be used as a proxy for the intermediation cost.[10] The cost of intermediation ratio is expected to be lower for more efficient

---

[9]Countries from Latin America in the sample have either excessively high real deposit rates (Argentina and Brazil) or significantly negative real rates (Mexico and Venezuela).

[10]This ratio is affected by the currency composition of the assets and liabilities of banks when valuation gains (or losses) owing to exchange rate developments are not taken into account in calculating the interest rate. Valuation problems are more distorting for the high-inflation economies.

financial systems. However, the findings in this table are puzzling. The cost of intermediation ratios for emerging economies in the table, except for Brazil, Mexico, and Syria, are lower than that of the Euro Area average, which is 2.1.[11]

In the third column of Table 4 the lending rate/T-Bill rate is reported. Suppose that banks treat government securities as a risk-free asset and loans are extended primarily to private agents. Then, this ratio will reflect the risk premium in lending to private agents. A high ratio, therefore, may indicate a weakness in the financial system's ability/willingness to finance private agents.

For the Euro Area, the average value of this ratio is 1.3 for the 1997–2001 period. Unfortunately, data are not available to calculate this ratio for most of the emerging countries in the sample. Data are available for three MENA countries and three other emerging economies. The ratios for Egypt and Mexico are below the Euro Zone average. The only exceptionally high ratio is for Brazil, which indicates that during the period in question the risk premium on private lending was extremely high.

2.4. Economic growth and financial development indicators

The next logical step is to see whether these three dimensions have some effect on economic growth in the MENA countries. In this exercise the MENA countries, irrespective of their per capita income, are treated within the world of developing countries and the following two questions are asked:

(1) Do these three dimensions contribute to the growth performance of developing economies?
(2) Is there a difference between the MENA countries and other developing countries with respect to the contribution of these direct channels on the their growth performance?

To answer these questions a set of indicators is defined to represent each dimension. The relation between these variables and the growth performance of the countries in the sample is tested by using cross-section data for developing countries. The choice of the indicators as well as the sample was restricted by data availability. The reason behind the choice of indicators is as follows:

---

[11] In the IFS data base, the "prime rate" data collected from banks is given as a proxy for the "lending rate." In practice such a rate may not be correlated at all with the actual rates that banks charge in their lending activities. First of all, the share of best customers may be too small to represent the actual rates. Secondly, banks may only be using the "prime rate" for official reporting and not in determining their actual lending rates. Finally, extension of a loan, in most instances, is a component of a basket of services that the bank offers to its client, where both parties are more concerned with the pricing of the basket and not its individual components.

2.4.1. *Resource mobilization function*

To represent this function the following variable is used:

$$RM = \frac{\text{Broad Money (Money + Quasi Money)}}{\text{GDP}}$$

The choice of such measure is based on the following assumption: the savings rate in an economy is determined by a set of economic, sociological, and political factors. The financial system development has little, if any effect, on the savings rate. What the financial system does is to transform financial savings and make them available to be used by economic decision makers.

The data for Broad Money is obtained from IFS, whereas the GDP figures are from WDI.

2.4.2. *Resource allocation function*

The following indicator is used to represent the resource allocation function:

$$RA = \frac{\text{Credit to the Private Sector}}{\text{Credit to the Private Sector + Claims on Government and Other Public Entities}}$$

This indicator is based on an asymmetric view of treating private and public sectors. The private sector, in this treatment, is assumed to attain the status of being credible through the quality of their operations. The public sector, in contrast, derives its credibility from being part of the government. Therefore, as the financial system extends more credit to the private sector, it can be considered as contributing more to the growth of the economy.[12]

The data are obtained from WDI.

2.4.3. *Operational efficiency*

The following, widely used, interest margin variable is used as a proxy for operational efficiency:

$$OE = \frac{\text{Lending Rate}}{\text{Deposit Rate}}$$

---

[12] In fact, this assumption can be challenged on various grounds. First of all, the banking system may play a purely passive role in channeling preferential credits to the private sector. In other words, volume and conditions of such credits may be administratively determined and financed through public sector funds. Secondly, but less likely in developing countries, credits to the public sector may be subjected to the same conditions as the private sector. In contrast, it is not necessarily true that credits to the private sector, by definition contribute to economic growth. They may be misused through schemes such as connected lending.

It is assumed that the closer this ratio to 1, the higher is the operational efficiency of the financial system.[13] Data are obtained from WDI.

To see whether these variables have an effect on the growth performance of the developing countries a cross-section study was conducted. The sample was chosen on the basis of data availability and consists of 97 developing countries. In this study, a set of control variables (such as per capita income, the inflation rate, the savings rate, and monetary growth) are used along with financial development indicators. In contrast, to answer the second question, intercept and slope dummies are introduced to see whether being a MENA country[14] makes a difference concerning the direct effects of the financial system. Since the aim of the exercise is to look at the long-run effects of financial development on growth, the averages of the relevant variables for the 1980–2000 period are used. Countries without sufficient data are eliminated. However, among the countries that remained in the sample, some have still missing observations for certain variables.

In the equation reported,[15] the control variables are per capita income (GDP/N), inflation (INF) and the savings rate (S/GDP). The expected signs of the coefficients for RM and RA are positive, whereas for OE it is negative. In contrast, statistical significance of the slope and interaction dummy variables will give an indication whether the MENA countries differ from other developing countries in the relation between financial development and economic growth. The regression equation was estimated by the OLS and the findings are reported in the Table 5.

The results reported in the table indicate that the coefficients of the three financial development indicators are statistically significant with the expected signs. Increasing the resource mobilization and resource allocation capacities of the financial systems and enhancing the operational efficiency of the financial system (measured by the decrease in interest margin) positively affect growth performances of developing countries. In contrast, the coefficients of all dummy variables that are introduced to distinguish the MENA countries are statistically insignificant. In other words, the findings do not point out a qualitative difference in the relation between financial development and economic growth in the MENA countries when compared with other developing countries.

---

[13] Interest margin may be quite misleading in high inflation countries where banks have open foreign exchange positions. As the effects of exchange rate movements are accounted for separately from interest payments, if a bank finances itself with foreign exchange deposits and extends loans in domestic currency, the above ratio automatically rises.

[14] The MENA countries included in the sample are Algeria, Bahrain, Egypt, Jordan, Kuwait, Morocco, Syria, and Tunisia.

[15] Different sets of control variables did not change the qualitative nature of the findings. In general financial indicators are statistically significant with the expected signs, but the control variables were not.

Table 5.   The Effect of Financial Indicators on the Rate of Growth in Selected Developing Countries

Parameter	Coefficients	T-Stat	Significance
Constant	−0.2451	−2.371	0.01996
Per capita GDP	−0.00056	−0.7148	0.4767
Inflation	−0.0051	−0.4079	0.6843
Savings rate	0.0203	1.3810	0.1709
Resource mobilization	0.03588	4.808	0.000006
Resource allocation	0.2613	2.5218	0.0135
Operational efficiency	−0.0072	−2.003	0.0482
MENA dummy (intercept)	0.2598	0.6001	0.5500
MENA dummy resource mobilization	−0.0560	−1.3842	0.1698
MENA dummy resource allocation	−0.2590	−0.5776	0.5651
MENA dummy operational efficiency	0.0089	0.5039	0.6156

Adjusted $R^2 = 0.3340$; $F(10, 86) = 5.8144$ (Significance level 0.000001); DW statistic: 1.925. The null hypothesis that the coefficients RMF, RAF, and OE are zero was also rejected, $F(3,86) = 11.23796$ (Significance level 0.000003).

3. Indirect contribution of financial markets to growth: The effectiveness of economic policy

Financial development, through broadening the spectrum of financial markets as well as inducing institutional developments is expected to create a better environment for monetary policy to be effective. Under normal assumptions, such a development is expected to have a positive effect on the growth potential of the economy.

Before examining the role and effectiveness of the monetary policy a logical issue needs to be addressed. Consider an economy with only an omnipotent central bank. Obviously, in such an economy both markets and institutions will be quite different from what is envisaged in financial development programs. Therefore, the information concerning the monetary aggregates may not shed sufficient light on the financial development level of the country in question. In contrast, the distinction made between direct and indirect contributions of a financial system to economic growth implies that the financial intermediaries are expected to operate efficiently in carrying out two different functions. The direct contribution of the financial system to growth requires financial intermediaries to be capable of taking decisions concerning financial resource mobilization and its efficient allocation. However, to carryout their second function, these institutions are expected to act as agents of economic policy makers, notably of central banks.

It is extremely difficult, if not impossible, to design an institution that can undertake these two rather diverse functions simultaneously in a perfect way. It can be argued that the former function is best served in a competitive environment accompanied by strong supervision. However, for the second function, assuming that internal informational and organizational problems can be solved, a gigantic central bank that controls both resource mobilization and resource allocation functions may suit better and serve the purpose. Such an institutional design may enhance efficiency of implementation of policy decisions for two reasons. First, it will eliminate the communication problems between the principal and the agents. Second, it may also lead to lower costs of operation when compared with an institutional setting based on principal (the central bank) and agents (banks) relation.[16]

These considerations highlight the importance of the financial system architecture and the recent financial reform efforts. Financial markets do not operate in a vacuum, but in an institutional environment. However, institutions are not neutral and they influence the working and the efficiency of the markets. Institutions are also human-made artifacts and change from one society to the other, owing to differences in cultural heritage, the legal system, and political factors. Therefore, it is neither realistic nor desirable to expect to design a uniform financial architecture applicable to all economies. Instead, the focus should be on delineating the functions to be carried out by the financial system and the tradeoffs that feasible structures impose on. As can be seen from the example given above, aggregating commercial banking and central banking under a single institution, even if it enhances financial systems' indirect contribution to growth, may hamper its direct contribution by eliminating competition among financial intermediaries.

Financial liberalization programs, one way or another, aim at enhancing a competitive environment for the financial system to develop. Therefore, the expected outcome of these programs is an increase in the role of financial intermediaries, in practice, notably banks. This implies a reduction in the relative size of monetary authorities, i.e., central banks.

One simple, albeit naïve, way of measuring the relative size of central banks vis-à-vis the financial system is to compare reserve money with broad money (money + quasi money). Reserve money can be considered as a proxy for the size of the central bank whereas broad money is a proxy for the financial system as a whole. Notice that central banks can increase reserve money, *ceteris paribus*, by increasing currency issued or by raising the reserve requirement ratio. In either case, the central bank's role in resource mobilization and allocation increases.

In Table 6, the ratios of reserve money to broad money are given as averages for 1977–1981 and the 1997–2001 periods for the MENA countries and a set of middle-income countries from other regions of the world. The periods are chosen to represent, vaguely, the initial periods of financial liberalization and its final stage. The five-year averages are taken to smooth the effect of outlying years.

---

[16] Agents may have their own preferences and institution-specific constraints that affect their behavior. Under certain circumstances, their private concerns and/or constraints may dominate their behavior and the desired policy outcome may not be realized. Therefore, devising and implementing a mechanism that relies on the performance of intermediaries may not sound attractive for central banks.

Table 6. Reserve Money/Broad Money

Country	1977–1981 Average	1997–2001 Average
MENA countries		
Algeria	43.64	33.04
Egypt	52.40	32.48
Iran[a]	45.28	39.84
Jordan	61.62	35.34
Kuwait	19.02	6.26
Lebanon	25.48	20.80
Morocco	36.28	27.34
Saudi Arabia	57.18	21.36
Syria	66.78	47.36
Tunisia	24.98	20.10
MENA average	43.27	28.39
Middle-income countries		
Argentina	34.38	19.84
Brazil	30.62	22.46
Chile	43.36	79.56
India	37.00	26.06
Korea	29.90	8.32
Malaysia	47.22	25.72
Mexico	60.72	21.18
Phillippines	53.54	19.96
Thailand	23.24	12.68
Turkey	55.14	17.38
Venezuela	31.40	40.20
Middle-income countries average	40.59	26.67

Source: International Financial Statistics Yearbook, 2002, Washington, DC: IMF, pp. 92–95.
[a] Data for 1978 is not available for Iran.

It is clear from the table that, this ratio exhibited a marked decline for all the countries (except Chile) between the two periods. It should also be pointed out that despite such a decline, the averages for both groups of countries remain high when compared with those of the financially advanced economies.[17] In contrast, MENA countries still exhibit a higher ratio when compared to other middle-income countries for the 1997–2001 period.[18]

---

[17] In 2001, this ratio was 13.4% for Japan, 9.5% for the USA, 6.2% for Canada, and 2.9% for the UK. Notice that the average of this ratio for 1997–2001 period is at the level of financially advanced countries for Kuwait and Korea.

[18] This result is strengthened if the outliers (Syria, Kuwait, Chile, and Korea) are excluded. In this case, the MENA countries' average increases to 30.85% and the average of middle-income countries declines to 22.83% for the 1997–2001 period.

This result can be interpreted in the following way: Financial development, indeed, led to an increase in the relative importance of the financial interme-diaries with respect to that of the central banks of the emerging economies. These countries made notable progress toward enhancing the role of financial intermediaries. This tendency is relatively weaker for the MENA countries (Kuwait seems to be an exception within the sample). However, for the MENA countries, it can be assumed that the monetary policy is increasingly conducted in an environment where central banks take into account the behavior of the financial intermediaries and financial market developments. In the light of this observation, the following exercise is undertaken to see whether the MENA countries' financial development level enables them to conduct monetary policy in an effective manner or not.

3.1. Monetary policy design

The first step of the empirical investigation is to determine how rational agents perceive that the design of monetary policy varies in response to policy makers' observations of economic conditions.[19] It is assumed that the monetary autho-rity's reaction function in period t is dependent on variables realized in period $(t-1)$ as follows:

$$Dmoney_t = \alpha_0 + \alpha_1 Dir_{t-1} + \alpha_2 Dp_{t-1} + \alpha_3 Dy_{t-1} + \alpha_4 Dgov_{t-1} + \alpha_5 dum_{t-1} + \eta_m$$

$$(1)$$

Here, $Dmoney_t$ is the growth of the money supply at time t and α_0 is a constant.

Agents expect the monetary authority to determine the growth of the money supply at time t in response to their observations at time t-1 of the growth in international reserves, Dir, price inflation, Dp, real output growth, Dy, and the growth of government spending, $Dgov$.[20] To account for possible structural change in the design of monetary policy, the empirical model accounts for a dummy variable, dum, that takes zero values prior to 1973 and 1 thereafter.[21] The term η_m is a random residual with a zero mean and a constant variance.

The growth of international reserves is likely to create monetary expansion. In contrast, a reduction in international reserves prompts the monetary policy authority to slow down monetary growth and raise the domestic interest rate to attract foreign flows.

The response of the monetary authority to price inflation is likely to vary depending on the policy objective. An increase in price inflation stimulates an

---

[19] For some discussion on the views governing the design of monetary policy, see Hoskins (1993). Empirical investigations of the reaction function for monetary policy in developing countries include Porzecanski (1979) and Joyce (1991).

[20] This list is not intended to be inclusive. Instead, the list aims at identifying major determinants of monetary policy subject to data availability.

[21] 1973 marks the energy price hike following the Arab–Israeli conflict.

addition, devaluation is likely to determine aggregate supply by affecting the cost of the output produced. The change in the domestic currency price of Special Drawing Rights (SDRs), *Dex*, affects, therefore, real output growth and price inflation with magnitudes β_{3_y} and β_{3_p}. In addition, changes in the oil price are likely to affect the cost of the output produced in oil-importing countries and stimulate aggregate demand in oil-exporting countries. Subsequent effects of the change in the oil price on real output growth and price inflation are measured by β_{4_y} and β_{4_p}. To account for possible structural break, the dummy variable *dum_t* is included in the empirical models for real output growth and price inflation.

To differentiate between the effects of anticipated and unanticipated monetary policy, monetary growth in equations (2) and (3) is replaced as follows:

$$Dy_t = \beta_{0_y} + \beta_{a_y} EDm_t + \beta_{u_y} Dms_t + \beta_{2_y} Dgov_t + \beta_{3_y} Dex_t + \beta_{4_y} Doilp_t + \beta_{5_y} dum_t + \eta_y$$

(4)

$$Dp_t = \beta_{0_p} + \beta_{a_p} EDm_t + \beta_{u_p} Dms_t + \beta_{2_p} Dgov_t + \beta_{3_p} Dex_t + \beta_{4_p} Doilp_t + \beta_{5_p} dum_t + \eta_p$$

(5)

Here, *EDm* and *Dms* are the anticipated and unanticipated components of monetary growth according to the monetary policy reaction function.[24] The parameters β_a and β_u measure the effects of the anticipated and unanticipated components of monetary policy on real output growth and price inflation. By construction, anticipated monetary policy, if significant, may have long-lasting effects on dependent variables. In contrast, random unanticipated changes in monetary policy are transitory in nature. Hence, their significant effects induce short-term fluctuations in the dependent variables.[25] The long-run neutrality of monetary policy is dependent on the effect of anticipated growth of the money supply on real output. If rational agents are able to anticipate and react to monetary policy, anticipated monetary growth is absorbed fully in price without determining real output, i.e., money is neutral. In contrast, prices do not adjust fully to unanticipated growth in the money supply in the short run. Accordingly, monetary surprises are distributed between real output growth and price inflation in the short run. The allocation is dependent on the flexibility to adjust prices and capacity constraints in the short run.

---

[24] By construction, *Edm* is a function of lagged values of output growth and price inflation. This eliminates the need to include the lagged dependent variables for possible persistence in empirical models.

[25] Tests of cointegration indicate that the non-stationary dependent variable is not jointly cointegrated with non-stationary independent variables. Hence, the empirical models are estimated without an error correction term.

3.2. Time-series results

The empirical models (1), (4), and (5) are estimated jointly for each of the countries under investigation to highlight determinants of monetary policy and the allocation of monetary growth between real output growth and price inflation. Based on data availability, the sample of countries under investigation includes Algeria, Egypt, Jordan, Kuwait, Morocco, Saudi Arabia, Syria, and Tunisia. The sample period varies between 1957 and 1997 across countries based on data availability.

Table A.1 (in the appendix) presents the results of estimating the empirical model that approximates the monetary policy reaction function. Monetary growth appears to increase in response to the change in international reserves. This relationship is statistically significant in Algeria, Saudi Arabia, Syria, and Tunisia. In these cases, the monetary authority is more inclined to pursue an expansionary monetary policy in response to the increased holdings of international reserves. In contrast, the depletion of international reserves prompts the monetary authority to contract the money supply in an effort to raise the interest rate and attract foreign funds. For other countries, changes in the money supply do not show any systematic correlation with international reserves.[26]

The response of monetary policy to price inflation varies across countries. Evidence of accommodating monetary policy is consistent with the positive and statistically significant signs for Jordan, Kuwait, and Saudi Arabia. Monetary policy attempts to counter inflationary pressures in the remaining countries with significant coefficients in Egypt and Tunisia.

The coefficients measuring the response of monetary growth to real output growth is generally insignificant, except in Jordan and Saudi Arabia. The positive response of monetary growth to output growth in Jordan and Saudi Arabia confirms the accommodating nature of monetary policy in these countries.

The positive response of the money supply to the increase in government spending provides evidence on monetizing the budget deficit. This response is statistically significant in Algeria and Tunisia. That is, the growth of the money supply is used to finance higher government spending in these countries.

Finally, the statistical significance of the dummy variable in the money reaction function is evident for Egypt, Morocco, Syria, and Tunisia. This evidence is consistent with a structural shift that leads to a significant increase in the average growth of the money supply after the oil price shock in 1973. That is, the monetary policy appears to have accommodated velocity shocks attributed to the inflationary pressure in response to the oil price shock of 1973.

---

[26] This may be indicative of the systematic policy of sterilization in these countries. The paper's evidence is robust with respect to a modification that measures the design of monetary policy in terms of domestic credit rather than the money supply.

Overall, the evidence indicates variation in the design of monetary policy in response to various determinants of monetary policy. Although central banks in most developing countries were originally established to finance government budget deficits, efforts are now devoted to make them more independent. Statistically significant coefficients in the reaction function indicate that central banks of the respective countries are still not independent.

Next, the real and inflationary effects of monetary growth in the countries under investigation are examined. The monetary policy reaction function is used to decompose monetary growth into two components. The predicted value measures the component of monetary policy that varies in response to economic conditions. Other random fluctuations in monetary growth are captured in the residual. The results of estimating the empirical models (4) and (5) present the real and inflationary effects of anticipated and unanticipated monetary growth. These results are summarized in Table A.2 (in the appendix).

Anticipated changes in the money supply are statistically significant in determining real output growth in Algeria, Jordan, and Tunisia. That is, anticipated changes in the money supply are capable of inducing non-neutral lasting effects on output growth over time. The non-neutral effects indicate failure of the financial system to transmit signals concerning the direction of monetary policy in light of available information. Other institutional rigidities (e.g., wage and price controls) may have further prevented nominal adjustment in the face of monetary shifts, providing a channel for an adjustment in real activity.[27] Similarly, random unanticipated fluctuations in the money supply have statistically significant effects on real output growth in Algeria, Jordan, and Tunisia. In the remaining countries, monetary policy is not statistically significant in determining real output growth.

The inflationary effect of anticipated monetary policy dominates that of unanticipated monetary policy in Jordan, Kuwait, and Saudi Arabia. The inflationary effect of unanticipated monetary policy appears significant only in Jordan. In the case of Algeria and Syria, the negative coefficients highlight price rigidity in response to anticipated and/or unanticipated monetary growth. This may be attributed to price control policies that prevent inflation from rising in response to expansionary monetary policy. Accordingly, price inflation is decreasing despite growth in the money supply. From the time-series evidence, there appears to be a tradeoff between the real and inflationary effects of monetary policy. Indeed, the correlation coefficient between the inflationary and real effects is -0.25 for anticipated monetary policy and -0.37 for unanticipated monetary policy, across countries.

---

[27] Along the same line, the literature citing institutional rigidity in industrial countries has provided evidence that anticipated monetary growth determines real activity in the US (see Mishkin (1983)).

3.3. *Policy design and the effects of monetary growth*

The evidence of this section will seek to evaluate the importance of the design of monetary policy to the real and inflationary effects of monetary growth across the countries under investigation. Table A.3 (in the Appendix) presents correlation coefficients between parameters of the monetary policy reaction function and the real and inflationary effects of monetary growth. These correlations highlight the importance of variation in the design of monetary policy to the real and inflationary effects of monetary growth across countries.[28]

In line 1, an increase in the response of monetary growth to international reserves decreases the real effects of monetary shifts. This is evident by the negative correlation coefficients, −0.17 and −0.19, between the response of monetary policy to international reserves and the real effects of anticipated and unanticipated monetary policy across countries. In contrast, an increase in the response of monetary growth to international reserves appears somewhat inflationary. This is evident by the positive correlation coefficients, 0.045 and 0.24, between the response of monetary policy to international reserves and the inflationary effects of anticipated and unanticipated monetary policy across countries.

In line 2, the policy response to price inflation appears important to the real effects of anticipated and unanticipated monetary policy, as evident by the negative correlation coefficients, −0.45 and −0.58. That is, where monetary policy is accommodating price inflation, the real effect of this policy is smaller. In contrast, where monetary policy aims at price stability, the real effect of this policy is larger. Consistently, the inflationary effects of anticipated and unanticipated monetary growth vary positively with the response of monetary policy to price inflation with correlation coefficients 0.27 and 0.57, respectively. That is, where monetary policy is accommodating price inflation, the inflationary effect of monetary policy is larger across countries. Similarly, disinflationary monetary policy decreases the inflationary effect of monetary policy across countries.

According to the evidence in line 3, the response of monetary policy to output growth does not appear to differentiate the real effect of monetary policy. This is evident by the small correlation coefficients, 0.059 and −0.11, between the response of monetary policy to output growth and the real effects of anticipated and unanticipated monetary growth. In contrast, an increase in the

---

[28] Cross-country correlations employ parameter estimates from the time-series regressions, multiplied by the inverse of the standard deviation in the time-series regressions. That is, parameters that are highly variable are weighted less heavily in the cross-country analysis. It should be emphasized, however, that cross-country correlations remain illustrative regarding variation in growth across countries. Country-specific factors are likely to differentiate these correlations. Nonetheless, cross-country correlations aim to identify whether a general pattern dominates this correlation despite variations across countries. For a detailed discussion of limitations of cross-country growth regressions, see, for example, Lee *et al.* (1997).

the experience with universal banking exhibits some variation among the countries of the region.[35]

The second problem concerning institution development is at the micro level. Changes in environment induce or require corresponding transformations in the mode of operation of the institutions. This is particularly important for financial intermediaries (banks), as they rely relatively much more on establishing credibility and sustaining reputation to do their business. In other words, the institutions need to be designed in such a way as to enable share-holders to compete successfully in a market system. These concerns increased interest in corporate governance in banking. In recent years, especially after the 1997 crisis, in line with developments in the world, efforts to restructure the authority and control structures of exiting banks in line with the guidelines of corporate governance are intensified in the MENA region.[36]

(iv) *Regulation and supervision.* MENA countries were no exception to the general trend in launching reforms to strengthen their regulatory and supervisory authorities' capabilities following the universal blueprint. In practice, there is not much dispute over the general concepts of prudential regulation. Therefore, the focus is more on ascertaining the effectiveness of supervision. In this context, delineating factors that limit the supervisory authorities from exercising their power becomes an important issue.

It is possible to distinguish two sets of factors that may hinder the supervisory authority from functioning properly. The first factor is the information processing and decision-making capability of such institutions. The second factor is the autonomy of the supervisory authority.

In most instances the most effective challengers of the autonomy of the supervisory authorities are governments. Governments' negative attitudes toward the autonomy of the supervisory authorities may stem from two different considerations. The first is the politicians' traditional unwillingness to share authority in policy design, which can be cured by developing democratic institutions. The other source of government's resentment to the existence of autonomous supervisory authorities is practical considerations. When state-owned banks play an important role as policy tools and/or when domestic borrowing is crucially important, the supervisory authority's decisions may directly affect governments. Under such conditions, a conflict between the government and the supervisory authority may lead to a *de facto* violation of the supervisory

---

[35] For example in Tunisia, the financial reform program, strengthened the universal banks by expanding the spectrum of their activities (Boughrara, 2002). In contrast, financial reforms in Egypt, although did not change the universal nature of her banking system, kept "a limited distinction between commercial and other banks", Bahaa Eldin and Mohieldin (1998, p. 121).

[36] There is an increasing literature on corporate governance in banking in Arab countries. See, for example, El-Kharouf, (2000); Suleiman (2000); Mohieldin *et al.* (2001); El Said (2002); and El-Kady (2003).

authority's autonomy and eventually its credibility in the eyes of the other players. It is clear that such a conflict is avoided if state-owned banks are privatized and if the domestic debt is not excessive. The interplay between the government and the state-owned banks highlights the importance of the interdependencies between the financial and public sector reforms. The excessive involvement of governments of MENA countries in their financial systems seems to be a crucially important factor behind their modest success in creating strong autonomous supervisory authorities.

The above factors deserve a careful study aimed at enhancing the contribution of the financial sector to the effectiveness of monetary policy and the promotion of steady economic growth in the MENA countries.

Acknowledgments

The authors gratefully acknowledge the comments and help of Alpay Filiztekin. The views in this paper are those of the authors and should not be interpreted as those of the affiliated institutions.

References

Aleskerov, F., H. Ersel and M. Mercan (2001), "Structural dissimilarities in Turkish banks: 1988–1999", *Bogazici Journal*, Vol. 15(1), pp. 57–69.

Allen, F. and D. Gale (1995), "A welfare comparison of intermediaries in Germany and the US", *European Economic Review*, Vol. 39(2), pp. 179–209.

Atiyas, I. and H. Ersel (1994), "The impact of financial reform: the Turkish experience", pp. 103–139 in: G. CaprioJr., I. Atiyas and J.A. Hanson, editors, *Financial Reform-Theory and Experience*, Cambridge: Cambridge University Press.

Bahaa Eldin, Z.A. and M. Mohieldin (1998), "On prudential regulation in Egypt", pp. 111–140 in: M. El-Erian and M. Mohieldin, editors, *Financial Development in Emerging Markets: The Egyptian Experience*, Cairo: ECES Publication.

Ball, L., N.G. Mankiw and D. Romer (1988), "The new Keynesian economics and the output-inflation tradeoff", in: *Brookings Papers on Economic Activity*, Vol. 2, pp. 1–82.

Boughrara, A. (2002), "The monetary policy of the Central Bank of Tunisia: an assessment", Paper presented at ERF 9th Annual Conference, October 26–28, Sharjah, UAE.

Creane, S., R. Goyal, A. Mushfiq Mobarak and R. Sab (2003), *Financial Development in the Middle East and North Africa*, Washington, DC: IMF Publication.

El-Kady, M.F. (2003), "Sound corporate governance for banks", Paper presented to The International-Arab Banking Summit for 2003, June 25–26, Montreal, Canada.

El-Kharouf, F.W. (2000), "Strategy, corporate governance and the future of the Arab banking industry", *The Arab Bank Review*, Vol. 2(2), October, pp. 30–39.

El Said (2002), "Aspects of corporate governance in the banking system", Paper presented at the conference on Institutional and Policy Changes Facing the Egyptian Economy, May 26–27, Cairo, Egypt.

ERF (2000), *Economic Trends in the MENA Region*, Cairo: Economic Research Forum Publication.

ERF (2002), *Economic Trends in the MENA Region, 2002*, Cairo: Economic Research Forum Publication.

Fischer, S. (1977), "Long-term contracts, rational expectations, and the optimal money supply rule", *Journal of Political Economy*, Vol. 85, February 1977, pp. 191–205.

Hoskins, W.L. (1993), "Views on monetary policy", *Review, Federal Reserve Bank of St. Louis*, March/April, pp. 43–55.

Joyce, J.P. (1991), "An examination of the objectives of monetary policy in four developing economies", *World Development*, Vol. 19(6), pp. 705–709.

La Porta, R. and F. Lopez de Silanes (1998a), "Banks, markets and structure: implications and determinants", pp. 29–57 in: S.J. Burki and G.E. Perry, editors, *Beyond the Washington Consensus: Institutions Matter*, Washington, D.C.: World Bank.

La Porta, R. and F. Lopez de Silanes (1998b), "Capital markets and legal institutions", pp. 99–117 in: S.J. Burki and G.E. Perry, editors, *Beyond the Washington Consensus: Institutions Matter*, Washington, D.C.: World Bank.

La Porta, R., F. Lopez de Silanes and A. Scheifer (1998), "Law and finance", *Journal of Political Economy*, Vol. 106(6), pp. 1113–1155.

Lee, K., M.H. Pesaran and R. Smith (1997), "Growth and convergence in a multi-country empirical stochastic Solow model", *Journal of Applied Econometrics*, Vol. 12, pp. 357–392.

Lucas, R. (1973), "Some international evidence on output-inflation tradeoffs", *The American Economic Review*, Vol. 63(3), pp. 326–334.

Lucas, R. (1975), "An equilibrium model of business cycle", *Journal of Political Economy*, Vol. 83, pp. 1113–1144.

Mishkin, F. (1983), *A Rational Expectations Approach to Macroeconometrics: Testing Policy Ineffectiveness and Efficient Market Models*, Chicago: University of Chicago Press.

Mohieldin M., N. Abulata and M. Lasheen (2001), "Corporate Government Country Assessment-Arap Republic of Egypt", Report on Observance of Standards and Codes, The World Bank, September, www.worldbank.org/ifa/rosc_cg.html.

Nelson, C. and C. Plosser (1982), "Trends and random walks in macroeconomic time series", *Journal of Monetary Economics*, Vol. 10, pp. 139–162.

Porter, R. and S. Ranney (1982), "An eclectic model of recent LDC macroeconomic policy analyses", *World Development*, Vol. 10(9), pp. 751–765.

CHAPTER 5

Labor Markets and Economic Growth in the MENA Region [☆]

Christopher A. Pissarides and Marie Ange Véganzonès-Varoudakis

Abstract

The labor market plays an important role in economic development through its impact on the acquisition and deployment of skills. This paper argues that countries in the Middle East and North Africa (MENA) region failed to deploy human capital efficiently despite high levels of education because of a large public sector, which has distorted incentives, and because of excessive regulation in the private sector. The education system is geared to the needs of the public sector, so the acquired skills are inappropriate for growth-enhancing activities. Excessive regulation of the private sector further removes the incentives for employers to recruit and train good workers. As a result, the MENA countries found it difficult to adapt to new conditions in the 1990s and their rate of productivity growth fell to very low levels. The group as a whole failed to keep up with countries that used to be at a comparable level of development such as East and South-East Asia.

Keyword: Middle East and North Africa economies, public sector employment, employment and growth, education and growth

JEL classifications: J45, E24, I20, O53

[☆] A first version of this paper was written by Christopher Pissarides in 1999 for the Growth Development Project of the World Bank as a "thematic" paper for the MENA region. The current version is fully revised and updated, following comments from anonymous referees.

CONTRIBUTIONS TO ECONOMIC ANALYSIS
VOLUME 278   ISSN: 0573-8555
DOI:10.1016/S0573-8555(06)78005-1

1. Introduction: the growth context

The labor market is given a key role in the literature on economic growth. This may not appear at first to be the case, as many models do not refer explicitly to the structure of labor markets. But on deeper examination of the most popular recent models, it is invariably found to be the case. A variety of "engines of growth" are usually discussed in the growth literatures, which are directly or indirectly related to human capital and the implementation of new ideas. The engine of growth in the baseline Solow model is unspecified labor-augmenting technology; what can labor-augmenting technology be if it is unrelated to human capital? In other models it is the ability to introduce new products, namely the knowledge on how to do new things. In addition, in others it is explicitly "human capital" without going into the specifics of what human capital does to output growth and how. The conclusion reached from a reading of the recent growth literature is that if we are to understand growth and development, we need to understand the creation and deployment of human capital.

Human capital is created and put into use in labor markets. The structure of the labor market is therefore critical for the quantity and quality of human capital that is created and for the uses to which it is put. The structure of the market will determine, for example, how much human capital is put into growth-enhancing activities and how much into other activities such as redistribution. It will also determine what types of human capital will be required in different environments. Yet, despite the wide appeal of the recent growth literature and the large number of economists who have been attracted to it, not many labor economists have switched from their traditional preoccupations to the study of growth. Research in growth has become the domain of macroeconomists whose data on labor markets amounts to two or three aggregate series – usually for employment, schooling and participation rates. As a result, progress in the integration of labor market institutions with aggregate growth has been slow. In fact, it has not progressed much beyond the insights that generated the initial interest in growth theory. Looking at what data macroeconomists have on labor markets, and what propositions have been put forward by growth theorists for the link between labor market outcomes and growth, it becomes obvious that not much progress can be made within the current cross-country research agenda.[1] Deeper country research is needed that pays attention to the institutional structure of the country in question and to the links between human capital, the institutional structure and the growth outcomes.

In light of this, research on growth and the labor market in the MENA region has to begin with an examination of the labor market institutions in the

---

[1] Similar conclusions were reached by Topel (1999) in his survey of research on labor markets and growth.

MENA countries that are likely to influence growth outcomes. Unfortunately, past literature provides little guidance in this respect. There is virtually no literature explaining which labor market institutions are likely to be good for growth and which are likely to be bad. Of course, economists have views on the matter, but there is no consensus founded on solid empirical research. For example, the thorough and comprehensive books on growth by Barro and Sala-i-Martin (1995) and Aghion and Howitt (1998) do not mention a single labor market institution that might influence growth. But in many variants of their models they do devote space to what they consider the key to growth, human capital. The same can be said for the recent survey on labor markets and economic growth by Topel (1999). The survey is devoted to human capital and growth, but not to labor market institutions. Of course, this reflects the current state of the literature, not an omission by the authors of those works.[2] In the case of the MENA region, although some recent studies analyze quite extensively the functioning of the labor market, there is very little discussion on the connections between the labor market and growth.[3]

Country research on growth can make a real contribution to our understanding of growth if it can produce new data that can identify labor market institutions that are conducive to the creation and deployment of good-quality human capital and institutions that are wasteful of human resources. The purpose of this "thematic" paper is to point out the links between human capital and growth that need empirical verification and discuss some summary data for the MENA region that might help point directions for research on individual countries. The role that human capital occupies in growth theory and its likely empirical contribution in the MENA region is first discussed. It is shown that despite rapid growth in human capital resources, it is unlikely that human capital has contributed significantly to growth in this region. The challenge facing research in this region is to find the reasons for the apparent wasteful use of human capital. We examine the sectoral composition of employment and the institutional structure that governs wage determination and employment and make some suggestions about the role of each and the directions for future research.

2. Human capital and economic growth

2.1. Human capital definitions

Human capital is created by formal education and formal training as well as by informal learning mechanisms. Each time someone develops the ability to do

---

[2] More recently, there has been increased emphasis on the role of institutions in growth and their empirical measurement. See, for example, Acemoglu *et al.* (2005).

[3] See, in particular, World Bank (2004) for a study of the functioning of labor markets in the MENA region and Agenor *et al.* (2003) for a more quantitative approach to the study of labor market institutions and reforms and outcomes.

something new, he or she increases his or her human capital. Of course, measuring human capital in its full dimension is an impossible task. For this reason, the literature usually confines itself to measuring the years of schooling in the working population and using the outcome as a proxy for all human capital in the country.

As a first step in the study of labor markets and growth we therefore need a series for the stock of human capital (years of schooling) in the labor force or the population of working age. This can be done by employing an inventory method to enrollment data, provided one or more points of reference are available for the stock from labor force surveys. The stock is augmented by the years of schooling of school leavers and depreciates by the education of those leaving the labor force. Data for the stock of human capital for the population of working age are also useful in making inferences about the likely changes in the supply of labor. A country with large amounts of human capital outside the labor force (e.g., with many educated women who are not participating) is more likely to experience changes in its participation rates than another.

Data for 5-year periods during 1960–1999 are available (Barro and Lee, 2000) and these data could provide a starting point for the research on the connection between human capital and growth in MENA. Table 1 reproduces some summary statistics for a selection of MENA countries, as well as by region. The main feature of these statistics is the steady growth of education in all the MENA countries of our sample throughout the period. In the 1960s, MENA educational attainment was one of the lowest in the world with an average of 1.6 years of schooling for each adult over the age of 15 years. This low attainment was comparable to the low attainment in the countries of Sub-Saharan Africa and South Asia. By 1999, however, the MENA region had closed the educational gap with the more advanced developing economies. With an average of 5.8 years of schooling, MENA is far ahead of South Asia and Sub-Saharan Africa, and less than one year behind Latin America and East Asia.

2.2. Growth theory

What specific role does growth theory give to human capital? Modern growth theory appears to give, at one and the same time, a large role to human capital but does not say enough about it. In some models, such as the Lucas (1998) model, human capital drives growth. Everything else – capital, output – adjusts endogenously to the accumulation of human capital. In other models, such as the imitation model of Rivera-Batiz and Romer (1991), it drives the imitation technology which ultimately determines the speed of convergence to the technological frontier. This model is of particular relevance to developing countries, especially those in proximity to more advanced trading partners. The MENA countries fall into this category in relation to the European Union. In the R&D models, such as the variant estimated by Benhabib and Spiegel (1994), human capital is the factor that is engaged in R&D and so its productivity determines the rate of growth. This model, however, is less relevant to MENA, as R&D activity is concentrated in a small number of advanced countries.

Table 1. ***Average number of schooling years, total population over 15 years old***

Country	1960	1980	1999
Algeria	1.0	2.7	5.4
Bahrain	1.0	3.6	6.1
Egypt		2.3	5.5
Iran	0.8	2.8	5.3
Iraq	0.3	2.7	4.0
Jordan	2.3	4.3	6.9
Kuwait	2.6	4.3	7.1
Syria	1.4	3.6	5.8
Tunisia	0.6	2.9	5.0

Region	1960	1980	1999
Sub Saharan Africa	1.7	2.5	3.5
East Asia	3.4	5.3	6.7
Eastern Europe	4.5	6.3	7.2
Developed Economies	6.7	8.3	9.5
Latin America	3.5	5.1	6.2
MENA	1.6	3.7	5.8
South Asia	1.5	2.9	4.2

Source: Barro and Lee (2000) and authors' calculation from Barro and Lee (2000) for regional averages.

But whereas human capital is postulated to be the factor that plays these roles, it has not yet been possible to empirically test any model with sufficiently detailed data to arrive at a smaller set of possible links between human capital and growth. The macroeconomic models that have been estimated, mostly with cross-country data, or with panel regressions making use usually of the Barro–Lee data set for human capital, cannot discriminate between these models.[4]

It can be argued that – as a first step in our attempts to understand the connection between labor market structure and growth – research should concentrate on the relation between labor market structure and the contribution of human capital to GDP growth, without trying to discriminate between the different roles that have been attributed to human capital in the literature. Of course, if the research could discriminate between some roles it would be an added bonus. But the more urgent need (and the one that will be of more policy relevance) is to identify institutional structures that are good for the productive use of human capital and for encouraging more investments in it and structures that are poor in this respect.

---

[4] The human capital by Nehru *et al.* (1993) have similar implications to those of the Barro–Lee data set where the two overlap.

To focus ideas, consider the neoclassical production function without human capital:

$$y = AK^{\alpha}L^{\beta}$$

Human capital in some models influences the technological parameter A, through for example, R&D or imitation of more advanced countries' technologies. Moreover, it augments the labor input L as a productive factor sometimes. In the first class of models it influences, at least temporarily, the rate of growth of A, and hence of output. But in the second class of models it influences the level of output with the same coefficient as the labor input.

Cross-country regressions have come under criticism for a variety of reasons, but whatever their merits, they cannot distinguish between these two variants of the model – does the level of human capital influence the rate of growth of output or its level? In fact, hardly any robust results have been derived from these regressions about the contribution of human capital to growth, though when human capital does not show up as a significant influence in cross-country regressions most authors blame the data. Such is the conviction that human capital must be an important influence on growth. We will argue below that it is possible for human capital to have a high private rate of return but not contribute to growth, when the institutional structure of the labor market is such that "rent seeking" or other less-productive activities yield a higher private return to the individual than do growth-enhancing activities. In some cases, the contribution of human capital to growth can be hampered by its low quality, or by its unsuitable nature, as when skill mismatches and market rigidities lead to the unemployment of qualified people.

The fact that the stock of human capital has been trending up in most countries of the world but the rate of growth of output has not, gives an indication that if the level of human capital influences the rate of growth of output over certain periods of time, it is likely to be a temporary phenomenon. But if this were to lead to adoption of the other extreme view that the human capital stock influences output with the same coefficient as labor, the role of human capital in production and the implied rate of return to human capital would be too small to be credible. The results of the cross-country empirical research are diverse, but they are not consistent with the hypothesis that human capital enters the production function with the same coefficient as labor.[5]

The capital stock is usually treated as endogenous in growth models and driven by the savings rate in the economy. In the models which make human capital the engine of growth, the rate of growth of the capital stock eventually

---

[5] See Topel (1999) for an evaluation and Barro and Sala-i-Martin (1995), Benhabib and Spiegel (1994) and Pritchett (1996) for empirical results and more discussion.

converges to the rate of growth of human capital. In addition, the capital/labor ratio is also influenced by the features of the human capital production function. The prediction of growth models is that a country with more human capital will eventually have more physical capital as well. As a first step, however, it might be worthwhile to explain the contribution of human capital to output growth net of the contribution of the capital stock, namely to the series $\log Y - \alpha \log K$, though ultimately a complete explanation of the contribution of human capital to growth will need to explain the dependence of investment on human capital.

2.3. Growth accounting

Growth accounting exercises decompose the growth of output into growth owing to capital, employment and total factor productivity (TFP). Their information content is limited and the decompositions they arrive at should not be treated as research findings that should guide policy but as suggestive of further research. Yet occasionally growth accounting exercises come up with surprising (when viewed through the OECD lens, perhaps) facts and cause controversy, as the work of Young (1995) on growth accounting for South-East Asia did. For the MENA research on growth and labor, growth accounting exercises can shed light on the level and rate of growth of TFP in each country and their relation to human capital. More specifically, how can we account for the fact that the human capital stock has grown rapidly since 1960, yet output growth seems to have stagnated?

Tables 2 and 3a show GDP growth rates for a selection of MENA countries and by region, gross and decomposed into growth in the capital stock, labor force and TFP. The share of capital in the TFP calculations is taken to be 0.4, although there are variations across countries and in deeper country research country-specific estimates could be given. The share of labor is correspondingly taken to be 0.6. In the absence of a time series for employment, we used a series for total labor force growth. TFP1 shows the results of the TFP calculations when the contribution of human capital is not netted out. The idea behind TFP1 is that human capital contributes to TFP growth; namely, that human capital is one of the factors that explains the path of TFP growth and not the level of output. TFP1 is calculated as the residual of the production function previously specified: $\log(\text{TFP1}) = \log(Y) - 0.4 \log(K) - 0.6 \log(L)$. In TFP2, however, we have treated human capital as a factor that improves the quality of the labor force and so we used data on human capital to augment the contribution of labor before deducting it from output growth. With a Cobb–Douglas production function this amounts to treating human capital as a factor of production. In this case, TFP2 is calculated as follows: $\log(\text{TFP2}) = \log(Y) - 0.4 \log(K) - 0.6 \log(L')$ where L' (the skilled labor) is the labor force (L) augmented by the number of years of schooling of the population over 15 years old (H), the rate of

Table 2. **TFP calculations for a selection of MENA countries (average annual growth rates in %)**

Country Year	GDP	Capital stock	Labor force	TFP1	Skilled labor force	TFP2
Algeria						
1970s	5.7	8.7	3.2	0.3	4.4	−0.4
1980s	2.5	4.9	3.8	−1.8	5.5	−2.8
1990s	1.5	1.0	3.8	−1.1	5.0	−1.8
Egypt						
1970s	8.0	9.8	2.1	2.8	4.5	1.4
1980s	4.9	8.8	2.5	−0.1	4.5	−1.3
1990s	4.3	3.4	2.9	1.2	4.2	0.5
Iran						
1970s	0.7	12.8	3.0	−6.2	4.3	−7.0
1980s	3.8	2.6	3.0	1.0	4.2	0.3
1990s	4.0	1.3	2.3	2.1	3.7	1.2
Jordan						
1970s	8.7	10.8	2.3	3.0	3.4	2.4
1980s	3.2	7.0	4.9	−2.6	6.7	−3.6
1990s	5.2	1.3	5.8	1.2	6.9	0.6
Morocco						
1970s	5.6	8.8	3.2	3.0	4.1	−0.4
1980s	3.6	4.9	2.6	−2.6	3.4	−0.4
1990s	2.2	3.5	2.5	1.2	3.4	−1.2
Tunisia						
1970s	7.4	7.0	3.6	2.4	5.1	1.5
1980s	3.7	4.6	2.7	0.3	3.7	−0.4
1990s	4.8	3.3	2.9	1.7	4.0	1.0

Source: Authors' calculations from World Bank data.

return to education being fixed at 0.1.[6] The results should be regarded as indicative of trends rather than accurate descriptions of reality, as data tend to be unreliable. There are more than one time series for GDP growth for these countries and they are not all consistent with each other, and the capital stock data sometimes exhibit implausible behavior.

Tables 2 and 3a show that GDP growth experienced a sharp decrease in the 1980s, after the fall in oil prices. This has been the case in all the MENA countries in the sample (except Iran, Table 2) and in all regions (except South Asia, Table 3a). Both investment and employment decreased during the period,

---

[6] Following Dasgupta *et al.* (2002), the exact way in which we augmented the labor input is $L' = L \exp(0.1\,H)$ where H is the number of years of schooling.

Table 3a. *TFP calculations by region (average annual growth rates in %)*

Region Year	GDP	Capital stock	Labor force	TFP1	Skilled labor force	TFP2
Africa						
1970s	3.7	5.5	2.5	*0.0*	3.1	*−0.3*
1980s	2.2	3.1	2.7	*−0.7*	3.4	*−1.1*
1990s	2.7	2.0	2.6	*0.3*	3.2	*0.0*
East Asia						
1970s	7.7	10.6	3.1	*1.6*	4.1	*1.1*
1980s	6.1	8.5	2.7	*1.1*	3.4	*0.7*
1990s	6.2	8.5	2.2	*1.4*	3.0	*0.9*
Eastern Europe						
1970s	5.7	8.2	1.6	*1.5*	1.4	*1.6*
1980s	4.4	4.7	2.5	*1.0*	1.3	*1.7*
1990s	3.8	4.1	2.6	*0.7*	2.0	*1.0*
OECD						
1970s	4.2	5.2	1.5	*1.2*	2.4	*0.7*
1980s	2.8	3.3	1.1	*0.8*	1.9	*0.3*
1990s	2.8	3.1	1.0	*0.9*	1.7	*0.6*
Latin America						
1970s	4.7	6.4	2.9	*0.4*	3.6	*0.0*
1980s	1.0	3.1	2.8	*−1.9*	3.5	*−2.3*
1990s	3.2	3.3	2.7	*0.3*	3.2	*0.0*
MENA						
1970s	6.1	9.6	2.8	*0.6*	5.0	*−0.7*
1980s	3.8	6.1	3.3	*−0.6*	5.4	*−1.9*
1990s	3.7	2.3	3.3	*0.8*	4.3	*0.2*
South Asia						
1970s	3.6	4.5	2.5	*0.3*	2.4	*0.3*
1980s	5.3	5.5	2.3	*1.7*	3.2	*1.2*
1990s	5.0	4.5	2.5	*1.6*	3.1	*1.3*

Source: Authors' calculations from World Bank data.

especially the former. But these declines do not fully account for the decrease in GDP growth, so our calculations show a sharp fall in TFP growth which becomes negative in the majority of our MENA sample. In this regard, the MENA region did not perform better than Africa, although in terms of GDP and human capital growth the region as a whole outperformed Africa.

In the 1990s, the MENA region experienced a small recovery of GDP and TFP growth, despite a further cut of investment projects (in the public sector in particular). The recovery, however, was not sufficient to allow MENA to close the gap with the more advanced developing countries, with which the MENA region was catching up in the 1960s (East and South Asia in particular, Table 3a).

The independent TFP estimates of Nehru and Dhareshwar (1994) show a low TFP growth in all countries in the period 1960–1990 and, more strikingly, a negative overall TFP growth rate for the MENA region as a whole (see Table 3b). TFP growth in the MENA region compares poorly even with the rest of Africa. Our calculations are consistent with the Nehru and Dhareshwar estimates, but show that the negative results are even more striking when the contribution of human capital to TFP is deducted (TFP2 series, Table 3b). Because human capital accumulation was higher in the MENA region than in the rest of Africa, its performance net of human capital was even worse than in the earlier estimates that ignored it. This suggests a low contribution of human capital to growth in the region when compared with the rest of the world.

The task faced by a researcher of economic growth in the MENA region is to explain why TFP growth in the region was so low, in view of the fact that other things equal, the low initial income should have returned the TFP growth rates to above the average of the world economy. The relatively high investments in human capital that took place in these countries since the 1960s should also have contributed to faster convergence dynamics, namely, faster TFP growth during the sample period. For research on labor markets and growth in particular, the task is to identify features of the labor markets of the MENA countries that contributed to the low return on human capital and the low overall TFP growth.

Table 3b.   TFP calculations by regions (annual percentage changes)

Nehru and Dhareshwar (1994)	1960–1990	
Region	ECM	FD
Africa	–0.8	–0.4
East Asia	0.5	1.2
OECD	0.5	1.3
Latin America	–0.6	–0.1
MENA	–1.2	–0.3
South Asia	0.3	0.8
Authors' Calculations	1960–2000	
Region	(TFP1)	(TFP2)
Africa	0.0	–0.3
East Asia	1.3	0.8
Eastern Europe	1.5	1.6
OECD	1.3	0.8
Latin America MENA	0.1	–0.3
MENA	0.5	–0.4
South Asia	1.1	0.7

Note: Unweighted averages of annual country rates.
ECM stands for "error-correction method" and FD for "first-difference method."
Both sets of calculations ignore human capital.

3. Labor market structure

Human capital in the MENA region grew steadily throughout the period of low TFP growth (see Table 1). Therefore, even in the absence of a careful statistical analysis and despite the other factors such as economic reforms, macroeconomic and political instability or governance that played a role in slowing down TFP growth, it is obvious that human capital will not be able to contribute much to growth in country regressions. This may be due to the fact that human capital in MENA has suffered either from low quality or from a misallocation that diverted it from employment in growth-enhancing activities. A lot of it must have stood idle, engaged in rent-seeking or less-productive activities (not properly recorded in national income statistics such as the running of social services). An analysis of this issue, with a view to finding ways to improve the situation if misallocations are found, requires an examination of the labor market's *static efficiency*.

3.1. Static efficiency

Static efficiency investigates the allocation of labor across sectors of the economy. The concern in the present context is whether the allocation of skilled labor is the one most likely to maximize the country's growth potential. Table 4a shows the allocation of labor across some broadly defined sectors. Manufacturing occupies a smaller fraction of the labor force than in other industrializing countries, and this is compensated for in the MENA region by a bigger public sector (Table 4b). Tables 5a and 5b show that MENA's government and public sector (excluding health and education in the case of Table 5b) employ a bigger fraction of the non-agricultural labor force than in any region outside Africa.

Another set of more detailed statistics shows that in Egypt (Table 6), government employs more than half of all degree holders in the country, with public enterprises also employing a large fraction. Public sector employment of this magnitude clearly interferes with the static efficiency of the labor market and deeper country studies need to investigate carefully the uses to which the public sector puts this human capital.

Recent studies show that low productivity is exacerbated in the public sector of countries in the MENA region by an increasing overstaffing (World Bank, 2004). In the early 1990s, the share of underutilized workers in the public sector ranged from 17% (Algeria) to 21% (Egypt) and to even more in the oil-exporting countries. This share, despite its substantial size, has increased recently to 35% in Egypt and 40% in Jordan. Berthelemy *et al.* (1999) estimated the average loss of GDP growth owing to public sector employment by making the admittedly strong assumption that the fraction of human capital employed in the administrative public sector does not contribute at all to growth. Their estimate is shown in the last column of Table 5b. The loss in the MENA and Sub-Saharan Africa regions is bigger than elsewhere by a large margin.

Table 4a.   **Sectoral distribution of employment (% of total employment)**

Country	Agriculture	Manufacturing & other Industries	Services
Algeria (1995)	12	30	58
Bahrain (1994)	1	54	43
Egypt (2000)	30	21	49
Iran (1996)	23	31	45
Iraq (1990)	16	18	66
Jordan (1993)	6	25	69
Kuwait (1988)	1	24	74
Morocco (1999)	44	21	33
Syria (1991)	28	25	46
Tunisia (2001)	22	34	44
WB & G (2000)	14	34	52
UAE (2000)	8	33	59

Source: World Bank (2004).

Table 4b.   **Public sector employment (% of total employment)**

Country	(1)	(2)
Algeria (1990–1999)	58	30
Bahrain (1991–2001)	68	80
Egypt (1988–1998)	27	38
Iran (1986)	31	
Jordan (1987–1996)	45	36
Kuwait (1989–2000)	42	75
Morocco (1991–1999)	12	8
Oman (1991–1999)	76	79
Quatar (1986)	37	
Saudi Arabia (1992–1999)	70	82
UAE (late 1980s)	31	
Tunisia (1997–2001)	24	21
Yemen (late 1980s)	16	

Note: (1) and (2) relate respectively to the first and the second year in the country list above.
Source: Shaban *et al.* (2001) and World Bank (2004).

Table 5a.   **Size of government in the 1990s**

Region	Employment (% total)	Wages (% GDP)
Sub-Saharan Africa	6.2	6.3
Asia	6	4.5
Eastern Europe	16	3.9
OECD	17.5	4
Latin America	9	5
MENA	17.6	9.8

Source: Schiavo-Campo *et al.*, (2003).

Table 5b. Share of public sector in non-agricultural employment and human capital

Region	Share of Public Sector	Estimated Loss GDP Growth (1985–1995)
Sub-Saharan Africa	32.9	8.8
Asia	19.8	4.9
OECD	20.6	5.1
Latin America	17.7	4.3
MENA	31.7	8.4

Table 6. Educational attainment by employment sector in Egypt (1988)

Sector	Below Intermediate	Intermediate and Above	University and Above	Total
All sectors	76.9	14.6	8.5	100
Government	7.0	47.2	55.6	16.9
Public enterprise	5.3	15.8	14.7	7.6
Private agricultural	57.6	9.6	2.6	45.9
Private non-agricultural	29.7	24.5	23.0	28.4
Total	100	100	100	100

Source: Shaban, *et al.* (1994), Table 11.

Another source of misallocation of skilled labor comes from unemployment of highly qualified people. Unemployment rates are generally high in the MENA region (Table 7a) but more importantly, the unemployment rates of people in the middle to the upper end of the educational distribution are even higher (Table 7b). The waste of human capital through the high unemployment rates must be a contributory factor to the low overall contribution of human capital to growth. Interestingly, despite the high unemployment rates, entrepreneurs in these countries regularly cite the lack of labor with suitable skills as an important constraint to hiring. The combination of high skilled unemployment and skill shortages at the industrial level provides support to those who have claimed that the education systems in the MENA region have mostly been geared to the needs of the public sector. The high wages and other job advantages (such as job security, worker protection and social allowances) offered by the pubic sector led to educated workers queuing for public sectors jobs, and so to the absence of pressure to reform the educational system according to the needs of industry.

How did the MENA countries find themselves in a situation of large public sectors and misallocation of their human capital resources? Country experiences differ and a full analysis requires an examination of the institutional structure of the countries in question and the historical context. For the region as a whole, however, there has been one big missed opportunity. Historically, the biggest influence in these countries has been the oil boom of the 1970s, which lasted up to about 1982, and which enriched the public sector and led to the large

Table 7a.   Unemployment rates

Country	% Labor Force
Algeria (2000)	29.8
Bahrain (2001)	13
Egypt (2000)	9
Jordan (2000)	14
Iran (2001)	13.8
Kuwait (2003)	2.6
Lebanon (1997)	8
Morocco (2002)	22
Oman (1996)	12
Quatar (2002)	12
Saudi Arabia (1999)	7.5
Syria (2001)	11
Tunisia (2001)	15.4
UAE (1999)	2.5
W-B & Gaza (2001)	25
Yemen (1999)	11.5

Source: World Bank (2004).

Table 7b.   Unemployment rates (by educational level)

Country	None	Primary	Secondary	Tertiary	All
Algeria (1995)	9.6	30.9	30.9	68.4	27.9
Egypt (1998)	4.1	5.7	22.4	9.7	11.4
Jordan (1991)	8.2	8.7	25.8	21.5	14.4
Morocco (1999)	9.4	26.3	32.4	37.6	15.6
Oman (1996)	5.6	13.4	24.8	2.8	10.8
Tunisia (1997)	10.2	20.8	15.4	6.4	15.7

Source: Shaban *et al.* (2001) and World Bank (2004).

education expansion. But the resources gained during the oil boom were used to expand and protect the public sector from market competition and not spent in a way that was favorable to growth. They contributed to the large expansion of public sector employment, to the misallocation of resources in the public educational systems and to the introduction of other institutional rigidities that the economies could afford (perhaps) when the oil revenues were abundant, but not when they dried up.[7]

---

[7] See Pissarides (1993) for more discussion of the historical context and the relation between oil revenues and public sector expansion. More recent discussion about the role of reforms can be found in Dasgupta *et al.* (2002) and more discussion about the role of social contracts, political regimes and wars and their influence on the economy of the countries in the MENA region can be found in World Bank (2004).

3.2. Institutional foundations

Labor market institutions influence the allocation of resources. In the present context the question is whether human capital is employed in growth-enhancing activities or elsewhere. There is a risk, when writing about labor market institutions to drift too far from the growth context. The focus of our discussion here is on the institutions that are likely to influence the allocations of labor in growth versus non-growth enhancing activities, even if other institutions appear more important at first sight. Two broad institutional structures appear most relevant for the allocation of resources and growth in the MENA region.

First, *wage setting* institutions and their implications for relative wages across sectors. Do high public sector wages explain why the public sector is so large in the MENA region? Table 8 shows that public sector wages relative to the private sector ones in the MENA region are higher than anywhere else (in addition, the public sector offers more non-wage benefits). Although this difference may partly reflect the higher educational background of the labor force working in the public sector, it also indicates the presence of distortions. If it reflected only the higher educational attainment of workers in the public sector there would have been no queues to enter the public sector and no higher unemployment of more educated workers. As it is, the public sector is obviously not competing with industry for qualified labor – it rather sets the agenda for wages and rations employment. The high wages and high non-wage benefits that we already mentioned constitute an important incentive for qualified workers to enter the public sector, with the poor results for the contribution of human capital to overall growth that we have already noted.

In addition to the waste of human capital in less-productive public sector employment, the large size of public employment in these countries inflates the public sector wage bill. The wage bill has to be met from the public budget and the debt and tax implications for private sector activity impose another large burden on the economy that works against growth.

Second, the institutional framework for hiring and firing employees and more generally the framework that regulates the *employment relationship*, including

Table 8.   Central Government wages (early 1990s)

Region	Central Government Wage Bill (% of GDP)	Ratio of Public Sector to Private Sector Wages
Sub-Saharan Africa	6.7	1.0
Asia	4.7	0.8
ECA	3.7	0.7
Latin America	4.9	0.9
OECD	4.5	0.9
MENA	9.8	1.3
Overall	5.4	0.8

Note: Table 3 of MNSED (1999).

Table 9a.   *Labor market regulation in developing regions*

Region	Composite Index
Sub-Saharan Africa	1.45
East Asia	1.6
Europe and Central Asia	1.95
Latin America	2.05
MENA	1.65
South Asia	1.25

Source: Doing Business Database (2003).

Table 9b.   *Labor market regulation in the MENA countries*

Country	Composite Index
Algeria	1.5
Egypt	1.85
Jordan	1.55
Iran	1.9
Lebanon	1.2
Morocco	1.35
Syria	1.3
Tunisia	1.7

Source: Doing Business Database (2003).

the legal framework for standards at work, minimum wages and trade union recognition and powers. This institutional framework is likely to be the result of government policy but workers' organizations may have their own rules on hiring and firing. In the MENA region, labor market regulations have historically been stringent and are still too tight compared with the other regions of the developing world, although not as high as the formerly planned economies or Latin America (Table 9a). The majority of the countries in the region are affected by this situation, which has introduced rigidities in the labor market (Table 9b). At the micro level rigidities of this kind lead to low productivity and removal of the incentive to innovate and start new businesses. At the macro level these negative consequences translate to slow growth, and to inertia in response to macroeconomic shocks, unemployment and misallocation of labor. More in-depth analysis is required of the implications of the regulation of employment and business for growth than can be pursued here, and the recent availability of the World Bank database provides a basis on which country papers can build.

3.3. Market flexibility

It is clear from the results obtained so far on TFP growth in the MENA countries (and elsewhere) that the way that we define and measure TFP gives a cyclical TFP series with downswings that can last for many years. This is a reflection of the well-known fact that labor productivity is procyclical. But unlike OECD economies, which are diversified and suffer from regular cyclical shocks of small intensity, developing countries have suffered mostly from more pronounced shocks associated with well-defined one-off events such as the debt crisis in Latin America, the fall of oil prices in MENA and the financial crisis in South-East Asia. The intensity and persistence of the resulting downswings in TFP growth are directly related to the ability of the economy to adjust to new long-term conditions with the minimum of waste. This is where the issue of market flexibility becomes key to growth. Consistent with this view it has been shown that, where labor markets are more rigid, countries tend to experience deeper recessions before adjustment as well as slower recoveries (Forteza and Rama, 2001).

Over the last 20 years, in the MENA region, the main economic shocks that seem to have affected TFP growth are the fall in the price of oil after 1982 and the Gulf War a decade later. Both these events reduced GDP growth for many years. The speed of response of the economy to the after-shock situation was generally slow, a fact that is at least partly due to the rigid institutional structure of the labor market. As with static efficiency, the institutional features that are likely to influence the dynamic adjustment are likely to be the wage setting institutions and how flexible they are in allowing wages to respond to changes in market conditions; the hiring and firing restrictions that govern the speed of labor turnover and the ease with which workers can migrate and change sector of employment. Of course, the economy sooner or later adjusts to a new steady state. The question in the present context is how fast it adjusts and whether policy can help it adjust faster and with less waste.

In the MENA region the adjustment to the oil shocks seems to have been slower than the adjustment to crises in other regions; for example, both Latin American and South-East Asian countries came out of their respective debt and financial crises faster than did the MENA countries out of their oil crisis. Although there has been some downward adjustment of real wages in the 1990s, the dominant role of government as employer has slowed down the adjustment. It requires a lot more research at the country level, however, to determine whether the labor market structure was responsible for the slow adjustment. In particular whether one or more of the three institutional features of the preceding paragraph – wage setting, employment flexibility and migration – played a role in slowing down the adjustment to the oil shocks. No general claims can be made for the region as a whole since the institutional structure is not well documented at the regional level.

4. Acquisition of skills

The discussion so far focused on the allocation of human capital between alternative uses, some of which are growth-enhancing and some less so. But equally important is the question of the acquisition of skills, and how effective are labor markets in generating a large amount of skills that are useful for growth. This requires first a discussion of the educational and training system and how it is organized in each country. It includes the coverage and quality of the education system, who pays for education and what incentives there are for individuals to engage in training. Has human capital grown in some countries because the state financed it and encouraged particular skills or because private initiative did it? Moreover, what can be said about the quality of the human capital stock?

The free market usually signals the need for skills through the relative wage system, namely, through the private rate of return to education and training. Are labor markets in the MENA region effective in this signaling function? Do individuals respond to the signals? The answers to these questions touch on the *dynamic efficiency* of the labor market. Under dynamic efficiency the emphasis is shifted to the efficiency of the labor market in the provision of adequate resources for education and training and to the recruitment of enough people for these purposes.

In MENA, these questions need special attention because of the distortionary labor market institutions that we have highlighted. The outcome appears to be low-quality education[8] and skill mismatches due to the bias toward public sector needs. The distortions in relative wages that we have highlighted increase the private rate of return to skill without a corresponding increase in its social rate of return, and its implications for dynamic efficiency are an issue that needs further investigation at the country level. Statistics on rates of return to schooling by sector of activity – available for different countries – confirm the attractiveness of the public sector. This is true at all levels of education, with the exception, recently, of Jordan and Yemen (Table 10).[9]

5. Conclusions

Human capital occupies a central role in modern thinking about growth. Despite a large literature on the matter, however, there is a lot to be learned: there is no consensus on its role in growth and development, probably because this role varies across different institutional settings and national environments. The labor market is the place where human capital is created and deployed. This paper has argued that the study of the links between labor markets and growth should concentrate on a study of labor market influences on the quantity,

---

[8] See for example, United Nations Development Program (2002, 2003), human development reports.
[9] It has not been possible to find easily accessible data sources for the quality of the human capital stock for the region as a whole. Psacharopoulos (1985) mentions virtually no MENA countries in his sample. Data on quality on a country basis are reported in the updated paper by Barro and Lee (2000), but the regional coverage for MENA is not satisfactory.

Table 10. Rate of return to schooling (% per year)

	Egypt		Morocco		Jordan	Yemen
	1988	1998	1991	1999	1997	1997
Primary						
Male (public)	8.2	6.4	12.4	6.1	3.5	2.7
Male (private)	2.3	3.6	3	3.4	2	2.7
Female (public)	1.9	5.3	28.2	10.5	−3.9	5.1
Female (private)	0.9	7.2	8.5	9.4	14.7	8
Lower secondary						
Male (public)	7	4.9	10.7	8.2	2.9	2.7
Male (private)	2.5	4.4	6.4	6.3	5.5	2.7
Female (public)	7.7	8.2	22.3	13.4	5.2	3.7
Female (private)	3.2	−11.2	13.9	10	9.8	7.4
Upper secondary (General)						
Male (public)	8.6	8.8	10.6	8.8	2.8	2.2
Male (private)	6.3	7.3	10.4	7.7	6	2.2
Female (public)	8.6	9.7	18.1	12.1	4.6	3.9
Female (private)	3.8	−1.5	16.4	11	10.4	12.1
Upper secondary (vocational)						
Male (public)	9.6	7.2	8.4	6.8	3.8	3.3
Male (private)	5.3	5	6.9	5.8	3.2	3.3
Female (public)	7.9	9.6	16.5	11.9	4.3	4.3
Female (private)	4.4	4.9	11.1	11.3	8.6	10.7
University						
Male (public)	10.1	8.8	10.8	8.9	4.6	3.8
Male (private)	8.5	7.3	12.5	9.5	10.2	5.2
Female (public)	8.9	10.7	15	12.8	6.8	4.4
Female (private)	9.1	10.9	15.2	9.3	12.9	6.8

Source: Assaad (2002) and World Bank (2004).

quality and productivity of human capital. This requires an investigation at the level of individual countries of the institutions that influence the acquisition and employment of human capital and their effectiveness in enhancing growth.

Our investigation of broad trends in the MENA region has revealed that there has been fast growth in the acquisition of skills through general education. But following the oil crises of the 1980s, the countries in the region have been unable to utilize their human resources to overcome the negative consequences of the crises for output and growth. In this respect, human capital in the MENA region has been less successful in contributing to growth than elsewhere, e.g., in East or South Asia. We argued that large and inflexible public sectors, wage inflexibility and excessive labor market regulation may be some reasons behind this failure. This opens up a number of issues about reform which require more and deeper research than can be given here on the role of labor market institutions at the country level.

References

Acemoglu, D., S. Johnson and J. Robinson (2005), "Institutions as the fundamental cause of long-run growth", in: P. Aghion and S. Durlauf, editors, *Handbook of Economics of Growth*, Amsterdam: North-Holland forthcoming.

Agenor, P.R., Nabli, M.K., Youssef, T.M. and Jensen, H.T., (2003), "Labor market reforms, growth and unemployment in labor-exporting countries in the Middle East and North Africa", World Bank (unpublished).

Aghion, P. and P. Howitt (1998), *Endogenous Growth Theory*, Cambridge, MA: MIT Press.

Assaad, R. (2002), "The transformation of the Egyptian labor market: 1988–98", in: R. Assaad, editor, *The Egyptian Labor Market in an Era of Reform*, Cairo: American University in Cairo Press.

Barro, R. and Lee, J.-W., (2000), "International data on educational attainment: updates and implications", Working Paper No. 42, Center for International Development, Harvard University, Harvard.

Barro, R.J. and X. Sala-i-Martin (1995), *Economic Growth*, New York: McGraw-Hill.

Benhabib, J. and M.M. Spiegel (1994), "The role of human capital in economic development", *Journal of Monetary Economic*, Vol. 34, pp. 143–173.

Berthelemy, J.-C., C.A. Pissarides and A. Varoudakis (1999), "Human capital and growth: the cost of rent seeking activities", in: T. De Ruyter van Steveninck, editor, *Economic Growth and its Determinants*, Dordrecht: Kluwer Academic Publishers.

Dasgupta, D., Keller, J., Srinivasan, T.G., 2002. "Reform and elusive growth in the Middle-East – what has happened in the 1990s?", MENA Working Paper Series No. 25, June, The World Bank.

Doing Business Database, 2003. Washington, DC: World Bank.

Forteza, A. and M. Rama (2001), "Labor market rigidity and the success of economic reforms across more than 100 countries", Policy Research Working Paper, No. 2521 (January), World Bank, Washington, DC.

Lucas, R.E. (1988), "On the mechanics of economic development", *Journal of Monetary Economics*, Vol. 22, pp. 3–42.

MNSED (1999), "Workers in crisis in the MENA region: an analysis of labor market outcomes and prospects for the future", Unpublished paper, World Bank.

Nehru, V., Dhareshwar, A., (1994), "New estimates of total factor productivity growth for developing and industrial countries", Policy Research Working Paper 1313, The World Bank, Washington, DC.

Nehru, V., E. Swanson and A. Dubey (1993), "A new database on human capital stock: sources, methodology and results", Policy Research Working Paper No. 1124, International Economics Department, World Bank.

Pissarides, C.A. (1993), Labor markets in the Middle East and North Africa", Middle East and North Africa Discussion Paper Series No. 5, The World Bank, Washington, DC.

Pritchett, L. (1996), "Where has all the education gone?", World Bank Policy Research Paper No. 1581.

Psacharopoulos, G. (1985), "Returns to education: a further international update and implications", *Journal of Human Resources*, Vol. 20, pp. 583–604.

Rivera-Batiz, L.A. and P.M. Romer (1991), "Economic integration and endogenous growth", *Quarterly Journal of Economics*, Vol. 106, pp. 531–555.

Schiavo-Campo, S., de Tommaso, G., Mukherjee, A., 2003. "An international statistical survey of government employment and wages," World Bank Policy Research Working Paper, No. 1806, World Bank, Washington, DC.

Shaban, R., R. Assaad and S. Al-Qudsi (1994), "Employment experience in the Middle-East and North Africa", Working Paper No.199401, Economic Research Forum, Cairo.

Shaban, R.A., A.R. Assaad and S. Al-Qudsi (2001), "Employment experience in the Middle East and North Africa", in: D. Saleha-Eshfahani, editor, *Labor and Human Capital in the Middle East*, Reading, UK: Ithaca Press.

Topel, R. (1999), "labor markets and economic growth", in: O.C. Ashenfelter and D. Card, editors, *Handbook of Labor Economics*, Amsterdam: North-Holland.

United Nations Development Program (2002, 2003), Arab Human Development Report, United Nations, New York.

World Bank (2004), Unlocking the Employment Potential on the Middle East and North Africa. Toward a New Social Contract, Washington, DC.

Young, A. (1995), "The tyranny of numbers: confronting the statistical realities of the East Asian growth experience", *Quarterly Journal of Economics*, Vol. 110, pp. 641–680.

CHAPTER 6

Microeconomics of Growth in MENA: The Role of Households [☆]

Djavad Salehi-Isfahani[*]

Abstract

This paper discusses whether households in the Middle East and North Africa (MENA) allocate their resources efficiently and in such a way as to promote growth. It focuses on the role of urban households because they form the majority and they are the main source of growth in human capital. I argue that an efficient and pro-growth allocation of household resources may not be feasible because of constraints that households face in their decisions to supply labor, and to accumulate human and physical capital. I identify two aspects of the environment in which MENA households operate as critical to conditioning their behavior: the large role of the state in the economy, which distorts the incentives in the education and labor markets, and social norms regarding gender, which influence the division of labor at home and in the economy. Patriarchal gender norms limit women's participation outside the home, resulting in higher fertility and lower labor force participation of women in MENA compared to countries with similar income. The strong role of the state affects incentives in three key markets for credit, education, and labor. Powerful central governments have inhibited the development of modern financial markets by preventing the emergence of private banking and an independent judiciary, which is critical for the enforcement of financial contracts. Distorted financial markets affect household savings by keeping interest rates low and often negative, and thereby discourage accumulation of financial assets relative to unproductive assets such as land. Of greater importance is state intervention in

---

[☆]This paper was prepared for the Global Research Project, Global Development Network, and was first presented in a GDN conference in Prague, June 2000.
[*]Corresponding author.

CONTRIBUTIONS TO ECONOMIC ANALYSIS
VOLUME 278   ISSN: 0573-8555
DOI:10.1016/S0573-8555(06)78006-3

the markets for education and labor, which determine the amount and type of human capital the MENA households accumulate. I argue that the prevalence of public-sector employment and the regulation of private employment have increased private returns to formal schooling over and above their social return, while at the same time reduced private returns to other types of productive skills below their social return. As a result, households invest in an inefficient portfolio of human capital with dire consequences for long-run growth.

Keywords: economic growth, middle east, household behavior, human capital, labor markets

JEL classifications: D13, J22, J24, O12, O15

1. Introduction

As the longest standing unit of social organization, the family is also recognized as an important agent of economic growth. Households make important decisions that affect production and accumulation of physical and human capital. Increased recognition of this fact in economics has led to a surge in theoretical and empirical models of household behavior in the last two decades. Manski (2000) considers the increased emphasis on households as one of the major recent innovations in neoclassical economics. A recent microeconomic view of growth in Sub-Saharan Africa by Collier and Gunning (1999) has produced important insights.[1] However, research on economic growth in the Middle East and North Africa (MENA) region has largely ignored the role of households, instead focusing on actions taken by governments. Historically, the region has been ruled by strong and dominant central governments, and often with negative effects on economic growth (Issawi, 1995). More recently, in the 20th century, socialist ideology and availability of oil revenues have helped maintain the image, if not the reality, of the all-powerful state. Nevertheless, we must understand the behavior of the micro units – households and firms – to reach a deeper understanding of aggregate outcomes, including the consequences of actions taken by powerful states.

In this paper I examine the role of households in economic growth of MENA. I focus on the incentives and constraints faced by households that help or hinder their role in fostering growth. The constraints I consider are those imposed by the two institutions that are not peculiar to the region, but have greater influence in MENA than elsewhere: the importance of central

---

[1] For a review of similar applications of microeconomics to economic growth around the world, see Guriev and Salehi-Isfahani (2003).

governments in economic life and social norms regarding gender. I show how these institutions define the incentives and the constraints that shape household behavior pertaining to growth. The strong presence of the state operates primarily in the form of extensive interventions in the markets for education and labor that create large gaps between private and social returns to human capital, leading individuals and households to invest more in formal education and diplomas than productive human capital. Social attitudes toward gender roles affect household behavior primarily by affecting the allocation of women's time between home production and market work. Women are discouraged from engaging in market work, thereby limiting the supply of labor and human capital to the economy and reducing incentives for investment in the education of girls. Limits on women's access to education and the labor market in turn promote population growth, reduce the education of the next generation, and thereby retard economic growth.

Throughout the paper I rely on the theory of household economics to guide the discussion, and on the rather limited body of empirical studies to relate the theory to the experience of individual countries in the Middle East. The most useful among the latter are those that use survey data. Learning from micro data is the most effective way to learn about household behavior in specific countries. Unfortunately, such data are only available for a handful of countries and researchers have only recently started to use them in micro econometric studies of households and markets in the Middle East. In the Appendix to this paper I provide a partial list of the micro data sets that exist for the MENA region, some of which are publicly available.

1.1. The role of urban households

I limit my discussion to the role of urban households in part to keep the discussion more focused, but more importantly, because urban households have greater influence on human capital accumulation and modern growth. Rural and urban households perform many similar economic functions – procreation, education, and labor supply – but they differ in important ways. Historically, the arid climate and the feudal system of surplus extraction have created urban centers that are quite distinct from rural communities. Rural and urban areas remain geographically and economically quite distinct even today. Because rural households operate both as firms and families, a proper treatment of the role of rural households in economic growth would require the widening of our scope considerably and the discussion of the role of agriculture in economic growth. It is best that the role of agriculture is treated separately. Furthermore, social norms interact with family decisions differently in rural areas because in rural settings the distinction between private and public space is more blurred, so rural women face less conflict between market-related activity and housework than urban women.

Table 1.   The importance of urban households in MENA

Country	Urban Population as % of Total		Labor Force in Agriculture (%)	
	1970	2002	1970	1990
Algeria	39.5	58.3	47.4	26.1
Egypt	42.2	42.8	51.8	40.3
Iran	41.9	65.4	43.8	38.8
Iraq	56.2	67.5	47.1	16.1
Jordan	50.5	79.0	27.8	15.3
Kuwait	77.8	96.2	1.8	1.2
Lebanon	59.4	90.3	19.8	7.3
Libya	45.3	88.2	28.9	10.9
Morocco	34.5	56.7	57.6	44.7
Oman	11.4	77.0	56.9	44.5
Saudi Arabia	48.7	87.1	64.2	19.2
Syria	43.3	52.1	50.2	33.2
Tunisia	44.5	66.8	41.9	28.1
Turkey	38.4		70.7	53.1
UAE	57.2	87.6	8.8	7.8
Yemen, republic	13.3	25.3	70.4	61.0
MENA	41.5	58.0	49.8	34.8
East Asia and Pacific	18.5	38.2	76.4	68.9
South Asia	18.7	28.0	71.1	63.4
Sub-Saharan Africa	18.7	33.1	78.5	67.5
LAC	57.4	76.4	41.0	25.5
Middle income countries	33.2	52.6	61.1	52.8

Source: World Bank, (2004a).

Fortunately, focusing on urban households only is less of a limitation in MENA than in the other regions because, next to Latin America and the Caribbean (LAC), the MENA countries are the most urbanized in the developing world (see Table 1). The degree of urbanization is even higher if we control for income per capita. Figure 1 shows that in the late 1990s all the MENA countries were at or above the (linear) conditional mean rate of urbanization.[2] For the greater part of the 20th century, the MENA countries have had a relatively high proportion of their population living in urban areas. In 1970 the share of the urban population in the MENA was 41%, compared to 19% each for South and East Asia; in 2002 the MENA share had increased to 58%, compared to 28% and 38% in South and East Asia, respectively. Except in Egypt and Yemen, in all the MENA countries the urban population exceeded the rural population (Table 1). Given that the average rural household is larger,

---

[2] The regression in Figure 1 (as well as in other similar figures) includes observations on all low- and middle-income countries. All data are from *World Bank Development Indicators*, 2004.

Figure 1.   Urbanization in the MENA countries

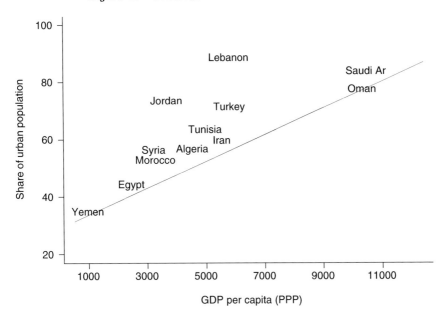

urban households must outnumber rural households in most MENA countries by a good margin. The share of the labor force in agriculture also lower in the MENA countries in 1990 (data for later years are sparsely available) compared to the other developing regions except Latin America and the Caribbean (Table 1), which further indicates the significance of the economic role of urban households in MENA.

Urban areas in MENA have historically been important centers of public administration, trade, and surplus extraction. Until the second half of the 20th century, those living in urban areas were not important as direct producers, but their positions as managers of the agricultural surplus placed them at the helm in capital accumulation and growth. Their decisions as landlords, tax farmers, and government bureaucrats affected how much was produced and collected in taxes and how the proceeds were used in the local economy as well as in international trade. The role of urban dwellers as managers of the agricultural surplus diminished as major land reform programs in the 1960s – notably, in Egypt, Iran, Iraq, and Syria – weakened the traditional land tenure systems and shifted the control of agricultural production to rural households.

In subsequent decades, with industrialization and globalization, the significance of human capital in production increased, and with it the role of urban households as its main producer. Finally, the dramatic increase in the flow of foreign exchange to the region after the oil price revolution of 1973 further tilted the balance away from the rural to the urban households. Although all

MENA countries did not benefit to the same extent from the oil price increase, labor migration to oil-rich countries and the resulting remittances spread the foreign exchange increase widely across the region. Foreign exchange inflow enabled more import of food and thereby diminished the role of rural households as the agents of economic growth. Thus, in the modern period, although urban households have lost their traditional roles, as producers and suppliers of human capital they remain at the center of the growth process.

2. Economic and social environment

Many aspects of the social and economic environment affect growth. My interest in this paper is in those aspects that constrain and distort household choices. I further narrow my attention to those that are exogenous to household choices (such as geography) because only these can be meaningfully said to limit choices. Some facets of the environment that are commonly believed to affect choice, such as low education, do not fit the criteria because they are themselves the result of household actions. Besides geography, two key features of the MENA environment that I believe fit the requirement of exogeneity are the strong role of the state in the economy and the social norms regarding gender. I argue that state interventions in the markets for education and labor are the greatest single source of distortion for household decisions. They distort incentives for investing in human capital and adversely affect growth. The state funds and directly provides much of the education and acts as intermediary in the relation between workers and employers. State interventions in the labor market reduce flexibility in wage setting and turnover, which not only reduce incentives to work and cause misallocation of workers to jobs (static misallocation), but also result in inefficient accumulation of human capital (dynamic misallocation).[3]

Social gender norms, too, affect growth by influencing static and dynamic allocations. Gender discrimination in the household and in the work place affects the allocation of time within the household by limiting women's access to market work outside the home. Social gender norms that govern the division of labor in the household can be considered exogenous to household decisions, and therefore constrain those decisions, to the extent that they have developed in an earlier period to serve a purpose which no longer exists. In a modern economy, restricting women to private spaces may inhibit economic growth by encouraging high fertility, reducing female labor supply, and lowering returns to female education. In this sense, as a constraint on household decisions, norms act in the same way as public sector domination of employment which distorts returns to human capital.

---

[3] Salehi-Isfahani and Murphy (2004).

2.1. Natural endowments and climate

The climate in MENA is arid and semi-arid. Scant and unreliable rainfall has forced settlers in most of the region to develop vast systems of irrigation based on rivers and underground aquifers. In 1997, about 31% of the MENA cropland was irrigated, compared to 3% in Sub-Saharan Africa, 21% in Latin America, and 38% in South Asia. The low proportion of irrigated land in Africa is one of the reasons why the African rural households face high risks, which Collier and Gunning (1999) argue has at the micro level caused poor economic growth. Irrigation is an important part of the response of farmers to the risky environment in the region. In some MENA countries where rainfed cultivation still contributes a large share of agricultural production, as in Syria, rural households must cope with a high degree of risk owing to variability of rainfall. In the more densely populated parts of the region, such as the banks of the Nile, irrigation is the only method of cultivation, and helps attenuate weather risks almost entirely.

In the last half a century, another geographic factor, the region's rich reserves of hydrocarbons have exerted an influence at par with the climate. With two-thirds of the world's oil and one-third of natural gas resources the economies of the region were to varying degrees affected by the rising price of crude oil in the second half of the 20th century. The oil wealth has greatly affected the course of economic growth by raising real wages faster than productivity and changing relative prices in favor of non-traded sectors through the well-known Dutch Disease phenomenon (Gelb, 1988).

2.2. Trade shocks

The largest trade shocks to the region result from fluctuations in the price of oil. A group of nine oil exporters in the region is directly affected by oil price fluctuations, and the rest through worker remittances and direct aid (El-Erian *et al.*, 1996). Oil prices quadrupled in 1973 and jumped again by a factor of three in 1979–1980, after which they started a gradual decline until 1986 when they collapsed, wiping out all but 10% of the gains made during the two previous price hikes. Since 1986 oil price fluctuations have continued (high in 1990–1991, low in 1998, and high again in 2003–2005), resembling price fluctuations for other primary commodities, with the obvious difference of the role played by political factors. There is no evidence available regarding how the variability in oil incomes enters household decision making. Governments, who are arguably better informed about oil price shocks than households, have so far failed to smooth over their own expenditures. Kuwait is the only country that systematically excludes a part of its oil revenues from current use by placing it in a fund for future generations. Several other countries, such as Iran, have oil stabilization funds that help smooth consumption over temporary price fluctuations, but not over generations (Davis *et al.*, 2001).

2.3. Institutional environment

2.3.1. Role of state

Central authorities have historically played a significant role in the economic life of the MENA societies. The reasons for the strong role of the state have changed over time and differ from country to country (Anderson, 1987). In the past the state dominated economic life because of its role as the manager of water resources, extractor of surplus, and protector of agricultural communities.[4] The role of Islam in the promotion of a patrimonial system may also have contributed to the rise of the state (Bill and Leiden, 1974). In the recent past, socialist ideology following independence (Iraq, Syria, and Tunisia), rise of nationalism (Egypt and Iran), and oil revenues that accrue to the state (Saudi Arabia, Iran, Kuwait, and other Gulf states), have helped the state continue its dominant role to date (Mahdavy, 1970, and Richards and Waterbury, 1996).

Although the state has contributed to economic growth by providing infrastructure and other public goods, it has also inhibited micro units – firms and households – from playing a more positive role in economic growth. For households state intervention in the markets for capital and labor has been the main inhibitor. Specifically, as we see below, the rise of public sector employment and interventions that reduced the flexibility of the labor market have distorted individual incentives for lending to firms and investments in human capital.

There is a large literature in economics that shows labor market regulations affect employment and growth, but they do not directly relate to the role played by households. Lazear (1990) shows how regulation in the form of severance pay hurts employment; Besley and Burgess (2004) show how manufacturing growth in Indian states with stricter labor regulation has lagged behind those with less regulation; and Botero *et al.* (2003) show that more regulation reduces labor force participation.

The large size of the public sector in MENA can be deduced from the share of public expenditures in GDP. In Figure 2, where this ratio is depicted for individual countries relative to a regression line for low and middle income countries, with the exception of Iran, Syria, Turkey, and Yemen, all MENA countries are above the regression line. The public sector in Iran is perhaps one of the largest in MENA, but the heavy underpricing of foreign exchange and energy products is responsible for the relatively small share of public expenditures reported in the World Bank data. Esfahani and Taheripour (2002) put the share of government expenditures closer to 50% of the GDP, which would make Iran an outlier in the other direction. State expenditures as

---

[4] The terms "Oriental Despotism" and "Asiatic Mode of Production" have been used to describe the economic systems at the helm of which stood the state. For an application to 18th century Iran, see Ashraf (1970) and Abrahamian (1974).

Figure 2. Size of government in the MENA countries

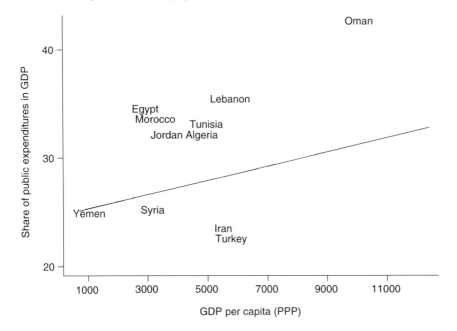

percentage of GDP range from a low of about 25% in Turkey to 35% for the North African countries, to 50% in Kuwait and Iran, compared to 12% in East Asia and 25% in Latin America (Table 2).

Not only are public expenditures high in relation to GDP, the share of wages and salaries of public employees in the GDP is also high relative to the other developing regions. Wages and salaries comprise about one-third of public expenditures in MENA compared to one-fourth in East Asia and Latin America (Table 2). The share of public sector wages and salaries in GDP, which ranges from 6.0% in Turkey to 15.4% in Jordan, is high compared to 2.6% for East Asia. Except for Turkey, the share of government wages and salaries in the GDP of MENA countries lies above the conditional mean represented by the regression line (Figure 3).

The heavy burden of public employment is correlated with overall intervention in the labor market. To start with, the state is by far the largest employer. If we consider public employment (civil service and state enterprises), the extent of the impact of public employment on the labor markets becomes evident. In 1990, public employment as percentage of total employment ranged from 21% in Morocco to 34% in Egypt, 44% in Jordan, 57% in Algeria, and 85% among the nationals in Kuwait (Said, 2001; Shaban *et al.*, 2001). Nearly one out of every three Arabs working outside agriculture is a public employee, compared to one out of five in the Organization for Economic Cooperation and

Table 2. Size of government

Country	Government Wages and Salaries as % of GDP		Public Expenditures as % of GDP	
	1977	1997	1977	1997
Algeria	–	8.30	–	31.8
Egypt	9.52	6.3	46.9	34.2
Iran	11.27	9.16	45.8	23.2
Iraq	–	–	–	–
Jordan	–	15.43	44.8	35.0
Kuwait	6.53	13.07	31.4	41.5
Lebanon	–	8.68	–	37.9
Libya	–	–	–	–
Morocco	10.44	11.34		–
Oman	4.95	10.23	40.2	–
Saudi Arabia	–		52.6	–
Syria	7.30	–	49.4	23.8
Tunisia	9.52	10.33	33.3	32.6
Turkey	5.98	6.08	20.9	26.9
UAE	–	4.15	8.0	11.8
Yemen, Republic	–	11.41	–	39.2
MENA	9.11	7.96	38.09	27.89
East Asia and Pacific	–	2.62	–	11.6
South Asia	2.11	–	12.7	17.7
Sub-Saharan Africa	7.08	–	23.0	–
LAC	6.09	–	19.1	–
Middle income	–	–	–	–

Source: World Bank, (2004a).

Development (OECD) countries (Said, 2001). Growth in public employment has come from access to oil revenues (Iran, Kuwait, Saudi Arabia, and UAE), job guarantees (Egypt and Morocco), and the government acting as the policy of employer of last resort during recessions (Algeria, Jordan, and Tunisia).

As the largest provider of formal employment and regulator of private sector employment, governments in MENA have radically affected the labor market and the economic environment. Public sector employment is characterized by low turnover and emphasis on formal education, especially high school and university degrees (Said, 2005). The share of state in the employment of the educated workers is even higher. In Iran, in 2001, 58% of men in the public sector had upper secondary education or more, compared to 20% in the private sector; for women, 75% in the public sector compared to 35% in the private sector (Salehi-Isfahani, 2005). The state is thus in a position to influence the structure of rewards to education out of proportion to its share in total employment. By emphasizing diplomas at the expense of productive skills, the state helps reinforce a system of education based on memorization and testing rather than acquisition of productive skills.

Figure 3. Share of government wages and salaries in the MENA countries

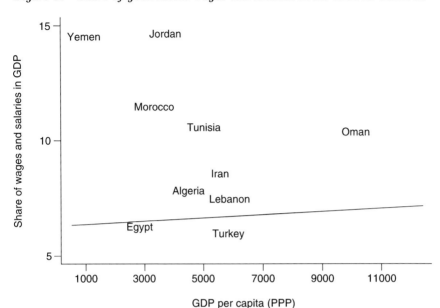

In addition to their role as the largest employer, most MENA states have further reduced the flexibility of the labor market through regulation of pay and rules for job termination. According to the Heritage Foundation index of wage and price flexibility, the MENA countries represented in the sample, with the exception of Jordan, Morocco, and Tunisia, had a labor market rigidity score above the median.[5] In Iran, which has a high score of 4 (only four countries in the sample had a higher score), the government sets the pay scales for private-sector jobs based on formal schooling, and the 1990 Labor Law places the burden of proof on the employers who lay off low-productivity workers (Salehi-Isfahani, 1999, 2000, 2002). In 2002, the Labor Law was amended to exempt firms with five or fewer workers. Egypt also has pay scales based on education and a system of compulsory arbitration between the employer and employees (Assaad, 1997; Said, 2001). According to Labor Law 137 (1981), all prospective employees must register at a district labor office where government officials evaluate skills and note ratings on an "employment certificate." Upon being hired or terminated, workers must notify the labor office of their change of status. In the event a firm is acquired by another, the obligation to continue employment falls to the new owner. Furthermore, the state has successfully used

---

[5] Heritage Foundation, *2002 Index of Economic Freedom*. Washington, DC and New York, NY: Heritage Foundation and Wall Street Journal.

the hierarchical union organization under its control to influence the employment relation in private enterprises (Posusney, 1997). In most other MENA countries the government places restrictions on firing of employees (Said, 2001). Egypt and Morocco adopted policies of job guarantees for educated workers in an effort to increase incentives for education (Assaad, 1997; Shaban, *et al.*, 2001). Recognizing the distortions that these policies have on incentives in the markets for education and labor, both Egypt and Morocco have in the 1990s backed away from their employment guarantee obligations. In 1990, Morocco provided exemptions from the stringent employment regulations that allowed businesses to hire, for up to 18 months, skilled workers without restrictions on wages and benefits or any obligation to retain them (Said, 2001).

The effect of state regulation of the labor market on human capital accumulation is exacerbated by its direct role in its production of education. The educational system in MENA is under heavy influence from the state, both in setting the curriculum and in financing of education. Except in Lebanon, where private schooling at all levels predominates, in all the MENA countries the state is the main provider of education. In 1992, only 7.2% of primary and 6.2% of secondary students in Arab countries were enrolled in private schools, compared to 11.7% and 41% for the upper middle-income economies (Barnett *et al.*, 1998). In Iran, in the mid-1990s the same figures were 1 and 2% only (World Bank, 1997a). Psacharopoulos and Nguyen (1997) show that in Arab countries private spending was only 10% of the total spending on education compared to 50% for East Asia and the Pacific.

The trend is for more privatization of education in MENA, but the environment for human capital accumulation may not be significantly affected by private provision of education as long as the labor markets remain inflexible. To the extent that educational institutions take their cues from the labor market, private schools may not behave very differently from public schools (Salehi-Isfahani and Murphy, 2004). In Iran, private schools only outperform public schools in test taking to prepare them for entry into universities, not in offering a more varied curriculum. After all, for parents and students success is still defined as passing the university entrance examinations and landing a job in a labor market that rewards diplomas rather than productive skills.

2.3.2. Social norms

It is commonplace to speak of the Middle Eastern societies as patriarchal and characterize their gender relations as less equal compared to other developing regions[6]. The veil has come to symbolize separation, and to many, the subordination of women in social and economic life in the MENA societies.

---

[6] There is a vast literature on this subject. For an excellent discussion of gender norms in the Middle East as it pertains to work and education, see World Bank (2004b).

Although the origins of these gender relations can be traced to pre-Islamic Middle East (Nashat, 1999), Islamic laws and edicts may have made them more resilient to change long after their purpose had disappeared, hence the designation of social gender norms as a constraint on household actions in the modern Middle East.

Although the importance of social norms in social outcomes is generally acknowledged, little is known about the precise way in which they influence micro decisions. Mason (1997) and McDonald (2000) divide gender relations into on family decisions into institutional stratification at the macro level and gender roles at the micro (household) level. Patriarchal gender relations exist at both levels in the MENA countries, in personal attitudes toward female education and work as well as at the level of social institutions (Kazemi, 2000). The state has often played an important role in promoting and enforcing social norms. In several countries gender norms have been "codified in law, especially in the region's personal status or family laws, such as those requiring women to obtain the permission of fathers or husbands to gain employment, to seek a loan, to start up a business, or to undertake any form of travel" (Moghadam, 1998). The ban against women driving in Saudi Arabia, lack of women's suffrage in Kuwait prior to 2005, and the sexual segregation of men and women in buses, classrooms, and workplaces in Iran are means by which the state enforces social norms. In Iran, where women have made strong gains in education, now outnumbering men in universities, former president Rafsanjani has complained of political pressures on him (while president in the 1990s) to limit women's access to the university.[7] Patriarchal gender roles at the household level, reinforced by the social image of men as breadwinners, have been blamed for low female participation in the labor market and wage rigidity (Karshenas, 2001).

The gap in gender relations between MENA and other regions of the world points to social norms as an important feature of the social environment in which micro units operate. The Gender Empowerment Measure (GEM) calculated by the United Nations, which measures the economic and social opportunities open to women relative to men, allows a comparison of gender relations across countries.[8] Figure 4 depicts mean GEM by income per capita

---

[7] "They asked why women should study if they are not going to work. And even some radical representatives spoke from the tribune of the Majlis asking why should we give the seats in universities to a woman who when she finishes her education must go home and take care of children. I said that an educated mother without a job would be effective in the society because of the children that she will educate." (Interview with M. H. Rafsanjani, author's translation from Persian, *Hamshahri* 1/10/00, p. 15)

[8] According to the *Human Development Report, 1999,* the Gender Empowerment Measure (GEM) "captures opportunities for women in selected economic and political areas. It examines whether women and men are able to actively participate in economic and political life and take part in decision making. It tracks the percentages of women in parliament, among administrators and managers and among professional and technical workers – and women's earned income share as a percentage of men's."

Figure 4. **Gender empowerment measure for the MENA countries**

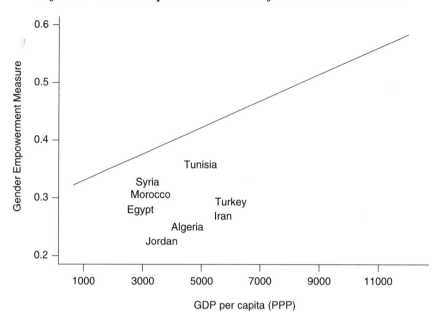

and shows that all MENA countries lie below the regression line. Interestingly, GEM in MENA is even below that of much poorer Sub-Saharan African countries (ERF, 2000). Around the world women live longer than men. The "Disability Adjusted Life Expectancy" (DALE) index calculated by the World Health Organization (WHO) shows the MENA countries among a select group in which men fare better than women (Murray and Lopez, 2000). Indeed, the top five countries in this category are the MENA countries. As one observer put it, the lack of "a sex gap in Egypt and Iraq, or the existence of a gap in favor of men in Turkey and Iran, may reflect a relative devaluation of women's well-being in those countries as well as large inequalities between the sexes in education, a variable that correlates highly with health."[9]

Gender norms are constraints on individual decisions, but they also change when enough individuals choose to defy them. Norms with respect to childbearing have gone through drastic change in many MENA countries, where fertility has declined precipitously in recent decades, notably in Iran where the slow pace of increase in women's work outside the home, despite improvements in health, reproduction, and education, might lead one to suppose very rigid gender norms sparingly as explanation of behavior (Salehi-Isfahani,

---

[9] *Washington Post*, June 12, 2000; p. A09.

2005). Since our understanding of how specific social norms arise and disappear is far from adequate, we must use social norms sparingly as explanation of behavior. Ironically, the oil boom that increased incomes and hastened modernization in the region may have strengthened the traditional gender contract because the inflow of oil revenues removed the need for women to work outside the home (Moghadam, 1998). This observation fits the pattern of gender norms across the region relatively well: norms have proved more resilient to change in oil exporting countries of Iran, Kuwait, and Saudi Arabia, where women have low labor force participation rates despite relatively high education, but shown less rigidity in Morocco, Tunisia, and Turkey where women have the highest activity rates with no apparent advantage in education or skills compared to women in oil-rich countries.

3. Household decisions

Economic theory identifies three household decisions with direct impact on economic growth: to save, to accumulate human capital, and to procreate. These decisions are interdependent. There is the well-known tradeoff between the quantity and quality of children, which derives from the scarcity of resources, mainly time, in the household (Becker, 1991). Children can be a substitute for other assets as means for old-age support. This interdependence implies that, in principle, all other household actions also indirectly affect growth. The allocation of household time between home production, leisure, and market work is the most important of such decisions. For example, rewards for market work for women influence household choices with regard to fertility and investment in human capital and thus indirectly affect growth. In this section I consider decisions with both direct and indirect impact on growth and two features of the environment that constrain these decisions – the interventionist state and social norms.

3.1. Household time allocation

The most important asset of the household is the total time available to its members. The household divides its total endowment of time between leisure, work for home production, and market work. For urban households home production primarily consists of 'child services' (Hotz *et al.*, 1997), which is itself a function of the number and quality of children. Modern economic growth is associated with a shift from home production of commodities to market work, especially for women, and from quantity to quality of children.

The allocation of time in MENA households differs in significant ways from households in other developing countries, and this is most noticeable in the gender allocation of tasks between married couples. Moghadam (1998) speaks of a specific "gender contract" which designates men as breadwinners and women as homemakers. The gender contract implies a low female labor force participation, at odds with which is the levels of fertility and education in the MENA societies. Whether low participation can be blamed on social norms is an empirical question for which we do not yet have a satisfactory answer. MENA gender norms inherited from the past can be said to constrain household choices – and thereby hinder growth – at present, if we can determine empirically that they prevent a more productive allocation of time between household members. I now examine how social norms affect time allocation in fertility and labor market participation decisions.

3.1.1. Fertility

Despite substantial decline in fertility in several MENA countries, notably Egypt, Iran, Lebanon, Turkey, and Tunisia, the region as a whole has been slow in its demographic transition (Rashad and Khadr, 2002). In 2002, fertility rates in MENA, averaging 3.2 births per woman, were exceeded only by fertility in countries of Sub-Saharan Africa (World Bank, 2004a). Delay in the transition and persistence of high fertility in the Arabian Peninsula where, despite high incomes and high education, fertility remains around 6 births per woman, has given rise to the notion of Islamic or Arab fertility (Caldwell, 1986; Obermeyer, 1992). As late as 1977, MENA births averaged 6.3 per woman (Table 3), nearly as high as in Sub-Saharan Africa (6.6) with much lower per capita income, and twice that of East Asia and the Pacific (3.3). Figure 5 shows that in 1977 the total fertility rate (TFR) in all but two MENA countries (Egypt and Turkey) was higher than indicated by the regression line which depicts mean TFR by income for all developing countries. Recently, fertility has declined in most countries of the region, lowering the TFR from 6.3 to 3.6 in the last 20 years (Table 3). In 1997 at least half of MENA countries were below the regression line (Figure 6).

Two implications of lower fertility for MENA growth are important to note. First, the move from high to low fertility provides these countries with a one-time bonus derived from a favorable age structure. Economic historians have labeled the benefits to growth from a more rapid labor force growth and a low dependency ratio (ratio of working to non-working population) that follow fertility transitions as a "demographic gift" (Bloom and Williamson, 1997) and a "window of opportunity" (Barlow, 1994). Salehi-Isfahani (2002, 2005), Tunali (1996), and Yousef (1998) show how the changing age structure can play a positive role in the MENA countries. Even though fertility has been on the decline in the last 20 years, the rate of growth of the labor force has remained high, averaging 3.2% during 1985–1995 and 2.9% during 1995–2002 (Table 3) and will likely remain above 2% for the next decade or so. Labor force growth rates could be even higher if female labor force participation rates increase. As noted earlier, although the effect of lower fertility and more female education on labor force participation of women in the formal economy is yet to fully materialize, it is only a matter of time before women begin to seek work outside the home.

Table 3. Population, labor force, and fertility

Country	Population Growth (annual %)			Growth of Labor Force (annual %)			Fertility Rate, Total (Births per Woman)		
	1997–1986	1987–1996	1997–2002	1975–1984	1985–1994	1995–2002	1977	1997	2002
Algeria	3.1	2.4	1.6	3.2	3.9	3.4	7.2	3.5	2.8
Egypt, Arab Republic	2.5	2.2	1.9	2.2	2.6	3.0	5.3	3.6	3.1
Iran, Islamic Republic	3.5	2.2	1.2	3.0	2.4	2.7	6.5	2.8	2
Iraq	3.3	3.0	2.1	2.8	3.2	3.0	6.6	4.7	4.1
Jordan	3.8	4.6	3.0	2.1	6.0	4.1	7.2	3.9	3.5
Kuwait	5.1	0.6	3.4	7.5	1.0	5.7	5.9	2.9	2.5
Lebanon	1.3	2.0	1.4	-0.1	3.2	2.7	4.3	2.5	2.2
Libya	4.3	2.1	2.0	4.3	1.9	2.1	7.4	3.8	3.3
Morocco	2.2	1.9	1.7	3.2	2.5	2.5	5.9	3.1	2.8
Oman	4.9	4.1	2.6	5.7	3.7	2.3	10.1	4.8	4
Saudi Arabia	5.4	3.6	2.7	5.1	4.3	2.9	7.3	5.7	5.3
Syrian Arab Republic	3.3	3.2	2.5	3.1	3.7	4.1	7.4	4	3.4
Tunisia	2.7	1.9	1.2	3.7	2.9	2.5	5.7	2.4	2.1
Turkey	2.3	2.0	1.7	1.4	2.8	2.5	4.5	2.6	2.2
UAE	8.7	5.2	4.9	21.8	5.0	4.4	5.7	3.5	3
Yemen, Republic	3.6	4.1	2.9	1.7	5.0	3.0	8	6.4	6
MENA	3.2	2.7	1.9	2.8	3.0	2.9	6.3	3.7	3.1
East Asia and Pacific	1.6	1.5	1.0	2.3	2.0	1.2	3.3	2.2	2.1
South Asia	2.3	2.0	1.8	2.3	2.2	2.4	5.5	3.5	3.2
Sub-Saharan Africa	3.0	2.7	2.4	2.6	2.6	2.6	6.6	5.5	5.1
LAC	2.2	1.8	1.5	3.2	2.7	2.2	4.5	2.7	2.5
Middle income	1.6	1.4	1.0	2.2	1.8	1.3	3.4	2.2	2.1

Source: World Bank, (2004a).

Figure 5. Total fertility rate for the MENA countries, 1977

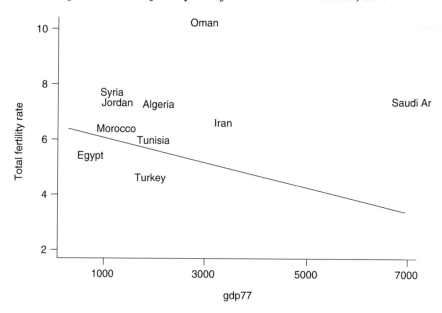

Figure 6. Total fertility rate for the MENA countries, 1997

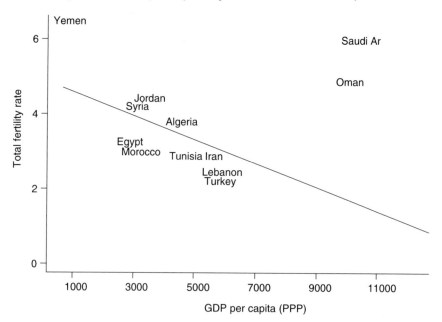

3.1.2. Participation of women in market work

Reliable data on labor force participation of women in the region is lacking. A few countries report data based on household surveys (Egypt, Kuwait, Iran, Morocco, and Turkey). As in other developing countries, accounting for women's work, especially in self-employment and in agriculture, is notoriously difficult. In addition, many women prefer to declare their occupation as housework (or are identified as such by their husbands if they are the respondent) rather than declare themselves unemployed, even though they would readily accept an appropriate job. Variation in the definition of what is meant by "work" reduces comparability of estimates, but this is a less severe problem in urban areas where own account workers form a smaller proportion of the workforce than in rural areas.

Comparison of urban women across the world reveals a much lower rate of participation for MENA. In 1990s female participation rates in urban Turkey was only 15% (Tunali and Baslevent, 2000), in Egypt about 16% (Assaad and El-Hamidi, 2002), in Jordan 12.1% (Flynn, 1999), and in Iran 8.6% (Statistical Center of Iran, 1998). These rates are all less than half the rates reported for East Asia. Even in the predominantly Muslim Malaysia female labor force participation has reached 40%. Table 4 presents a more complete comparison of the MENA female participation rates based on the share of women in the labor force as reported in World Bank (2004). The participation rate for the MENA women is the lowest among any region and is not changing as fast as one would expect given the rise in education and decrease in fertility. The sharpest contrast is with Sub-Saharan Africa where, despite higher fertility and lower education, women comprised 42.2% of the workforce in 2002, compared to 28.6% for MENA. The fact that Africa is more rural explains a part but not all the difference. The share of MENA women in the labor force appears low even taking into account their higher fertility. Although labor force participation, female education, and fertility are obviously interrelated, it is still informative to compare labor force participation rates conditional on education and fertility. Figures 7a and b present the regression for the share of women in labor force and depict the relative positions of MENA and Sub-Saharan African countries. In this regression, the shares of women in African countries appear well 'explained' by their high fertility and low enrollment rate in secondary school, whereas in the MENA countries they appear as outliers. Finally, changes in participation over time in MENA suggest a slow response to falling fertility. During 1977–2002, a period when fertility dropped by more than half (Table 3), the share of women in the labor force increased very modestly, from 23.4% to 28.6% (Table 4).

Given the declining trend in fertility and rising female education in the MENA region, future increase in female labor participation has the potential to contribute to the MENA growth. If the proportion of women who work outside the home were to gradually increase to the level in East Asia,

Table 4.   Women in MENA labor force

Country	Labor Force, Female (% of Total Labor Force)		
	1977	1997	2002
Algeria	21.1	25.7	29.0
Egypt, Arab Republic	26.3	29.4	31.0
Iran, Islamic Republic	20.0	25.4	28.4
Iraq	17.0	18.7	20.4
Jordan	14.3	22.6	25.6
Kuwait	11.6	31.2	32.1
Lebanon	21.4	28.8	30.1
Libya	17.9	21.7	24.0
Morocco	32.9	34.6	34.9
Oman	6.2	15.1	18.9
Saudi Arabia	6.8	14.2	17.7
Syrian Arab Republic	23.3	26.2	27.6
Tunisia	27.3	30.9	32.1
Turkey	36.2	36.7	38.1
UAE	4.8	13.8	15.9
Yemen, Republic	30.9	27.9	28.3
MENA	23.5	26.6	28.6
East Asia and Pacific	42.1	44.4	44.5
South Asia	33.8	33.0	33.6
Sub-Saharan Africa	42.0	41.9	42.0
LAC	26.4	34.1	35.2
Middle income	40.2	42.0	42.2

Source: World Bank, (2004a).

three times as many women would be participating in the labor market. This increase in the rate of growth of the labor force has the potential to generate economic growth.

These observations indicate that, given their levels of education and fertility, the low rate of market work of the MENA women is an anomaly, but they do not explain it. Social norms are frequently advanced as an explanation (see, for example, El-Sanabary, 1993), but convincing evidence that they do in fact act as a constraint is still lacking. An alternative hypothesis for the low participation of women in MENA is the importance of oil income (World Bank, 2004b). Oil income permits the average MENA family to enjoy a higher standard of living given their education and productivity, thereby reducing the need for women to work. Non-wage family income is well known as a negative influence on the labor force participation of women. The question is whether oil income at the national level acts on household behavior the same way as unearned income. The answer depends on how oil income is distributed. To the extent that households receive transfers from the government, their real income rises without changing the price of leisure. Direct transfers to households, as in

Figure 7(a). **Share of women in labor force, conditional on GDP per capita, total fertility, and female school enrollment in Sub-Saharan Africa; (b) Share of women in labor force, conditional on GDP per capita, total fertility, and female school enrollment in MENA**

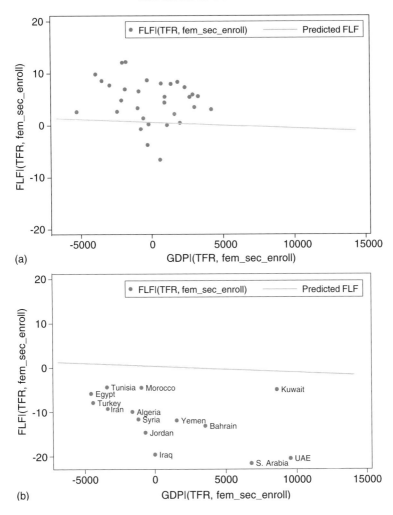

(a)

(b)

Kuwait, and subsidies for consumer goods, as in all oil-exporting countries, fall into this category. But transfers that occur through the labor market, e.g. higher pay for public sector jobs, do not because they raise the price of leisure which would increase labor supply. Anecdotal evidence suggests that the income effect on women's labor supply may be negative. For example, we read that, coping with hard times, "reluctantly, men allow their daughters to work until marriage or allow their wives to go on working until the mythical day when they can afford to forgo a second salary," (Al-Sayyid-Marsot, 1989, p. 121). But systematic evidence for this view is lacking. Assaad and El-Hamidi (2002) find evidence from micro data from Egypt which indicates the opposite – that female wage workers are more likely to be found in households with a male wage worker and one with higher earnings.

The search for cultural reasons for differences in the labor force participation of women with different ethnic backgrounds in the US has produced mixed results. Ortiz and Cooney (1984) find that the influence of Hispanic culture on the rate of participation of women works mainly through education, fertility, and language. Reimers (1985) confirms this finding for Hispanic women, but concludes that the difference between US-born whites on the one hand and Asian and blacks on the other is due to "direct cultural effects on the parameters of the labor force participation function." In contrast, decline in the female labor force participation during industrialization has been explained by social norms that prevent women from accepting blue-collar jobs (Mammen and Paxson, 2000). Goldin (1995) argues that in the US blue-collar jobs are shunned because they stigmatize the husbands as unable to care for their wives, whereas women holding white-collar jobs do not face such a situation.

Gender norms may influence labor supply of married women through the relative power of men and women in the household. The literature on the division of labor within the household suggests that the relative bargaining position of men and women influences the labor force participation of women, but the direction of influence is not obvious. More power to women may raise or lower their likelihood of market work. Grossbard-Schechtman (1993) presents evidence of circumstances in which women *increased* their participation in response to a decrease in their share of the gains from marriage, this itself being caused by a decline in the ratio of males to females. It is equally plausible to imagine, as indeed the prevailing wisdom on obstacles to women's participation goes, that increased female power within marriage would lead to higher participation. This version appears to be more true in MENA where female labor force participation declines with marriage (World Bank, 2004b). In Egypt, Assaad and El-Hamidi (2002) show that women's market work drops sharply with marriage rather than with childbearing. In Iran, married women have the lowest participation rates, followed by single and widowed women. In Kuwait, Shah and Al-Qudsi (1990) find that the labor force participation of single women aged 25–39 years is more than twice that of married women (60% compared to 30).

Where the rise in education has increased labor force participation rates, social norms may have forced occupational segregation. In MENA, where they have evolved to allow women to work outside the home, gender norms continue to restrict choice by defining what jobs are appropriate for women. However, although job segregation appears to discourage women from participation, it does not appear to be out of line in comparison to other regions (World Bank, 2004b, p. 93). As in most other regions of the world, educated women in MENA predominate in teaching, nursing, and clerical work.

Table 8. Savings and interest rates

Country	Average Real Interest Rates (%)			Gross Saving/GDP (%)	
	1968–1977	1978–1987	1988–1997	1977	1997
Algeria	–	–	–	35.7	34.5
Egypt	4.6	4.5	5.9	18.5	13.0
Iran	–	–	–	37.0	34.1
Jordan	–	–	2.9	−9.7	5.5
Kuwait	–	1.3	1.6	51.9	25.2
Lebanon	–	6.3	15.9	–	−16.7
Libya	3.1	1.8	1.5	50.0	–
Morocco	–	1.0	0.5	11.6	15.2
Oman	–	1.4	2.6	44.9	26.7
Saudi Arabia	–	–	–	54.9	34.6
Syria	–	–	–	13.0	19.0
Tunisia	–	4.1	2.5	22.1	24.2
Turkey	–	2.4	–	13.3	19.3
UAE	–	–	–	69.9	27.4
Yemen, republic	–	–	–	–	12.8
MENA	–	–	–	36.6	25.5
East Asia and Pacific	–	–	–	28.0	37.7
South Asia	–	–	–	18.1	18.2
Sub-Saharan Africa	–	–	–	23.4	16.7
Middle income	–	–	–	25.7	25.7

Source: World Bank, (2004a).

East Asian countries. Private sector investment in MENA is below other countries, about 10% in the 1990s compared to 18% for developing countries and 22% for Asian countries (IMF, 1996). No data are available on the part of this investment that is financed by household savings as opposed to retained earnings of firms. In developed countries household savings is a significant source of finance for firms, but not so in developing countries, where weak financial intermediation cannot channel household savings toward investors. Policies to liberalize the financial markets and deepen financial intermediation intend to raise the ability of small savers, such as households, to contribute to growth. Several MENA countries, mainly in North Africa, have attempted financial reform as part of their structural adjustment, but studies that can show if household savings have increased as a result do not exist.

Economic theory does not give a clear indication of the impact of interest rates on personal savings (Deaton, 1997). Neither of the main theories of why households save – life cycle, permanent income, or consumption smoothing – predicts unambiguously that savings should increase with interest rates. What we do know is that a well-developed system of financial intermediation is associated with a more effective use of household savings. It is generally agreed that with low and negative real rates of interest it is difficult to raise long-term finance from personal sources. Table 8 shows that for those countries that report the real interest rate in World Bank (2004), it has increased over time and is positive. In Iran, until recently, real interest rates averaged negative, and as recently as 2000 were about 5% points below zero (Jalali-Naini, 1997). Easterly (1999) notes a similar rise in the rate of interest for developing countries as a whole, showing that real rates, which were negative before 1980, were on average positive afterward.

The financial environment in which MENA households generally operate not only suffers from lack of depth, they are also insecure due to the heavy influence of the public sector and a weakly developed legal system overseeing financial contracts. As a result, households may prefer to place their savings in unproductive assets such as gold and land rather than in the financial system. The risks of nationalization and loss of value owing to inflation, even in countries undergoing reform, deter savers from depending on the financial system for long-term savings.

4. Conclusions

The question posed in this paper is whether households in MENA allocate their resources efficiently and in a way as to promote growth. To answer this question, I focused on the role of urban households, because they form the majority of households and are the main source of growth in human capital and therefore of modern economic growth. I argued that an efficient allocation of household resources which would maximize growth may not be feasible because of constraints that households face in their decisions to supply labor, and human and physical capital. I identified two aspects of the environment in which MENA households operate as key to conditioning their behavior: the large role played by the state in the education and labor markets and the social norms regarding gender. I argued that this environment has affected an important static decision of the households, namely the division of labor within the household, resulting in high fertility and low labor force participation of women. Given the declining trend in fertility and rising female education, increase in female labor force participation has the potential to raise MENA growth rates. If the proportion of women who work outside home were to gradually increase to the level in East Asia, three times as many women would be participating in the labor market, resulting in a lasting positive impact on economic growth.

I then identified the implications of the same environment for the dynamic aspects of household decisions – human capital accumulation and savings. Although little evidence exists regarding the magnitude of household savings in MENA, we know that their effectiveness for growth has been compromised by lack of confidence on the part of the households in the financial markets, which is itself the result of arbitrary actions by governments and the absence of the rule of law. I argued that the impact of state interventions and social norms on household actions were much greater in the accumulation of human capital than in the physical capital. The role of the public sector in MENA in education and the labor market has created a system of incentives in which households strive hard to accumulate formal education, but not enough in productive human capital.

There are several implications of the analysis of this thematic paper for future research. First, studies focused on individual countries should examine the extent to which characteristics of the environment identified here – the large role of the state and social norms – apply in specific cases. As far as the role of the state is concerned, a description of employment policies and labor market regulations is a good place to start. For social norms, indicators of restrictions placed on women in schools, the workplace, and public space should be developed to define the environment in which the households make decisions regarding fertility, female education, and labor force participation. If these constraints are judged as relevant and adequate descriptions of the environment in which households operate, their effect on household behavior should be the next item on the research agenda.

Micro studies of household behavior can be very useful in understanding the impact of the environment on the static and dynamic decisions of the households. In particular, they are indispensable in disentangling the effects of individual preferences and social norms as constraints on household behavior. For example, it is important to distinguish gender discrimination owing to parental preferences from that which is a rational household response to the gender discrimination in the labor market. Evidence on the static decisions could come from aggregate data on fertility and labor force participation of women, but ideally, one would need micro data to link individual characteristics, such as income and education, to fertility and labor force participation decisions. By controlling for observed individual characteristics, micro studies can provide a closer link between social norms and demographic and labor market outcomes.

For decisions to save and to accumulate human capital, the focus should be on the institutions of markets for credit, education, and labor. With respect to physical capital accumulation, the efficiency with which credit institutions can channel household savings toward productive investments should be determined. Do banks and other mechanisms of financial intermediation provide households with good alternatives to investments in unproductive assets such as land? Micro studies of consumption smoothing over the life cycle and intergenerational transfers through inheritance and dowries can provide valuable information on the household motives to save. With respect to human capital, which is produced within households as well as in schools, two questions should guide country studies. First, to what extent is the productivity of human capital affected by state interventions in the labor market? Second, to what extent household investments in the education of boys and girls are driven by the gender inequalities owing to social norms? Studies of returns to education which compare returns to formal schooling in private versus public sector, large establishments regulated by labor laws versus those unregulated, can reveal how state interventions in the labor market affect household choices in the amount and type of human capital to accumulate.

Acknowledgments

I am grateful to Francois Bourguinon, Angus Deaton, Valery Makarov, Heba Handoussa, Hashem Pesaran, Lyn Squire, and two anonymous referees for helpful comments. They have no responsibility for my views or errors.

References

Abrahamian, E. (1974), "Oriental despotism: the case of Qajar Iran", *International Journal of Middle East Studies*, Vol. 5(1), pp. 3–31.

Ashraf, A. (1970), "Historical obstacles to the development of a bourgeoisie in Iran", pp. 308–332 in: M.A. Cook, editor, *Studies in the Economic History of the Middle East from the Rise of Islam to the Present Day*, Oxford: Oxford University Press.

Al-Sayyid-Marsot, A. (1989), "Women and social change", in: G. Sabbagh, editor, *The Modern Economic and Social History of the Middle East in its World Context*, Cambrigde, UK: Cambridge University Press.

Anderson, L. (1987), "The state in the Middle-East and North Africa", *The Journal of Comparative Politics*, Vol. 1(3), pp. 1–18.

Assaad, R. (1997), "The effects of public sector hiring and compensation policies on the Egyptian labor market", *World Bank Economic Review*, Vol. 11(1), pp. 85–118.

Assaad, R. and F. El-Hamidi (2002), "Female labor supply in Egypt: participation and hours of work", in: I. Sirageldin, editor, *Population Challenges in the Middle East and North Africa: Towards the Twentieth First Century*, London: I.B. Tauris and Cairo: American University of Cairo Press.

Barlow, R. (1994), "Population Growth and Economic Growth: some More Correlations", *Population and Development Review*, Vol. 20(1), pp. 153–165.

Barnett, S., S. Eken, M. Lockheed, and W. V. Eegen (1998), "Effective financing of education: role of public and private sectors", Paper presented at the 1998 Annual Seminar of the Arab Monetary Fund and the Arab Fund for Economic and Social Development, February 21–22, 1998, Abu Dhabi.

Becker, G.S. (1991), *A Treatise on the Family*, second ed., Cambridge, MA: Harvard University Press.

Besley, T. and R. Burgess (2004), "Can labor regulation hinder economic performance? Evidence from India", *The Quarterly Journal of Economics*, Vol. 119(1), pp. 91–134.

Bill, J.A. and C. Leiden (1974), *Politics in the Middle East*, Boston: Little, Brown and Company.

Bishop, J.H. (1996), "Incentives to study and the organization of secondary instruction", pp. 99–160 in: W.E. Becker and W. Baumol, editors, *Assessing Educational Practices*, Cambridge MA: MIT Press.

Bloom, D. and J. Williamson (1997), "Demographic transitions and economic miracles in emerging Asia", *World Bank Economic Review*, Vol. 12(3), pp. 419–455.

Botero, J., S. Djankov, R.L. Porta, F.L. de Silane, and A. Shleifer (2003), "The regulation of labor", NBER Working Paper No. 9756, National Bureau of Economic Research.

Bray, M. and P. Kwok (2003), "Demand for private supplementary tutoring: conceptual considerations and socio-economic patterns", *Economics of Education Review*, Vol. 22, pp. 611–620.

Caldwell, J. (1986), "Routes to low mortality in poor countries", *Population and Development Review*, Vol. 12(2), pp. 171–220.

Collier, P. and J.W. Gunning (1999), "Explaining African economic performance", *Journal of Economic Literature*, Vol. 37(1), pp. 64–111.

Davis, J., R. Ossowski, J. Daniel, and S. Barnett (2001), "Stabilization and savings funds for nonrenewable resources: experience and fiscal policy implications", International Monetary Fund Occasional Paper No. 205, IMF: Washington DC.

Deaton, A. (1997), *Analysis of Household Data*, Baltimore: The Johns Hopkins University Press.

Easterly, W. (1999), "The lost decades: explaining developing countries' stagnation 1980–1998", World Bank, mimeo.

El-Erian, M., S. Eken, S. Fennel, and J. Chaurfour (1996), *Growth and stability in the Middle East and North Africa*, International Monetary Fund: Washington DC.

El-Sanabary, N. (1993), "Middle East and North Africa", pp. 136–174 in: E.M. King and M.A. Hill, editors, *Women's Education in Developing Countries: Barriers, Benefits and Policies*, Baltimore and London: The Johns Hopkins Press.

ERF (2000), *MENA Indicators 2000*, Cairo: Economic Research Forum.

Esfahani, H. and F. Taheripour (2002), "Hidden public expenditures and the economy in Iran", *International Journal of Middle Eastern Studies*, Vol. 34(3), pp. 691–718.

Flynn, D. K. (1999), "Reconceptualizing the female labor force in Jordan: accounting for the informal sector", Paper presented in the ERF Sixth Annual Conference, October 28–31, 1999, Cairo.

Gelb, A. (1988), *Oil Windfalls: Blessing or Curse?*, Oxford, UK: Oxford University Press.

Goldin, C. (1995), "The U-shaped female labor force function in economic development and history", in: T.P. Schultz, editor, *Investment in Women's Human Capital*, Chicago: University of Chicago Press.

Grossbard-Schechtman, A. (1993), *On the Economics of Marriage: A Theory of Marriage, Labor and Divorce*, Boulder, CO: Westview.

Guriev, S. and D. Salehi-Isfahani (2003), "Microeconomics determinants of growth around the world", in: G. McMahon and L. Squire, editors,

Explaining Growth: A Global Research Project, IEA Conference Vol. No. 150, London: Palgrave, MacMillan.

Jalali-Naini, S.A.R. (1997), "A look at inflation and monetary, foreign exchange, and credit policies", in: M. Nili, editor, *The Iranian Economy*, Tehran: Institute for Research in Planning and Development (in Persian).

IMF (1996), Building on Progress, Reforms and Growth in the Middle East and North Africa, Middle East Department.

Issawi, C. (1995), *The Middle East Economy: Decline and Recovery*, Princeton: Markus Wiener Publishers.

Karshenas, M. (2001), "Economic liberalization, competitiveness and women's employment in the Middle East and North Africa", in: D. Salehi-Isfahani, editor, *Labor and Human Capital in the Middle East: Studies of Labor Markets and Household Behavior*, Reading, UK: Ithaca Press.

Kazemi, F. (2000), "Gender, Islam and politics", *Social Research*, Vol. 67(2), pp. 453–474.

Lazear, E.P. (1990), "Job security provisions and employment", *Quarterly Journal of Economics*, Vol. 105(3), pp. 699–726.

Mahdavy, H. (1970), "Patterns and problems of economic development in rentier states: the case of Iran", in: M. Cook, editor, *Studies in the Economic History of the Middle-East*, Oxford, UK: Oxford University Press.

Mammen, K. and C. Paxson (2000), "Women's work and economic development", *Journal of Economic Perspective*, Vol. 14(4), pp. 141–164.

Manski, C. F. (2000) "Economic analysis of social interactions," *Journal of Economic Perspectives*, Vol. 14(3) (Summer), pp. 115–136.

Mason, K.O. (1997), "Gender and demographic change: what do we know?", pp. 158–182 in: G.W. Jones, R.M. Douglas, J.C. Caldwell and R.M. D'Souza, editors, *The Continuing Demographic Transition*, Oxford: Clarendon Press.

McDonald, P. (2000), "Gender equity in theories of fertility", *Population and Development Review*, Vol. 26(3), pp. 427–439.

Moghadam, V.M. (1998), *Women, Work, and Economic Reform in the Middle East and North Africa*, Boulder, CO: Lynne Reinner Publishers.

Nashat, G. (1999), "Women in the Middle East, 8000 B.C.E.-C.E. 1800", pp. 5–72 in: G. Nashat and J.E. Tucker, editors, *Women in the Middle East and North Africa*, Bloomington and Indianapolis: Indiana University Press.

Obermeyer, C.M. (1992), "Islam, women and politics", *Population and Development Review*, Vol. 18(1), pp. 33–57.

Ortiz, V. and R. Cooney (1984), "Sex-role attitudes and labor force participation among young Hispanic females and non-Hispanic White females", *Social Science Quarterly*, Vol. 65(June), pp. 392–400.

Pissarides, C., and Veganzones-Varoudakis (this volume), "Labor markets and economic growth in the MENA Region", Explaining Growth in the Middle East. J. B. Nugent and M. H. Pesaran, editors, London: Elsevier.

Posusney, M.P. (1997), *Labor and the State in Egypt*, New York: Columbia University Press.

Pritchett, L. (1999), *Has education had a growth payoff in the MENA region?* MENA Working Paper Series, No. 18, Washington DC: World Bank.

Psacharopoulos, G. and X. Nguyen (1997), *"The role of government and the private sector in fighting poverty*, Washington D. C.: World Bank Publications.

Rashad, H., and Khadr, Z. (2002). "The demography of the Arab region: new challenges and opportunities", in: Sirageldin, I. editor, *Human Capital: Population Economics in the Middle East.* London: I.B. Tauris, 2002.

Reimers, C.W. (1985), "Cultural differences in labor force participation among married women", *American Economic Review Proceedings*, Vol. 198575(2), pp. 251–255.

Richards, A. and J. Waterbury (1996), *A Political Economy of the Middle East*, 2nd ed., Boulder, Colorado: Westview Press.

Said, M. (2001), "Public sector employment and labor markets in Arab countries: recent developments and policy implications", in: D. Salehi-Isfahani, editor, *Labor and Human Capital in the Middle East: Studies of Labor Markets and Household Behavior*, Reading, UK: Ithaca Press.

Salehi-Isfahani, D. (1999), "Labor and the challenge of restructuring in Iran", *Middle East Report*, Vol. 28(210), pp. 34–37.

Salehi-Isfahani, D. (2000), "Demographic factors in Iran's economic development", *Social Research*, Vol. 67(2), pp. 599–620.

Salehi-Isfahani, D. (2002), "Population, human capital, and economic growth in Iran", in: I. Sirageldin, editor, *Human Capital: Population Economics in the Middle East*, London: I.B. Tauris and Cairo: American University of Cairo Press.

Salehi-Isfahani, D. (2005), "Human resources in Iran: potentials and challenges", *Iranian Studies*, Vol. 38(1), pp. 117–147.

Salehi-Isfahani, D. and R. D. Murphy (2004), "Labor market flexibility and investment in human capital", Working paper, Department of Economics, Virginia Tech.

Shaban, R., R. Assaad and S. Al-Qudsi (2001), "Employment experience in the Middle East and North Africa", in: D. Salehi-Isfahani, editor, *Labor and Human Capital in the Middle East: Studies of Labor Markets and Household Behavior*, Reading, UK: Ithaca Press.

Shah, N. M. and S. S. Al-Qudsi (1990), "Female work roles in traditional oil economy: Kuwait", in: Vol. 6, 213–246 I. Sirageldin, editor, *Research in Human Capital and Development*.

Statistical Center of Iran (1998), *Employment and Unemployment of Households*, Tehran, Iran.

Tansel, A. (1994), "Wage–employment, earnings and returns to schooling for men and women in Turkey", *Economics of Education Review*, Vol. 13(4), pp. 305–320.

Tansel, A. and F. Bircan (2004), "Private tutoring expenditures in Turkey", IZA Working Paper No. 1255, Bonn, Germany. URL: http://ssrn.com/abstract = 560283.

Tunali, I. (1996), "Labor market implications of the demographic window of opportunity", *The Forum*, Vol. 3(4), p. 3. ERF: Cairo.

Tunali, I. and Baslevent, C., (2000), "Estimation of female labor supply parameters when self-employment is an option", Mimeo.

United Nations (1999), *Human Development Report CD-Rom*, New York: United Nations.

UNDP (2002), *Arab Human Development Report 2002*, New York: United Nations Development Program.

Wahba, J. (2001), "Returns to education and regional earnings differentials in Egypt", in: D. Salehi-Isfahani, editor, *Labor and Human Capital in the Middle East: Studies of Labor Markets and Household Behavior*, Reading, UK: Ithaca Press.

World Bank (1997a). "Education in MENA: benefits and growth payoffs now and then", Mimeo

World Bank (1997b). "Spending on education in selected MENA countries", Mimeo, Washington DC

World Bank (1999), *Education in the Middle East & North Africa: A Strategy towards Learning for Development*, Human Development Sector, MENA region.

World Bank (2002), *Arab Republic of Egypt: Education Sector Review – progress and Priorities for the Future*, Washington, DC: The World Bank.

World Bank (2004a), *World Development Indicators CD-ROM*, Washington DC: The World Bank.

World Bank (2004b), *Gender and Development in the Middle East and North Africa Women in the Public Sphere,* MENA Development Report, Washington, DC: The World Bank.

Young, M.E. (1995), *Early Childhood Development: Investing in the Future*, Washington DC: The World Bank.

Yousef, T. (1998), "Demography, capital dependency, and growth in MENA", ERF Working Paper No. 9801, ERF: Cairo

PART II:
Country-Specific Studies

CHAPTER 7

Sources of Economic Growth and Technical Progress in Egypt: An Aggregate Perspective

Hanaa Kheir-El-Din* and Tarek Abdelfattah Moursi

Abstract

Egypt's economic growth record has been uneven during the period 1960–1998. The mean rate of growth was consistently high with an average of about 6 percent per annum. Recurrent fluctuations in the annual growth rate of real output were observed, associated with frequent changes in the political environment and in socioeconomic conditions. In this paper, the traditional total factor productivity (TFP) methodology is used to analyze sources of aggregate economic growth in Egypt. Two sources of growth in output are identified: changes in physical inputs (capital and labor) and disembodied technical innovations measured by growth in TFP. Unlike other studies postulating arbitrary estimates for factor shares liable to misrepresent actual TFP changes, a simple integrated approach is used. It is based on the Kalman filter algorithm (Hamilton, 1994), which allows for simultaneous estimation of the parameters of the aggregate production technology and of TFP within a multi-equation system framework. Based on these estimates, an aggregate growth accounting analysis for the role of physical inputs and of technical progress in economic growth is presented. TFP estimates are further used to provide a detailed chronological characterization of the structural pattern of economic growth. Then, employing regression analysis, the correlation between technical progress and a set of selected policy-related macroeconomic variables is examined. This helps in identifying stylized facts that are useful for pinpointing specific strategies to accelerate growth. The paper concludes with some reflections on the sources of economic growth in Egypt during the period of study.

*Corresponding author.

CONTRIBUTIONS TO ECONOMIC ANALYSIS
VOLUME 278   ISSN: 0573-8555
DOI:10.1016/S0573-8555(06)78007-5

Keywords: economic development, technological change, economic growth, aggregate productivity

JEL classifications: O10, O30, O40

1. Introduction

Egypt's economic growth record has been uneven from the early 1960s until the late 1990s. During the period 1960–1998, the mean rate of growth was consistently high with an average of about 6 percent per annum. Nevertheless, that period exhibited recurrent fluctuations in the annual growth rate of real output because of frequent changes in the political environment and in socioeconomic conditions.

Early in 1960 and further in 1961, a big nationalization wave brought the public sector in control of around 90 percent of the total investment, in what became known as the "Socialist Revolution." In the First Five-Year Comprehensive Plan (1960–1965), the public sector dominated all nonagricultural activities. There was also significant expansion in the provision of free education and health services and in securing guaranteed jobs for all "secondary technical" schools and university graduates. The main lines of the socialist economic policy orientation prevailed until the next major political turning point: the *Infitah* (or opening-up) of President Sadat in 1974.

Under *Infitah*, starting in the late 1970s through the 1980s, there were new policies attempting to encourage private sector initiatives to develop and upgrade the infrastructure, to expand new urban and industrial clusters in the desert and to control population expansion. However, Egypt's institutional and management setup remained unchanged. Consequently, a number of these policies proved to be too expensive and required revision. Moreover, macroeconomic imbalances, which were partly brought about by the high costs of implementing these policies, threatened the stability of the economy.

The year 1991 witnessed a key turning point in Egypt's modern economic history with initiation of an economic reform and structural adjustment program (ERSAP). The program aimed at removing macroeconomic imbalances and promoting economic efficiency. This was envisaged through market-oriented strategies based on elimination of price distortions, on relieving government budget from hefty consumption subsidies, on foreign trade deregulation, on intensifying the role of private sector in economic activity, on financial and capital market reform and on encouraging foreign trade openness and improving Egypt's potentials for more solid foreign trade relations especially with the West. While the program was successful in reducing both internal and external imbalances, its impact on economic growth during 1991–1998 has been disappointing for the government and for the Egyptian people, as it could not raise the average growth rate back to the pre-1991 levels, despite modest recovery in the level of economic activity by the beginning of 1992/93.[1] The pivotal factor underlying this recovery appeared to hinge on increasing domestic supply of typically scarce foreign currency as a result of external debt forgiveness in return for Egypt's political role in the Gulf War. That is, the success of the reform measures and apparent stability of the macroeconomic framework were not sufficient to generate high sustainable levels of growth. This is not at all surprising. It has been known for quite some time that macroeconomic stabilization and reform are only necessary, but not sufficient prerequisites for growth (Fischer, 1993).

Recent years have witnessed extensive endeavors to find ways to salvage the Egyptian reform program by reviving the previous high rates of growth. Various attempts have focused on identifying different aggregate variables and policy instruments that are conducive to the creation of an enabling macroeconomic environment, which in turn would stimulate economic growth. In this paper, we use the traditional total factor productivity (TFP) methodology to analyze sources of aggregate economic growth in Egypt during the period from 1960 to 1998. We identify two sources of growth in output: one that is attributed to changes in physical inputs (capital and labor) and the other owing to disembodied technical innovations measured by growth in TFP.

The conventional TFP approach presupposes existence of prior information on factor shares in income. The information is typically available from one of two sources: detailed national accounts surveys or reliable studies that provide accurate estimates for the parameters of an aggregate production function (APF). Because of unavailability of regular time series data, both sources are inaccessible in the Egyptian case for the period that is examined. Alternatively, unlike other studies, we find ourselves reluctant to postulate arbitrary estimates for factor shares, which are liable to misrepresent the actual TFP changes. Instead, we introduce a simple integrated approach based on utilizing the Kalman filter (KF) algorithm (Hamilton, 1994). Our approach allows for simultaneous estimation of the parameters of the aggregate production technology and of TFP within a multi-equation system framework.

The main objective of the paper is to use the TFP estimates, derived from that system, to provide a detailed chronological characterization of the structural pattern of economic growth during 1960–1998. Then, employing regression analysis, we examine the correlation between technical progress and a set of selected policy-related macroeconomic variables. Understanding the relation between technical progress and these variables should be helpful in identifying stylized facts that may be useful for pinpointing specific strategies to accelerate growth.

The paper begins in Section 2 with a presentation of Kalman-filtered estimates for TFP and for the parameters of the APF. Based on these estimates, Section 3 presents an aggregate growth accounting analysis for the role of

---

[1] The average real rate of growth declined to about 4.6 percent per year during 1991–1998.

physical inputs and of technical progress in economic growth. The relation between technical progress and each of the selected macroeconomic indicators is
explored in Section 4 with the help of regression analysis. Section 5 concludes
with some reflections on the sources of economic growth in Egypt from 1960 to
1998. The paper includes two appendices. In Appendix A, we provide a short
review of the technique that is developed for the joint multi-equation system
estimation of TFP and the parameters of the APF by Kalman filtering. It also
includes a comparison between the system results vis-à-vis analogous estimates
from a standard single-equation regression and from a model based on an autoregressive moving average (ARMA) in the errors specification. Appendix B
documents the sources of data used in the study.

2. Total factor productivity estimates (1960–1998)

The standard neoclassical model presumes two potential sources of growth in
the aggregate amount of output. They can be identified by decomposing the
growth rate of real output into two parts.[2] The first is that which can be explained by the growth in the quantity of physical inputs used in production. The
second is a residual that is left after accounting for the growth in inputs. Under
the assumption of competitive markets, this residual growth is typically taken to
represent gains in output that can be explained by improvements in the level of
technological efficiency with which physical inputs are used. Hence, the residual
growth, dubbed TFP growth (TFPG), measures disembodied factor-neutral
technical progress that emanates from production process innovations that do
not necessarily require input quality improvements and/or from improvements
in the quality of inputs because of mutations of unknown and known origin in
the production process associated with exogenous impulses. Such impulses may
include changes in factors affecting the motivation of workers and the productivity of capital and changes in levels of education, health and standard of living
of members of the society. The residual growth would also contain measurement
and any other unknown statistical errors in the output or input data.

Putting it formally, we assume that output (Y) can be adequately approximated by a two-factor linearly homogenous Cobb–Douglas APF with Hicks-
neutral technical progress, which describes the relation between output and
factor inputs – capital stock (K) and labor force (L) – represented in physical
units. Under the assumption of competitive equilibrium and marginal changes in
output and factor inputs, the APF can be written in the form

$$Y_t = A_t K_t^\alpha L_t^{1-\alpha} \tag{1}$$

---

[2] The decomposition process is commonly known as growth accounting.

where the coefficient α, $0 < \alpha < 1$, is the share of capital in income and A_t denotes TFP. The exponents of capital and labor in the production function are set to add up to unity in compliance with the constant returns to scale (CRS) assumption. By dividing by L, taking natural logs and differentiating equation (1) totally with respect to time, we can express the production function in its intensive (per-worker) form

$$\dot{y}_t = a\,\dot{k}_t + \dot{a}_t \qquad (2)$$

such that the lower case letters, $\dot{y}$ and $\dot{k}$, measure the logarithmic growth rates of output (dy) and of capital (dk) per-worker (where $y = \ln(Y/L)$ and $k = \ln(K/L)$) and the variable $\dot{a}$ is an unobserved index of technical progress (TFPG) or dA/A where $a = \ln(A)$.

In standard applied aggregate growth accounting studies for individual countries, it is critical to establish *a priori* information on the size of the elasticity of output with respect to capital, α, before estimating TFP residually from a production function.[3] Information on the size of α is often postulated on the basis of estimates for capital's share of income obtained from different empirical studies and international evidence from developed as well as developing countries (Collins and Bosworth, 1996; Harrison, 1996; Maddison, 1987). Given the selected value of α, an estimate of TFPG in period t can be numerically computed as a residual from equation (2), after rearranging terms, conditional on observed (logarithmic) changes in the time series $\{y_t\}$ and $\{k_t\}$ over some sample period $t = 1, \ldots, T$, by using the formula

$$\dot{a}_t = \dot{y}_t - \alpha\dot{k}_t \qquad (2')$$

When the residually calculated TFPG estimates are averaged over the sample period, the mean gives a cumulated estimate of the effect of shifts in the production function over the relevant sample horizon that are not explained by the growth rates of inputs.

Apart from high probability of being biased (Chen, 1997), the estimates of TFPG derived from equation (2') are also sensitive to the arbitrarily predetermined size of the capital share. Alternatively, recent studies confirm that the TFP estimates are also highly sensitive to the chosen magnitude of α (Dowling and Summers, 1998). Naturally, such findings cast doubt on the efficiency and robustness of estimates of technical progress derived using the conventional growth accounting methodology.

---

[3] Regression models have been used occasionally, as an alternative to growth accounting exercises, to estimates TFP. In such models, TFP estimates are based on the size of the estimated constant term and/or time trend from an APF regression. Such estimates are usually subject to several statistical limitations including sensitivity to selected sample period and multicollinearity between explanatory variables (Dowling and Summers, 1998).

We think that these limitations may be overcome by simultaneous estimation of TFP and the parameters of the underlying APF (Solow, 1957). In this way, subjective determination of the value of α is completely circumvented. More specifically, the innovation of this paper is estimating jointly both unobserved TFP and the share of capital income (α) using observed output and capital per-worker time series. The estimation is based on a state-space representation of the multi-equation system composed of the APF, equation (1) and of a process explaining the temporal dynamics of TFP. Sequential estimates of a_t for the period 1960–1998 are derived from the state-space model by means of the KF algorithm. We present a review of this technique in Appendix A.

TFP is estimated with annual time-series data for Egypt on output and capital per-worker during 1960–1998. The series y_t and k_t are obtained by dividing real GDP and physical capital stock, throughout the selected sample period, by the number of employed workers. This number is determined by adjusting the total labor force by the unemployment rate in each year. Appendix B lists the sources of data on real GDP, real capital stock, total labor force, unemployment rate and on the other variables that are used in the rest of the study.

The successive KF estimates for (logged) TFP measured up to a scalar from 1960–1998 are portrayed in Figure 1. Each estimated value for a_t represents the shift factor of the APF in a given year.[4] Following Solow (1957), the estimates of a_t can be employed to construct an APF that is represented by drawing a scatter plot of y_t-a_t against k_t, with a_t valid only up to a scalar measure. The APF is sketched in Figure 2. The diagram discloses a remarkably smooth and tight fit for the estimated functional relation.

Figure 2 reveals two striking characteristics of the APF for Egypt during the period 1960–1998. First, the plotted function exhibits visible evidence of diminishing marginal returns to capital, k, which is marked by an apparent concave curvature. Second, a set of observations in the plot tend to lie distinctly higher, parallel and toward the right of the points in the main scatter such that values of capital per capita (k) around 6 seem to match with more than one value for y-a. In addition, it appears that these maverick points encompass observations pertaining to the last 8 years in our sample (1991–1998).

It is perhaps important to note that the displacement of the observations for 1991–1998 cannot be attributed to an upward shift in the APF, as any upward shift in that function is already totally taken into account by means of the variable, A_t. Solow (1957) provides three possible views on the sources of such displacement, a couple of which seem relevant here. One explanation is related to the possibility of existence of measurement errors in the time series involved in

---

[4]In general, the level of TFP *per se*, as opposed to TFPG, is not analytically useful since a_t is determined arbitrarily. Hence, our interest in the TFP level series is confined to examining changes in its trend, to identifying disturbances and upturn and downturn points in the course of its historical evolution and, naturally, to computing TFPG.

Figure 1.   Kalman Filter estimates for TFP (a) (1960–1998)

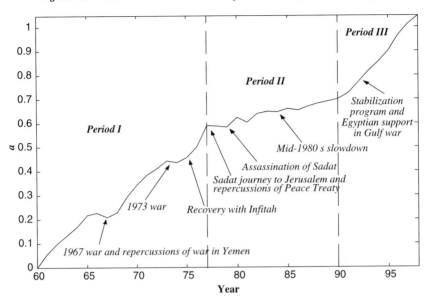

Figure 2.   Aggregate production function

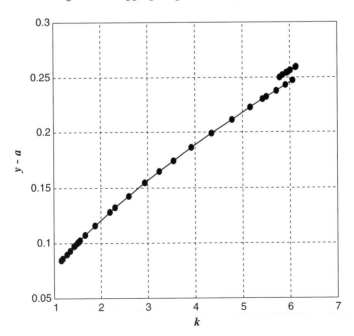

estimation, especially those with respect to physical capital. Undoubtedly, such errors are highly probable due to the crudeness of the methodology used in the construction of physical capital stock (Nehru and Dhareshwar, 1994) and/or to problems generated in the process of aggregation of physical inputs.

Aside from errors in measurement, another explanation pertains to overestimation of the productivity increase because of the unusual decline or underestimation of physical capital input services per-worker. The continued contraction in aggregate investment expenditure that started a few years before the mid-1980s through the early 1990s – partly in response to the decrease in government investment in public sector companies in view of rising fiscal deficits – led to a decline in the stock of capital. Moreover, two years during the period 1991–1998 (specifically 1993 and 1996) witnessed marked increases in the level of employment to popularize newly instated governments.[5] This resulted in a sharp fall in the capital-labor ratio, k. Yet, ostensibly limited labor efficiency may cause a fall in k to deceptively represent a rise in the productivity of capital.

Additionally, speeding up the pace of the privatization program in the early 1990s eventually led to an increase in the supply of shares available on the market (EFG-Hermes, 1997). Hence, stock prices started tumbling in mid-October 1994 and continued to fall until June 1996. Throughout most of this period, many trading companies were considerably undervalued, with the stocks of several privatized companies trading at prices below their initial public offering price. However, cheap deals and falling prices at the time were still not sufficient to induce the public to increase their demand for stocks. It is likely that underestimation of capital inputs, resulting from undervaluation of stock prices, led to overestimation of productivity increases, as reflected in the displacement of the 1991–1998 observations in the production function scatter diagram (Figure 2).

3. Role of input changes and technical progress in economic growth

Following the mainstream literature, we assume two sources for growth in output; the first is associated with growth in physical inputs and the second with technical progress. In this section, the contribution of physical inputs and technical progress to the process of economic growth in Egypt from 1960–1998 is examined within an aggregate growth accounting framework.

3.1. Role of physical inputs

During the period 1960–1998, the annual rate of real GDP growth averaged 5.90 percent. In that period, the growth of GDP was characterized by considerable volatility and frequent fluctuations around its average with values ranging

---

[5] In 1993 and 1996, new governments came into office. Dr. Sidki's government was reinstated in 1993 and in 1996, government responsibilities were transferred to a new Prime Minister, Dr. El Ganzouri.

between a minimum of −0.25 percent (1967) and a maximum of 15.44 percent (1976), with a standard deviation of 3.20 percent.

Analysis of the impacts of changes in TFP and in physical inputs on output growth over a relatively long time horizon requires cautious periodization that permits identification of broadly homogenous subperiods during which the main drivers of growth are rather stable. The high frequency and volatility of changes in real GDP generate extreme unevenness in the pattern of economic performance that precludes the possibility of relying on aggregate growth to dichotomize the entire period, 1960–1998, meaningfully into homogenous subperiods.

Alternatively, important interactions among technical progress, aggregate growth and sociopolitical development processes make it reasonable to rely on TFP to provide a benchmark for periodization. Despite its smooth positive trend, the TFP graph displays two main breaks in aggregate productivity in 1977 and 1991 (Figure 1).[6] They divide the entire period into three principal subperiods: 1960–1976, 1977–1990 and 1991–1998. While each of the three subperiods witnessed some turning points, the behavioral pattern of TFP seems uniform within each one of them. We adopt this periodization for our growth accounting study.

Table 1 and Figures 3–5 display the behavior of output (y), labor and capital (k) in the three subperiods. With few exceptions, Table 1 as well as Figure 4 show that average employment growth during the whole period 1960–1998 is noticeably stable, with only marginal increase from one subperiod to the next.[7] Excluding the extreme values of 1976 as well as 1977, the average employment growth is even more stagnant with a relatively small standard deviation of less than 1.1 percent.[8] The other peaks and troughs in the employment growth series are relatively infrequent, mainly arising because of unanticipated shocks (e.g. the 1967 war) or changes in the political environment (e.g. those causing the employment increases of 1993 and 1996).

There are several reasons underlying steady employment growth rates in spite of rapid population expansion and high fertility rates. One reason is due to

---

[6]The year 1977 designates the beginning of a period of generous government social and investment spending following the bread riots of January 17–18, 1977, whereas 1991 marks the beginning for the implementation of ERSAP.

[7]The average rate of growth of employment during 1960–1998 is about 2.26 percent (with values ranging between −3.34 percent in 1976 and 7.19 percent in the following year) with a modest standard deviation of 1.61 percent.

[8]Employment rates for 1976 and 1986 are obtained from the Population Census (PC). The rest of the data in the series come from the Labor Force Sample Survey (LFSS) (Moursi and Kamel, 1989). PC and LFSS data are not comparable. To overcome the incompatibility without losing pertinent information embodied in the PC data for the two census years, we adopt the following procedure. Adaptive exponential smoothing bias minimizing forecasts for census years are estimated using the combined LFSS/PC unemployment series. We use the *forecasted* estimates for census years, 1976 and 1986, in lieu of census figures from which the magnitude of the forecast differs significantly from the corresponding actual PC data.

Table 1. *Annual and average growth rates of output and inputs in selected sub-periods[a]*

	Period I (1961–1976)	Period II (1977–1989)	Period III (1990–1998)
Average (trend) growth (percent) of			
Output	4.88	6.08	4.55
Labor	1.96	2.07	2.86
Capital	5.01	10.08	2.38
Output per-worker	2.92	4.02	1.69
Capital per-worker	3.05	8.01	−0.49
Annual average growth (percent) of			
Output	5.74	6.40	4.57
Labor	1.92	2.45	2.61
Capital	5.95	10.06	2.80
Output per-worker	3.81	3.95	1.96
Capital per-worker	4.03	7.61	0.19

[a]All averages are calculated as a simple arithmetic mean.

Figure 3. *Real output (GDP) per-worker growth (1960–1998)*

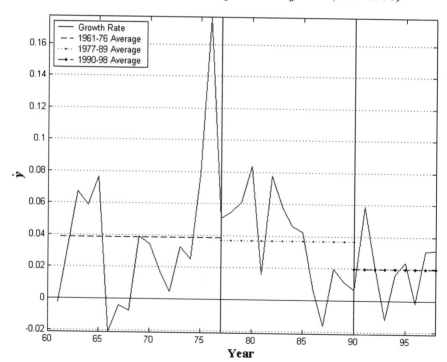

Figure 4.   Labor growth (1960–1998)

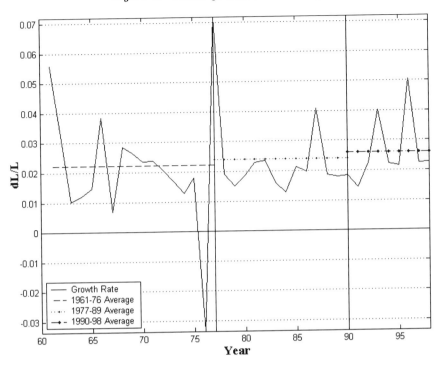

underestimation of employment figures, which include civilian labor only and omit military force employment and consequently its fluctuations. In addition, the extension of the compulsory schooling program – though largely unenforced – caused a decline in the number of children who are employed. The decrease of children participation in the labor market has recurrently slowed down employment growth especially during the 1970s and the early 1980s. In the 1990s, Egypt's commitment to structural reform had a significant effect on employment growth. Though the private sector was given the chance to play a more dominant role in the country's development program, its share in employment increased only marginally because of a limited supply of skilled human resources. Slow employment growth in that period was aggravated by fiscal budget problems that almost completely hampered the government's historical commitment to hire all fresh graduates in context of what is known as the employment drive.

Two conclusions may be drawn in light of the above discussion. First, the stability of average employment growth leads to significant covariability between output and output per-worker and between capital and capital-labor ratio growth rates. Hence, abstracting from productivity fluctuations, the growth of physical capital would be sufficient to characterize the behavioral structure of real output changes. Second, stability of employment growth accompanied by

In the last few years of the first subperiod, the level of investment started to rise again and remained comparatively high on average until the mid-1980s. Investment growth stimulated new production opportunities. The reasons for the increase in investment primarily included implementation of a number of proinvestment laws within the context of *Infitah* as well as an increase in the country's hard currency resources because of rising world petroleum prices, a regional boom that encouraged inflow of workers' remittances from abroad, reopening the Suez Canal and expansion in tourism. The rise in inflow of Arab aid and capital also permitted a large increase in investment. Thus, by 1988, investment reached a peak of 34 percent of GDP. The investment surge, translated into a rise in physical capital growth between 1973 up until 1985 (Figure 6), led to expansion in GDP growth. However, toward the end of the second subperiod (from the mid-1980s to 1990), investment started to fall sharply because of the collapse of international petroleum prices and domestic market distortions that overburdened the government budget. At the same time, these distortions undermined the efficient allocation of investment across sectors and activities. Again, the fall in investment was reflected in the decline in the growth rates of capital stock as well as real output.

Conversely, the third subperiod marked a fundamental reversal in the relation between capital expansion and output growth in contrast with the previous subperiod. During 1991–1998, the rate of capital growth relatively slowed down because of several reasons. Among these reasons are the sharp reductions in public investment associated with implementation of the reform program and contraction in private investment as a consequence of low domestic savings.[10] Nevertheless, despite its low level, GDP growth started to rise by 1992/1993 (see Figure 6), mainly because of enhancements in TFP that were presumably associated with implementation of the stabilization program.

The above discussion suggests that large investment allowances may frequently have promoted economic growth during the period 1960–1998. In Egypt, there has always been a domestic resource gap. The discrepancy between domestic savings and investment has usually been bridged by external financial resources. Considering these facts, it sounds plausible, at first glance, to infer that higher levels of investment, which may be achieved through raising the domestic saving rate and encouraging foreign financial capital inflow, would result in an immediate increase in economic growth.

Indeed, it is rather hard to imagine that such an inference could be questionable. After all, most technical innovations are in a way embodied in some new forms of machinery, equipment and acquisitions that can only be made available through accumulation of investment (Solow, 1957). Our results,

---

[10] The fall in investment is partly seen as an outcome of lower inflow of workers' remittances from abroad and poor performance of the export sector.

however, give an unambiguous impression that accumulation of physical capital – though necessary – is not always sufficient to sustain efficient growth. Diminishing returns to physical capital (per-worker), illustrated by the curvature of the production function in Figure 2, reveals that increasing investment and thereby capital per-worker is not always conducive to growth. It also raises serious concern that the capital-labor ratio often may have exceeded its maximum efficient threshold.

The above findings suggest that aggregate economic efficiency in Egypt would not necessarily be hampered by decreasing capital intensity. This evidence downplays arguments that attribute slow growth to investment deficiencies and physical capital shortages.[11] Nevertheless, it accentuates the importance of addressing problems underlying unproductive investment and poor economic and institutional management of the existing capital stock as the crucial element constraining growth in Egypt.[12] Our results dwell, therefore, on the central role that TFPG and the factors that affect it have to play in the process of economic growth.

3.2. Role of technical progress

While TFP is now playing an increasingly vital role as a major source of development in the Egyptian economy,[13] from 1960 until 1990, the contribution of TFP to aggregate production growth was negligible. However, with the implementation of ERSAP in 1991, technical progress became the dominant contributor to real GDP growth during the 1990s. We examine that contribution in this section.

Table 2 is more or less self-explanatory. It records the large contribution of capital to growth (especially in (sub)period II) and provides further justification for diminishing returns to capital (Figure 2). It also reveals that the considerably larger role of TFP in output growth is a direct consequence of the sharp decrease in the contribution of physical capital rather than a result of the deterioration in the share of labor in growth, which actually almost doubled between the two (sub) periods II and III.

Figure 7 shows that during the period 1960–1998, TFP was sensitive not only to variation in the level of input growth but also, more importantly, to changes in the aggregate economic and political environment. The diagram shows that temporary dips in TFP coincided with political disturbances resulting from (a) the repercussions of military involvement in Yemen, (b) the two major wars in

---

[11] It is interesting, for example, to observe the similarity of output growth rates for the subperiod between 1967–1976 and the subperiod between 1990–1998 together with the marked dissimilarity of capital per-worker growth rates across the same subperiods, really helping us appreciate the significance of this evidence.

[12] Such problems include choice of unsuitable and/or outdated machinery, deficient maintenance policies for equipment and incompetent laborers who are unable to deal with modern technology.

[13] Recently, Easterly and Levine (2001) document the critical role of TFP and argue that it accounts for most cross-country differences in growth and income.

Table 2.   Input and TFP contributions to economic growth

	Period I (1960–1976)	Period II (1977–1989)	Period III (1990–1998)
Contribution of labor to GDP growth (percent)	0.69	0.73	1.01
Share of labor in GDP growth (percent)	14.10	11.94	22.12
Contribution of capital to GDP growth (percent)	3.25	6.54	1.54
Share of capital in GDP growth (percent)	66.57	107.45	33.88
Annual average growth of TFP (percent)	3.48	1.42	3.98
Growth of TFP (percent)	2.96	0.89	4.58
Contribution of TFP to GDP growth (percent)	0.94	−1.18	2.00
Share of TFP in GDP growth (percent)	19.33	−19.40	44.00

1967 and 1973 and (c) the cold-shoulder treatment and withdrawal of investment inflows from Arab countries to Egypt and assassination of President Sadat by fundamentalist militants in the aftermath of the Camp David Peace Treaty with Israel. The graph suggests, however, that productivity is influenced by economic forces,which, unlike political events, are liable to have somewhat more lasting impact on TFP. The economic slowdown of the 1980s – instigated by the decline in petroleum and tourism revenues and Arab aid and by investment cuts – had a lingering effect on TFP during 1977–1989. Alternatively, recovery with *Infitah* and then the reform program accompanied by increase in hard currency availability, because of debt forgiveness, sent TFP rising a little bit above the pre-1977 levels. These observations are underscored in Figure 7, which shows that the average annual TFPG remained almost the same during 1960–1976 and 1990–1998, despite serious military turbulence that occurred in (sub) period I.

Moreover, looking at Figure 6 and Table 2, we observe that the first and third (sub) periods were characterized by relatively higher shares of TFP in GDP growth; and unlike the second (sub) period (II), the rate of output growth exceeded that of the capital in both (sub) periods (I and III). Our observation discloses an inverse relation between the contributions of capital and TFP to output growth, at least within the period under examination.

The estimates of TFPG, portrayed in Figure 7, provide further knowledge about the behavioral characteristics of technical progress that are not discernible

Figure 7. TFP growth (1960–1998)

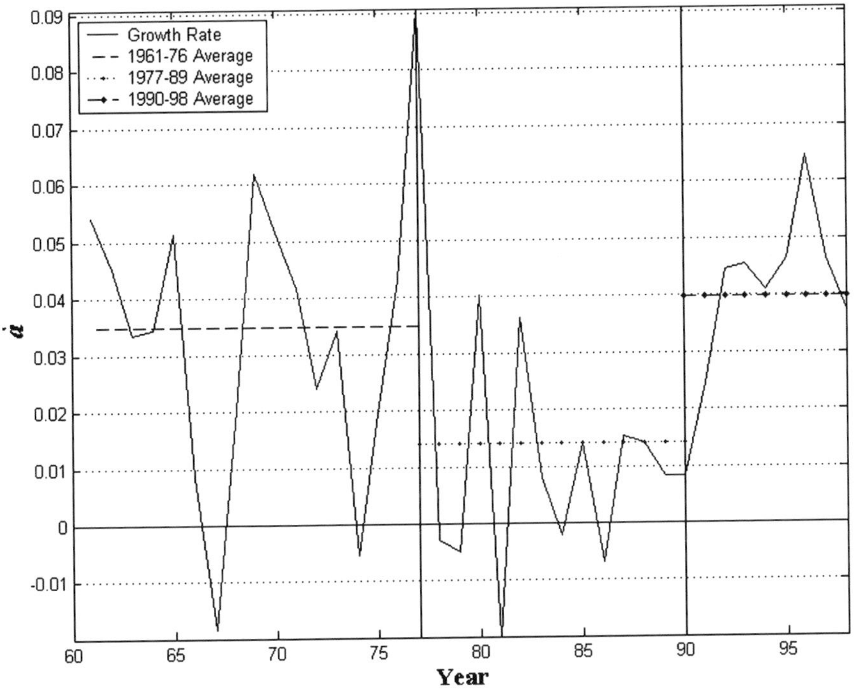

from an examination of the TFP levels alone. We start by presenting three stylized facts that are deduced from the observed behavior of technical progress during 1960–1998.

First, despite an abrupt decline in the average TFPG during the economic slowdown of the late 1970s and the 1980s (Figure 7), on the whole, the dynamics of technical progress appear to be smooth and normal. Normality is confirmed by the rejection of significant skewness and kurtosis in the TFPG series. In addition, TFPG is stationary during 1960–1998, with random fluctuations around a constant mean of approximately 2.83 percent. The stationarity of TFPG is confirmed by means of a Dickey–Fuller (DF) test. The test coefficient and some basic descriptive statistics for technical progress are reported in Table 3. Second, TFPG is uncorrelated with the amount of available capital per-worker. This is revealed by means of an excessively small coefficient of determination (approximately 0.67 percent) obtained from a linear regression of capital per-worker, k, on TFPG and a constant term. Third, because of variations in the relative contribution of inputs, output growth may not always be positively associated with TFPG.

These facts are important for understanding the nature of the contribution of technical progress to aggregate growth. The stationarity of TFPG unveils information about its behavior when the economy is temporarily subjected to

Table 3. Descriptive statistics for TFPG

Statistic	Estimate	Statistic	Estimate
Mean (percent)	2.829	Kurtosis[a]	−0.939
Standard error of mean (percent)	2.552		(0.953)
Skewness[a]	0.113	t-test (with constant term)	−4.269
	(0.784)		

[a]Significance level reported in parentheses.

unanticipated disturbances. On average, the effects of transient exogenous shocks (e.g. war and assassination of President Sadat) on technical progress are typically short-lived and tend to dissipate quickly, in spite of their considerable impact on TFPG. Thus, while ephemeral impulses associated with introduction of technological innovations or new economic policy (e.g. announcement of *Infitah*) might have a big impact on technical progress, they would undoubtedly fail to leave an everlasting impression on the average level of TFPG. Indeed, TFPG series, during the period 1960–1998 incorporate only two AOs (in 1976 and 1980) with no encounters of either TC or LS. The small number of AOs, present in TFPG series, rules out the possibility of perpetual introduction of technological or institutional improvements during the 39 years under consideration.

Finally, comparing Figures 1 and 7 emphasizes the correspondence between the major turning points in the TFP and TFPG series. The smooth trending pattern characterizing the behavior of TFP, however, suggests that the series could be useful to identify *major* upturns and downturns in technical progress. So although the nonstationary nature of *a* masks the specific details pertaining to the structural behavior of technical progress, the TFP series should be useful for identifying turning points associated with main technological shocks and breaks in production processes. This supports our earlier decision to employ TFP for periodization to avoid *ad hoc* splitting-up of the sample period into subperiods.

The absence of a significant positive correlation between GDP changes and TFPG indicates that net shifts in the APF (that averaged approximately 2.83 percent per year over the entire period 1960–1998) are to a great extent associated with changes in the output scale. This result is a bit discouraging. In a sense, it is suggestive of the impotence of Egyptian economic policy (implemented under both planned and market-oriented systems) and of recent reform measures to fully exploit technical progress as a vehicle for promoting economic growth. In the following section, we try to identify different economy-wide variables that, if appropriately controlled, could contribute to raising TFPG and, hence, assert its importance as a key element for motivating the aggregate production and growth processes.

4. Relation between technical progress and selected macroeconomic indicators

The growth literature cannot propose compelling theoretical justifications regarding the selection of a unique group of determinants for growth. Thus, the process of choosing specific explanatory variables from the set of possible determinants of growth has been essentially based on results from an ever-growing body of empirical cross-country inquiries (see for example, Barro, 1991; Barro and Lee, 1993; Barro and Sala-i-Martin, 1995; Sachs and Warner 1997, Makdisi *et al.*, 2000; O'Connell and Ndulu 2000).

We follow a conventional approach for selecting the control variables for our technical progress equation. Our choices come from a collection of economy-wide control variables proposed by other researchers, which are known to have more or less robust effects on growth, and, at the same time, have purportedly played an important role in shaping up the productive performance of the Egyptian economy since the 1960s.[14] No causal order is implied by our choice of explanatory variables for the regressions. The dearth of specific information about socioeconomic forces that simultaneously affect growth and the selected regressors precludes any attempt to impose arbitrary assumptions that may erroneously enforce structural causal relations between the dependent and the independent variables. The remainder of this section presents the estimation results for the TFPG equation regression using the sample period 1960–1998.

Our regression model considers six aggregate explanatory variables: general government consumption (*GOV*), exports (*EXP*) and imports (*IMP*) of goods and services, gross domestic fixed investment (*GDFI*), foreign aid (*AID*) and credit to the private sector (*CRPRIV*), each defined as a ratio to GDP.[15] Inflation (*INFLAT*) is incorporated in the regression to represent macroeconomic stability. With the exception of inflation, the regressors are expressed in logarithmic first differences. The (logarithmic) change in population ($\Delta \ln POP$), two dummy variables (*DWAR* and *D91*) and a constant term are added to the list of regressors. The dummy variable *DWAR* that takes on the value 1 in the war years (1967 and 1973) and 0 otherwise, is supposed to capture the destabilizing effects of war exigencies. The other dummy variable, *D91* – set to unity

---

[14] Brock and Durlauf (2001) maintain that a fundamental problem in growth analysis – referred to as open-endedness – relates to absence of a formal approach for choosing a unique set of explanatory variables that must be included in regressions. At the present, there does not seem to be a satisfactory way to deal with this problem. Nevertheless, we think that selection of regressors based on country-specific growth-related experience should provide some justification for our choices.

[15] It would have been important to include budget deficit and real interest rate in the list of explanatory variables that are likely to be correlated with technical progress. This might have allowed us to capture the crowding-out effect on private investment by public spending on public investment projects and by current expenditures. We expect such effect to be important given the weight of the public sector and the scope of government intervention in the Egyptian economy. We are unable to introduce these variables in the regression model, however, in view of the unavailability of the required data for a significant subset of the estimation horizon.

Table 4. OLS regression estimates for aggregate variables (1961–1998)

Parameter	Value	Parameter	Value
Δln GOV/Y	−0.111 (−2.128)	INFLAT	−0.003 (−4.699)
Δln EXP/Y	0.082 (2.447)	Δln POP	0.007 (0.146)
Δln IMP/Y	−0.131 (−3.164)	DWAR	−0.028 (−2.358)
Δln GDFI/Y	0.091 (3.233)	D91	0.027 (3.618)
Δln AID/Y	0.007 (2.309)	Constant	0.049 (7.509)
Δln CRPRIV/Y	−0.077 (−4.449)		

Note: Robust t-statistics in parentheses.

in 1991 and 0 in other years[16] – is designed to account for the influence on technical progress of introducing reform measures at the beginning of the 1990s.

The regression is estimated by means of the ordinary least squares (OLS) method.[17] The estimated coefficients and relevant robust t-statistics are exhibited in Table 4. The estimated R^2 (percent) for the regression is 59.13. In general, the estimated relationship between the explanatory variables in the regression and technical progress are economically sensible. With the exception of population growth, the reported t-ratios are all statistically significantly different from 0 at conventional levels.

Tables 5a and 5b present a battery of statistical specification and stability tests for the aggregate indicators regression (Johnston and DiNardo, 1997). Overall, the test results support the rejection of misspecification and of instability of parameters of the estimated equation.

First, the one-step forecasts for the period 1985–1992, reported in Table 5a, reveal that the standard error range about the technical progress forecast, $\hat{a}$, in each year includes the actual value of TFPG. Second, the Ramsey RESET test – substantiates rejection of specification error.[18] Third, Table 5b records Hansen test statistics for joint and for individual coefficients stability. The tests could not reject the null hypotheses of joint and individual parameter constancy.[19] Fourth, panel 8. i, Figure 8, sketches the recursive residuals and relevant ± 2.0 standard error (SE) bands for the regression. Except for 1993, the recursive residuals lie

---

[16] This dummy has been first assumed to take the value 1 in all years starting from the implementation of the reform program in 1991 till the end of the period in 1998; however, its coefficient was insignificant. The significance of the coefficient of the dummy variable, as defined in the text, precisely reflects the instantaneous effect of policy changes introduced in 1991 and confirms further that reform is a continuous process which warrants successive and sustained measures that have not been undertaken by the Egyptian government.

[17] A DF statistic is computed to test for a unit root in the time series of each explanatory variable. All the test results (not reported) significantly reject nonstationarity of the selected control variables.

[18] The RESET test is implemented using only $\hat{a}^2$.

[19] The p-values for all the reported stability statistics could not reject the null hypothesis as they exceed the top significance level (0.20) for the test.

Table 5a. *One-step forecasts analysis and parameter constancy and specification tests[a]*

Year	$\dot{a}$	$\hat{\dot{a}}$	$\dot{a} - \hat{\dot{a}}$	Forecast SE	t-Value
1985	0.014	0.024	−0.010	0.020	−0.480
1986	−0.007	0.007	−0.014	0.023	−0.610
1987	0.015	0.006	0.009	0.030	0.313
1988	0.014	0.001	0.013	0.024	0.554
1989	0.008	0.017	−0.009	0.021	−0.414
1990	0.008	0.022	−0.014	0.023	−0.614
1991	0.024	0.019	0.006	0.025	0.224
1992	0.045	0.007	0.037	0.022	1.665

Tests of Parameter Constancy (significance level in square brackets):
(i) Over 1985–1992: Chow test statistic $F(8,16) = 0.319$ [0.947].
(ii) Over 1961–1998: RESET test statistic $F(1,27) = 1.686$ [0.205].
[a]One-step forecasts are estimated based on the observations from 1960–1998.

Table 5b. *Hansen's instability test*

Test	Statistic	Test	Statistic	Test	Statistic	Test	Statistic
Joint	1.779	GOV/Y	0.046	$INFLAT$	0.055	$CPRIV/Y$	0.075
Variance	0.052	EXP/Y	0.052	AID/Y	0.161	WAR	0.079
Constant	0.079	IMP/Y	0.137	$GDFI/Y$	0.204	$D91$	0.041

between the SE bands, thereby corroborating the previous evidence on parameter stability. The same result is again confirmed by a Chow test (see Table 5a).

Finally, panels 8 (a–h) (Figure 8) portray the time varying parameter (TVP) estimates and ±2.0 SE bands for the right side variables in the regression.[20] A solid line is drawn in each panel to mark the level of the relevant OLS coefficient reported in Table 4. As expected, the diagrams show negligible time variation for almost all the estimates of the explanatory variables in the regression within the sample period.

The above statistical tests provide support for using the OLS results. Hence, they are employed to explain the relation between TFPG and the selected aggregate variables.

During 1960–1998, public expenditures were generally allocated to pay wages and salaries for a massive number of civil employees and to support public sector industries and large-scale development projects (e.g. the High Dam and heavy industry projects). Furthermore, large fiscal expenditures were allocated to meet social welfare targets (e.g. subsidizing basic commodities consumed by people in low-income brackets and securing social services for a considerable

---

[20] The TVPs are estimated by means of the ordinary KF technique.

Figure 8.   Time-varying parameter (TVP) and recursive residuals for the TFPG regression.

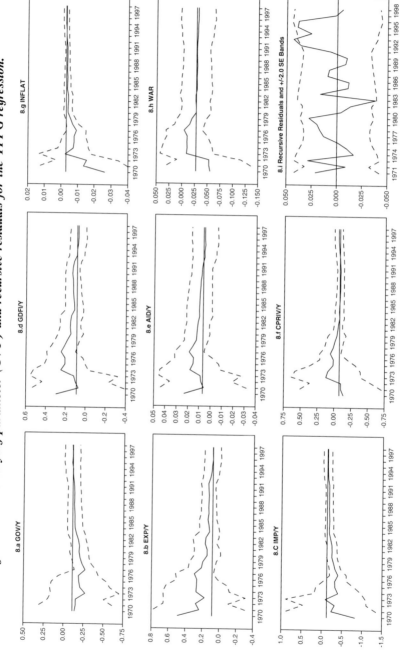

fraction of the population). Thus, our measure of government consumption is likely to pick up the adverse effects of distortions associated with nonproductive fiscal expenditures and with the size of government (Barro and Sala-i-Martin, 1995). Table 4 depicts a significant negative correlation between government consumption (as a share of GDP) and TFPG with a large estimated coefficient that is equal to −0.11. To offset this negative effect, the government ought to consider modifying the current structure of fiscal spending. Government expenditures must be geared more toward productive uses (e.g. investments in infrastructure, decentralized institutional development programs and scientific research) and less toward distortive uses (e.g. excessive government employment and conspicuous fiscal consumption).

Foreign trade openness – measured as the ratio of imports and exports of goods and services to GDP – is frequently cited as a determinant of growth that is capable of promoting improvements in economic performance through stimulation of price competitiveness and technological diffusion and spillover benefits. Because most countries in the MENA region have high trade ratios, Makdisi *et al.* (2000) argue that openness may not be an appropriate explanatory variable in growth regressions. Instead, they suggest using Sachs and Warner's (1997) index that rates a country's openness on the basis of a set of criteria related to the levels of tariff and nontariff barriers (NTBs) and to the degree of free trade and state control. We do not feel that Sachs and Warner's index can be accurately computed in the case of Egypt. One reason is related to the paucity as well as the inaccuracy of the available data on NTBs. Instead, we capture the relation between foreign trade and technical progress by introducing export and import ratios, EXP/Y and IMP/Y, separately in the regression. This dichotomy allows us to take account of differences in the contribution of export and import ratios to TFPG arising from variance in the economic behavior of export and import industries.

The negative correlation between IMP/Y and TFPG (Table 4) is interpreted as follows. On one side, the share of consumer goods in total imports is quite high, especially after the *Infitah*. On the other side, imports of physical capital goods, in the form of machinery and equipment, are often outdated. Therefore, while capital imports carry little technological spillover benefits, high-tech imported consumer goods compete viciously with domestic production to the extent of restricting the economy's production and technical capabilities.

In contrast, export promotion compels domestic producers to adopt progressive modes of production to penetrate world markets. In addition, a portion of hard currency export revenues is frequently recycled to promote efficiency in exporting industries with further favorable impacts on productivity. These gains encourage technological spillover and know-how benefits for other domestic producers. Together, all these spell significant positive association between TFPG and the export ratio, as demonstrated in Table 4.

Egypt is one of the largest recipients of foreign financial assistance (*AID*) that has been needed to bridge the gap between the supply and demand for hard currency. Apart from being used to promote large economic development projects and welfare programs, foreign aid funds are regularly utilized to finance importation, particularly of basic staples (e.g. wheat), to build up foreign reserves, to stabilize the exchange rate and to ease balance of payments crises. Table 4 illustrates that foreign aid share in GDP is positively related to TFPG with a coefficient estimate of less than 0.01. This weak relation seems somewhat puzzling, bearing in mind Egypt's prominent position as a recipient of aid. The result, however, confirms that some foreign assistance funds directed to the government or to the public sector are used unproductively. Frequently, bureaucratic and red tape constraints prevent effective utilization of these funds.[21]

The importance of the private sector in Egypt varied during 1960–1998 because of changes in the country's political orientation. The changes are reflected on the amount of credit available to the private sector as a ratio to GDP $(CRPRIV/Y)$.[22] From 1960 to 1980, $CRPRIV/Y$ was fairly low as public sector companies dominated production activities and received most of the available credit. Liberalization measures that were launched in the early 1980s gave a larger and more pivotal role for private sector investment in the economy. Accordingly, $CRPRIV/Y$ increased, reaching a peak in 1998. The increase was not entirely benign. A great deal of that credit was indulged in unproductive high-returns activities including investment in the construction and contracting industry, in speculation on land and real estate and in importation of luxury goods. Moreover, corruption, lax judicial system and absence of a regulatory mechanism to control capital outflows permitted some business tycoons to illegally transfer a part of the credit funds abroad. Such transfers had perverse effects on economic performance as well as on the credibility of the private business environment in Egypt. We find, therefore, that the private sector credit to GDP ratio and technical progress were significantly negatively correlated with an estimated coefficient of −0.08 (Table 4).

According to Fischer (1993), inflation ($INFLAT$) reduces growth through its negative effect on investment and productivity expansion. In addition, he argues that the inflation rate unequivocally provides a reasonable measure for uncertainty of the macroeconomic environment. During 1960–1998, the average annual inflation rate in Egypt (measured by the consumer price index (CPI)) was approximately 10.0 percent with a large variance of 49.1 percent. The economic slowdown of the 1980s was accompanied by a sharp rise in the annual inflation rate, reaching a maximum of 23.9 percent in 1986. From the mid-1980s until

---

[21] For example, the European Union (EU) recently warned the Egyptian government of the possibility of withdrawing foreign assistance funds intended to develop the Egyptian industrial sector – in compliance with the EU – Egypt Partnership Agreement – if Egypt failed to utilize these funds productively.

[22] According to World Bank (2000), for some countries $CPRIV$ may include credit to public enterprises. We have no clue if this were the case for Egypt. Anyway, we assume that the share of credit to public sector firms in $CPRIV$ is negligible.

1998, the annual inflation rate gradually fell to 4.3 percent in 1998. On average, the level of inflation and its variance were above what would have been desired for providing a stable economic environment. For instance, uncertainty proceeding from large inflation-induced distortions in the market for foreign exchange frequently spawned increases in the country's real exchange rate. The real exchange rate increases led to a reallocation of factors toward production of nontradable goods and against export promotion. Such pattern of resource allocation reduced Egyptian producers' competitiveness in both international and domestic markets with obvious negative effects on productivity and domestic investment.

Table 4 shows that inflation is significantly – though weakly – inversely correlated with TFPG. The estimated coefficient of *INFLAT* implies that a rise in the yearly inflation rate of 100 percent is associated with a modest decrease in the rate of technical progress of only 0.3 percent per annum. It is possible that the low correlation is a statistical illusion caused by the deliberate doctoring of CPI data to keep official inflation figures below actual levels as a means of assertion of political and social stability.[23]

Apart from that, during most of the period under consideration, the prices of essential inputs and of basic goods and services were subjected to extensive subsidization and/or mandatory control measures purportedly designed to achieve national welfare targets. The rental values of agricultural land and housing were subjected to similar controls. In addition, the large fraction of labor force holding tenured jobs in government and public sector and labor laws that nearly prohibit dismissal of employees, except in highly unlikely situations, reduced the variability of wages and household labor income. Together with price controls, stability of income and wages may have restrained volatility of the inflation rate, which, in turn, artificially reduced macroeconomic uncertainty and hence the degree of correlation between price fluctuations and TFPG.

GDFI (as a percentage of GDP) contains public and private investments in plant and equipment, in industrial buildings, schools, hospitals, construction of roads and railways, etc. and in land improvements. These investments play a catalytic role in facilitating the development process. The productivity of public and private investments differs. It would have been more interesting to capture the selective impact of those differences on TFPG. Unavailability of suitable data rules out this option. According to our regression results, the expansion of domestic fixed investments has the strongest positive correlation with technical

---

[23] Perhaps the following data may help – at least in part – substantiate this allegation. We note that during the last quarter in 2003, annualized CPI inflation was about 3.54 percent according to official estimates (IMF, 2004). Meanwhile, Information and Decision Support Center (IDSC) (unpublished) estimates reveal that (annualized) increase in prices of basic food commodities such as rice, flour, oil, sugar and tea reached about 64.09 percent, 15.18 percent, 24.37 percent, 26.42 percent and 27.38 percent, respectively, for the same quarter.

progress. The relatively large parameter estimate confirms the importance of investing in infrastructure and new machinery and equipment for encouraging TFPG (Solow, 1957).

It is usually proposed that the increase of population (*POP*) has an unfavorable effect on technical progress, especially in developing countries. The main intuition behind this proposition is that with a fixed amount of resources (land, capital, savings, etc.), the growth of population would immediately imply fewer resources per person and, thus, lower growth potential. Pritchett (1996) rejects this proposition because resources, primarily, the amount of physical capital and the level of education, are not fixed. Furthermore, his evidence – using cross-section country data – suggests a positive correlation between physical capital growth and rapid population expansion.

Figure 5 demonstrates that during the 30-year period from 1961 to 1990, with the exception of the interwar years 1967–1973, the annual growth rate of capital per-worker was high in absolute terms and exceeded the rate of population growth (roughly 2–2.5 percent per year).[24] In contrast, the interwar years and the last subperiod 1991–1998 were characterized by low absolute levels of capital expansion and reversal in the relation between physical capital accumulation and population growth. Besides, the education drive (beginning with the 1952 revolution) has definitely increased educational standards through compulsory primary education and through raising the average number of years of schooling per person. Nevertheless, illiteracy and school dropout rates remain above acceptable levels, partly because of teaching facilities and resource constraints that limit the potential to increase educational opportunities. Together with the change in the relation between capital growth and population expansion, limited educational opportunities forestall the potential for a significant positive correlation between TFPG and population growth.

The estimated coefficient for population growth is positive (approximately 0.01), but not statistically significant (Table 4). The result implies a weak nonnegative association between TFPG and population expansion. Furthermore, it supports the proposition that fast population growth did not hurt the rate of technical progress much, since increases in population were accompanied by – albeit insufficient – rise in the level of education.

Finally, the estimated coefficients of the two dummy variables, *DWAR* and *D91*, are statistically significant and have the expected sign. The estimate for the (1967 and 1973) war dummy variable verifies that Egypt's persistent conflicts with Israel had moderate negative impacts on technical progress. Not only were the two wars politically destabilizing, but they also represented a severe drain on the country's economic resources. Frequently, investments and foreign

---

[24] Concavity of the APF provides further support for the proposition that the absolute level of accumulation of physical capital per worker was high.

assistance from Arab and other countries were withdrawn from productive uses to finance the military forces. The hazardous repercussions of war discouraged domestic and foreign direct investments and encouraged their diversion to other countries in the region, e.g. Tunisia, Qatar and Oman, which provided safe havens for these investments in the region. At the same time, the wars motivated many skilled workers and some of the best Egyptian professionals and experts to migrate to Arab and Western (e.g. USA, Canada and Australia) countries in pursuit of better employment opportunities and higher living standards away from military hostilities. It is easy to understand how such resource and brain drains had adverse effects on the country's potential for innovation and technical progress.

On the whole, the stabilization program and the steps taken for raising economic competitiveness improved macroeconomic management and reduced both internal and external imbalances (World Bank, 2001). The combined effect of improved economic management and increased supply of financial resources – spurred by foreign debt forgiveness – raised TFPG. This is demonstrated in Table 4 by a statistically significant positive coefficient estimate for the dummy variable *D91* (0.027), which almost counterbalanced the negative association between war and technical progress (−0.028).

5. Conclusion: reflection on sources of economic growth in Egypt (1960–1998)

In this paper, we provide a synopsis of key factors that influenced the behavior of economic growth in Egypt during the period 1960–1998. This was done in two stages. In the first, we studied the contributions of physical inputs (capital and labor) and TFP to aggregate production within a growth accounting framework. Then, using regression analysis, we studied the correlation between technical progress and a selected set of key macroeconomic variables that affect the aggregate performance of the economy. Statistical results from the regression analysis confirmed that all, save one, of the chosen explanatory variables were significantly associated with technical progress.

Our findings indicated that from 1960 until the end of the 1980s, capital accumulation was the main driving force behind economic growth. It is puzzling why a country like Egypt with abundant labor and chronically low savings rate would opt for capital-intensive modes of production. We offer two explanations.

First, despite tenacious domestic savings shortages, the availability of investment expenditures was not always a significantly binding constraint. The geopolitical role of Egypt in the MENA region in general and in the Arab–Israeli conflict in particular constantly secured regular foreign investment inflows from Arab countries, from the West and/or from the ex-Soviet Union. Significant fractions of these inflows were allocated to build capital for production and to finance major national projects.

Second, during the peak of the socialist era, in the 1960s, much of the foreign inflow that accrued to the state was invested either in newly nationalized or in public sector companies. The companies were economically inefficient and badly managed. The inefficiencies resulted in small marginal returns on investments and losses in profitability. However, output growth was reasonably robust during that period as the government poured more and more investments into losing public companies. On the consumption side, the inward-looking orientation of the country generated perpetual increases in demand for domestic output regardless of quality. Almost the same setting prevailed in the 1970s and the 1980s because of dominance of the public sector and of government intervention in production and in the distribution and allocation of inputs.

The substantial quantities of unqualified labor and prevailing employment laws fostered the adoption of capital-intensive production techniques, which kept the growth rate during 1960–1989 on average above 6 percent per annum. High levels of output growth, initiated by accelerated capital utilization, were helpful in hiding some of the negative effects of productive inefficiency and mismanagement on economic profitability. The increase in capital intensity, however, was incapable of generating a sufficient level of technological dynamism that could continuously induce positive technical progress (Steindel and Stiroh, 2001). The lack of dynamism, together with limited labor productivity, which is probably the main source for diminishing returns to capital exhibited by our APF estimates, caused a gradual reduction in the level of investment.

The decrease in investment led to an unprecedented fall in the contribution of physical capital to growth after 1991, and, a consequent increase in the share of TFPG in economic growth from 1991 to 1998. The increasing importance of technical progress is better seen as an outcome of the decline in the rate of capital accumulation rather than as a result of basic improvements in the management and organization of the production sphere in the economy. That is why the rise in TFPG in that period has not been quite sufficient to stimulate sustainable economic growth.

Low saving and investment growth rates in Egypt curtail the prospects for a substantial increase in the rate of capital accumulation in the near future. Enhancing labor productivity requires radical repair of the educational system and implementation of human capital development programs, which by nature are not feasible in the short run. Thus, by elimination, it seems natural to focus on analyzing the behavior of technical progress and on the variables that influence it. We concentrate on macroeconomic variables. Our results show that TFPG is significantly correlated with the main aggregate policy variables in Egypt. In particular, during the entire period from 1960 to 1998, reductions in inflation, government spending, imports and increases in exports, foreign aid and domestic fixed investment are significantly correlated with positive variation in technical progress.

In sum, the relative abundance of inexpensive physical capital historically encouraged the adoption of capital-intensive methods of production. The accessibility of low-cost capital allowed a national political target of supporting unprofitable producers to be maintained, especially in the public sector and to encourage industrial production. Excessive use of capital inputs gave rise to diminishing marginal returns to capital. Hence, human capital and skilled labor shortages imposed serious constraints on aggregate production capacity. These constraints could be relaxed by introducing tangible improvements in the quality of human labor capital via suitable long-run education and training programs. In the short run, however, stimulating technical progress, through appropriate macroeconomic policy intervention, seems to be the most viable alternative that is available – at present – for raising economic growth.

Acknowledgments

The authors would like to thank Hashem Pesaran, Jeffrey Nugent, Nadeem Ul-Haq, Sherine El-Shawarby, Alaa El-Shazly and two anonymous referees for their extremely helpful comments. We are also grateful to Mai Ashraf, Mai El-Mossallamy, Sally Farid, Iman El-Shair and Rasha Reda for their valuable research assistance. Naturally, all errors and omissions remain exclusively our responsibility.

References

Abdellatif, L. (2003), "Egypt's manufacturing sector: factor inputs and TFP over half a century", GDN Library: Research papers from GDN activities, revised version, http://www.gdnet.org/activities/global_research_projects/explaining_growth/country_studies/#G.

Barro, R. (1991), "Economic growth in a cross-section of countries", *Quarterly Journal of Economics*, Vol. 104, pp. 407–433.

Barro, R. and J. Lee (1993), "International comparisons of educational attainment", *Journal of Monetary Economics*, Vol. 32, pp. 363–394.

Barro, R. and X. Sala-i-Martin (1995), *Economic Growth*, New York: McGraw-Hill.

Bisat, A., M. El Erian and T. Helbing (1997), "Growth, investment and saving in the Arab economies", IMF Working Paper, WP/97/85.

Brock, W. and S. Durlauf (2001), "Growth empirics and reality", *The World Bank Economic Review*, Vol. 15, pp. 221–224.

CAPMAS (various issues), *Labor Force Sample Survey*, Cairo: CAPMAS.

Chen, E. (1997), "The total factor productivity debate: determinants of economic growth in East Asia", *Asian-Pacific Economic Literature*, Vol. 11, pp. 18–38.

Collins, S. and B. Bosworth (1996), "Economic growth in East Asia: accumulation versus assimilation", *Brookings Paper on Economic Activity*, Vol. 2, pp. 135–203.

Dowling, M. and P. Summers (1998), "Total factor productivity and economic growth-issues for Asia", *The Economic Record*, Vol. 74, pp. 170–185.

Easterly, W. and R. Levine (2001), "It's not factor accumulation: stylized facts and growth models", *The World Bank Economic Review*, Vol. 15, pp. 177–219.

EFG-Hermes (1997), *Country and Capital Market Update March 1997*, Cairo: Egyptian Financial Group.

Fischer, S. (1993), "The role of macroeconomic factors in growth", *Journal of Monetary Economics*, Vol. 32, pp. 485–512.

Gómez, V. and A. Maravall (1997), "TRAMO and SEATS: instructions for the user," Banco de España, www.bde.es.

Hamilton, J. (1994), *Time Series Analysis*, Princeton, New Jersey: Princeton University Press.

Harrison, A. (1996), "Openness and growth: a time-series, cross-section analysis from developing countries", *Journal of Development Economics*, Vol. 48, pp. 419–447.

Information and Decision Support Center (IDSC) (unpublished), *Daily Prices for Basic Commodities Database*, Information Sector, Cairo, Egypt: Information and Decision Support Center.

IMF (2004), *International Finance Statistics* on CD-ROM, May edition, IMF.

Johnston, J. and J. DiNardo (1997), *Econometric Methods*, Fourth Edition, New York: McGraw-Hill, International Editions.

Maddison, A. (1987), "Growth and slowdown in advanced capitalist economies: techniques of quantitative assessment", *Journal of Economic Literature*, Vol. 25, pp. 649–698.

Makdisi, S., Z. Fattah and I. Limam (2000), "Determinants of growth in The MENA countries", Paper for World Bank Global Development Network.

Moursi, T. and A. Kamel (1989), "The relationship between unemployment and its dispersion and the rate of change of money wage rates and of prices in Egypt", Proceedings of the First Conference of the Economics Department, February 20–22, Faculty of Economics and Political Science, Cairo University.

Nehru, V. and A. Dhareshwar (1994), "New estimates of total factor productivity growth for developing and industrial countries", Policy Research Working Paper No.1313, The World Bank.

O'Connell, S. and B. Ndulu (2000), "Africa's growth experience: a focus on sources of growth", Paper for World Bank Global Development Network.

Pissarides, C. (2000), "Labor markets and economic growth in the MENA region", Paper presented at the Global Research Project: Explaining Growth sessions held in Cairo, Egypt, March.

Press, W., B. Flannery, S. Teukolsky and W. Vettering (1988), *Numerical Recipes in C*, New York: Cambridge University Press.

Pritchett, L. (1996), "Population growth, factor accumulation, and productivity", Policy Research Working Paper, R/1567, The World Bank.

Sachs, J and A. Warner (1997), "Natural resource abundance and economic growth", Center for International Development and Harvard Institute for International Development.

Solow, R. (1957), "Technical change and the aggregate production function", *Review of Economics and Statistics*, Vol. 39, pp. 312–320.

Steindel, C. and K. Stiroh (2001), "Productivity: what is it, and why do we care about it?", Federal Reserve Bank of New York, *http://www.ny.frb.org/rmaghome*.

World Bank (1994), "Private sector development in Egypt, the status and the challenges", A World Bank Report prepared for the Conference Private Sector Development in Egypt: Investing in the Future, Cairo, October 9–10, 1994, The World Bank.

World Bank (2000), *World Development Indicators 2000*, on CD ROM, The World Bank.

World Bank (2001), Egypt social and structural review, Report No. 22397-EGT, The World Bank.

Appendix A: Review of the methods used to estimate the APF

Consider an $(n \times 1)$ random vector of variables, z_t, containing the observed values of n variables at date t with $t = 1, \ldots, T$. A *state-space representation* of the dynamics of z in terms of observed (x_t) and unobserved (ξ_t) vectors can be given by the following system of equations

$$z_t = Bx_t + C\xi_t + w_t \tag{A.1a}$$

$$\xi_t = D\xi_{t-1} + v_t \tag{A.1b}$$

where x_t is a $(k \times 1)$ vector of predetermined random variables, ξ_t is an unobserved (or state) vector of dimension $(r \times 1)$ and B' and C' are $(n \times k)$ and $(n \times r)$ matrices of parameters, respectively. The observation equation (A.1a) relates the observable variables z_t to the unobservable states, such that w_t is a vector of white noise measurement errors. The state equation (A.1b) describes the dynamics of the evolution of the vector of states over time. The matrix of parameters D is of dimension $(r \times r)$ and v_t is a vector of random shocks. Assume that the disturbances vectors v_t and w_t are uncorrelated at all lags and that

$$E(w_t w_\tau') = \begin{cases} G \text{ for } t = \tau \\ 0 \text{ otherwise} \end{cases} \tag{A.2a}$$

$$E(v_t v_\tau') = \begin{cases} H \text{ for } t = \tau \\ 0 \text{ otherwise} \end{cases} \tag{A.2b}$$

where G and H are matrices of dimension $(n \times n)$ and $(r \times r)$, respectively.

The unknown value of TFP in period t can be computed by casting it within a state-space representation. Drawing on Solow's (1957) highly touted study, a Cobb–Douglas APF, in intensive form, can be written as

$$y_t = \beta + \alpha k_t + a_t \tag{A.3}$$

The initial guesses for the capital share in income, α, and the coefficient β are estimated from a double-log OLS regression of y_t on real capital per-worker and a constant. In addition, a dummy variable ($D91_t$), that takes on the value unity in 1991 and 0 otherwise, is added as an explanatory variable in the regression to account for variance in the level of utilization of capital per-worker owing to the introduction of economic reform measures. The highly significant statistical estimate of the dummy variable coefficient in that regression (Table A.1) strongly suggests modifying the observation equation. Accordingly, equation (A.3) and the vector $\boldsymbol{B}'$ are rewritten, respectively, as follows:

$$y_t = \beta + \alpha k_t + \phi D91_t + a_t \tag{A.3'}$$

and $\boldsymbol{B}' = [\beta \ \alpha \ \phi]$ where ϕ is any parameter. The initial guess for ϕ that is employed in the Kalman-filtering algorithm is taken from the same OLS production function regression from which α is estimated.

The estimates of α and ϕ from the production function regression are also used to compute a crude estimate of TFP ($\hat{a}_t$) during the sample period such that

$$\hat{a}_t = y_t - \hat{b} - \hat{\alpha} k_t - \hat{f} \, D91_t \tag{A.5}$$

where $\hat{\alpha}$, $\hat{b}$ and $\hat{f}$ are the parameter estimates of α, β and ϕ, respectively. The Akaike Information Criterion is employed to guide the selection of an appropriate order (p,q) of an ARMA process for $\hat{a}_t$. Our results (not reported) suggest that $\hat{a}_t$ may be adequately described by an $ARMA(1,5)$ model. The same order (1,5) is selected for the state equation (A.4) in our empirical state-space representation of TFP. Furthermore, the estimated coefficients from the ARMA equation for $\hat{a}_t$ are used in the Kalman-filtering algorithm as initial guesses for δ and γ_i ($i = 1, \ldots, 5$) in equation (A.4).

There is no commonly accepted procedure to determine an initial guess for the variance–covariance matrix $\boldsymbol{H}$. We stipulate that the estimated square standard error (SSE) from the $ARMA(1,5)$ regression equation (A.4) for the $\hat{a}_t$ process is a reasonable initial value for σ^2. The SSE estimate is used to construct the initial matrix $\boldsymbol{H}$.

Employing the initial guesses, the estimation of the APF parameters and unobserved state variable (a_t) is carried out using the standard KF by means of the maximum likelihood (ML) method.[27] Convergence is achieved smoothly after 13 iterations. The estimates of the parameters, their t-statistics and the log-likelihood function (Ln F) are displayed in Table A.1. The parameter estimates, exhibited in Table A.1, are used to provide estimates for TFP during the period under consideration.

On observing the pattern of significant coefficients, the table delineates that – with the exception of γ_4 – all the parameter estimates of the production function and

---

[27] The Broyden, Fletcher, Goldfarb and Shanno (BFGS) algorithm (Press *et al.*, 1988) is used in ML estimation.

Table A.1.   KF system, OLS, ML and ARMA in the errors estimated parameter values of the per-worker aggregate production function

Parameter	OLS	ML[a]	System[a]	ARMA$_\varepsilon$[b,c]	Parameter	ML[a]	System[a]	ARMA$_\varepsilon$[b,c]
β	0.008	0.008	−2.058		γ_3		0.327	0.153
	(1.411)	(1.900)	(−4.121)				(1.692)	1.011
α	0.606	0.606	0.649	0.549	γ_4		0.166	0.437
	(6.815)	(13.624)	(4.223)	(3.758)			(1.120)	3.716
δ			0.991	0.508	γ_5		0.289	0.705
			(74.270)	3.402			(1.655)	(5.480)
γ_1			0.605	–	ϕ		0.042	0.039
			(3.261)	–			(1.883)	(1.793)
γ_2			0.344	−0.202	σ^2	0.001		
			(1.589)	(−1.263)		(4.116)		
R^2 (%)	56.33			43.26	Ln F	122.363	137.924	

Note: (*t*-Statistics in parentheses.)

[a]BFGS algorithm employed in estimation.

[b]Gauss–Newton algorithm employed in estimation.

[c]For succinctness, the state-space parameter notation, α, δ, $\gamma_1 \ldots \gamma_5$ and ϕ is borrowed to denote the ARMA$_\varepsilon$ parameters α_{ARMA}, δ_{ARMA}, $\gamma_{ARMA1}, \gamma_{ARMA5} \ldots \gamma_{ARMA5}$ and ϕ_{ARMA}, respectively.

the state equation are significant at conventional levels. In particular, the coefficient estimates of the APF and the autoregression (AR) coefficient (δ) of the state equation are of high quality according to the reported t-statistics. The estimated value of δ is notably near unity, suggesting that the state variable TFP process is characterized by a substantial degree of persistence. This finding provides some statistical support for the assumption maintained in the construction of the state equation that TFP exhibits a high degree of persistence over time.

The estimate of the share of capital in income reported in Table A.1, roughly 0.65, is above the commonly assumed value, 0.4, for growth accounting exercises and other studies on the Egyptian economy (see for example, World Bank, 1994 and Pissarides, 2000). Our result, however, is consistent with recent international evidence as well as with other findings for the Middle East and North Africa (MENA) region, which suggest that the capital share in income is considerably higher than 0.5 (Bisat et al., 1997). Abdellatif's (2003) study of the industrial sector in Egypt provides further support for our finding. Using micro-data for the industrial sector, she shows that the share of capital in industrial output (value added) is on average – for different plant sizes – greater than 0.65.

Table A.1 also contrasts our KF system estimates of the parameters of the APF with standard (single-equation) estimates of α and β, obtained directly from equation A.3[28] The latter estimates are derived by means of the OLS and the ML methods. As expected, while both OLS and ML yield the same estimates for α and β, the ML estimates tend to be relatively more efficient as indicated by the t-statistics reported in Table A.1. Moreover, we find that the value of α estimated from the single-equation regression (0.606) is quite close to the analogous estimate resulting from the KF system (0.649). However, a comparison between the computed log-likelihood functions, exhibited in Table A.1, provides evidence confirming that the multi-equation system outperforms the single-equation regression. The only qualm associated with this result is that – contrary to the estimate of β – the single-equation ML (as well as the OLS) estimate of α is somewhat more efficient than the multi-equation system estimate. This should not be too alarming for two reasons. First, relative efficiency of the single-equation estimate of α is most likely the spurious result of omitting some of our a priori knowledge about the dynamic behavior of a. Second, the short sample period (1960–1998) involved in estimation is not sufficient to allow us to attach large significance to differences between the estimates of the t-statistics obtained from the single- and multiple-equation models.

Figures A.1 and A.2 sketch the TFP and TFPG series, respectively, calculated on basis of the different single- and multi-equation system parameter estimates. In addition, the two series are recalculated for an ad hoc value for α equal to 0.4,

---

[28] The single-equation APF is estimated without the dummy variable D91. Introducing the dummy variable does not have any qualitative effect on any of the results.

Figure A.1.   Sensitivity of TFP to the value of α

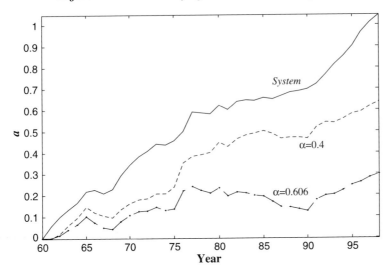

which has been adopted frequently in the earlier studies (World Bank, 1994). Visual inspection reveals that the TFP level is sensitive to the selected value of α.[29] In general, the TFP level series computed with the system and the ML/OLS estimates of α are more or less comparable. Figure A.2, however, shows that the single-equation model could not distinctly resolve variances in TFPG associated with values of α ranging between 0.4 and 0.6. In contrast, the TFPG series, based on the richer dynamic behavior of the underlying system estimates, appears to capture variations in technical progress associated with different values of α as well as some of the distinctive realities of Egyptian economic performance such as the rise in TFPG during the 1990s.

Alternatively, the system results reported in Table A.1 suggest the presence of a unit root in a, which is indicated by the parameter estimate of δ (0.991). This may affect our inference based on the KF approach. We notice that the KF approach that we use in this paper is equivalent to fitting equation A.3 with ARMA specification in the errors.[30] The latter approach has the

---

[29] The nonmonotonic sensitivity of (log) TFP estimates to the value of α disclosed by Figure A.1 follows from the difference in the functional specification of the single-equation (OLS/ML) and of the multiple-equation (system) models (see Table A.1) used to derive those estimates.

[30] We thank Hashem Pesaran and Jeffrey Nugent for pointing out that equivalence and for suggesting the procedure for comparing our KF estimates with the ARMA in the errors estimates of the parameters of the APF.

Figure A.2.   Sensitivity of TFPG to the value of α

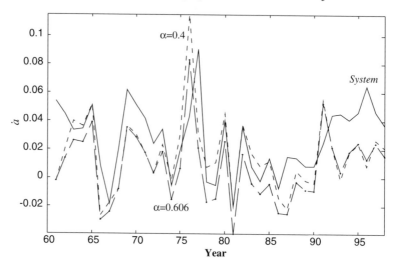

advantage that it can be easily adapted to deal with the possibility of a unit root in TFP.

To compare the results from the two approaches, we employ the ARMA specification in the errors ($ARMA_\varepsilon$) to estimate the coefficients of the APF. We begin by taking the first difference of both sides of equation A.3. Then we estimate the regression of dy on dk without an intercept, but inclusive of the 1991 dummy variable in first difference form (d$D91$)

$$\mathrm{d}y_t = \dot{a}_{ARMA_t} + \alpha_{ARMA}\mathrm{d}k_t + \phi_{ARMA}\mathrm{d}D91 \tag{A.6}$$

We assume, also, that the residuals from the regression A.6 ($\dot{a}$), which measure the TFP growth, are allowed to have an ARMA(p,q) specification

$$\dot{a}_{ARMA_t} = \sum_{i=1}^{p} \delta_{ARMA_i}\dot{a}_{ARMA_{t-i}} + \varepsilon_{ARMA_t} + \sum_{j=1}^{q} \gamma_{ARMA_j}\varepsilon_{ARMA_{t-j}} \tag{A.7}$$

Similar to the empirical KF system, we choose the order $(p,q) = (1,5)$ to describe the $ARMA\varepsilon$ process and we invoke the Gauss–Newton procedure to estimate the parameters of equations A.6 and A.7.

Despite many tedious trials with different initial guesses, the selected $ARMA_\varepsilon$ (1,5) model failed to converge after a reasonable number of iterations. Repeated attempts, however, have suggested that the convergence properties of the model are significantly enhanced when the first coefficient of the MA process (γ_{ARMA1}) is restricted to 0. We impose that restriction directly by excluding the MA(1) process from the estimation of the empirical analog of equation A.7. Following that strategy, the estimated $ARMA_\varepsilon$ (1,2-5) model converges smoothly after 21

Figure A.3.   *TFP estimates from the KF system and the ARMA specification in the errors model*

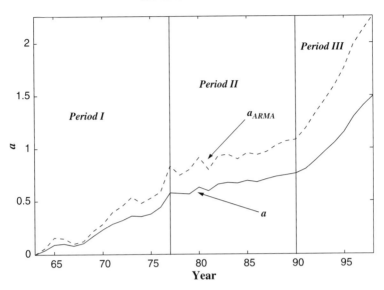

iterations. The parameter estimates obtained from this model are exhibited in Table A.1 along with the corresponding t-statistics and the R^2 (percent) for the regression.

Table A.1 shows that the system and the $ARMA_\varepsilon$ estimates are qualitatively equivalent. (In particular, the estimate of the share of capital in income (0.55) is still above the commonly assumed value, 0.4, and is relatively close to the value estimated from the KF system, 0.65.) To be sure, we compare the TFPG and the TFP estimates derived from the state-space system ($\dot a$ and a) with the corresponding estimates ($\dot a_{ARMA}$ and a_{ARMA}) resulting from the $ARMA_\varepsilon$ model. The a_{ARMA} series are obtained by accumulating the residuals from equation A-6 ($\dot a_{ARMA}$) from some given value (say 0) to compute estimates of TFP (a_{ARMA}) up to a scalar. The two sets of TFP and TFPG series are depicted in Figures A.3 and A.4, respectively. Visual inspection of the two diagrams substantiates the similar behavior of the TFP and of the TFPG series (particularly their respective turning points) estimated by means of the two approaches. This result is further confirmed by a set of Ljung-Box Q-statistic tests (not reported).

Appendix B: Source of data

(A) *World Development Indicators (2000).* GDP at market prices [*GDPMP*]; real GDP at constant 1987 prices [*GDP (Y)*]; total labor force; inflation [*INFLAT*]; general government consumption [*GOV*]; gross domestic fixed

Figure A.4.   TFP growth estimates from the KF system and the ARMA specification in the errors model

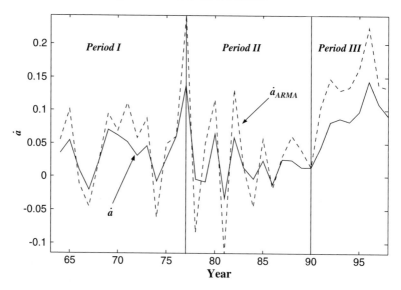

investment [*GDFI*]; credit to private sector [*CRPRIV*]; exports [*EXP*] and imports [*IMP*] of goods and services; foreign aid [*AID*] and population [*POP*].

(B) *Other sources.* Data on unemployment rates are obtained from Moursi and Kamel (1989) and CAPMAS (various issues); real capital stock at constant 1987 prices (LE) [k_{87}] data for 1960–1990 from Nehru and Dhareshwar (1994) and data after 1990 are updated using real fixed investment at constant 1987 prices [FI_{87}] (World Bank, 2000) and assuming a depreciation of 4 percent per annum as follows:

$$k(t+1) = FI_{87}(t) + (1 - 0.04)k_{87}(t-1), t = 1991, \ldots, 1997.$$

CHAPTER 8

Sources of Growth and the Output Gap for the Turkish Economy

Kıvılcım Metin Özcan, Ümit Özlale* and Çağrı Sarıkaya

Abstract

In this study, we analyze the growth dynamics of the Turkish economy. After investigating the sources of growth and comparing both the output and the inflation performance with the other MENA countries, we find that the Turkish economy has not achieved a sustainable growth path and has a much worse inflation performance. Then, we take a closer look at the volatile output performance and discuss the role of the wrong macroeconomic policies on the unsustainable output performance. Utilizing an output gap measure, we find that the short-term capital flows seem to be the main driving force in generating excessive fluctuations in the output. Based on these findings, we can say that the high economic growth rates, which the Turkish economy has achieved in the recent years owe much to massive short-term capital inflows. At this stage, it is too early to evaluate the effects of the recent structural reforms on the long-term output dynamics.

Keywords: Turkish economy, emerging markets, output gap, economic growth

JEL classifications: C1, E3, O4

---

*Corresponding author.

CONTRIBUTIONS TO ECONOMIC ANALYSIS
VOLUME 278   ISSN: 0573-8555
DOI:10.1016/S0573-8555(06)78008-7

1. Introduction

Despite several stabilization and structural adjustment programs, all of which were backed by the World Bank and the International Monetary Fund (IMF), the Turkish economy can be characterized as having an unsustainable output growth and an inflationary environment over the last four decades. Similar to other emerging market economies, a boom–bust cycle on the output dynamics can be observed. After the collapse of the exchange rate-based stabilization program in 2001, which was followed by the deepest financial crisis that Turkey has ever experienced, the economy has started to recover with very high economic growth rates. Moreover, unlike the previous recovery periods, the price stability objective of the monetary authorities seems to have been achieved, with inflation rates being under 10% as of mid-2005.

However, it is an open question whether these recent positive developments after the crisis stem from a major structural change in the macroeconomic dynamics or simply reflect the expansionary phase of the boom–bust cycle. On the one hand, with the IMF's supervision, the government and the central bank took important steps to achieve fiscal discipline and low levels of inflation, which are the two necessary preconditions for a sustained long-run growth performance. While the government followed a tight fiscal policy to put the debt stock on a sustainable path, the central bank started to implement a form of inflation targeting, where it is clearly stated that the main objective of the monetary policy is price stability.

On the other hand, it can be argued that the still-high real interest rates and the increasing appetite of the investors to invest in the emerging market economies have induced massive short-term capital inflows, thus helping the Turkish economy to perform at high economic growth rates without any pressure on price dynamics. As the recent experiences in the emerging markets suggest, high growth rates that are mainly driven by short-term capital flows are not sustainable and generally lead to excessive fluctuations in the macroeconomic dynamics in the long run. Moreover, with short-term capital inflows, pressure on exchange rates is relieved, which clearly affects inflation performance positively both through the lower cost of imported intermediate inputs and the prices of the imported final goods. However, as soon as the concerns regarding the financing of the current account deficit increase, a possible adjustment in the exchange rates has the potential to disrupt the price dynamics and generate lower economic growth. As a result, it is not clear whether the recent positive developments in the Turkish economy imply a sustainable long-run growth performance or simply signal a temporary improvement.

To address the above-mentioned issue, this study analyzes the output dynamics of the Turkish economy. First, beginning with the 1960s, we present an overview of the economy from a growth perspective. Then, we provide a brief comparison of the Turkish economy with the other MENA countries. The main finding in these two sections is that the Turkish economy has been far from having a sustainable growth path especially during the last two decades. Therefore, following the comparison of the Turkish economy with the other MENA countries, we discuss the negative outcomes of the macroeconomic policies implemented over the last two decades, with special reference to the financial crises in 1994 and 2001. One main result of this discussion is that the short-term capital flows are becoming increasingly important in shaping macroeconomic dynamics. Thus, we continue our analysis with an empirical investigation of the influence of short-term capital flows on the excessive fluctuations in the output. In this respect, we utilize an output gap measure and show its comovement with the capital inflows. Using this gap measure, we also display the business cycle characteristics of the Turkish economy. Such an exercise will not only enable us to develop an idea about the recent macroeconomic framework, but it will also reveal which macroeconomic variables are procyclical or countercyclical as well as whether these variables lead or lag behind the fluctuations in the output. Section 6 concludes the discussion.

2. An overview of the Turkish economy from a growth perspective

This section provides a brief historical overview of the Turkish economy from a growth perspective by identifying periods by stabilization policies and the growth path followed.[1] In this section, we will mainly focus on capital formation and the sources of growth. The evaluation of the Turkish economy is analyzed by dividing the entire period into three phases: 1963–1980, 1980–1999 and from the millennium onward.

2.1. Inward-oriented strategy: 1963–1980 period

While there was no conscious planning or coordination of economic policies in the 1950s, a new constitution was formulated under the revolutionary government in 1960–1961. One of its key changes was social and economic development planning. The role of the state gained importance by following the import substitution policies together with economy-wide planning. During the First and Second Five-Year Plans, the traditional strategy of modernization and industrialization in a mixed economy was attempted systematically. In both plans, the main aim was to achieve a higher rate of growth and investment in a balanced economy. Some social issues addressed in the plans were more equitable income distribution, better regional balance, land reform, economic organization and

---

[1] See, for example, Aricanli and Rodrik (1990), Celasun and Rodrik (1989), Ekinci (1990, 2000), Metin-Ozcan *et al.*, (2001) and Özatay (1999) among others for more detailed analyses and discussions of these and related issues of the Turkish economy.

the efficiency of the State Economic Enterprises (SEEs) (for more detail, see Celasun and Rodrik (1989), Şenses (1991) and Metin (1995, pp. 17–18)).

The pace of economic growth accelerated during the 1960s and most of the 1970s was also good. In fact, the GDP increased at an average annual rate of 6.4% during the First Plan period (1963–1967), 6.7% during the Second Plan period (1968–1972) and 7.2% during the Third Plan period (1973–1977). In the 1960s, development occurred with moderate reliance on foreign aid. In the 1970s, it was supported by large increases in workers' remittances, but after 1974 by excessive reliance on foreign borrowing.

The long-term growth of industry has been particularly rapid, averaging 9.2% between 1963 and 1977. This led to a substantial structural change in the economy. Agricultural output growth averaged 3.3% per annum during this period, somewhat above the annual population growth rate of 2.5%. Population growth remained fairly high (2.5% per annum). Since GDP growth was fairly high, this allowed a relatively fast growth in per capita income. However, the rising income level does not appear to have been accompanied by a better income distribution. In fact, the 1973 household income survey showed that the income was unequally distributed. The top 10% of the population received at least 40% of the income while the bottom 40% received about 11.5%. Considerable inequality within the agricultural sector (owing largely to extremely unequal land distribution) was the main cause of the overall income inequality (World Bank Country Study (1980, p. 11))

During the 1963–1977 period, both real private investment and real public investment increased at almost the same pace, averaging 10.8% and 11.4% per annum, respectively. This revealed the crowding-in effect in both sectors, which is in line with inward-oriented strategy (see İsmihan (2003, p. 144). From 1973 to 1979, public sector investment increased tremendously with a 22.1% annual rise, while private investment grew by 10.2%.

During the 1960s, the macroeconomic environment was stable compared to that in the 1970s. In fact, the inflation rate, which is regarded as an important indicator of macroeconomic instability, was quite low during the 1960s (5.2% per annum) compared to that in the 1970s (27% per annum). Starting in the mid-1970s, the economy become even more unsteady since Turkey had delayed its internal adjustment to the external shocks of this period via reserve decumulation initially and excessive short-term borrowing later on (Celasun and Rodrik, 1989). In addition to macroeconomic instability, from the mid-1977 onward, the political environment became more unstable owing to successive weak coalition governments. In 1978–1979, the crisis in the economy deepened on account of inflation and balance of payment difficulties, so the government needed to implement more effective policies. On January 24, 1980, the government announced a major stabilization program, which included a series of new economic measures that were intended to solve the high inflation, economic stagnation and unmanagable balance of payment problems.

Table 1.   Selected indicators of the Turkish economy (1980–1999)

Output and capital formation	
Annual average growth rate	
Real GNP	4.2
Real private fixed investment	6.1
Real public fixed investment	1.6
Real public fixed core infrastructural investment	2.7
Real public fixed non-core infrastructural investment	0.8
Composition of public investment[a]	
Core infrastructural investment (as % of total)	50.5
Non-core infrastructural investment (as % of total)	49.5
Macroeconomic instability[a]	
Inflation rate[b](%)	61.8

Source: İsmihan *et al.* (2005), Table 1, p. 241.
[a]Simple period average.
[b]Percentage change in the GNP deflator.

2.2. The 1980s and the 1990s

Turkey began taking serious steps to liberalize and strengthen its economy a full 25 years ago. In 1980, Turkey made a fundamental decision to switch its economic strategy from an inward-oriented growth to an outward-oriented one. Prior to the reform program, tariff barriers were high, state ownership prevailed in key sectors and competition was strangled by regulations. The 1980 program had stabilization as well as structural aspects with efforts to liberalize trade and finance. During the outward-oriented period of 1980–1999, the real GNP grew at an average annual rate of 4.2% (see Table 1 which provides summary information on the Turkish economy for the 1980-1999 period).[2]

The economic growth rate was higher during the 1980s (5.2% per year) compared to that in the 1990s (3.2% per year). Capital formation performance in the private sector was better compared to that of the public sector during this period. Real private (public) investment grew at an average annual rate of 6.1% (1.6%) from 1980 to 1999. The most important development in this period was the changing role of the state in the investment process. The share of core public infrastructural investment in total public investment rose from 37.3% in the inward-oriented period to 50.5% in the outward-oriented one. While the private investment to GNP ratio (in current prices) rose from 12.8% in the 1980s to 18.1% in the 1990s, the public investment/GNP ratio dropped from 8.8% in the 1980s to 6.2% in the 1990s owing to budgetary pressures.[3]

---

[2] For further discussion, see İsmihan *et al.* (2005, p. 241).
[3] See Conway (1990), Uygur (1995) and İsmihan *et al.* (2005, p. 242) for a detailed discussion of private and public investment behavior in Turkey.

Turkey experienced a very severe financial crisis in early 1994 mainly owing to unsustainable fiscal balance and monetization of the domestic debt. GNP contracted by 6.1% during 1994, which is the peak rate of contraction of the Turkish economy during the 1963–1999 period. Similarly, real public investment fell dramatically by about 40% from 1993 to 1994. This is evidence of the negative effect of macroeconomic instability on the fiscal "ability" of governments to make investments. Real private investment, in contrast, contracted only moderately (about 5%). Inflation peaked in 1994 with 107.3% per annum and the Turkish lira depreciated by > 70% against the US$ in 1994 (İsmihan et al., 2005, p. 242).

Following this major crisis in mid-1994, Turkey adopted an IMF-based stand-by agreement to eliminate the severe financial crisis. The inflation rate decreased from 107.3% in 1994 to 87.2% in 1995. However, macroeconomic instability continued until the late 1990s, and public sector balances were unsustainable owing to heavy reliance on domestic borrowing. In addition, the East Asian and Russian crises of 1997–1998 and the two devastating earthquakes of 1999 had a negative impact on the Turkish economy. In December 1999, Turkey signed a 3-year IMF-based stand-by agreement.[4] The objectives of the program were tight fiscal and monetary policies, ambitious structural reforms and the use of a predetermined exchange rate path as a nominal anchor. The disinflation program had a major impact on banks' balance sheets. At the end of 2000, the Turkish banking system was seriously affected by increasing interest, exchange rate and credit risks because of the short-term maturity structure of financial sources used in the banking sector and the open positions of the Turkish banks. Owing to a major banking crisis, unfortunately, this program failed in the early 2001 and the real GNP contracted by 9.4% in 2001. Then, backed by the IMF and the World Bank, Turkey signed another program, called "Transition to a Strong Economy," to eliminate the confidence crisis and financial instability. The strategy was strongly based on market orientation and openness to the world economy. An important pillar of the program consisted of a renewed effort to eliminate structural weaknesses that had not been fully tackled by the 2000 program, particularly by strengthening governance and improving economic management.

2.3. The millennium onward

The trend in economic growth during the period from 1998, the year prior to the economic crisis that affected the early 2000s, to the end of 2004 may be analyzed in two subperiods: 1999–2000 and 2001–2004. In the first subperiod, the average annual increase in the GDP was around 1.1% and in the second subperiod 3.7%. If the 1999–2004 period is taken as a whole, the rates of growth of the GNP and GDP are 2.9% and 2.3%, respectively. In spite of the improvement throughout

---

[4] See Ekinci (2000) for the details of program.

the 2002–2004 period, the negative effects of the two banking crises experienced in 1999 and 2001 were still being felt (see Figure 1 to observe the GDP growth rates). A high GDP growth rate of 7% was achieved in 2002, followed by 4.8% in 2003 and 9% in 2004. The Turkish economy displayed an especially high growth performance in 2004. After the 2001 banking crisis, inflation had been on a steady downward trend and came close to the single-digit level as of 2004. Starting from the first quarter of 2002, high growth figures were achieved without interruption over a period of 10 quarters. Therefore, there are indications that the Turkish economy has been free of the structure, which is characterized by boom–bust cycles since the 1990s and has embarked on a high-growth process (*Pre-Accession Economic Programme*, State Planning Organization (SPO) (2004, p. 27)).

At this point, it is necessary to discuss whether these positive developments caused expectations to change permanently. The course of Turkish economy has clearly seen improvement in expectations since 2001 (see Figure 2 below).

The upper-left panel of the figure indicates that business confidence has been stable and dominated by optimists since the beginning of 2002. Moreover, the consecutive achievements in reaching the year-end inflation targets since 2002 have increased the credibility of macroeconomic policies and have helped in-flation expectations maintain a downward trend since then. In line with the robust economic growth and disinflation process, improved economic funda-mentals have led to a more conducive environment for employment and invest-ment decisions (right panel of the figure). However, although business tendency survey results point to a significant improvement in the expectations, it is too early at this stage to claim that the changes in these expectations are permanent.

Private fixed capital investment emerged as the other element that drove growth in 2004 (see Independent Social Scientists' Alliance (ISSA) Report, 2005 and *Pre-Accession Economic Programme*, State Planning Organization (SPO) (2004) for further discussion).

Figure 1. GDP growth rates

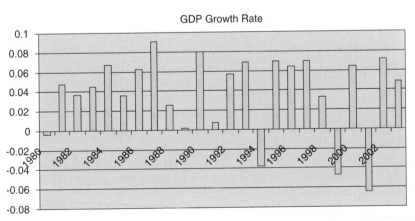

Figure 2.   Selected indicators from the CBRT business tendency survey

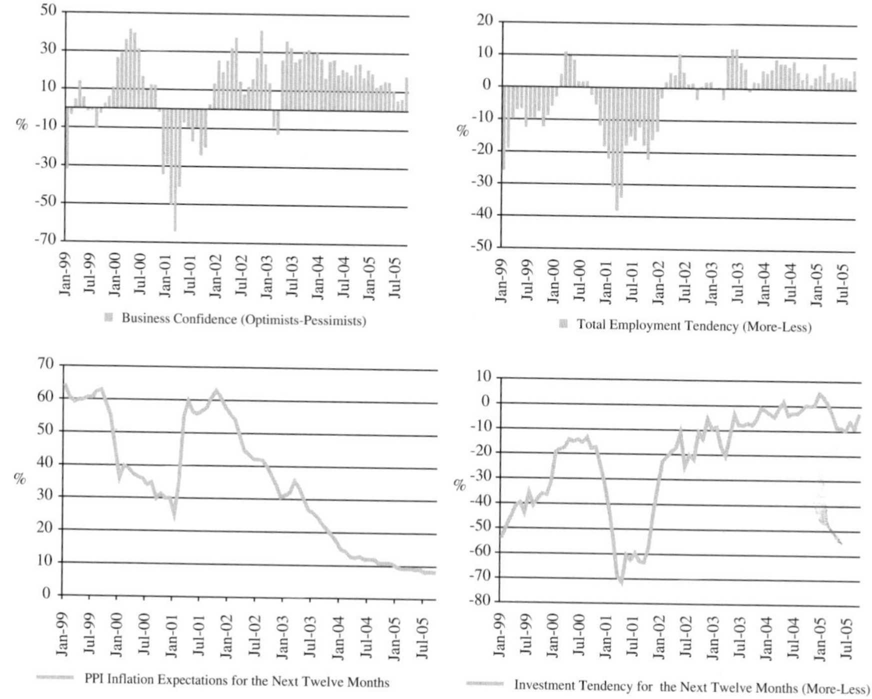

■ Business Confidence (Optimists-Pessimists)

■ Total Employment Tendency (More-Less)

——— PPI Inflation Expectations for the Next Twelve Months

——— Investment Tendency for the Next Twelve Months (More-Less)

When the total savings–investment balance, which is given in Table 2 is considered, the first point to be noted is that some revival in private sector fixed capital investment has been observed (13.7%) in 2004. However, this figure is still far behind the averages of the private fixed investment to GDP ratios of 1990–1994 (17.9%) and 1995–1999 (17.4%) periods. It is also observed that this revival is largely financed by increases in external resources (4.6% in 2004) and that the domestic savings/GDP ratio, which was showing an increasing trend since the 2000s remained at the same level as during 1990–1994.

The second point to be raised is that the ratio of private investment to GDP was realized at 11.3% in 2002 and maintained at this level in 2003 along with a significant increase recorded in private investment in 2004 (13.7%). The third point is that the ratio of public investments to GDP, which was around 5%–6% during the 1990s (see Table 2), decreased to as low as to 4.0% in 2004 as a result of the tight fiscal policy implemented. In addition, stocks are rising and investments, especially public investments are steadily declining. In fact, there is no possible economic explanation of the observation that stock increases have become a considerable determining factor in economic growth. However, Independent Social Scientists' Alliance (ISSA) Report (2005, p. 11) put forth two reasons, which shed light on the phenomenon. First, it seems that the fact that

Table 2.   Total savings–investment balance (as percentage of GDP)

Year	1990–1994	1995–1999	2001	2002	2003	2004
Total investment	23.0	23.2	15.9	21.3	22.8	25.9
Fixed capital investment	24.2	22.9	17.2	16.6	15.5	17.7
Public investment	6.3	5.5	5.3	5.3	4.2	4.0
Private investment	17.9	17.4	11.9	11.3	11.3	13.7
Stock changes	−1.2	0.3	−1.3	4.7	7.3	8.2
Total savings	23.1	23.3	15.9	21.3	22.8	25.9
Domestic savings	21.3	19.2	18.2	19.8	19.5	21.3
Foreign savings	1.8	4.1	−2.3	1.5	3.3	4.6

Note: The savings–investment balance is based on State Institute of Statistics (SIS) figures of the GDP by expenditures. Public investments in the table include the investments of the SEEs in addition to those of the general government.Source: Pre-Accession Economic Programme (2004, p. 31, Table 2.1).

the economy has recently become more dependent on imported inputs and consequent decreases in value added/gross production value ratios in all sectors including industry in the first place is not duly considered by the SIS, which still uses the technical coefficients of the 1990s. Hence, when high estimations are made for GDP growth (based on gross production values), final demands, which cannot be explained by changes in investment, consumption and net exports turn into virtual demand elements and reflect themselves in stock changes as a residual (see also Somçağ (2004)). A less likely second possibility is the under-estimation of private consumption expenditures, which are not as closely followed as investments by the State Planning Organization (SPO), and carrying the impact of this faulty estimation to stock changes (see Independent Social Scientists' Alliance (ISSA) Report (2005, p. 11)).

Finally, the total domestic savings had an upward trend after 2000. The large increases of domestic demand that were observed in 2003 and 2004 have increased the economy's need for foreign savings.

The most unpleasant result of the high growth rate was its failure to generate employment. Throughout 2004, unemployment remained a problem of the economy awaiting solution (see State Institute of Statistics (SIS), 2004). An important observation relating to labor market data for the period following 2002 is the presence of sharp increases in the national income together with overly slow expansion in employment, which is known as jobless growth in the literature (see UNCTAD, 2002, 2003).[5] Therefore, while the contribution of employment to growth was negative owing to the decline in employment, the contribution of

---

[5] Turkey's jobless growth starting from the late 1990s and the early 2000s is believed partly to have been due to tightening labor market regulations so as to be more like the EU. The labor market will be one of the key factors in ensuring a sustainable growth environment and enhancing the competitiveness of the economy during the process of EU accession (see further discussion, *Pre-Accession Economic Programme*, State Planning Organization (SPO) (2004, p. 80).

The basic conclusion to be drawn regarding the Turkish economy is that, from 1990 onward, while the contributions of capital and labor to the economic growth rate are below the average of the MENA as well as the non-oil MENA countries, the Turkish economy performs remarkably well in terms of TFP. The important contributions of both capital and labor to the economic growth rates between 1960 and 1990 were replaced by TFP in the following years.

Consequently, our message from this section is clear: despite recent improvements, when the MENA countries are taken as a benchmark, the Turkish economy suffered a high and volatile inflation for the whole sample. In addition, in terms of growth performance, it should be noted that the contribution of TFP to the output growth rate is much higher for the Turkish economy, despite the fact that the contributions of labor and capital are below the average. Finally, in terms of output, it should also be added that the growth performance of Turkey changes significantly over time, which leads to excessive fluctuations in output around its potential level. Such a finding necessitates further focusing on these fluctuations. For this purpose, in the following sections, we first elaborate on the effects of the macroeconomic policies implemented in generating these negative outcomes. Then, we try to build a link between short-term capital flows and the output gap.

4. Macroeconomic policies and the financial crises

Several studies point out that macroeconomic problems intensified during the 1990s. Thus, it is not surprising to witness two financial crises for this particular period, which resulted mainly from incorrect macroeconomic policy decisions.[11] In this section, we investigate these policy mistakes. In addition, we focus on two important negative characteristics of the economy for this particular period: specifically, the lack of fiscal discipline and the untimely liberalization of the financial markets. As will be clarified below, these two interrelated factors are significant, but not solely responsible for the two financial crises, which could have been avoided with the right macroeconomic policy decisions. We start our discussion with the currency crisis of 1994.

4.1. The 1994 currency crisis

As mentioned in the second section, in April 1994, the Turkish economy suffered a major currency crisis, during which the domestic currency depreciated by almost 70% against the US dollar, interest jumped overnight to 700%, and as a result, economic growth decreased by 6%. As discussed in Özatay (2000), despite the worsening macroeconomic fundamentals in the economy such as the

---

[11] For a detailed analysis of the Turkish economy for the sample period, see Ertuğrul and Selçuk (2001), Özatay (1999) and Şenses (1991).

Figure 3.   *Actual output, potential output and output gap*

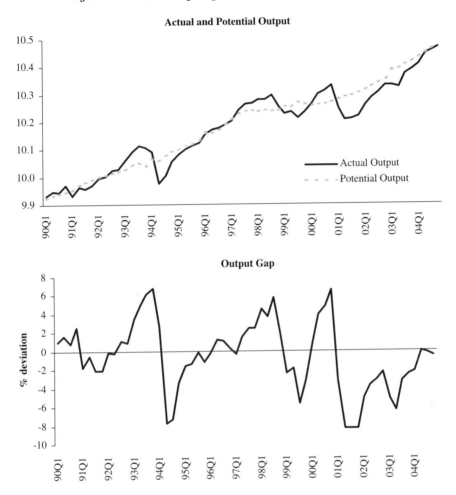

5.1. *Role of short-term capital flows*

Emphasis can be placed on the significance of short-term capital flows as a major determinant of the above-mentioned output gap, especially after the capital account liberalization of 1989. Capital flows that are accompanied by weak financial structure have led to a number of economic crises with severe social and economic costs in many emerging market economies. A similar argument can be valid for Turkey considering the growth performance in the aftermath of the financial liberalization policy. The experiences of the last decade especially point to the dependence of growth performance on capital flows (Figure 4).

In fact, economic conditions providing speculative arbitrage opportunities were a result of unsuccessful disinflationary efforts, which dragged the economy

Figure 4. Capital flows and GDP growth

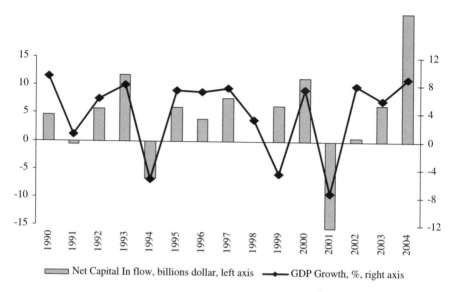

into "slowed down depreciation-correction" cycles (Ertuğrul and Selçuk, 2001). In this respect, the fluctuations during the 1990s can be characterized as a financial cycle determined by capital movements. Therefore, periods of capital inflows coincided with high economic growth periods followed by subsequent real depreciation and crisis periods. In an effort to control inflation as well as ease domestic borrowing, the policies focused on slowing down the depreciation of the Turkish lira.

However, policies oriented toward controlling the exchange rate generally lead to an initial decline in interest rates and a real appreciation of the domestic currency owing to the slow catch-up of the inflation rate. As a stylized fact, similar to the general characteristic of exchange rate-based stabilization programs, an initial upsurge in domestic demand and real activity along with real appreciation give rise to an increase in imports. The subsequent deterioration of the current account balance and concerns regarding its sustainability reverse the process and trigger capital outflows. Hence, the economy comes to its initial point again with high interest rates, depreciated domestic currency, contracted domestic demand and an improved current account balance. Such a macroeconomic instability results in the rising volatility of the growth rate and thus creates *mini* business cycles, the duration of which shortens as a result of the huge and rapid changes in the size and direction of short-term capital flows.

Figure 5 demonstrates the tight relationship between net capital inflows and the real exchange rate, except for the years 1998 and 1999. During the 1995–1998 period, capital flows had been quite stable at positive levels and the real exchange was appreciating. It was possible to sustain the appreciation of the

6. Conclusion

Unsustainable output growth and high inflation are the two prevailing macroeconomic characteristics of the Turkish economy. These two factors also indicate a boom–bust cycle, which the economy has experienced more severely in the last decade. In this respect, as of mid-2005, after the negative effects of the 2001 crisis were partly eliminated, there has been considerable discussion about whether the recent positive developments in the output and the inflation dynamics are the result of a new macroeconomic policy framework or whether they simply reflect an expansionary phase of such a business cycle.

Taking this discussion as our reference point, we tried to analyze the growth dynamics in the Turkish economy. Throughout the study, we handled the issue in three ways. First, we presented an overview of the Turkish economy from a growth perspective and compared its performance in terms of output and inflation with the other MENA countries. The main finding from this approach is that Turkey has not followed the right macroeconomic policies to have a sustainable growth path. Moreover, the Turkish economy has suffered from high and volatile inflation. In addition, the growth accounting exercise shows that the TFP is the main cause behind the recent increase in output growth rates for the Turkish economy. Then, we discuss the characteristics of these incorrect macroeconomic policies, with a special reference to the two financial crises in 1994 and 2001. This discussion brings to the fore an important link between short-term capital inflows and excessive output fluctuations. Finally, we performed an empirical investigation of the role of the short-term capital flows in generating these fluctuations. It can be seen clearly that there is a very close relationship between the output dynamics and the capital inflows. The periods of high growth rates also coincide with the periods of massive short-term capital inflows. The fact that these capital inflows reached a maximum by mid-2005 makes us think that the recent positive developments owe much to the increases in the capital inflows. Thus, we can say that it is too early to judge the success of the new macroeconomic policy framework that was put into effect after the 2001 crisis. The effects of this new framework will be better understood when the short-term capital inflows decrease to moderate levels.

Lastly, based on the output gap measure, we analyzed the business cycle characteristics of the Turkish economy. As a result, we found that most of the major output components tend to move with the cycle. Moreover, the indicators of resource utilization move with the output gap simultaneously. Finally, a positive output gap exerts an upward pressure on the marginal costs through the labor demand channel.

References

Aguiar, M. and G. Gopinath (2004), Emerging market business cycles: the cycle is the trend, Mimeo, University of Chicago.

Akyüz, Y. and K. Boratav (2001), "The making of the Turkish financial crisis", prepared for a conference on Financialization of the Global Economy, PERI, December 7–9, University of Massachusetts, Amherst, MA.

Aricanli, T. and D. Rodrik (1990), *The Political Economy of Turkey: Debt, Adjustment, and Sustainability*, London: Macmillan.

Boone, L., M. Juillard, D. Laxton and P. N'Diaye (2001), "How well do alternative time-varying parameter models of the NAIRU help policy makers forecast unemployment and inflation in the OECD countries?", IMF Working Paper, Draft version.

Boratav, K. and E. Yeldan (2002), "Turkey, 1980–2000: financial liberalization, macroeconomic (in)-stability and patterns of distribution", Mimeo, January.

Bosworth, B. and S.M. Collins (2003), *The empirics of growth: an update*, Brookings Institution.

Butler, L. (1996), "A semi-structural method to estimate potential output: combining economic theory with a time-series filter", The Bank of Canada's New Quarterly Projection Model (QPM), Part 4.

Celasun, M. and D. Rodrik (1989), "Debt, adjustment and growth: Turkey", in: J. Sachs and S.M. Collins, editors, *Developing Country Debt And Economic Performance, Country Studies*, Chicago: University of Chicago Press.

Conway, P. (1990), "The record on private investment in Turkey", in: T. Aricanli and D. Rodrik, editors, *The Political Economy of Turkey: Debt, Adjustment, and Sustainability*, London: Macmillan.

Dees, S., F. Di Mauro, M.H. Pesaran and L.V. Smith (2005), "Exploring the international linkages of the Euro area: a global VAR analysis", CESifo Working Paper No. 1425.

Ece, D., H. Kara, F. Öğünç, Ü. Özlale and Ç. Sarikaya (2005), "Estimating output gap for the Turkish economy", Unpublished Manuscript, The Central Bank of the Republic of Turkey, Research Department, Ankara, Turkey.

Ekinci, N. (1990), "Macroeconomic developments in Turkey: 1980–1988", *METU Studies in Development*, Vol. 17(1–2), pp. 73–114.

Ekinci, N. (2000), "The IMF and reforming the public sector in Turkey", METU E.R.C. Working Papers in Economics, No. 00/04, Ankara, METU.

Ertuğrul, A. and F. Selçuk (2001), "A brief account of the Turkish economy 1980–2000", *Russian and East European Finance and Trade*, Vol. 37(6), pp. 6–28.

Femise Report on the EURO Mediterranean Partnership (2003), ERF, Cairo, Egypt and Institut de la Mediterranee, France.

Hakura D. S. (2004), "Growth in the Middle East and North Africa", IMF Working Paper WP/04/56.

Independent Social Scientists' Alliance (ISSA) Report (2005), "On economic and social life in Turkey in early 2005", http://www.bagimsizsosyalbilimciler.org.

İsmihan, M. (2003), "The role of politics and stability on public spending dynamics and macroeconomic performance: theory and evidence from Turkey", Unpublished PhD Thesis, The Graduate School of Social Sciences of Middle East technical University, Ankara.

Ismihan, M. and K. Metin-Özcan (2005), "Sources of growth in Turkish economy, 1960–2004", ERF 12th Annual Conference Paper, Cairo, Egypt.

İsmihan, M., K. Metin-Özcan and A. Tansel (2005), "The role of macroeconomic instability in public and private capital accumulation and growth: the case of Turkey 1963–1999", *Applied Economics*, Vol. 37, pp. 239–251.

Kydland, F. and E. Prescott (1990), "Business cycles: real facts and a monetary myth", Federal Reserve Bank of Minneapolis Quarterly Review, Spring, pp. 3–18.

Ljung, L. and T. Soderstrom (1983), Theory and Practice of Recursive Identification. The MIT Press.

Makdisi, S., Fattah Z. and I. Limam (2000), "Determinants of growth in the MENA countries", The World Bank sponsored project on the Global Development Network.

Maraşlıoğlu, H. and Tiktik, A. (1991), *Türkiye Ekonomisinde Sektörel Gelişmeler : Üretim, Sermaye Birikimi veİstihdam 1968–1988*, Devlet Planlama Teşkilatı, İktisadi Planlama Başkanliği, DPT: 2271- İPB: 428.

Metin, K. (1995), *The analysis of inflation: the case of Turkey (1948–1988)*, Ankara: Nurol Publishing Co., Capital Markets Board Publication No. 20.

Metin-Ozcan, K., E. Voyvoda and E. Yeldan (2001), "Dynamics of macroeconomic adjustment in a globalized developing economy: growth, accumulation and distribution, Turkey 1969–1998", *Canadian Journal of Development Studies*, Vol. 22(1), pp. 219–253.

Özatay, F. (1999), "Populist policies and the role of economic institutions in the performance of the Turkish economy", *Yapi Kredi Economic Review*, Vol. 10(1), pp. 13–26.

Özatay, F. (2000), "The 1994 currency crisis in Turkey", *Journal of Policy Reform*, Vol. 3, pp. 327–352.

Pamukçu T. and Yeldan, E. (2005), "Country profile: Turkey, public sector and fiscal policy issues", Mimeo, March 2005.

Saygili, Ş. (1999), *Technical change efficiency, growth and exports: the case of Turkish economy*, Unpublished PhD thesis, University of Kent at Canterbury, England.

Saygili, Ş., C. Cihan ve H. Yurtoğğlu (2005), "Türkiye Ekonomisinde Sermaye Birikimi Verimlilik ve Büyüme: 1972–2003, DPT yayin No. 2686, Ankara.

Sekkat, K. (2003), "The sources of growth in Morocco: an empirical analysis in a regional perspective" ERF Working Paper, Cairo.

Senhadji, A. (2000), "Sources of economic growth: an extensive growth accounting exercise", *IMF Staff Papers*, Vol. 47(1), pp. 129–157.

Şenses, F. (1991), "Turkey's stabilization and structural adjustment program retrospect and prospect", *The Developing Economies*, Vol. 29, pp. 210–234.

Somçağ, S. (2004), "Confession of imaginary stock by the SIS", http://www.selimsomcag.org.

State Institute of Statistics (SIS) (2004), *Household Labor Surveys*, Ankara, Turkey.

State Planning Organization (SPO) (2004), *Pre-Accession Economic Programme*, Ankara: Republic of Turkey: SPO, November 2004.

Temel, A., ve Ş. Saygili (1995), "An estimation of gross fixed capital formation", in: T. Bulutay, editor, *Investment and the Labour Market in Turkey: Proceedings of a Seminar Held in Ankara 7 December 1995*, Ankara; SIS.

Temel, A., E. Boyar and Ş. Saygili (2000), *Türkiye Ekonomisinde Büyüme ve Ekonomik Yapi Değişmeleri: 1946-1999*, Unpublished Manuscript, State Planning Organization, Ankara, Turkey.

UNCTAD (2002, 2003), *Trade and Development Report, 2002 and 2003*, New York: UNCTAD.

Uygur, E. (1995), "Recent estimates of investment and private investment behaviour in Turkey", in T. Bulutay, editor, *Investment and The Labour Market in Turkey: Proceedings of a Seminar Held in Ankara 7 December 1995*, Ankara; SIS.

World Bank Country Study (1980), *Turkey: policies and prospects for growth*, Washington, DC, USA: The World Bank.

Appendix A: The output gap estimation for the Turkish economy

This appendix briefly introduces the output gap model and the methodology that is used in Ece *et al.* (2005). The system of equations, in which the output gap is derived as the difference between the actual output and the potential output, is as follows:

(1) Inflation-output gap dynamics:

$$\pi_t = \alpha_{1,t}\pi_{t-1} + \alpha_{2,t}\pi_{t-2} + \alpha_{3,t}gap_{t-1} + \alpha_{4,t}reer_t + v_t$$

(2) Actual output decomposition:

$$y_t = y_t^* + gap_t$$

(3) Potential output equation:

$$y_t^* = y_{t-1}^* + \mu_{t-1} + \eta_t$$

(4) Potential output growth rate equation:

$$\mu_t = (1 - \rho_t)\mu_0 + \rho_t\mu_{t-1} + \varepsilon_t$$

(5) Output gap dynamics:

$$gap_t = \gamma_{1,t}gap_{t-1} + \gamma_{2,t}r_t + \gamma_{3,t}DI_t + \gamma_{4,t}reer_t + \varsigma_t$$

where π_t is the inflation rate defined as the logarithmic difference of quarterly seasonally adjusted consumer price index (CPI), gap_t the unobserved output gap, $reer_t$ the logarithmic difference of the real effective exchange rate, y_t the logarithmic seasonally adjusted real gross domestic product, y^*_t the unobserved potential output, μ_t the potential output growth rate, r_t the *ex post* real interest rate based on 3-month Treasury auction rates and DI_t the demand index, which is constructed from the Business Tendency Survey of the Central Bank of the Republic of Turkey. In contrast, v_t, η_t, ε_t and ξ_t represent shocks to the system, which are assumed to be i.i.d. with zero mean and constant variances.

It is important to remind that the parameters of the system are time varying. Therefore, one has to make a time-series specification for the evolution of these parameters. It is assumed that each time-varying parameter follows a random walk. Such a specification can be defended on theoretical grounds: Since any structural change on the dynamics of the model–thus the system parameters–cannot be known *a priori*, it is intuitive to specify a random-walk process for each parameter. As a result, the system includes nine more equations, where each time-varying parameter follows a random-walk process.

Finally, it should be noted that the output gap variable, which needs to be estimated within the system, appears in multiplicative form with the time-varying parameters, which, again, are to be estimated. Thus, the model has a non-linear characteristic, where the standard Kalman filter is inappropriate and should be replaced by the extended Kalman filter algorithm, which is designed for estimating non-linear state space models. For details about the extended Kalman filter algorithm, one can either read the appendix in Ece *et al.* or "Theory and practice of recursive identification" by Ljung and Soderstrom (1983), from which the appendix in Ece *et al.* (2005) is derived.

Appendix B: Robustness tests with the output gap measure from Dees et al. (2005)

Table B.1.   *Cross correlations of GAP_t with $STCF_{t \pm i}$ (1992Q1–2003Q4)*

$(t-5)$	$(t-4)$	$(t-3)$	$(t-2)$	$(t-1)$	(t)	$(t+1)$	$(t+2)$	$(t+3)$	$(t+4)$	$(t+5)$
−0.17	−0.09	0.09	0.23	0.49	0.47	0.24	0.04	−0.17	−0.21	−0.07

Table B.2.   *Granger causality test between GAP and STCF (1992Q1–2003Q4)*

Dependent variable: GAP		
Excluded	χ^2	P-value
STCF	7.7550	0.0207
Dependent variable: STCF		
Excluded	χ^2	P-value
GAP	2.0692	0.3554

Table B.3. Cross correlation of output gap (Gap$_t$) with selected variables (1988Q2–2003Q4)

	$(t-5)$	$(t-4)$	$(t-3)$	$(t-2)$	$(t-1)$	(t)	$(t+1)$	$(t+2)$	$(t+3)$	$(t+4)$	$(t+5)$
Private consumption	-0.17	-0.16	-0.02	0.13	0.35	0.52	0.44	0.32	0.17	0.02	-0.04
Durable consumption	-0.21	-0.19	-0.02	0.12	0.30	0.47	0.38	0.28	0.17	0.05	0.00
Private investment	-0.11	-0.13	0.00	0.12	0.32	0.45	0.43	0.35	0.20	0.04	-0.03
Machinery equipment	-0.13	-0.12	0.00	0.15	0.36	0.48	0.46	0.34	0.18	0.00	-0.07
Construction	-0.01	-0.07	-0.08	-0.09	-0.07	-0.05	0.03	0.11	0.16	0.24	0.29
Capacity utilization	0.18	0.22	0.33	0.46	0.60	0.68	0.43	0.21	0.00	-0.15	-0.17
Number of workers	-0.07	-0.04	0.05	0.18	0.29	0.40	0.40	0.30	0.15	0.00	-0.08
Working hours	-0.04	-0.02	0.07	0.21	0.34	0.45	0.39	0.28	0.13	-0.04	-0.09
Labor productivity	-0.04	-0.05	0.08	0.10	0.31	0.36	0.19	0.11	-0.03	-0.08	-0.06
Real wage[a]	-0.54	0.09	-0.38	-0.21	0.03	0.29	0.48	0.43	0.37	0.22	0.18
Real unit wage[a]	-0.45	-0.47	-0.37	-0.22	-0.01	0.22	0.47	0.48	0.42	0.29	0.15

[a] Correlation in 1999Q1–2004Q4.

CHAPTER 9

Economic Growth and Economic Policy in Iran: 1950–2003

Ahmad R. Jalali-Naini[*]

Abstract

The Iranian experience reveals, in a number of ways, the potentials, problems, and challenges that have been confronted by other populated oil-exporting countries – a tale of high expectations turning into mediocre performance. Three distinct growth periods, with different political and policy environments, are identified over the 1950–2003 period. From the 1960s up to the first oil boom (1973–1974) the economy exhibited high GDP growth and low inflation rates. The oil boom brought in large financial resources, but also induced soft-budget constraints, and expanded the public sector. The huge increase in oil-financed government spending raised growth temporarily above its trend; however, by creating inflation and opportunities for rent seeking, it resulted in economic and social instability. The positive wealth and saving effects of the oil boom did not have a long-lasting effect on either economic growth rates or on per-capita income levels. Since 1974 economic growth has been volatile and factor-intensive and total factor productivity did not make a significant contribution to economic growth. The evidence also does not support that human capital accumulation has strongly contributed to economic growth. While fixed investment/GDP ratios in Iran compare favorably with high growth economies, the growth performance does not; too many resources have been spent to produce only an average growth performance. It is argued that Iran's relatively rich resources, high rates of accumulation of physical and human capital, but a mundane growth performance and continued dependence on oil reflect inadequate economic institutions, price/incentive distortions, policy coordination and rent-seeking problems, and the effect of the Iran–Iraq war. In the episodes with superior

---

*Corresponding author.

CONTRIBUTIONS TO ECONOMIC ANALYSIS
VOLUME 278   ISSN: 0573-8555
DOI:10.1016/S0573-8555(06)78009-9

growth performance, economic and institutional uncertainty and transaction costs were lower, the price structure was more rational, and government policies allowed wider participation by the private sector.

Keywords: Economic growth, Iran, government policy

JEL classifications: O40, O53, Q38

1. Introduction

Iran's growth experience over the 1950–2003 period is, in many ways, similar to the opportunities, problems, and challenges that have been confronted by other populated oil-exporting countries. It is a case of high expectations turning into mediocre performance. The positive wealth and saving effects of the oil boom did not have a long-lasting effect on economic growth rates. Since 1974 economic growth has been volatile and factor-intensive and total factor productivity (TFP) did not make a significant contribution to economic growth. While fixed investment/GDP ratios in Iran compare favorably with high growth economies, the growth performance does not. In this paper we will argue that Iran's relatively rich resources, high rates of accumulation of physical and human capital (HC), but mediocre growth rates and continued dependence on oil reflect inadequate economic institutions, price/incentive distortions, policy coordination, and rent-seeking problems – and the effect of the Iran–Iraq war in the 1980s.

This paper identifies three distinct phases of economic growth in Iran during the 1950–2003 period, compares the growth performance of the Iranian economy with other developing countries (DCs), identifies the sources of growth, and examines the influence of oil and government economic policies on economic growth.

The paper is organized as follows. Section 2 reviews three distinct growth periods in Iran and sectoral growth patterns. Section 3 reviews the modern "stylized facts" of growth and their empirical relevance in Iran. In Section 4 we use the conventional growth accounting methods to measure the sources of economic growth. In Section 5 the influence of important growth correlates such as oil, fiscal variables, macroeconomic uncertainty, price distortions, and financial deepening for the Iranian economy will be tested through standard growth regressions. Section 6 discusses oil, the state, and rent seeking and growth performance. Section 7 presents a summary and some policy options.

2. Aggregate growth performance and sectoral growth patterns: 1950–2003

Modern economic growth is predicated on a number of social, economic, and institutional transformations; first and foremost being the growth of the domestic market. Market production increasingly supplanted "natural economy" during the first half of the 20th century in Iran. Demographic changes, migration, urbanization, oil discovery, and transportation breakthroughs accelerated this process. Population growth, particularly in the urban areas picked up: the share of urban population rose from around 20 percent at the turn of the 20th century to 40 percent in 1955 – while the size of the population nearly tripled. Trade between rural areas and the towns expanded as expansion of road networks and highways reduced transportation costs quite significantly (Issawi, 1971). Safer and more secure roads facilitated greater local and regional trade. Growing oil revenues stimulated urbanization and monetization of the economy. The rural areas supplied growing quantities of food and agricultural cash crops to the urban areas.

During the early 1920s to the mid-1950s a justice system was created and a set of legal codes for trade and commerce was enacted. Moreover, a public administration system, a fiscal system, and a national bank were created. The number of small and large manufacturing firms increased significantly during the 1930s; oil revenues financed imports of capital and intermediate goods for this sector.[1] This period also witnessed growth in wage-laborer employment on a significant scale. Back-cast projections put the GDP growth rate estimates during the 1937–1950 period at 4.42 percent *per annum* and indicates that the growth rate had picked up in the 1950s.[2]

Based on the available data, we can distinguish three different growth phases or growth cycles in Iran: 1959–1977 (Persian calendar years 1338–1356), 1978–1988, and 1989–2003. The time trend for real GDP, non-oil GDP, and *per-capita* GDP are shown in Figures 1 and 2. The average growth rates and growth fluctuations, measured by their standard deviations, are shown in Table 1. The average growth rate of non-oil GDP in constant prices during the first period was 10.2 percent per annum. A clear fall in the growth trend can be observed in the 1978–1988 interval covering the revolution and the Iran–Iraq war. In the third period, there is another break in the trend as economic growth resumes following the end of the war. The average annual growth rate of non-oil GDP in the third period was 5.4 percent. On a *per-capita* basis, the distinctions between the three different periods are starker. The average non-oil GDP *per-capita* growth rate in the second period is about -4 percent.

3. Stylized facts of growth

The main features of the economic growth of nations are described by the stylized facts. The original stylized facts of growth (Kuznets and Kaldor) focused on a number of "grand" ratios and their evolution through time, specifically: potential

---

[1] In 1926 only 30 manufacturing establishments employing > 50 workers including the oil industry were in existence. By 1956, the total number of large manufacturing units had grown to 114. Total employment in this sector had grown to around 520,000 persons by 1956; the great majority of the employees worked in small artisan-type workshops (Bharier, 1971).

[2] The above period is equivalent to the 1316–1329 period in the Persian calendar, see, Khavari (2001).

Ahmad R. Jalali-Naini

Figure 1.   Real GDP Trend Iran

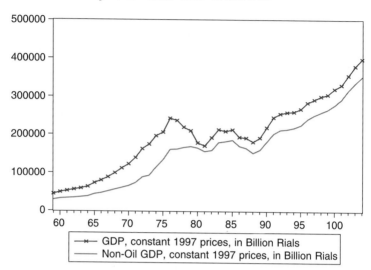

Source: The Central Bank of the Islamic Republic of Iran, henceforth BMI

Figure 2.   Per capita Real GDP and Non-Oil GDP in Iran

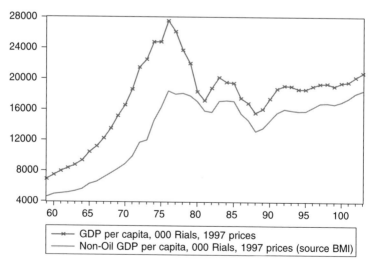

Source: BMI

Table 1. Economic growth in Iran, selected periods (in percentages)

	1959–2003		1959–1977		1978–1988		1989–2003	
	Non-oil GDP[a]	GDP[a]	Non-Oil GDP	GDP	Non-Oil GDP	GDP	Non-Oil GDP	GDP
Mean	5.93	5.27	10.2	9.91	−0.424	−2.1	5.47	5.13
Standard deviation	6.90	7.26	6.6	4.84	6.006	8.21	3.41	3.84
	Non-oil GDP per worker	Non-oil GDP per population	Non-oil GDP per worker	Non-oil GDP per population	Non-oil GDP per worker	Non-oil GDP per population	Non-oil GDP per worker	Non-oil GDP per population
Mean	3.4	3.17	8.0	7.06	−2.67	−3.93	2.31	3.72
Standard deviation	6.4	6.8	5.9	6.65	5.4	−5.59	2.54	3.11
Observations	44	44	18	18	11	11	15	15

Source: BMI.
[a]Constant 1997 prices.

output and *per-capita* income grow steadily over the long run; capital stock growth is about the same as output; capital labor ratio grows at a fairly steady rate; the shares of profit and wages in output are fairly stable in the long run. Chenery and Syrquin (1975) detected a general pattern of structural transformation and sectoral shift in the DCs in the process of growth. More recent empirical works (Mankiw et al., 2000; Mankiw, 1995; Klenow and Rodríguez–Clare, 1997; Barro, 2001; Easterly and Levine, 2001) have given rise to a number of other empirical findings on whether growth is driven by factor accumulation or productivity increases over time, on the effects of HC, national economic policies, and institutions on growth. Among these findings are:

(a) Non-convergence in large cross-country samples: *per-capita* incomes diverge over the long run among developed countries and DCs because growth rate differentials persist.
(b) Growth is highly volatile and not persistent, but factor accumulation is persistent.
(c) TFP (or more appropriately the "residual") rather than factor accumulation accounts for much of the growth differentials among countries.
(d) National policies and good institutions have a significant effect on economic growth performance.

For the specific case of economic growth of Iran, we elaborate the changes in the "grand" ratios and other stylized facts in the following paragraphs.

3.1. Grand ratios and structural change

In the course of economic growth capital per worker and output per worker grow steadily over time. In a standard production function setting, higher capital per worker and (Hicks-neutral) technical progress are the main determinants of output per worker. The data indicates that the main determinant of output per worker in Iran (as measured by real non-oil GDP per non-oil worker) is capital per worker and the contribution of technical progress to higher output per worker is positive but very little. Figure 3 shows that the indexes of capital per worker and non-oil output per worker during the 1959–2003 period have similar trends. The long-run comovement between these two non-stationary variables is empirically verified by the existence of a co-integrating vector between the log of output per worker and the log of capital per worker.[3] Output per worker increased at a quicker pace than capital per worker during 1964–1974. This trend was reversed during the 1975–1987 period.

---

[3] The trace statistics test indicates the existence of a cointegrating vector between the two variables at the 1 percent level for the 1959–2000 period. The trend variable capturing the effect of TFP or technical progress is positive, but has a very low value of 0.0016.

Figure 5.   Gross Fixed Investment Rate in Iran

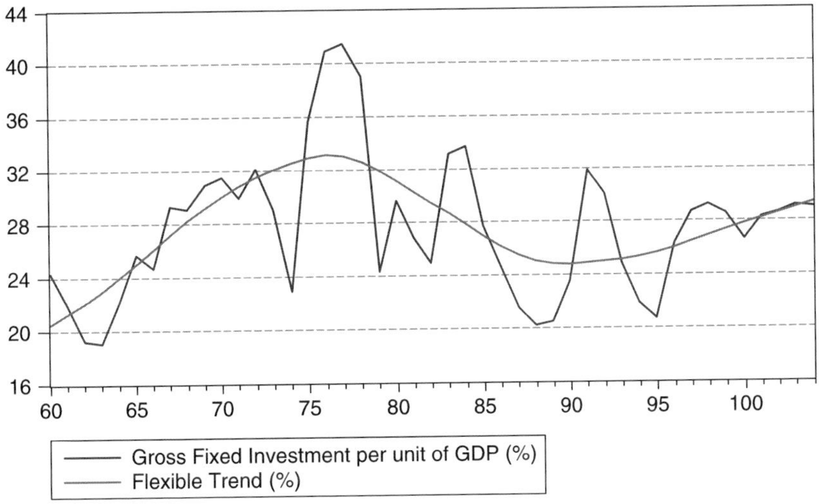

——— Gross Fixed Investment per unit of GDP (%)
——— Flexible Trend (%)

Source: BMI

developed financial market and budgetary rent seeking. As a consequence, the huge wealth transfer and positive government-saving boost from higher oil prices during 1974–1985 in Iran and in most other oil-exporting countries did not result in a significant and permanently higher *per-capita* income level or a higher growth path – as implied from either conventional (Solow–Swan) or endogenous growth models. There has not been a growth miracle story for the oil exporters, and it does not seem that there will be one in the offing.

3.3. Growth volatility and shock persistence

Economic growth in Iran like most MENA countries and other DCs is unstable and shows significant fluctuations. Growth rate volatility in Iran is nearly twice as much as in the industrial countries.[7] Unlike South and East Asia, growth in MENA (and Latin-America) has been volatile. Output series and estimates for TFP in the MENA region are twice as volatile as those in developed countries (Senhadji, 1999). These observations are consistent with the findings of Easterly *et al.* (2000) that the volatility of growth for DCs is much higher than that in the OECD countries.[8]

---

[7] For details see Jalali-Naini (1999).
[8] They also found that employment and real wages are also more volatile in the DCs.

Ahmad R. Jalali-Naini

Table 4. Measures of persistence for GDP series in selected MENA countries

Country	Egypt	Iran	Morocco	Saudi Arabia	Tunisia	Turkey
ARIMA	1.89 (1,1,0)	2.41 (1,1,0)	0.641 (0,1,1)	1.44 (1,1,0)	0.258 (0,1,2)	0.905 (1,1,0)
Spectral density	1.75	2.68	0.264	1.98	0.256	0.94

Note: the sample period for Iran is 1959–2000, and for other countries is 1960–1999.
Source: calculated from real GDP series, World Bank.

Aside from volatility, economic growth in Iran shows a significant degree of shock persistence. The estimates of persistence, based on spectral density and auto regressive integrated moving average (ARIMA) are given in Table 4. The order of ARIMA and the associated measures of persistence for Iran and some selected countries are presented.[9] The estimates of persistence based on spectral density and ARIMA for Iran during the 1959–2000 period are both substantially higher than unity – which is the measure of persistence for a random-walk process. These imply persistence of growth shocks; a pick up in the growth rate is followed by movements in the same direction.[10]

What could be behind shock persistence? In the mainstream macro models (excluding RBC) nominal shocks are presumed to have only temporary effects on output, though nominal or real rigidities can prolong their effects. Easterly *et al.* (2000) argue that, given that real wages are more flexible in DCs, the orthodox Keynesian and monetarist interpretation that monetary shocks have a long-lasting effect on output growth cannot be maintained. In their opinion, the shallowness of financial institutions rather than incomplete wage flexibility in the standard macro models is the cause of excess output volatility.[11] Jalali-Naini and Nazifi (2002) provide indirect support for this view by showing that the effects of positive as well as negative nominal shocks on output die out quickly and there are

---

[9] The results of the ARIMA specification with the highest value of Akaike Information Criterion and Schwarz Bayesian Criterion are reported here (Pesaran and Pesaran, 1997). In most cases, a first-order autoregressive process in the first difference of the log of GDP (*ARIMA* 1,1,0) gave the best fit. In Morocco and Tunisia a moving average process was selected.

[10] Some words of caution are worth mentioning here. Given that our sample of observations is limited, the statistical problem of determining long-run characteristics (e.g. permanent component to output fluctuations) from finite samples exists. The evidence cited here cannot be taken as the evidence of the existence of a permanent component – even though the evidence is consistent with such an interpretation. Given the length of our sample, the evidence of shock persistence in Iran can also be consistent with a mean reversion story, that is, a slow reversion of output to a deterministic trend. What can be established with the evidence produced here is that, even if trend reversion cannot be rejected owing to finite data, trend reversion does not occur quickly.

[11] Countries can smooth shocks with greater capital account openness and this might result in less growth volatility. Greater openness, however, might increase volatility through sudden capital outflows. In any event, a better access to international capital markets can partially be achieved through a more developed domestic financial sector.

Table 5.   Estimates of production function parameters, selected regressions

	I	II	III	IV	V
	Phillips–Hansen	Phillips–Hansen	OLS	OLS	OLS
K	0.416	0.452	0.519	0.479	0.509
L			0.430		0.420
HL	0.577	0.490		0.513	
RSINTM		0.159	0.0005		

Note: sample period, 1959–2000.

no significant dynamic multiplier effects. If not attributable to monetary variables, persistence of shocks could have resulted from the real variables (e.g. major economic policy shifts, institutional instability, and terms of trade shocks).[12]

4. Sources of growth: factor accumulation or productivity

Growth studies have been interested in finding out whether *per-capita* income differentials across countries are due to different saving and investment rates in physical capital or differences in productivity growth and HC accumulation.[13] Some cross-country studies show that capital formation is the main driver of growth (Mankiw, 1995; Young, 1995), but others (Klenow and Rodríguez–Clare, 1997; Easterly and Levine, 2001) argue that it is TFP. In this section, we attempt to provide an answer to this question by examining the sources of growth in Iran and use standard methods to examine the relative importance of capital accumulation and TFP in the growth process.

Several forms of aggregate production functions with slightly different factor specifications were estimated for Iran. The Cobb–Douglass function yielded superior results and the estimated coefficients from five different regressions covering 1959–2000 are reported in Table 5. Each column in the table specifies the estimation methods used: Phillips–Hansen, 1990 (PH) and ordinary least squares.[14] The inputs in the production function are physical capital stock (K), employed workers (L), and in regression I, III, and IV the number of workers

---

[12] Makdisi *et al.* (2005) point to the significance of the terms of trade shocks in the Arab countries.
[13] These factors influence growth via a higher pace of innovation, quicker adaptation, creation of stronger incentives for investment, and improved resource allocation.
[14] The estimated parameters of regression I in Table 5 are a PH estimate of a Cobb–Douglass production function for non-oil GDP (value-added). The PH method is appropriate for estimation when a single cointegrating vector exists between a set of I(1) variables. Augmented Dicky Fuller test determined that the elements of the production function are I(1). A cointegration test indicated the existence of a single vector between them.

weighted by their HC.[15] The capital stock was estimated using perpetual inventory method.[16] We follow the general practice in the literature by taking a stock measure of education, that is, the average educational attainment of the labor force, as the proxy for HC.[17] A period dummy variable is included to capture the break in the production function owing to the war and revolution in the post-1977 period. In regressions II and III we added the deviation of real imported intermediate goods from trend as a capacity adjustment factor (a shift variable) to improve the fit.[18] When lower oil revenues and foreign currency shortages result in import rationing, imported intermediate goods/raw materials are below trend, thereby reducing the capacity utilization rate of the production units that have insufficient inputs and materials for further processing. In these periods the shift factor assumes a negative value. Different specifications and estimations resulted in slightly different factor elasticities and TFP estimates.[19] The elasticity of GDP with respect to the capital stock for the post-revolution period (1978–2003) was also estimated; its value is close to the average of the estimates in Table 5.[20]

The impact of HC in the growth accounting exercise was tested. First, HC was included as a separate factor of production. However, the coefficient of HC was not statistically significant. Inclusion of HC as a weighting factor for labor (education-augmented labor) yielded better results. In regression I, the elasticity of output with

---

[15] Lucas (1988) developed an intertemporal optimizing model that incorporates externalities (spillovers) originating from HC. A simplified Lucas-type production function is:

$$y_t = AK_t^{\alpha}[uh_t]^{1-\alpha}$$

where y is output per worker, k the capital per worker, u the fraction of time devoted to production of goods, and $(1-u)$ is the time allocated for production of h (HC per worker). The increment to capital stock is equal to savings. An estimate of this function for 1966–2000 yielded $\alpha = 0.518$, slightly larger than the capital elasticity obtained in Table 5 regressions, but the estimated elasticity of HC per worker was not statistically significant.

[16] The gross fixed capital formation series used for estimating K is based on the Central Bank data.

[17] Empirical studies have used a variety of proxies for education: enrollment ratios, the ratio of educated adults to the adult population, and the average years of schooling, that is, past educational attainment as a measure of current stock of HC. The estimated time series for HC stock in Iran was extracted from the Iranian household budget surveys for the 1972–1998 period and was extended forward for 1999 and 2000.

[18] The production function specification here is of the following form:

$$Y_t = A_t[K^a(H_tL_t)^{1-a}]f(.)$$

where f(.) measures the factors that cause a shift in the production function aside from productivity shocks. It has a general functional form; the specific form is ascertained through empirical estimation.

[19] The homogeneity condition was not imposed, but the estimated elasticities are very close to 1.

[20] The estimated value is 0.483 and it was obtained from a simple intensive form of a Cobb–Douglass function. Note that, the reliability of the estimates is dependent on the quality of the data, which is not very high.

Figure 8. Short and Long-term Deposit Rates

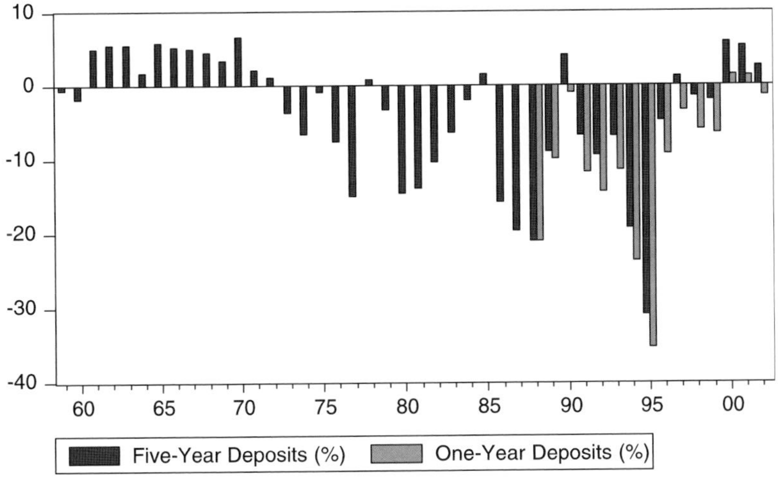

Note: Prior to 1988 only intermediate-term deposit rates, calculated from BMI data on deposit rates and prices

billion or > 14.5 percent of GDP.[33] The official exchange rate had remained unchanged for a long time despite a relatively higher domestic inflation rate. Consequently, the black-market premium in 1989 had increased to 2000 percent (Pesaran, 1992), creating and encouraging vast rent-seeking opportunities and activities. A highly overvalued domestic currency had drawn resources out of tradables, and domestic production at the prevailing exchange rates was no longer profitable in many sectors.

(6) Domestic real interest rates, particularly on short-to-intermediate certificates of deposits, were negative (Figure 8). Moreover, like other "repressed" financial markets, banking sector resources were widely used for quasi-fiscal operations. Moreover, state-directed (and subsidized) credit programs had done little to spur private investment (Jalali-Naini and Khalatbari, 2003).

(7) Foreign savings (current account deficits) of the mid-1980s were largely used to finance government current expenditures or the war efforts. Rationing the dwindling oil revenues was sufficient neither to significantly increase the domestic investment rate nor to recapitalize public enterprises and to finance reconstruction of the economy, including the oil sector.

---

[33] For more details see Iran Energy Report (2005).

The options for the economic planners were to:

(a) Mobilize and generate savings in excess of what the existing heavily state-controlled economic structure could deliver. This required the creation of incentives through price signals for additional supplies of capital and conservation of valuable resources such as energy. Subsidized energy prices had (and since then have) induced a high rate of growth of fuel consumption and its cost was financed out of government savings.

(b) Reduce the degree of real exchange rate misalignment to manageable proportions to economize its use in domestic production and consumption of imported goods and shifting relative prices in favor of tradables. Moreover, some restrictions on exported commodities were lifted. These measures were meant to encourage movement of capital and labor into non-oil exports and domestic production of import competing goods, hence increased supply of much needed foreign exchange by the private sector. However, no comprehensive measure to lift protection of domestic industry was attempted. Domestic protection emanated largely from a quantitative import control system, which cut imports during 1993–2000 by more than one-third of the levels in 1990–1992. Import tariffs were of secondary importance since the average level of tariffs in Iran was not high compared to that of the other DCs.[34]

(c) Reform and implement measures to develop the domestic financial sector.

(d) Resort to foreign borrowing as another avenue through which additional resources could be mobilized. External borrowing was exercised though not managed efficiently.

To remove tradable price distortions, several rounds of partial devaluation were implemented to unify various currency rates around the free-market rate during 1990–1993. These attempts were largely unsuccessful because they were inconsistent with the expansionary fiscal stance and low foreign currency reserves of the Central Bank. Put differently, the expenditure-switching policies (devaluation) were not backed with expenditure-reducing (monetary and fiscal) policies to achieve a real depreciation. Falling oil prices, foreign debt repayment, and limited access to international financial markets, in the absence of the appropriate fiscal measures rendered the inflation tax as the balancing variable in the system.[35] The inflation rate picked up significant momentum in 1993 and reached its height in 1995 (Figure 9). As a consequence, a real depreciation was not achieved by the exchange rate unification policy in 1992 and the Central Bank had to implement several rounds of additional nominal devaluations. The subsequent pickup in the inflation rate turned the social and political

---

[34] A major opening up of the economy for imports materialized only as a result of a huge increase in oil revenues during the 2002–2005 period.

[35] Fiscal measures to boost public savings are the most effective method to raise national savings (Easterly et al., 1994).

Figure 9.   Inflation Rate Trends

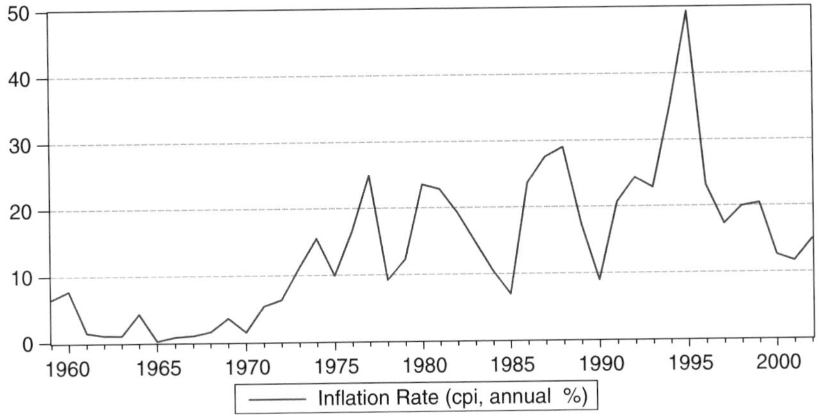

Source: calculated from CPI index (BMI)

environment against the reform package, and the process was stalled. With the election of a new president, the critics of the reform strategy gradually took charge of the majority of economic policy-making organizations. However, falling oil prices and economic realities forced the new group to opt for the same reform agenda. The Third Plan was based on a low oil price estimate of around $12 per barrel. Consequently, it called for privatization, exchange rate unification, elimination of quantitative trade restrictions, reform of the financial markets, privatization of banks, and more private sector (domestic as well as foreign) investment to achieve external balance and higher growth.

The general economic policies in the post-war period became more market-friendly compared to those in the 1978–1988 period; the relative price and exchange rate distortions were partially corrected, incentives for wider private sector participation became stronger, and the extent of property rights' uncertainties diminished. In this environment growth performance improved. Persistence of relatively low oil prices until the early 2000 was one reason policy makers pushed for greater economic efficiency, higher non-oil exports, and greater private sector investment. While government investment outpaced private investment, mainly owing to higher costs of acquisition of capital goods and crowding out of private investment by an expansionary fiscal policy in the mid-1990s, private investment rose significantly since 1996 as a share of aggregate fixed capital investment (Figure 10).[36] Note that, in general, the government's

---

[36] One should bear in mind that some of the private companies are first- or second-generation companies created by some government entity. There is no data to separate the purely private ones from those whose lineage goes back to some government organization or ministry.

Ahmad R. Jalali-Naini

Figure 10.   Government Share of Fixed Capital Investment

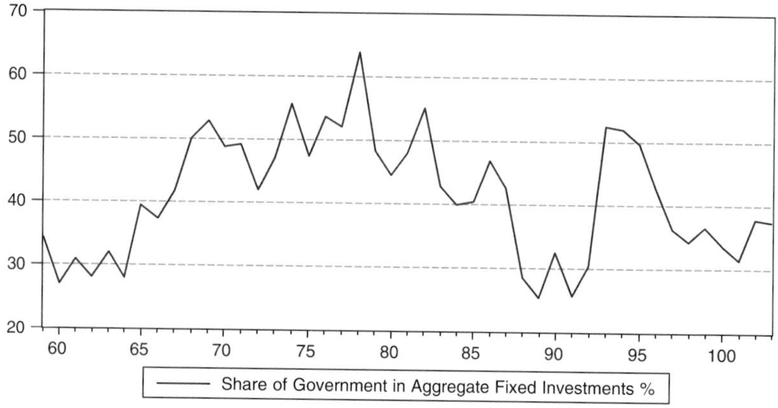

Source: calculated from GNE data (BMI)

share of aggregate investment in the Iranian economy has been large in the pre-
as well as post-revolution years. The shares were 41.9, 45.5, and 37.2 percent in
the first, second, and third periods, respectively.

Although growth performance improved in the post-war period, no major
progress was achieved to improve income distribution, in spite of huge subsidies
paid out by the government. The reform policies mentioned above have been
relegated and distributional issues and extension of subsidies have assumed a
higher priority since 2003 owing to a significant and sustained increase in oil
revenues. Large oil price changes usually pre-date major shifts in economic
policies in Iran.

5.3.1. National economic policy variables and growth: the evidence

One way to model the influence of economic policies is to relate them to growth
via their influence on TFP. This was the approach used in the growth accounting
section earlier.[37] An alternative is to use a number of institutional and policy
factors that influence growth performance as growth correlates. We follow the
literature on the growth correlates (Barro, 1995, 2001; Easterly and Levine,
2001). They include fiscal variables, the exchange rate, financial development,
measures of economic openness, proxies for the effect of macroeconomic im-
balance and uncertainty, and institutional variables. In the case of Iran, the
magnitude of oil revenues could be an important growth correlate. Owing to the

---

[37] A more general approach is to model how institutions, markets being an important subset, affect
the growth process. However, there is no comprehensive growth model to integrate even a subset of
these variables in a unified framework.

6. *Oil, rent-seeking, and economic growth*

In the standard growth models with perfectly competitive markets, the effects of institutions and policies on growth are reduced to the first-order conditions.[41] Under this setting, factor accumulation and technical progress are just what are needed to explain growth.[42] The bench mark optimal growth model generates results similar to the competitive model when the growth regulator is a benevolent government – a government devoid of self or group interest. Once the benevolence assumption is relaxed, a number of factors such as the quality of institutions, property rights, and rent seeking can affect growth performance. Hall and Jones (1999) and Stigliz (1989) argue that a significant proportion of the *per-capita* income gap between LDCs and DCs can be attributed to qualitative differences in organizations and the institutions through which the individuals interact.

Because of a historically weak private sector, missing markets, and monopoly of oil revenue, the government in Iran has had an enormous effect on the matrix of social institutions. The institutional matrix in an economy influences the allocation rules, development of non-governmental institutions, and economic incentives, hence it affects economic behavior and performance.[43] Economic performance in state-led economies has varied quite significantly ranging from "collapse" to "miracle," depending on the institutional matrix and the governance structure. Governments that have undertaken to establish an institutional framework with credible rules; limited economic uncertainty; low transaction costs; efficient provision of public goods; and conducted sensible economic policies, have been successful in promoting high rates of capital accumulation, higher productivity levels, and sustained growth.[44] Under this model, the commitment and reputation of the state to uphold the rules of the game provide private agents with a frame of reference to form "social capital" which is pro-growth.[45] Few populated oil states have been successful in creating this type of

---

[41] The government finds a place in the competitive model when externalities (learning, knowledge, public goods, provision, ...) are taken into account. When competitive markets and prices, as regulators and disciplinarians of the economic process are totally or partially absent, a host of factors, e.g. transaction costs, information asymmetry, and credit rationing can influence growth.

[42] If the differences were due to factor accumulation, then the rates of return on HC and physical capital would be significantly higher in DCs and that massive foreign capital should have flown to the poor instead of the rich countries. The evidence is clearly contrary to this pattern of factor reward and capital flows based on differential factor endowments (Stiglitz, 1989).

[43] Institutions are social constraints that structure incentives and human interaction. See North (1994) on institutions.

[44] For more details, see World Bank Report (1997).

[45] For more details, see Ismail Serageldin and Christiaan Grootaert, "Defining Social Capital: An Integrating View," Joseph Stiglitz, "Formal and Informal Institutions", Richard Rose, "Getting Things Done in an Antimodern Society: Social Capital Networks in Russia," and Partha Dasgupta, "Economic Progress and the Idea of Social Capital," in Dasgupta and Serageldin (2000).

economic environment. Gylfason (2001) argues that economic performance in oil-exporting countries is not satisfactory owing to widespread rent seeking, policy failures, and the Dutch disease. These tend to dampen the growth-inducing effects of government spending.

A bureaucratic/rentier system limits the allocation of resources through markets and economic transparency. Price distortions in a bureaucratically controlled allocation process imply greater inducement for rent-seeking opportunities and behavior and designing private networks to extract rent become an attractive economic activity. In this environment, extracting benefits from bureaucratic allocations of economic resources dominates the working agenda or the goals of business/formal organizations. "Social capital networks" can penetrate organizations and further affect allocation of resources through favoritism and rent seeking. Instead of following the laws and responding to price signals, rules are sidestepped by personal contacts and politics.[46] The payoffs to rent seeking can be very significant and in many instances greater than what could be obtained through competition and efficiency. Those who distribute rents and the firms collecting it can form interest groups to oppose reform and contest with outside groups for a share of the benefits. The by-products of such an economic environment can be large unproductive expenditures such as military spending, large government payoffs to groups with political and military clout, and (numerous) government investment programs with low social rates of return (Gelb, 1988) and low TFP.[47]

Attempts to undertake some reforms in the economic sphere (in the context of the development plans) to foster non-government institutions, including incomplete and missing markets, to correct price signals, to reduce the degree of trade protection, and to improve economic-policy consistency have been made in Iran, but these were not accompanied by the complementary political and institutional reforms. These attempts have been resisted by the vested interests – and sometimes by the social groups that were not the direct beneficiaries – particularly during oil

---

[46] See Rose (2000). This kind of model can also result in incredibility (or instability) of the rules Incredibility gives rise to contract uncertainty and low credibility. The effectiveness of the enforcement of contracts is one of the most important determinants of economic performance and a crucial difference between developing and developed economies (North, 1990). Uncertainty and low credibility of economic policies result in lower investment rates and adoption of costly strategies by the private sector. Countries with higher credibility tend to have a higher investment rate (as a percentage of GDP) and a higher growth rate (World Bank Report, 1997). As shown in Tabibian (2002) little or no growth in the average size of the private firms which can be due to economic uncertainity and property rights' concerns. Salehi-Isfahani (2002) describes the relationship between contract uncertainty and growth in Iran.

[47] The average duration of government investment projects in Iran is unusually high.

booms.[48] Well-functioning economic institutions have a higher probability of developing in an environment in which small groups do not have privileged access to natural resource revenues. As mentioned in Sections 5.1–5.3, every major improvement in the terms of trade of oil, while improving the potential for rent seeking, has significantly altered the posture of economic policies in Iran, making reform initiatives less credible.

Based on the above discussions, we expect that economic rents made available through the government budget to be significant and rent-seeking activities are likely to increase during an oil boom when the state distributes the windfall gains through bureaucratic channels. Karimi (2002) calculates the Katz and Rosenberg (KR) index of budgetary rent seeking and shows that this index is relatively high in Iran, as is the case for all populated oil-exporting countries. Jalali-Naini and Karimi (2003) show that the KR index of budgetary rent seeking is relatively high in Iran compared to a sample of developing and oil-exporting countries. Moreover, the value of the KR index increases after the oil boom of the mid-1970s and is highly correlated with changes in *per-capita* oil revenues and the size of the government. Furthermore, it is shown that the KR index negatively influences economic growth in Iran (Jalali-Naini and Karimi, 2003). This finding is consistent with the conjecture that a *rentier* system generates an incentive structure not conducive to growth (Easterly, 1993; Brixiova and Bulii, 2001). The above arguments also partially explain why Iran's relatively rich resource endowments and high investment rates were not converted into high-growth performance.

7. Summary and conclusion

Three distinct growth periods can be distinguished in Iran: 1959–1977, 1978–1988, and 1989–2003. The superior growth performance during the first period reflected more favorable external and internal environments. During the first period the share of the oil sector in GDP was not high until 1973, but oil revenues were growing. The growth of oil revenue and domestic expenditure prior to 1973, while boosting real aggregate demand and financing imports of intermediate and capital goods and hence capacity output, were non-inflationary. Growth in domestic output was mainly due to growth in domestic

---

[48] The masses and the intellectuals in Iran, as in a number of the MENA countries, have historically looked to the state as a medium for bringing about equity and social justice without sufficient scrutiny under what kind of governance structure and policy regime the state can deliver the results. At various times there has been a significant degree of resentment or opposition to the growth of private institutions and market-oriented economic policies in Iran. Not enough attention is given to the possibility that bureaucratic allocations and pervasive rent seeking associated with big governments can contribute to both inequality and inefficiency.

demand and non-oil exports grew at moderate to low rates. In spite of an extensive state presence in the economy, stable property rights, low uncertainty, and market-friendly policies allowed for the growth of the private sector. The sharp rise of the price of crude oil in 1974 fueled economic growth and inflation; it also induced rent-seeking activities and behavior. At the end of this period, growth came to an abrupt end owing to a political crisis, in part caused by income distribution concerns and inadequate social representation and participation in the socioeconomic system. The poor growth record in the second period is due to the debilitating effects of the war with Iraq and over-bureaucratization of the economy. Moreover, a higher level of uncertainty at the macro as well as micro levels and adverse incentive/price signals were the main reasons for lower rates of the private sector participation in the economy. Per-capita GDP growth rates were negative in this period. During the 1989–2003 period, economic growth resumed and TFP rose. The improved economic growth during the third period partly reflects the unwinding of government controls, a more conducive environment for private sector participation in the economy, and a partial correction of the price system. However, the weight of a large and inefficient bureaucracy, an institutional setup that limits internal competition and openness and encourages rent seeking, has limited the growth potential of the economy.

Like other populated oil-exporting countries, the positive wealth and saving effects of the mid-1970s did not have a long-lasting effect on economic performance. Economic growth in Iran has been relatively volatile and factor-intensive during most of the 1959–2003 period and TFP did not significantly contribute to economic growth. TFP's contribution to growth was small, but positive during the 1961–1973 and 1989–2000 but negative during the oil boom of 1974–1977 and even worse during the 1978–1988 period. HC accumulation, as in the other MENA countries, did not make a significant direct contribution to economic growth (reflecting inefficient labor allocation mechanisms and markets); it made an indirect contribution through TFP growth. We used a number of policy and economic variables to explain movements of TFP. The rate of inflation and government size had a negative influence on TFP. The results from growth regressions indicate that economic growth is responsive to greater participation by the private sector in the economy, as measured by the ratio of private investment to (non-oil) GDP. They also show it to be negatively associated with proxies for price distortions, but no definitive effect could be ascertained with regard to the size of the government. Coordination and rent-seeking problems have contributed to a significant increase of the average gestation period of government investments, which constitutes a large share of gross domestic fixed capital formation in Iran.

The international experience suggests that an economy characterized by the combination of a very substantial natural resource income; big government; extensive control of the economy; large price distortions as a by-product of inefficient bureaucratic allocation schemes; an underdeveloped financial market;

and limited domestic and foreign competition[49], has a high probability of having an inferior growth performance. Economic performance is further undermined when coordination problems and rent seeking become pervasive. Such an environment is in most likelihood associated with low rates of increase in TFP and unsustainably high economic growth rates. Properly functioning institutions tend to flourish when the rules limit rent seeking as well as impose credible checks and balances on those who control resource allocation via the political process.

Economic growth in Iran has been adversely affected by large shifts in policy stance, motivated politically and/or by large shifts in the terms of trade of oil, resulting in uncertainty and high transaction costs. The consequence of a large and active government in both production and distribution spheres, relying on administrative allocation with disequilibrium prices, has been to undermine the development of social institutions for efficient allocations of credit, capital, and labor, and the protection of property rights. Short-term jumps in growth rates owing to higher oil prices are not sustainable within the current economic structure. The experience suggests that the current oil boom will not have a long-lasting positive growth effect unless institutional reforms to encourage wider participation of non-government institutions in the economic process, credible price/incentive reforms policies to improve resource utilization and allocation, and improved governance standards are in place. These reforms have a higher likelihood of success in an open economic and political environment.

Acknowledgments

I would like to thank Hashem Pesaran, Jeff Nugent, and two anonymous referees for their helpful comments on earlier drafts of this paper.

References

Arrow, K.J. (1962), "The economic implications of learning by doing", *Review of Economic Studies*, Vol. 29(3), pp. 155–173.

Aschauer, D.A. (1989), "Is public expenditure productive?", *Journal of Monetary Economics*, Vol. 23(2), pp. 177–2000.

Barro, R.J. (1991), "Economic growth in a cross-section of countries", *Quarterly Journal of Economics*, Vol. 106(2), pp. 407–443.

Barro, R.J. (1995), *Economic Growth*, New York: McGraw–Hill.

---

[49] The estimated Herfindahl indices demonstrate a high concentration ratio in the Iranian manufacturing industry and are indicative of a significant degree of market power by government-owned enterprises. Moreover, government-owned companies account for a very large share in sales, value-added, and employment. As the scale of operations becomes larger, the number of private firms decline, see Salehi and Mozhdehi (1999).

Ahmad R. Jalali-Naini

Barro, R.J. (2001), "Human Capital and growth", *American Economic Review*, Vol. 91(2), pp. 12–17.

Benhabib, J. and M. Speigel (1994), "The role of human capital in economic development: evidence for aggregate cross-country data", *Journal of Monetary Economics*, Vol. 34(2), pp. 143–173.

Bharier, J. (1971), *Economic Development in Iran 1900–1970*, London: Oxford University Press.

Brixiova, Z. and A. Bulii (2001), "Growth slowdown in bureaucratic economic systems: an issue revisited," IMF Working Paper, WP/01/6, IMF, Washington, DC.

Chenery, H.B. and M. Syrquin (1975), *Patterns of Development 1950–1970*, London: Oxford University Press.

Dasgupta, P. and I. Serageldin (editors) (2000), *Social Capital: a Multifaceted Perspective*, Washington DC: The World Bank.

Dos Santos, T. (1971), "The structure of dependence", *American Economic Review*, Vol. 60, pp. 231–236.

Easterly, W. (1993), "How much do distortions affect growth?", *Journal of Monetary Economics*, Vol. 32(2), pp. 187–212.

Easterly, W., R. Islam and J. Stiglitz (2000), "Shaken and stirred: explaining growth volatility", Annual World Bank Conference on Development Economics, Washington, DC 2000, Oxford University Press.

Easterly, W. and R. Levine (2001), "Its not factor accumulation: stylized facts and growth", *World Bank Economic Review*, Vol. 15(2), pp. 177–219.

Easterly, W. and S. Rebelo (1993), "Fiscal policy and economic growth: an empirical investigation", *Journal of Monetary Economics*, Vol. 32(3), pp. 417–458.

Easterly, W., C.A. Rodriguez and K. Schmidt-Hebbel (editors) (1994), *Public Sector Deficits and Macroeconomic Performance*, New York: Oxford University Press.

Fischer, S. (1993), "The role of macroeconomic factors in growth", NBER Working Papers 4565.

Frank, A.G. (1967), *Capitalism and Underdevelopment in Latin America*, New York: Monthly Review Press.

Gelb, A. (editor) (1988), *Oil Windfalls: Blessing or curse?* New York: Oxford University Press.

Ghosh, A. and H. Wolf (1998), "Threshold and context dependence in growth", NBER Working Papers 6480.

Gylfason, T. (2001), "Nature, power, and growth", Manuscript, Center for Economic Studies (CESIFO).

Hall, R.E. and C.I. Jones (1999), "Why do some countries produce so much more output than others?", *Quarterly Journal of Economics*, Vol. 114(1), pp. 83–116.

Hirschman, A.O. (1968), "The political economy of import substituting industrialization in Latin America", *Quarterly Journal of Economics*, Vol. 82(1), pp. 2–32.

Iran Energy Report (2005), International Institute for Energy Studies, Tehran, Iran, 2005 edition.

Islam, N. (1995), "Growth empirics: a panel data approach", *The Quarterly Journal of Economics*, Vol. 110(4), pp. 1127–1170.

Issawi, C. (editor) (1971), *The Economic History of Iran 1800–1914*, Chicago: University of Chicago Press.

Jalali-Naini, A.R. (1999), "Business cycles in selected MENA countries", Research Project, ERF, www.erf.org.eg.

Jalali-Naini, A.R. and M. Karimi (2003), "Rent seeking and economic growth", ERF 10th Annual Conference, December 2003, Marrakech, Morocco.

Jalali-Naini A.R. and F. Khalatbari (2003), "Financial markets and growth in Iran", GDN, *gdnet.org/pdf2/gdn_library/.../Iran_financial_final.pdf.*

Jalali-Naini and Nazifi, F. (2002), "Inflation-output tradeoff and asymmetric effects of monetary shocks", *Plan and Development Quarterly*, Vol. 3(2), June, pp. 13–41.

Karimi, M. (2002), "Budgetary rent seeking in Iran", Unpublished M.S. dissertation, IRPD, Tehran.

Karshenas, M. and M.H. Pesaran (1995), "Economic reform and the reconstruction of the Iranian economy", *The Middle East Journal*, Vol. 49(1), pp. 89–111.

Khan M.S. and A.S. Senhadji (2000), "Threshold effects between inflation and growth", IMF Working Paper, WP/00/10.

Khavari N.A. (2001), "An estimate of the gross domestic product of Iran: 1936–1958", Collected Monthly Lectures 2001, Monetary and Banking Research Institute, the Central Bank of Iran, Tehran, 2002.

Klenow, P.J. and A. Rodríguez–Clare (1997), "The neoclassical revival in growth economics: has it gone too far?", pp. 73–102 in: B. S. Bernanke and J. J. Rotemberg, editors, *NBER Macroeconomics Annual 1997*.

Klenow, P.J. and A. Rodriguez-Clare (2004), "Externalities and growth", NBER Working Paper No. 11009.

Knight, M.N., Loayza and D. Villanueva (1993), "Testing the neo-classical theory of economic growth", *IMF Staff Papers*, Vol. 40(3), pp. 412–441.

Kongsamut, P., S. Rebelo, and D. Xie (1997), "Beyond balanced growth", NBER Working Paper 6159.

Kuznets, S. (1971), *Economic Growth of Nations: Total Output and Production Structure*, Cambridge, MA: The Belknap Press of Harvard University Press.

Levine, R., N. Loayza and T. Beck (2000), "Financial intermediation and growth: causality and causes", *Journal of Monetary Economics*, Vol. 46(1), pp. 31–77.

Lucas, R.E. Jr. (1988), "On the mechanics of economic development", *Journal of Monetary Economics*, Vol. 22(1), pp. 3–42.

Mankiw, N.G. (1995), "The growth of nations", *Brookings Papers on Economic Activity*, Vol. 1, pp. 275–310.

Mankiw, N.G., D. Romer and D.N. Weil (2000), "A contribution to the empirics of growth", *Quarterly Journal of Economics*, Vol. 107(2), pp. 407–437.

Makdisi, S., Z. Fattah and I. Limam (2005), "Determinants of growth in the MENA countries", chapter 2 in: J.A. Nugent and M.H. Pesaran, editors, *Explaining Growth in the Middle East*, Amsterdam: Elsevier.

Nelson, R.R. and E.S. Phelps (1966), "Investment in humans, technological diffusion, and economic growth", *American Economic Review*, Vol. 61(2), pp. 69–75.

North, D.C. (1990), *Institutional Change and Economic Performance*, Cambridge: Cambrige University Press.

North, D.C. (1994), "Economic performance through time", *The American Economic Review*, Vol. 84(3), pp. 369–395.

Pesaran, M.H. (1992), "The Iranian foreign exchange policy and the black market for dollars", *International Journal of Middle Eastern Studies*, Vol. 24, pp. 101–125.

Pesaran, M.H. (2000), "Economic trends and macroeconomic policies in post-revolutionary Iran", chapter 2 pp. 63–100 in: P. Alizadeh, editors, *The Economy of Iran: Dilemmas of an Islamic State*, London: I.B. Tauris.

Pesaran, M.H. and B. Pesaran (1997), *Microfit 4.0*, New York: Oxford University Press.

Phillips, P.C.B. and B.E. Hansen (1990), "Statistical inference in instrumental variables regression with I(1) processes", *Review of Economic Studies*, Vol. 57, pp. 99–125.

Pritchett, L. (1996), "Where has all the education gone?", Policy Research Working Paper Series 1581, The World Bank, Washington, DC.

Romer, P. (1986), "Increasing returns and long-run growth", *Journal of Political economy*, Vol. 94(5), pp. 1002–1037.

Romer, P. (1990a), "Increasing returns and long-run growth", *Journal of Political Economy*, Vol. 94(5), pp. 1002–1037.

Romer, P. (1990b), "Endogenous technological change", *Journal of Political Economy*, Vol. 98(5), pp. S71–S102 Part two.

Rose, R. (2000), "Getting things done in an antimodern society: social capital networks in Russia", in: P. Dasgupta and I. Serageldin, editors, *Social Capital: a Multifaceted Perspective*, Washington D.C.: The World Bank.

Saedi, A.S. (2002), "An analysis of the factors influencing wages in the Iranian services sector", Unpublished M.A. thesis, Tehran: IRPD.

Salehi-Isfahani, D. (2005), "Microeconomics of growth in MENA: the role of households", chapter 6 in: J.B. Nugent and M.H. Pesaran, editors, *Explaining Growth in the Middle East*, Amsterdam: Elsevier.

Salehi-Isfahani, H. (2002), "The political economy of growth in Iran", Paper prepared by GRP project, Global Development Network. ww.erf.org.eg/html/grp/GRP_Sep03/Iran-Pol_Econ.pdf

Salehi H. and A.J. Mozhdehi 1378 (1999), "Review of the market structure in Iran", *The Iranian Economy*, in: M. Tabibian, editor, Tehran: the Institute for Research in Planning and Development.

Senhadji A. (1999), "Sources of economic growth: an extensive growth accounting exercise", IMF Working Papers, WP/99/77.

Solow, R.M. (1956), "A contribution to the theory of economic growth", *Quarterly Journal of Economics*, Vol. 70(1), pp. 65–94.

Stigliz, E.J. (1989), "Markets, market failures, and development", *American Economic Review*, Vol. 79(2), pp. 197–203.

Tabibian, M. (2002), "Manufacturing sector's long-term strategy and development in Iran", GRP Country Paper, www.erf.org.eg.

Tanzi, V. and H.H. Zee (1997), "Fiscal policy and long-run growth", *IMF Staff Papers*, Vol. 44(2), pp. 179–209.

World Bank Report (1997), *The State in a Changing World*, Washington, DC: World Bank.

Young, A. (1995), "The tyranny of numbers: confronting the statistical realities of Asian growth experience", *Quarterly Journal of Economics*, Vol. 110(3), pp. 641–680.

CHAPTER 10

The Political Economy of Development Policy in Tunisia

Mohamed Z. Bechri* and Sonia Naccache

Abstract

During the last five decades Tunisia managed to achieve a robust long-run GDP growth of about 5% per year, against 3.5% only, for the MENA region as a whole. However, Tunisia failed to reduce obvious inefficiencies such as high protection, financial repression, and a highly regulated economy in general. The present study attempts to explain why the country was unable to do better in this respect, even though it was a top performer in social modernization and it started its economic reforms relatively early. The study adopts the political economy approach to explain independent Tunisia's development policy choices, based on the theory of collective action and an analysis of contracting problems of representation, coordination, and commitment. The paper draws on some lessons from Tunisia for the other MENA countries. It stresses the importance of women's rights, population control, and modern education. In addition, it refers to the recent examples of Morocco and Kuwait regarding women status reform to argue that action is still possible. It argues that even though no efforts should be spared to get influential groups on board, the reforming governments in MENA today cannot afford to be paralyzed by anti-reform groups – such as Islamist groups in Parliaments – either.

KEYWORDS: political economy, economic development, interest groups, collective action, Tunisia

JEL classifications: D78

---

*Corresponding author.

CONTRIBUTIONS TO ECONOMIC ANALYSIS
VOLUME 278   ISSN: 0573-8555
DOI:10.1016/S0573-5555(06)78010-5

1. Introduction

When Tunisia gained independence from France in 1956, the economy was largely based on subsistence farming, food processing, and mining. In this respect, independence undoubtedly ushered in an unprecedented era of economic and social development.

The policies pursued to that end shifted from State intervention (1956–1960) to socialism (1961–1969) to export promotion (1970–1985). Then following a severe balance of payments crisis in 1986, Tunisia adopted a structural adjustment program under the guidance of the International Monetary Fund (IMF). The liberal policies implemented under this framework were further boosted with the signing of a free-trade agreement with the European Union in 1995.

The main features of Tunisia's development during the past five decades are: (1) an early and sustained focus on social modernization and population control, (2) a heavy involvement of the State in the economy, even after the abandonment of collectivism in 1969, and (3) a robust long-run GDP growth of about 5% per year.

But Tunisia's performance remained well below that of Southeast Asia and other fast-growing economies, which means that the country could have done much better. Hence, the relevant questions for the present study are: how did Tunisia manage to achieve a robust growth over such a long period of time? And why was the country unable to do better?

In the present study, we attempt to answer these questions, by explaining Tunisia's policy choices as the outcome of interaction between institutions and interest groups, taking into account contracting problems and the way they impeded groups' ability to implement efficient policies. The policy variables we focus on are: the role of the private sector, foreign trade, and credit and exchange rate policies, in addition to gender issues and population control, which make Tunisia an exception by regional standards.

The study is structured as follows: Section 2 summarizes the main policy episodes since 1956 and the political economy approach. Section 3 analyzes the establishment of a State-led economy, which paved the way to socialism in the early 1960s until its end in 1969. The adoption of a two-track strategy is analyzed in Section 4. Section 5 studies the populist experiment of 1981–1985, the crisis-triggered reforms of 1986, and the signing of the Association Agreement with the European Union. Section 6 contains the main conclusions.

2. Policy episodes and the political economy approach

2.1. Policy episodes: 1956–2004

The main episodes of Tunisia's development policy since independence are summarized in Table 1. The first 5 years (1956–1960) were characterized by State intervention. Monopolies, inherited from the colonial rule, became State-owned.

Table 1. Tunisia's development policy episodes

		1961–1969	1970–1980	1981–1985	1986–1991	1992–1995	1996–2000	2001–2004
A. Role of the state	Number of public enterprises	25 (1960)	185 (1970)	285 (1984)	n.a.	219 (1993)	203	187
	Share of the public sector in total investment (in %)	68.08	59.37	54.05	50.89	50.79	47.80	43.26
B. Private sector development	Share of the private sector in total investment (in %)[a]	31.92	40.63	45.95	49.11	49.21	52.20	56.74
C. Trade policy	Nominal protection rate (in %)	n.a.	n.a.	34.33	[41.29]	37	46.66	36
	Effective protection rate in (in %)[b]	n.a.	n.a.	75	[70.44]	56	67.66	50
D. Credit policy	Real deposit interest rates	1.15	−1.25	−3.92	−4.98	−5.73	−5.01	−4.08
	Real lending interest rates	6.7	5.33	4.28	7.77	7.22	4.83	4.49

Mohamed Z. Bechri and Sonia Naccache

Table 1 (continued)

		1961–1969	1970–1980	1981–1985	1986–1991	1992–1995	1996–2000	2001–2004
E. Exchange rate (annual change in, for depreciation)	REER[c]	n.a.	n.a.	-1.39	-6.57	0.297	-0.052	-1.785
	Exchange rate equilibrium[d]	n.a.	0.5 (1970–1979)	2.0 (1980–1985)	-6.0 (1986–1990)	4.0 (1991–1997)	n.a.	n.a.
	Black-market premium[e] (%)	81.0	15.7	102	5.0	9.2	0.7	0.7

n.a. Not available.

Notes:

(1) Nominal and effective rates relate to the whole economy, hydrocarbons excluded. Estimates began only in 1983 and were interrupted during the years 1987–1989, 1991–1994, 1996, and 1998. Therefore, average rates relate to the years for which estimates are available.

(2) Average rate for the years 1983–1985. Source: *Cahiers de l'Institut d'Economie Quantitative*, No. 5, March 1988, p. 92.

(3) Between 1986 and 1990, respectively. Source: *Institute d'Economie Quantitative*.

(4) Figure of 1995.

(5) cf. footnote b.

(6) Given different lending rates across industries, during the period 1962–1986, we take the *taux du decouvert bancaire* as a proxy. Since 1987, the rate is the money market rate + 3 percentage points.

(7) For nominal interest rates, the source is Statiques Financieres de la Banque Centrale de Tunisie. The inflation rate is the rate of growth of the GDP deflator (100 = 1990). Sources: International Financial Statistics 2004, IMF and *Statistiques Financieres de la Banque Centrale de Tunisie*.

(8) Since 1987, nominal rates on deposit have been freely set by banks.

[a] Share of private firms and households in gross fixed capital formation, at market prices. Sources: Annual Report of the Central Bank of Tunisia and National Accounts.

[b] The preceding notes on nominal rates apply to the corresponding effective rates.

[c] Real effective exchange rates, Source: International Financial Statistics, IMF.

[d] Based on economic fundamentals. Source: Achy (2000) Appendix 2.

[e] Black-market premium. Sources: Levine and Renelt: *World's Currency Yearbook* (for 1985, 1990–1993), and Adrian Wood, Global trends in real exchange rates: 1960–1984, World Bank Discussion Paper No. 35, 1988.

And the creation of the Central Bank and of two government-owned banks in 1958 ensured public control of the financial sector.

At the social level, a radical reform of women's status was adopted, population control was integrated in the development strategy of the country, and a modern educational system, based on the French curricula, was promoted all over the country, including the remote rural areas. Moreover, Zeitouna University, which had been the guardian of Sunni Islam since the Islamic conquest of the country, competing in influence with Al-Azhar in Cairo, was abolished in 1956 when its students integrated the public system.

Meanwhile, at the economic level, State intervention was further strengthened, with the adoption of central planning in 1962 and collectivization in 1965, a disappointing experience that was abandoned in 1969. This was followed by the adoption of a "two-track" approach, with the establishment of an offshore industrial sector for exports, in addition to a traditional local and highly protected sector. With the passage of time, however, the system proved to be unsustainable. Despite the high protection of the onshore sector, the populist policies adopted in the early 1980s resulted in a severe balance of payments crisis. As a result, the country had finally no choice but to sign a Stand-by Agreement with the IMF in August 1986, and to adopt a stabilization-cum-structural adjustment program.

As a result, macroeconomic stability was rapidly achieved, but institutional reforms remained hesitant, and private investment failed to recover. Under these circumstances, the authorities decided to take a bold decision by signing an association agreement with the European Union in 1995, being the first country in the South-Mediterranean region to do so.

In this framework, an ambitious program to upgrade domestic industries was launched in 1996. But again institutional reforms, especially regarding the civil service, the labor code, and banking and telecommunications, remained limited. A political economy approach will help to explain this failure.

2.2. Political economy approach

Why do countries persist in adopting inefficient policies? One explanation is that these inefficiencies may benefit some powerful interest groups. In what follows we present the theory of collective action and its limits to explain reform, followed by a presentation of contracting problems as a potential source of inefficiencies.

2.2.1. Interest groups and collective action

The main thrust of the theory of collective action is that policy choices are outcomes of interest groups' pressures and lobbying (for a survey on the subject, see for instance, Nabli and Nugent (1989) and Isfahani (2002)).

First, success in collective action is enhanced with the small size of the group and its geographic concentration. Otherwise, it would be difficult to mobilize its members. Farmers in the developing world, as an example, constitute a large share of the population and they are thinly spread in the rural areas, which makes it difficult for them to mobilize. As a result, they fail to get the kind of subsidies that are prevalent in the industrial world, where it is easier for farmers to communicate and lobby for their common good.

Second, sector concentration helps to do away with free riders, since a small number of large beneficiaries will be willing to undertake all the needed lobbying. Third, homogeneity of both background and goal enhances the focus on a specific set of claims. In a situation of rationing with price set below the market clearing one, as for example with regulated credit markets, business groups tend to focus more on credit availability than on preferential interest rates. Moreover, they may consider protection to be more sustainable than subsidies, since the tariffs can also serve as an important source of revenue for the government.

2.2.2. *Limits of the theory of collective action in explaining reforms*

Despite its appeal, the theory presented so far does not do well in explaining the timing of reforms, since it is unlikely that relative strength of different interest groups' influence would have changed dramatically at that particular period of time. We also observe that countries with similar economic conditions may adopt different policies. As we will see below, a failed collectivist experiment led to radical reforms in Tunisia in 1969, whereas neighboring countries with similar problems did not follow Tunisia's lead.

Several factors may explain the failure to reform. First, groups may not be able to figure out the type of policies that better serve their interests in the long run. For example, Rodrik (1998) argued that import-substitution industrialists in Korea and Taiwan resisted the reforms that these countries introduced in the mid-1960s. An alternative explanation is that high redistribution costs may be involved, as is generally the case in trade reform. In this case, politicians hesitate to reform precisely because they perceive a high "political cost–benefit ratio," i.e., a high ratio of redistribution to efficiency gains. Under these conditions, only a severe crisis that makes the *status quo* unsustainable may succeed in triggering reforms.

Another alternative that may have lower political costs is to follow a two-track reform strategy, whereby new opportunities are created, without unduly altering the old system. Examples include the promotion of a private sector while maintaining State-owned enterprises and the creation of special processing zones for exports.

2.2.3. *Institutional dimensions of governance: representation, coordination and commitment*

The failure to remove inefficiencies to have access to a larger surplus may also be explained by contracting problems, which depend on representation, coordination, and commitment (Castanheira and Isfahani (forthcoming)).

Representation requires the government to have a power delegated to it by the people. This enhances the government's ability to appropriately assess the needs of society to make the appropriate tradeoff between competing demands. Furthermore, groups will cooperate better in implementing government policies when they feel they are part of the decision-making process.

But, a government setup aimed at enhancing representation may end up reducing efficiency at the implementation level. This is of particular importance in the Arab countries owing to the powerful impact of tradition, tribalism, and regionalism factors.

Coordination is needed to prevent excesses like high taxes and overspending for government provision of goods and services that the private sector can better provide. In this respect, trade unions, as an example, could play a very constructive role in participating to wage negotiations and in ensuring social stability.

The tradeoff between competing demands depends first and foremost on the degree of government intervention in the economy. When the government plays an important role, regions will compete more to attract public projects and social groups lobby more for handouts (subsidies, access to bank credit, protection, etc.). That is why the first-best solution is to have an institutional framework that leaves most choices to the market. The adoption of vouchers in education and private sector financing of infrastructure, as an example, may dispense the government from having to make difficult choices. Low taxes would also limit the amount the government will have to spend and, as a consequence, the coordination needed in that respect. Moreover, the same is true with the adoption of some *ex-ante* rules like a balanced budget law. In all circumstances, decentralization is very effective. Furthermore, decisions that could be made at the community or the regional level should not be left to the central government.

Commitment indicates the extent to which announced policies are effectively implemented. Credibility is particularly difficult to accomplish in developing countries known for weak institutions and past histories of failures by government officials to fulfill promises. Some alternative solutions exist, however. Under these circumstances, the presence of a visionary leadership with historical legitimacy may be an effective mechanism to implement policies that improve significantly the well being of the people, as pointed out by World Bank (2003) with a specific reference to Bourguiba in Tunisia and Lee Kuan Lew in Singapore. But, this should not be a justification for dictatorship either. Many historical precedents show how one-man rule may not be sustainable and how democracies can indeed achieve reform.

Recent successful MENA cases in social modernization include Morocco and Kuwait. Morocco failed for years to adopt a modern legal code for women owing to Islamist opposition. The latter mobilized hundreds of thousands of followers in street protests during the late 1990s to sabotage the socialist government's attempts in this respect. However, the king seized the aftermath of the May 16, 2003 terrorist bombings of Casa Blanca, to present the *Moudawana*, which made polygamy impossible to practise and better protected women rights. Cornered and isolated, the Islamist deputies in Parliament had no choice but to vote for it. Moreover, for years, tribal leaders in Kuwait's Parliament turned down the Emiri decree of 1999 that gave women the right to vote. But, after long negotiations, Islamist terror that struck neighboring Saudi Arabia and Kuwait itself, and several democratic steps in neighboring Bahrain, Qatar, and Oman, the government finally succeeded in obtaining a vote in favor of the law on May 16, 2005.

Once the political backing is secured to overcome local opposition, the selection of a competent technocratic team can significantly enhance the probability that the reforms are implemented. In the case of economic liberalization, for example, the appointment of a technocratic pro-market team like the "Chicago boys" in Chile, can significantly enhance the chances of success.

3. Establishment of a State-led economy (1956–1969)

In addition to its agricultural potential, Tunisia has succeeded for centuries in producing and even in exporting some manufacturing goods such as textiles, ceramics, leather, and other handicrafts. Production processes remained, nevertheless, artisanal in nature (Bellin, 1989). In the mid-nineteenth century, the establishment by Ahmed Bey of light weaponry and food processing plants gave a temporary boost to industrialization. But this attempt was halted by the French invasion of 1881.

In 1904, a customs' union with France was established but within a colonial vision in which Tunisia was to be kept as a safe market for French consumer products. At the time when the country gained independence in 1956, the economy remained based largely on subsistence farming, a few other import-substitution industries, and non-tradables.

3.1. Political setup and interest groups

After a long and protracted struggle, taking the form of both peaceful resistance and military insurgencies, Tunisia won its independence from France in the mid-1950s. The resistance was first organized by the Destour Party, which was founded by Sheikh Abdelaziz Thaalbi, a prominent scholar at Zeitouna University. But the movement failed to outline a clear strategy for independence. A French-educated young lawyer, Habib Bourguiba, seized the opportunity to break ranks with the old guard and created the Neo-Destour in 1934. It was a preventive action that would gradually marginalize the historic influence of the traditional Zeitouna-based establishment. Later on, this gave Bourguiba a free hand in negotiating independence with France, and in implementing his modernization agenda, once the country became independent.

The first French offer of "internal independence" of Tunisia came in 1955. Bourguiba accepted it, but a nationalist wing of the Neo-Destour, headed by its

Secretary General Salah Ben Youssef, vehemently opposed it. In a speech delivered at the Zeitouna Mosque, Mr. Ben Youssef considered the offer as "a step backward." The conflict took a violent turn and brought the country to the brink of civil war. But an extraordinary congress of the Neo-Destour fully supported Bourguiba, and Mr. Ben Youssef was sacked. One year later, in 1956, Tunisia was granted full independence. This event proved Bourguiba right and gave a final blow to the rebellion.

Tunisia's accession to independence greatly enhanced the legitimacy of its leadership. Moreover, Bourguiba's hold on power was further strengthened with the co-option of the national associations and the proclamation of the Republic in 1957.

At the interest group level, the groups expected to play leading roles in the policy debate during this period were producers' associations, labor, and the ruling Party elite. Producers' associations were limited to the *Union Tunisienne de l'Artisanat et du Commerce* (UTAC, to become UTICA later on) for manufacturing and commerce, and the *Union Nationale des Agriculteurs de Tunisie* (UNAT), for farmers. UTAC was founded in 1947, by the Neo-Destour, in reaction to the communist party's *Federation des Artisans et Petits Commercants de Tunisie*, which was created in 1945. But while UTAC's leadership was elected during the colonial era, since independence, the organization's president was handpicked by the authorities. In addition, UTAC was asked to encompass all types of industries, handicrafts, and commerce as well as the service sector since the mid-1960s. This strategy of amalgamation further weakened the organization's ability to mount collective action (Nugent, 1989).

Moreover, UNAT was in no better position. Large farms, formerly in the hands of European nationals, became State-owned. This left the union membership limited to small rural farmers among whom organization was difficult and to a handful of urban-based members more interested in (non-agricultural) lucrative activities such as trade, handicrafts, and manufacturing. As a result, the financially squeezed organization had no choice but to rely on staff hired from the Agriculture Ministry and on government handouts.

With their leadership neutralized, producers' organizations became a mere instrument of State influence. This left organized labor and the ruling Party elite as the only players with the potential to effect coherent government policy.

The national labor union *Union Tunisienne des Travailleurs de Tunisie* (UGTT) was created in 1946 by Farhat Hached, a popular figure who was later assassinated by the French. Its nationalist stand and large membership base made it the only organization really capable of challenging Bourguiba for the Neo-Destour Party political leadership. Some UGTT activists started the ideological struggle well before the country's access to independence. For example, in 1955 at a congress of the Neo-Destour that was held in Sfax to give its support to Bourguiba, a young UGTT leader, Ahmed Ben Salah, seized the opportunity to present an "Economic Report," which detailed his vision for a socialist development strategy for independent Tunisia.

UGTT's strategy from the beginning was to infiltrate the ruling Party and thereby to orient economic policy from within. This became clear in 1956 when UGTT leadership called for the constitution of an "organic union" with the Neo-Destour in an attempt to turn the latter into a labor Party. Since the ruling Party's strategy was to co-opt national associations so as to dilute dissent, it was easy for UGTT to increase its influence within the party. Indeed, at the first legislative election of independent Tunisia, a "National Front" was constituted, including UTICA, UNAT, and UGTT, under the leadership of the Neo-Destour. The UGTT was the main beneficiary from this participation since it succeeded in securing 35 out of the 98 seats in the new Parliament.

However, it is worth noticing that the Neo-Destour's natural inclination remained in favor of a liberal policy. Its membership base came mainly from the rural areas, where the basic activity is subsistence farming and in urban areas, merchants constituted its main support. Furthermore, the market economy is the natural choice of its Western-educated leadership. Indeed, even before the country's access to independence, Habib Bourguiba expressed on many occasions his apprehension about UGTT-advocated socialism.

3.2. Representation, coordination, and commitment

Tunisia's independence raised expectations about a better popular representation. Indeed, the debates that took place at the National Assembly during the early years of independence reflected to a large degree the concerns of the population and gave the appearance of representative rule. The real power, however, was concentrated in the hands of Habib Bourguiba, who was so confident about his status that he dared to announce on August 13, 1956 revolutionary measures in favor of women, and on July 20, 1957 the abolition of the monarchy. In both cases, the rubber-stamp parliament was urged to adopt the changes. But Bourguiba was the real driving force behind this. Indeed, it is a well-known fact that he personally drafted the Women Code and for the announcement of the republic, the long sessions organized by the parliament played no more than a ceremonial role, since no serious debate took place, and no referendum was organized.

From Bourguiba's speeches and behavior during this period, one could easily sense how, like any other autocrat, he saw himself, from the start, as having a better grasp of the country's priorities than the elected representatives. Moreover, his action in favor of women, education, and the overall development and his ability to co-opt labor and business associations, raised his status as the supreme leader of the country. Furthermore, his insistence on "national unity," indicates just how he views representation as a threat, a view that was probably shared by a large section of the population at that time. In addition, the centralized nature of the system enhanced the coordination process, and Bourguiba's secure position gave him a strong incentive to commit himself to efficient policies. However, the newly independent Tunisia clearly lacked the technical skills it needed to manage its economy. Tunisian reformists of the nineteenth century, once they became disillusioned about the ability of the Zeitouna Mosque to modernize, created a new model of French-curricula-based schools. Some of their graduates (like Bourguiba himself) continued their studies in France. But they remained limited in number, especially in the field of economics and business management. These weaknesses, together with the failure of the liberal wing of the Neo-Destour to come up with a consistent plan for economic reconstruction, explain to a large extent the chaotic situation that prevailed during 1956–1961. This provided an opportunity for the trade union leader Ahmed Ben Salah to advance his socialist agenda.

3.3. Policy choices

Two basic choices were made during the post-independence period: State intervention and social modernization.

3.3.1. State intervention

The post-independence years of 1956–1961 were generally, but mistakenly, considered a period of liberalism. In fact, State intervention was prevalent. In public utilities (electricity and water) and other lucrative businesses like tobacco, government monopolies were maintained. The rate of protection of domestic industries increased, with some tariffs reaching prohibitive levels. In addition, the two banks created in 1958 were government-owned banks, guaranteeing government dominance over the financial sector.

There was obviously no shortage of arguments to justify this option, for it could be argued that: (1) the private sector was, at that stage, in no position to own and manage large units like public utilities, (2) the government was in a better position to allocate the scarce resources to priority sectors, and (3) what Grissa (1989) had called "the need for the State to establish itself" all required State ownership of the means of production to provide jobs and distribute rents. Likewise, public-sector banks would enhance the government's ability to allocate credit to priority activities.

But while making political sense, these interventions sent a negative signal to private entrepreneurs. Business took a "wait and see" attitude, and in some instances it took refuge in real estate speculation such as buying abandoned French properties. This understandable response to the prevailing set of incentives at that time was, however, mistakenly perceived by some observers as a disappointing response, and even a proof of the "parasitic nature" of the Tunisian private sector (Bellin, 1989).

3.3.2. Social modernization

As already indicated, President Bourguiba took the lead by adopting some extremely bold measures in favor of women's rights. First, Bourguiba set up a special commission to review the status of women, and, when the latter could not agree on the thorny issue of polygamy (though their consensus was to limit the right to two wives only instead of four), the President took the matter in his own hands, by introducing the needed changes to the draft law, which was first adopted in August 1956, and integrated later into the Woman's Code in 1958. This would be by far the most progressive reform of women's status in the Islamic world. The new code outlawed polygamy, tightly regulated divorce, and fixed the minimum age of marriage for girls at 18.

The move to announce these measures was so swift that it caught the remnants of the traditional establishment off guard. But, Bourguiba knew that, for these reforms to be effective, he had to use his prestige, historical legitimacy, and oratory gifts in an attempt to change people's attitudes toward women. Hence, the issues of women's liberation and population control became a recurrent theme of his regular speeches to the nation.

Social modernization required also modern education. Bourguiba himself was educated in the "Sadiki College" created in reaction to the failure of Zeitouna University's traditional system. Bourguiba's first action, in this respect, was to generalize free public education, with the adoption of the French curriculum. This was obviously at the expense of the "Madrassas" (religious schools) system. Moreover, once the new system became popular among parents, Bourguiba took a second bold decision, namely, to abolish Zeitouna University altogether. It was only in the early 1990s that a new Zeitouna University was created, modeled on Western theology departments where the focus is on comparative religious studies.

3.4. Rise and fall of collectivism

After a period of economic stagnation, Bourguiba appointed the trade union activist Ahmed Ben Salah as the Minister of Social Affairs and Economy, in 1961. The decision made political sense, since the move was meant to defuse the threat of a unified leadership by labor, which would include three figures: Habib Achour, Ahmed Tlili, and Ahmed Ben Salah and things worked out very well. For once he became minister, Ben Salah used his insider knowledge of the union, with the help of some of his former comrades, to neutralize UGTT (Khiari, 2000).

This was a milestone in Bourguiba's quest to destroy any potential source of organized resistance to his leadership. But this "cooption" also had a major drawback in that the integration of UGTT leadership into the Neo-Destour gave the former a precious opportunity to introduce policy changes from within.

3.4.1. Adoption of central planning

With Bourguiba's blessing secured, Ben Salah had obviously no reason to give himself an executive role. Soon, he started maneuvering to shift policy toward central planning, which was introduced in 1962 with the publication of the

"Perspectives Decennales." Meanwhile, a populist policy led to a large increase in wages. As a result, the fiscal deficit widened and a balance of payments crisis erupted. In 1964, Tunisia had no choice but to adopt a stabilization plan and to devalue the dinar, for the first time since independence.

The 1964 debacle was a sufficient reason for the dismissal of Ben Salah. As pointed out above, Bourguiba needed him in the government to keep UGTT leadership divided. But there was no need to give him the portfolio of the economy either. Bourguiba's failure to act at that time remains a puzzle. One reason may be that the technicalities of economic management were not a priority for the President who was known first and foremost as a veteran politician. In addition, the failure of the liberal wing of the Neo-Destour to come up with a credible alternative may have left the President with no other choice. Furthermore, the economic mess may have been presented to the President as a technical matter to be corrected with the adoption of appropriate stabilization tools alone. In any case, Bourguiba seemed to have bought the argument. So much so, that as soon as the economy showed signs of recovery, the President gave a *carte blanche* to Mr. Ben Salah to go ahead with the collectivization of the economy, an adventure terminated only by an economic collapse that came to threaten Bourguiba's own hold on power.

3.4.2. Population control and family planning

Unlike the chaos on the economic front, social modernization continued unabated. The revolutionary measures promulgated in the late 1950s were further consolidated by setting up a family planning program, which was integrated to the National Development Plan, starting in 1962–1963. To this end, an *Office National de Planning Familial* (ONPF) was created to disseminate information. Important investments were made in reproductive health and incentives were structured so that social security benefits were limited to those families with no more than three children.

Population control is obviously a long-term endeavor. Nevertheless, as early as in 1970, Tunisia's total fertility rate (the average number of births per woman) declined to 6.4 compared to 7.0 in Morocco and 7.4 in Algeria (Table 2). Meanwhile, Tunisia boasted the highest rate of girl's education at the primary level in the region (61.9%, compared to 49.4% for Egypt and 33.9% for Iraq). More importantly, population control allowed Tunisia to enter a "virtuous circle." Less demographic pressure enhanced socioeconomic development, which in turn helped reduce population growth.

3.4.3. Shift to collectivism

The political decision in this respect came at the Neo-Destour Congress in 1964 where Ben Salah scored a clear success. This owed much to his personal qualities, particularly his dynamism, relative integrity, and commitment. But these qualities would not have been enough, had Bourguiba been better advised, and

Table 2. Social development indicators: Tunisia and MENA countries

Indicator	Expected Life at Birth				Total Fertility Rate			Schooling (in %) Primary				Secondary				Higher			
Year	1970	1980	1998	2002	1970	1980	1998	1970	1980	1996	2001	1970	1980	1996	2001	1970	1980	1996	2001
Tunisia	54	62	72	73	6.4	5.2	2.2	100.4	102.1	118.0	117.0	22.7	27.0	64.63	78.0	2.6	4.8	13.7	15.0
Algeria	53	59	71	71	7.4	6.7	3.5	76.1	94.5	107.5	112.0	11.2	33.0	63.3	71.0	1.8	5.9	13.4	–
Jordan	54		70	72		6.8	3.6	72.0	81.6	70.6	100.8	32.8	59.1	57.4	87.7	2.1	13.4	17.9	28.6
Egypt	51	56	67	69	5.9	5.1	3.5	67.6	73.1	101.1	100.0	28.4	50.5	78.3	86.0	6.9	16.1	22.6	–
Morocco	52	58	67	68	7.0	5.4	3.0	51.5	83.0	86.0	94.0	12.6	26.0	39.1	39.3	1.4	5.9	11.1	10.0
Syria	56	62	70	70	7.7	7.4	3.7	77.5	99.6	100.8	109.0	38.1	46.4	42.5	43.0	8.3	16.9	15.1	–

Source: Arab Monetary Fund, the Arab Unified Report, 2004.

the producer organizations in a better shape. Indeed, as pointed out by Nugent (1989, p. 295) "cooperativization of private property would not have been possible if producer organizations had been strong." In addition, the liberal wing of the Neo-Destour failed to seize on the failure of collectivism experiments, which were showing disastrous results at that time, in other countries such as Egypt and some Sub-Saharan countries.

With their associations in shambles, the only way for producers to effectively voice their concerns was outside the official organizations. But this was very risky. The government's intolerance of any type of dissidence was made very clear by its decision to disband the Communist Party in 1962, and by responding with overwhelming use of force to quell the violence that erupted in some regions to protest against cooperatives. This does not mean, however, that producers' interests were irrelevant to the government. Interestingly enough, it was the weakest groups in terms of collective action that were the first to be targeted for collectivism (farming, transportation, and local commerce).

3.4.4. Fall of collectivism

After 4 years of collectivism, Bourguiba dismissed Ben Salah and abolished the cooperatives. It was an abrupt move that changed dramatically the way Tunisia will develop during the following decades. Bourguiba's decision followed a World Bank Report on Tunisia in 1969, which focused on the severe fiscal crisis that the country was facing. The experience of the year 1964 showed, nevertheless, that an economic crisis by itself was in no way sufficient to bring down the government, and it is even less likely to engineer a radical shift in policy. The difference this time is that the crisis was aggravated by popular discontent about expropriations, shortages, and a severe drought for 3 years in a row. But, one could still argue that similar problems were encountered in other countries in the region, without having the same impact.

To understand Bourguiba's decision, we need to keep in mind that for the Western-educated, liberal-minded Bourguiba (at least as long as his own grip on power was not concerned), the puzzle remains his adoption of the socialist orientation in the early 1960s, not its abandonment in 1969. This is indeed in contrast to many other Third World countries, where dogmatic socialist leaders implemented collectivism. More importantly, the large popular discontent at that time required a strong response from the security apparatus and, eventually, a need to call in the army. The latter option would have been particularly horrifying for Bourguiba, given his well-known distrust of the military.

As soon as Ben Salah was dismissed, the government started a reversal of the most damaging and unpopular aspects of the former policy, namely cooperatives. Private initiative was reinstated and hailed as an engine of growth. Furthermore, a two-track strategy was adopted to promote export industries.

4. The two-track strategy

To implement his grand scheme of economic reconstruction, Bourguiba needed new competencies. In 1971, he appointed the then Governor of the Central Bank, Hedi Nouira as the new Prime Minister.

The system that Mr. Nouira became in charge of had lost much in popular representation and support. The disastrous adventure of the previous decade showed clearly that the leadership was not immune from making terrible mistakes. But, the new government had no choice but to take some bold initiatives. In particular, an offshore company law was adopted in 1972, which facilitated the establishment of special industrial zones devoted to exports.

4.1. Offshore Company Law and export promotion

With collectivism dead, the alternative could be either the adoption of *laissez-faire* or of a hybrid system combining both private initiative and government intervention. In practice, the Nouira team implemented a two-track strategy. The idea here was to create new opportunities, but without unduly destroying the pillars of the old system (Lau *et al.*, 2001). The Mauritius experiment with the development of an offshore enclave for exporting industries in tandem with a protected onshore sector was receiving considerable attention and may have served as a model for Tunisian decision makers.

The other alternative was to radically liberalize the system, as Chile successfully did in the mid-1970s. At that time, however, these reforms were met with suspicion in much of the rest of the world (Edwards, 1998). Hence, they could have been easily discarded as extremist or irrelevant for the Tunisian context, if they were at all contemplated. In addition, Tunisia lacked an economic team capable of providing a coherent master plan for economic liberalization. Unlike Chile's "Chicago boys," the members of the Nouira team were mostly from legal and engineering background. Hence, they lacked a formal training in economics in the Anglo-Saxon tradition that favors market mechanisms.

4.2. Financial repression and exchange controls

The development strategy described so far was implemented in a context of financial repression. Banks were tightly regulated. Interest rates were administratively set at below-equilibrium levels, which discouraged savings, and led to credit rationing and misallocation of resources.

Exchange controls were also prevalent, but as indicated in Figure 1, overvaluation of the local currency was limited. The real effective exchange rate of the Tunisian dinar was quite stable during the 1970s.

The new Tunisian strategy of amalgamation of private initiative and export promotion, on the one hand, with heavy government intervention, on the other, was viewed by some economists as fundamentally inconsistent (Moussa, 1995).

Figure 1.   ***Nominal effective exchange rate (NEER) and real effective exchange rate (REER) of the dinar***

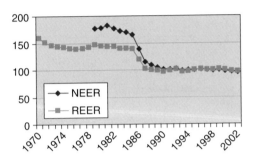

Source: International Financial Statistics, the IMF

This "inconsistency" will be better understood with the flowing analysis of interest groups.

4.3. Role of interest groups

To assess this role, we start with an assessment of groups' *expected* success in collective action, followed by an estimate of their *actual* success.

4.3.1. Expected success

Producer groups are classified in the following three categories: (1) non-tradables, (2) import substitution, and (3) exportables. Based on the theory of collective action presented above, the expected degree of success of these groups in the Tunisian context, is presented in Table 3 (low, L; medium, M; and high, H).

4.3.2. Actual success

Two indicators were selected to assess the actual success of different interest groups, namely, (1) the effective rate of protection and (2) the ratio of access to bank credit (Nugent, 1989). The latter indicates the ratio of the sector's share in bank total credit to its share in GDP. Accordingly, a ratio higher than 1 means that the activity gets more credit than its contribution in economic activity would justify. This may just mean that the sector is more capital intensive or it gets less government funds. Nevertheless, the ratio would indicate, to a large extent, the political influence of the group. If an activity scores L according to one indicator and H according to the other, the score that appears in Table 4 will be M. Otherwise, the first score refers to the first indicator (protection) and the second refers to the credit ratio. M/H, as an example, indicates that the activity has an average effective protection, but higher than average credit ratio.

Table 3. *Group characteristics and expected success in collective action*

	Size/Concentration	Homogeneity	Expected Success in Collective Action
Non-tradables			
Construction	Sector dominated by a few large enterprises, concentrated in the main cities	Homogeneity of goals	H
Non-tourism services	very large number, spread all over the country	Lacking homogeneity of background, difficult to mobilize	L
Import substitution			
Agriculture	Very large number, members spread all over the country	Heterogeneity of background and objectives	L
Food processing	Small number, relatively concentrated	Similar objectives	H
Wood and paper	Limited number of firms	Homogeneous goals	H
Construction products	Large firms are dominant	State-owned enterprises (cement factories and others)	H
Exportables			
Textile and leather	Concentrated activity	Different goals according to whether the activity is import substitution or export oriented	M
Mechanical and electrical	Small number	Shift overtime from import substitution to exports	H
Chemicals	Concentrated and public sector dominated	Homogeneous	H
Mining	Public sector activity	Homogeneous	H
Tourism	Large number	Heterogeneous	M

The comparison between expected success (Table 3) and actual success (Table 4) shows some differences. Textile and leather turn out to have been more successful than expected during the 1970s. Textiles and leather finished products were highly protected in the local market, and the activity's access to bank credit was higher than average. This is not surprising since the sector was boosted by the Offshore Company Law of 1972 after which it became the main exporting activity in manufacturing.

For some other activities, however, actual success turned out to be lower than expected. This is the case for construction, food processing, mechanical and electrical equipment, chemicals, and mining. This result is surprising for construction since this activity is of low risk to banks and it enjoys natural protection from foreign competition. During this period, however, the financing of

Table 5. Adjustment programs in MENA countries

Country	Pre-adjustment	Adjustment Year	Post-adjustment	Recent Situation
Morocco	1982	1983	1984–1985	Average: (2000–2003)
Budget deficit[a]/GDP (%)	–11.4	–7.7	–7.0	–4.1
Current account deficit/GDP (%)	–12.5	–7.3	–5.4	–3.6
Inflation (%)	10.7	6.3	9.6	1.64
Tunisia	1985	1986	1987–1989	
Budget deficit[a]/GDP (%)	–5.0	–7.1	–4.2	n.a.
Current account deficit/GDP (%)	–6.2	–7.1	–0.2	–2.7
Inflation (%)	7.2	6.2	7.7	2.6
Jordan	1988	1989	1990–1999	
Budget deficit[a]/GDP (%)	–9.0	5.8	+1.2	–2.2 (2000–2002)
Current account/ GDP (%)	–6.1	+10.5	–9.6	+6.2
Inflation (%)	6.5	25.7	6.8	1.66
Egypt	1990	1991	1992–1997	
Budget deficit[a]/GDP (%)	–5.7	–4.9	+1.0	2.1 (2002–2002)
Current account / GDP (%)	+0.4	+5.7	+1.7	0.0
Inflation (%)	16.7	19.7	10.2	3.05

n.a. Not available.
Source: International Financial Statistics, IMF, January 2005.
[a]For both the Government budget and the current account, a sign (+) means a surplus.

One should also notice that the new President was in a privileged position, at the Interior Ministry, to monitor the deteriorating situation of the country since the early 1980s. Once in charge, he should have been aware of the need for institutional arrangements to ensure better governance. First, he turned down suggestions to create a new political Party, preferring instead to "rejuvenate" the Neo-Destour. Second, a "National Charter" was signed in 1988 by all major political parties, including the Islamists. Moreover, coordination was strengthened with centralized power, a domesticated trade union, and co-opted business associations. The latter had long grown used to protection but eventually realized that they had no other choice but to adapt to the new orientation. The newly appointed President of UTICA as well as the entire Bureau was among the most successful Tunisian exporters and therefore favorable to greater openness even though several of them were also involved in import-substitution activities.

As regards credibility, the country still lacked institutional enforcement mechanisms. But, the general consensus to open up the economy, the appointment of pro-export leaders within UTICA, and the signing of the Stand-by Agreement with the IMF in 1986, all made return to protection unlikely.

The stabilization program succeeded rapidly. In particular, the strong devaluation was accompanied by restrictive monetary, fiscal, and income measures. As a result, the nominal devaluation translated into a real depreciation of the dinar by 14.5% in 1986 and an additional 8.6% in 1987. The current account turned into a surplus in 1988, followed by moderate deficits in the subsequent period.

Structural reforms were also adopted to liberalize the price, investment, and trade regimes. As a result, private investment, shifted from non-tradables to exportables (especially manufacturing) and to a lesser extent to importables (Bechri and Lahouel, [1999]). Nevertheless, deeper institutional reforms were hesitant and in some instances clearly lacking, especially in critical areas like public administration, education, banking, telecommunications and the labor market (Bechri, 1999).

5.3. Post-adjustment uncertainties (1992–1994)

The post-adjustment years (1992–1994) witnessed some policy reversals, mainly in foreign trade. Temporary surcharges were established in 1992, on some manufactured consumer goods like clothing and footwear, "technical controls" under the so-called *Cahiers des Charges* regime were imposed on other imports. These reversals sent an unfortunate signal about the government's commitment to reforms by indicating to the private sector that protection can always be restored by one type of restriction or another.

These reversals and the lack of institutional reforms help explain the decline in private investment from 13.5% of GDP in 1992 to 12.7% in 1993 and 11.6% in 1994. The decline in the volume of private investment was particularly pronounced in 1993 for food processing (–20.0%) and in 1994 for textiles and leather (–13.0%), mechanical and electrical equipment (–20.0%), and chemicals (–27.3%). Foreign direct investment (outside energy) was also weak, <1% of GDP. This decline occurred despite the adoption of a unified investment code in 1993 and the removal of import licensing in 1994. Thus, the authorities realized that additional bold measures were needed. In 1995, Tunisia was the first South-Mediterranean country to sign an Association Agreement with the European Union, which provided for the establishment of a free-trade area.

5.4. The association agreement with the european union

The Tunisian official rationale in this respect was that as the first signatory from the South-Mediterranean region, Tunisia would benefit the most from: (1) EU financial support, (2) industrial relocation, (3) enhanced credibility, by locking the economy into an irreversible set of reforms, and (4) an advantage in terms of determining the content of the agreement (Bechri, 1999). But, one should notice that this rationale might also be valid for countries like Egypt, Morocco, and Jordan. So to understand Tunisia's decision, we need to look at some differences in interest group characteristics.

First, the three decades-old export-oriented strategy in Tunisia ended up creating a whole constituency that had a stake in openness. For example, according to the most recent available estimates for the textiles and clothing sector, out of a total of 1540 exporting firms, only one-third (536 firms) is foreign-owned, 333 firms are partnership companies, and the remaining 671 firms are locally owned. Other sectors, like mechanical and electrical equipment shifted gradually from import substitution in the 1970s to export by the late 1980s. This is a sign of a better performance, but it also means that with the passage of time these activities became more interested in export promotion than in protection.

The second major difference relates to the domesticated labor union. UGTT was allowed to renew its activities in 1988, but under the condition of a cooperative leadership. As a result, strikes and violent protests became rare. Nevertheless, both UTICA and UGTT were concerned about the costs of adjustment. These concerns may explain why Tunisia chose a long implementation period of 12 years for tariffs removal.

So far, the implementation of the association agreement is proceeding as planned and without major disruptions. A technological upgrading program *Programme de Mise de Niveau* (PMN), funded by the European Union, started in 1996. As of April 2003, upgrading was approved for 1448 firms with investments amounting to 2.4 billion dinars, of which 24% was allocated to agribusiness, 20% to construction products, 18% to textiles and clothing, 14% to mechanical and electrical equipment, 8% to chemicals, and 5.2% to leather and other industries.

From a labor point of view, things also went smoothly. No major bankruptcies took place, worker layoffs were rare and there have even been reported instances where restructuring led to job creation. The long implementation period of the free-trade agreement, however, also had major economic drawbacks. First, by announcing the opening up of the economy to European competition by 2008, the agreement sent a wrong signal to business about the urgent need to adjust. Second, restructuring in import-substitution activities remained limited. This is harmful to consumers and did not bode well for the competitiveness of these industries. Third, the bureaucracy and other entrenched interests (especially protected business and trade unions) managed to postpone badly needed reforms in crucial activities like trading boards, telecommunications, and banking.

Trading boards in Tunisia have a monopoly on foreign trade in specific products like edible oil, cereals, tea, coffee, and sugar. The *Office de l'huile* clearly outlived its usefulness, since its monopoly on olive oil exports was lifted in the early 1990s. The same could also be said about the *Office du commerce*, following the withdrawal of sugar from the list of subsidized items. But, the *Office des Cereales* continues to have a monopoly on the imports of cereals that is unlikely to be eliminated as long as food subsidies are in place.

As regards telecommunications, this sector used to be managed by the government until the mid-1990s. This resulted in poor quality of services and high costs. In an attempt to modernize the sector, the authorities created Tunisie-Telecom, as an independent entity from the ministry. However, the public monopoly failed. Thus, Tunisia ended up lagging behind countries like Morocco, which successfully liberalized its telecommunications in the 1990s. In 2002, a second license for GSM services was granted to the Egyptian company ORASCOM and further opening of the sector to competition is expected, including the withdrawal of the State from Tunisie-Telecom.

The banking sector, however, remains dominated by State-owned institutions. Costs for banking services remain high by international standards, and non-performing loans (NPLs) a major source of fragility of the system. Despite the introduction of prudential regulations in 1992, their ratio remained at 22% in 2002–2003, and increased to 24% in 2004 (compared to an international standard of 6%). There has also been a merger of three public banks. One public sector bank (UIB) was sold to the French *Societe Generale* in 2004, and the *Banque du Sud* is expected to follow suit in 2005. But these attempts remain insufficient to create an internationally competitive banking sector.

6. Conclusion

During the last five decades, Tunisia clearly outperformed other MENA countries. This exceptional performance in economic and social development owes much to its visionary leadership, its early emphasis on modernization and economic progress, and its better technical abilities to implement economic policy. The leadership averted Tunisia's involvement in regional conflicts that proved costly to other countries in the region like Egypt, Syria, Iraq, Algeria, and others.

The Tunisian experience showed, indeed, the instrumental role of leadership in isolating traditional groups, and in rallying the support of women, trade unions and the other liberal fringes of the population. Once freed from the shackles of backward teachings of the traditional establishment, constituted around Zeitouna, Tunisia was able to improve the status of women, modernize its education, and adopt population control. This is in contrast to the other MENA countries, such as Egypt, where Al Azhar and similar institutions continue to influence public opinion and to oppose serious attempts (by parliament and other institutions) to take action in favor of women and educational reform.

The gains were very important: lower population growth and higher GDP growth, compared to MENA averages. The combined effect was an acceleration of annual *per-capita* GDP from 2.1% in the 1960s, 2.5% in the 1990s, and about 4% at present, which gives the country the status of a top performer in the region.

Indeed, demographic explosion turned out to be a chief culprit in the other MENA countries, as Bourguiba has been arguing for decades. The decline in fertility was slow. As recently as 1998, the average for Jordan, Egypt, Morocco, and Syria, was 3.5, against only 2.2, for Tunisia. The implication was enormous. Egypt's population, as an example, would have been about 54 millions only, against 68 millions in 2000, had it experienced the Tunisian demographic growth of the last five decades.

Population control and social modernization, therefore, would seem to have played an important role in explaining Tunisia's high annual average growth of 6.0%, compared to Egypt's 4.6%, Morocco's 4.5%, and Jordan's 2.7% during 1985–2003. Better health and education created a more productive labor force, which was strengthened with better women participation.

Tunisia also did particularly well in starting early its reforms, especially its policy shift from import substitution to export promotion as early as the early 1970s. Current laggards in the region currently face serious challenges, although the recent examples of Morocco and Kuwait regarding women status reforms indicate that action in this respect is still possible.

The Tunisian case also shows the clear dangers of co-option. In the case of the trade union, the ruling Party ended up adopting UGTT policies not the other way around. In most MENA countries, Islamists groups in parliaments are nowadays the main obstacle to social and educational reforms. Even though no efforts should be spared in seeking cooperation from these groups, neither can reformist governments afford to be paralyzed by them.

For years, Tunisia tried to bypass business opposition by adopting a two-track strategy that is no longer feasible. The only option left for laggards in the MENA region today is to adopt a wide range of social and economic reforms. In this respect, due consideration should be given to sequencing. It may be prudent to start with actions that are expected to face less opposition. For reforms that involve huge redistribution, governments need to start by explaining the long-term benefits to the public and provide appropriate compensation schemes for losers.

References

Achy, L. (2000), "Misalignment and exchange rate arrangement against the euro", Paper presented at the ERF Annual Conference, Amman, Jordan.

Bechri, M.Z. (1999), "Institutional obstacles, reform uncertainty and Tunisia's integration in the European Union", Paper presented at the Euro-Med partnership seminar in Cairo, February.

Bechri, M.Z. and M.E.H. Lahouel (1999), "Trade liberalization and the behavior of private investment in Tunisia", Paper presented at the ERF Annual Conference, Cairo, October 28–31.

Bellin, E. (1989), "Tunisian industrialists and the state", *World Development*, Vol. 22(3), pp. 1994.

Castanheira, M. and H.S. Isfahani (forthcoming), "Political economy of growth: lessons learned and challenges ahead", in: L. Squire and G. McMahon, editors, *Explaining Growth*, Washington, DC: International Economics Association.

Edwards, S. (1998), "The political economy of unilateral trade reform in Chile", available on Professor Sebastian Edwards Website.

Grissa, A. (1989), "The Tunisian state enterprises and privatization policy", Mimeo, unpublished.

Isfahani, H.S. (2000), "Political economy of growth in MENA: a framework for country case studies", Global Development Network Working Paper.

Isfahani, H.S. (2002), "Political economy of growth in Iran, 1963–2002", Department of Economics, University of Illinois.

Khiari, S. (2000), "La place de l'UGTT dans le systeme politique Tunisien", Mimeo, unpublished.

Lau, L., J.Y. Qiau and G. Roland (2001), "Reform without losers: an interpretation of China's dual-track approach to transition", available on Stanford University website.

Moussa, H. (1995), "Economic policy and economic development in Tunisia", Paper presented at the International Economic Association World Congress, December, Tunis, Tunisia.

Nabli, M.K. and J.B. Nugent (1989), "Collective Action, Institutions and Development", in: M.K. Nabli and J.B. Nugent, editors, *The New Institutional Economics and Development: Applications to Tunisia*, Amsterdam: North-Holland (Chapter 3).

Nugent, J.B. (1989). Collective action in Tunisia's producer's organizations. in: M.K. Nabli and J.B. Nugent, editors, The New Institutional Economics and Development: Applications to Tunisia. Amsterdam: North-Holland.

Rodrik, D. (1998), "Why is trade reform so difficult in africa?", in: I. Zubair and M. Khan, editors, *Trade Reform And Regional Integration in Africa*, The International Monetary Fund.

World Bank (2003), Better Governance for Development in the Middle East and North Africa.

CHAPTER 11

Algeria's Macroeconomic Performances from 1962 to 2000

Mohamed Abdelbasset Chemingui* and Moataz Mostafa El-Said

Abstract

The paper examines Algeria's economic growth performance with an effort to explain its performance over the period 1962–2000. The paper considers prevailing economic policies and changes introduced to the economic environment over the same time period. In addition, the paper conducts a Solow's accounting exercise to break down growth in output into growth in capital, labor, and total factor productivity (TFP) and at key determinants that influence Algeria's growth performance. Over the past four decades, Algeria's growth performance has been characterized by high fluctuations and generally slower growth than that in the neighboring developing countries. The poor economic growth performance that Algeria experienced is a result of a slow growth in productivity which can be attributed to the following factors: (i) the inefficient management of the country's natural resources; (ii) the country's macroeconomic policies, specifically price deregulation and economic reforms aimed at increasing investment; (iii) structural impediments limiting the private sector contribution to the country's economic activities; and (iv) an overall economic environment dominated by the public sector, a weak financial sector, slow and non-transparent privatization process, and other factors that limited the progress of economic reforms.

Keywords: economic growth, productivity, technological change, government policy, trade policy, foreign exchange policy

JEL classifications: F43, O47, O33, 038, 024

---

*Corresponding author.

CONTRIBUTIONS TO ECONOMIC ANALYSIS
VOLUME 278   ISSN: 0573-8555
DOI:10.1016/S0573-8555(06)78011-7

1. Introduction

Growth has been one of the most active fields of research in economics since the mid-1980s. Economists seek answers to explain why there are very rich countries at the same time as very poor countries. For example, why do rates of economic growth vary substantially across countries? Finding answers as to what are the sources of economic growth and what can be done to improve it can help explain how countries can grow from rags to riches, and how economic policies can play a role in achieving rapid economic growth. In the 1950s and 1960s, it was accepted that inventing massively was sufficient for achieving high economic growth rates. However, the 1970s showed that investment alone was not enough, which led to a search for the sources and determinants of economic growth. The economics of "ideas" and of human capital and the economics of technology were introduced to growth theories and much of the 1990s was spent in quantifying and testing those theories.

In this paper Algeria's economic growth performance is examined over the period 1962–2000. The paper makes use of a Solow accounting exercise to break down growth into growth in capital, labor, and total factor productivity (TFP).

Over the past four decades, Algeria's growth performance has been characterized by high fluctuations and generally slower growth than that in neighboring developing countries. At times, Algeria even experienced growth rates lower than those of poor Sub-Saharan African countries. Four different periods in Algeria's growth over the past four decades can be distinguished: (a) a period from 1962 to the early 1970s characterized by high growth rates averaging 8.3 percent per year; (b) a period of more volatile growth from the early 1970s until 1986, during which growth rates averaged at ∼5 percent; (c) a period from 1987 to 1994 during which growth rates were negative in some years and averaged only 0.2 percent and (d) a fourth period since the mid-1990s when the economy exhibited modest but progressively positive growth (averaging 3.2 percent *per annum*).

Analyzing the main determinants of the Algerian growth achievements was a first step toward identifying what needs to be done to make growth more sustainable. The empirical literature suggests a wide range of growth correlates. This list includes research and development (R&D), technological transfer from abroad mainly through foreign direct investments (FDI), population growth and unemployment rates, the level of human capital development, level of physical investment, infrastructure development, degree of factor allocations, government size, financial market development, natural resource endowment, institutions, politics, technical barriers, income distribution, economic base, rates of returns on investment in physical and human capital, level of integration in the world economy, and the level of development of market institutions. The empirical literature indicates that most of these determinants of growth are as important as the proximate factors of growth namely physical capital, labor, and the efficiency with which these factors are combined. In this respect, a detailed examination of the determinants of

Algeria's slow growth performance was carried out. The list of factors that impede Algeria's economic growth include low labor productivity, high inflation rates, high levels of external debt, weak institutional development, non-transparency in administrative practices, inadequate infrastructure, and underdeveloped financial markets.

Furthermore, growth patterns are believed to be inextricably linked to various economic policies such as fiscal policy, labor policy, trade policy, exchange rate policy, interest rate policy, government spending in human capital, and infrastructure development and competition policy, among others. Algeria introduced substantial reforms in several of these respects beginning in 1986, and has since then undertaken a number of policy and regulatory changes to liberalize what was previously a highly protected and centrally planned economy. These changes included progressive liberalization of trade policy, privatization of state-owned enterprises (SOEs), and fiscal policy reform.

The format of the paper is as follows: Section 2 of the paper considers an overview of economic growth in Algeria, while Section 3 presents a growth accounting exercise to quantify the sources of economic growth and to determine the contribution of each factor to the growth of output. This is followed by Section 4, which looks at some structural and economic policy obstacles behind Algeria's sharp fall in economic growth rate and TFP. Finally, Section Y_5 concludes with an assessment of the Algerian experience.

2. Overview of Algeria's economic growth

Algeria represents a rather special case among countries of the Middle East and North Africa (MENA) region. Although endowed with abundant natural resources, mainly crude oil, Algeria was not successful in fully reaping the potential exemplified by the country's low GDP growth and high unemployment rates. Compared to Tunisia, a neighboring MENA country, Algeria's income *per capita* was 60 percent higher than that of Tunisia in 1960. However, 30 years later, Tunisia's *per capita* income is higher than that of Algeria by 7 percent even though Tunisia is not endowed with natural resources (Tunisia is not an oil-exporting country) like Algeria. To provide an answer as to why this is the case, the paper looks at Algeria's growth path over the period 1962–2000 and considers the prevailing economic policies and changes introduced to the economic environment over the same time period.

Algeria's growth record over the 1962–2000 period can be broken down into four subperiods in terms of the country's economic growth and economic policy orientations:

1962–1973:   A period of high and stable economic growth.

1974–1986:   A period of macroeconomic instability, difficult adjustments, and more volatile growth rates, and falling GDP *per capita* growth rate (Figure 1).

Figure 1.   GDP per capita growth rate

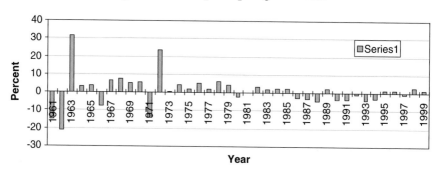

Year

1987–1994:   A period of structural adjustment programs coupled with
                    declining economic growth.
1995–2000:   A period of modest economic growth and a new wave of
                    economic reforms.

2.1. 1962–1973: High but unstable economic growth

Since independence in 1962, Algeria's economic orientation followed a model of
a socialist economy dominated by public sector industrialization-based development strategy. In general, the Algerian government favored state monopolies
in a centralized economic planning system. In terms of economic growth, by the
end of the 1970s, Algeria was on a path of high and fluctuating growth in *per
capita* income, with total investment accounting for a large share of national
income (about 45 percent). Hydrocarbon exports provided the bulk of the revenue that financed these efforts, and helped create a large network for public
enterprises (PEs) and an extensive infrastructure base. The period was marked
by improving social indicators, falling illiteracy, increasing life expectancy, and
high school enrollment.

Following an industrialization-based development strategy led to the allocation of a large proportion of total public investment (about 54 percent) toward
manufacturing, mining, energy, and hydrocarbons, while the share for agriculture remained relatively constant at around 10 percent. The heavy industry,
notably hydrocarbons, played a major role in Algeria's economic activity, as it
contributed to the construction of the industrial sector by endowing it with raw
materials and provided agriculture with inputs and energy.

However, as is the case with most state-run enterprises, Algeria's public
sector quite often followed contradictory political, ideological, economic, and
social objectives. In general, public firms lacked managerial autonomy and had
to attend to other objectives like having to aid in reducing regional disparities,
absorb the growth in the labor force, and take care of the social necessities of the

employees (consumer goods with low costs, habitation, health, transportation). To a large degree the private sector was crowded out by state-owned enterprises. However, some private sector activities existed, mainly relying on subcontracting for public sector activities.

In summary, Algeria was able to achieve high growth rates during this period as a result of a mix of factors, mainly from an intensive public investment program carried out by the state and an expansion in oil and energy production that was coupled with increasing international oil prices.

2.2. 1974–1986: Macroeconomic instability, difficult adjustments, and volatile economic growth

By the late 1970s, the inefficiencies of the central planning system became apparent. For agriculture, state farms, which accounted for the major part of Algeria's agricultural output, suffered from low productivity growth and stagnating crop yields. Inefficiencies in state management were evident as many large public investment projects took unnecessary long time for completion and a large number of new industrial plants were running substantially below capacity because of weak domestic and foreign demand. In addition, the inefficiency of investment was reflected in an abnormally high incremental capital/output ratio (Table 1) which, despite investment levels averaging ~40 percent of GDP, resulted in annual real *per capita* output growth of slightly <2 percent on average.

Since the beginning of the 1980s, Algeria's macroeconomic balances deteriorated rapidly in large part because of falling oil prices. By 1986, the deterioration reached a climax as export revenues from oil collapsed as a result of a Saudi-inspired lowering of world prices and depreciation in the value of the US dollar. Algeria's terms of trade declined by almost 50 percent. The Government of Algeria had to borrow to maintain consumption levels, while the volume of imports declined by almost one-third between 1985 and 1987. In the meantime, investment was reduced and the level of domestic industries activities decreased significantly. This includes almost all sectors of the economy with the exception of hydrocarbon and agriculture. Toward the period 1986–1988, real GDP growth averaged <1 percent per year (compared to 5.4 percent per year in 1978–1985). Unemployment and inflation rates increased, and *per capita* consumption declined. An acute social and political crisis was brewing, which

Table 1. **Investment shares, capital/output ratios, and per capita GDP growth**

	1975–1976	1977–1978	1979–1980	1981–1982	1983	1984	1985
Gross investment/GDP (percent)	44.0	49.5	41.0	37.0	38.0	35.0	33.0
Capital/output ratio	3.5	4.5	5.5	7.0	8.0	8.0	6.0
Per capita GDP growth (percent)	3.5	3.9	1.3	1.6	1.9	2.2	2.3

Source: Authors' calculations on the basis of data from World Bank (1994).

prompted the authorities to initiate a broad-ranging program of macroeconomic stabilization and structural reform.

2.3. *1987–1994: Structural adjustment programs and economic recession period*

The adoption of the structural adjustment and macroeconomic stabilization program became necessary to achieve macroeconomic stability. By 1987, the program was initiated with an aim to establish the "right" conditions for sustainable long-term growth and at the same time to correct the macroeconomic imbalances and price distortions, and to contain inflation in the short term.[1] In addition, reforms that covered the legal and institutional framework of the productive sector and the factor markets were introduced. These aimed at creating an incentive structure to stimulate supply response and to provide a source of competition for PEs, especially from the private sector. The reforms also included a program to restructure PEs and the banking sector.

The structural reforms encompassed an overhaul of the incentive framework, including price, tax, and trade reforms. In January 1992, a major tax reform was enacted; a value-added tax (VAT) was introduced to simplify the indirect tax structure, while unified corporate and individual income taxes replaced a series of tax schedules and special tax regimes. In addition, the tax reform included a reduction in the maximum tariff from 120 percent to 60 percent, and a unification of the compensation tax rates on imports and domestically produced goods. Nevertheless, the reform efforts remained ineffective because of significant distortions that remained. While the tariff structure became more neutral, the overall incentive structure continued to distort border prices and to accord a relatively high rate of protection to domestic PEs. In addition, two key distortions remained: an overvalued exchange rate and a negative real interest rate.

Despite the progress achieved in implementing reforms, the economic crisis persisted. Weak economic growth lowered *per capita* consumption and exacerbated unemployment. Over the 1985–1992 period, aggregate GDP growth averaged only 0.4 percent annually, and 1993 and 1994 were two years marked by very poor economic performance.[2] The only exception came from the agriculture sector, averaging an encouraging 5.4 percent growth rate per year. This was

---

[1] The priority objectives of structural reform included:

- Promoting private sector development;
- Reforming and restructuring PEs;
- Deepening agricultural reform;
- Developing a competitive financial sector, and a well-functioning labor market;
- Strengthening the social safety net, and adapting it to the needs for a market economy; and
- Integrating the economy into world markets.

[2] During the 1990–1994 period, annual real growth was negative, averaging −0.9 percent (IMF, 2000).

taking place while value added by the core "enterprise sector" (industry, construction, and services) was declining by an average of ~3.2 percent *per annum*. *Per capita* private consumption declined annually by about 3 percent over the 1985–1992 period. The industrial sector continued to be dominated by large, inefficient, and heavily protected PEs, enjoying monopoly power and access to official foreign exchange and domestic credit at subsidized rates. Privatization prospects remained difficult as the economy stagnated and the unemployment record worsened (the number of unemployed workers tripled over that period) and the official open unemployment rate reached an estimated 21 percent.

In summary, the adopted reforms had at best a short-lived positive impact on economic performance.

2.4. 1995–2000: A new wave of economic reforms and economic growth

With the implementation of the 1994 reform program supported by the World Bank and the IMF, Algeria's economic performance started to show signs of improvement. The program was put in place following a severe external payment crisis, in the wake of the oil price drop in 1993. The Government introduced swift stabilization and adjustment measures, including a strong fiscal adjustment; tight monetary policy; an active exchange rate regime; and price liberalization. The program was accompanied by a debt rescheduling agreement with the Paris and London clubs, and the initiation of structural reforms, including privatization of a number of PEs.

To date, the main parameters of the reform program remains in place. This reform program has been successful in bringing about macroeconomic stability. Inflation dropped from 39 percent in 1994 to ~5 percent by the end of the 1990s. The fiscal deficit was significantly reduced (from a high of 8.7 percent of GDP in 1993 to a surplus of around 2.5 percent by 1997) with the exception of 1998 when the state budget recorded a deficit of 4 percent of GDP because of the sharp drop in oil prices. However, as oil prices started to recover along with significant expenditures cuts, the fiscal stance was reversed yielding a close-to-balanced budget by 1999.

Regardless of the reform efforts, the supply response failed to materialize. The economy remained vulnerable to oil price changes. The reform program succeeded in reversing the past decline in GDP growth, but the recovery remained slow and subject to large fluctuations provoked by weather and oil price variability. Real GDP growth rate in the 1995–1996 period averaged 4 percent (mostly driven by the hydrocarbons sector), followed by a sharp slowdown in 1997 to ~1 percent, reflecting the drought-induced decline in agricultural production and a continued decline in the state-owned industrial sector. Manufacturing value added decreased by 2 percent in 1995, 13 percent in 1996, and 7 percent in 1997, implying a cumulative loss during the period 1990–1997 of ~40 percent in real terms.

Despite a second oil price shock in 1998, the Algerian economy achieved a real GDP growth rate of 5.1 percent, mainly owing to agricultural growth (an exceptionally high rainfall record and an overall good harvest) along with a slight recovery in manufacturing in response to the restructuring efforts of the previous 4 years. However, in 1999 real GDP growth dropped to 3.5 percent owing to a substantial slowdown of the non-hydrocarbon sectors (mainly construction and services sectors), which grew at only 2.7 percent in real terms owing to the budgetary impact of the sharp drop in oil prices. This was compounded by a severe slowdown in agriculture caused by a drought that mostly affected the cereal sector. Still the hydrocarbon sector grew by 6 percent as a result of improving oil prices to compensate for the slowdown in the non-hydrocarbon sectors.

3. Sources of economic growth in Algeria: a growth accounting exercise

The incomes of countries increase as they accumulate more factors of production (labor, capital, and human capital) and as they use their resources more efficiently. There is a substantial literature that considers the relative contribution of the different factors of production and their productivity to output growth across countries (Page and Underwood, 1996). Growth accounting is an approach to decompose the growth of output into the growth of individual factors of production and TFP growth.

This exercise is carried out to quantify the contribution of the different factors of production to Algeria's total growth and to better understand what has prevented the country from achieving the rates of economic growth needed since its independence.[3] As explained by Keller and Nabli (2002), in Algeria, accumulation and productivity have often gone in opposite directions, as seen during the period of massive public sector investments. Examining growth alone will mask these very different effects and the somewhat anemic growth that has characterized the country, especially considering that the observed effects of reform may be more a reflection of significantly lower investments than of poor productivity performance.

Using a constant returns to scale Cobb–Douglas functional form and assuming that the capital share, and hence technology, is the same across countries

---

[3] An alternative econometric estimation of the production function was performed with the data used for the growth accounting carried out in this study as well as the database established by UNIDO. The estimation results using both data sources were not fruitful and arriving at conclusions could not be drawn using the estimated results. The production function used has GDP as output and labor and capital as input; alternative data were taken from Penn World Tables 6.1 (UNIDO). Data on capital were generated by UNIDO staffs from investment data (using PPP investment deflators, assuming 13.3 percent depreciation rate following Leamer). To compute TFP growth, the Data Envelopment Analysis (DEA) was used to obtain the change in technical efficiency and technical change, and the Malmquist index to obtain TFP growth. The advantage of this method is that it does not assume any functional form and no assumptions about perfect competition, profit maximization, etc. are needed. Technically, DEA involves the use of linear programming methods to construct a non-parametric piece-wise frontier. Furthermore, a global study on determinants of productivity in developing countries was carried out last year (2004) by UNIDO, and also their estimation for Algeria was not promising and consequently Algeria was dropped from the project while it was included in the MENA countries to be covered by the project.

the share of physical capital in real output. The higher this share, the higher is the contribution of capital to economic growth. In both countries, there is a significant contribution of capital to economic growth, but the difference between both of them is in the contribution of labor and TFP to economic growth. For Algeria, the contribution of labor growth to GDP growth is higher than that in Tunisia whereas Tunisia realized a much higher TFP contribution to economic growth as a result of technological changes, improvements in human capital, and many other structural reforms both at the macro as well as the micro levels[8].

4. Structural weaknesses in the Algerian economy

The potential for growth depends to a large extent on the resources that a country has, but for a country's economy to grow, the "right" conditions have to be created. In this respect and in some of the recent contributions to the growth literature (Hall and Jones, 1999; Rodrik, 2003) a distinction has been drawn between two different layers of factors underlying growth: the "proximate" sources of factor accumulation and of productivity, and a few "deep" determinants. The latter can be divided into three groups, namely, geography, integration, and institutions (Rodrik *et al.*, 2002).[9] The present section will focus on the proximate sources. As far as the deep determinants go, all three groups (and also human capital) will play important roles; however, in a way that is different from that encountered in the standard analysis of aggregate growth.

In Algeria and during the first period (1962–1973) of economic development the hydrocarbon sector remained the backbone of the economy, accounting for ~57 percent of the government revenues, 25 percent of GDP, and almost 100 percent of export earnings. This is not surprising as Algeria has the fifth-largest reserves of natural gas in the world, is the second-largest natural gas exporter, and ranks 14th in terms of oil reserves.

In this context, the impact of the higher oil prices observed during the past few years has been blurred by the internal political unrest that characterized the country since 1988.[10] In what follows we consider some of the other structural barriers to achieving high economic growth in Algeria. These include weak institutions and administrative capacity, high external debt and debt servicing, high inflation rates, low productivity, an underdeveloped banking sector, and inadequate infrastructure.

---

[8] For a detailed discussion of the labor factor and human capital contribution to economic growth in Algeria, the reader may refer to Keller and Nabli (2002).

[9] Another view (represented by Lucas, 2002), would move one of the proximate sources, namely human capital to the level of deep – in fact, deepest – determinants.

[10] To isolate the impact of oil on the growth performance of the Algerian economy given its political instability, one could choose a similar oil country or a counterfactual that did not experience the same instability and estimate what would have happened to the Algerian economy in the absence of this political instability. This exercise, however, is beyond the scope of this paper.

4.1. Weak institutions and administrative capacity

The recent growth literature strongly emphasizes the role of good (i.e., high-quality) institutions for speeding up growth, and of poor ones for retarding it.[11] Unfavorable institutional factors – such as the degree of regulation and corruption in the government – are recognized as critical factors that can stand in the way of sustained economic growth. In this context, an important dimension for creating an investment climate conducive to growth is to have a governance system that honors contracts and property rights and works on reducing corruption.

Surveys of existing enterprises and potential investors consistently rank various elements of institutional capability as among the major factors determining the ability of developing economies to attract new private investment (Dasgupta *et al.*, 2002). Along the same lines is the work by Gwartney *et al.*, (2004) which shows a positive correlation between investment and the quality institutions.[12] Institutions affect performance primarily by fostering better policy choices and enhancing the sustainability of policies. Moreover, weak institutions tend to undercut the resilience of economies to exogenous shocks. Hence, poor institutions may lead to more volatile, crisis-prone economies compared to situations where institutions are better developed.

Good governance is fostered through regulatory institutions that promote competition, support efficient resource allocation, and protect property rights. Furthermore, empirical studies show a robust effect of institutions on volatility: the higher the quality of institutions, the lower the volatility of growth. The role of institutions has become a stronger determinant of growth as investors have become better informed about other countries and therefore, can compare institutional performance more easily than they could in the past.

In Algeria, the quality of institutions is considered one of the main determinants of growth mainly because of the pervasive role of the state in the economy. There is a need for improving transparency and fair competition so as to attract external financing.[13] Typically, countries characterized by high returns, transparent investment procedures and regulations, low political risk, and accountable economic regimes and institutions are better able to attract external financing. The ten-point index of Economic Freedom published by the Heritage

---

[11] Rodrik *et al.* (2002).

[12] According to Noth (1990), institutions are defined as the formal and informal constraints on political, economic, and social interactions. From this perspective, good institutions are viewed as establishing an incentive structure that reduces uncertainty and promotes efficiency–hence contributing to stronger economic performance.

[13] Many indicators of institutions' quality and governance are available for such assessments. The World Bank suggests evaluative and quantitative measures which are available for a large selection of countries including Algeria. But given that reliability of these measures depends on data accuracy and whether or not subjective perceptions are at play, rating measures seem useful for assessing both actual and potential performance and risk.

subject to diminishing returns to scale, a sustained rise in the growth rate of productivity will require the continued introduction of new goods, not just continued learning on a given set of goods. One measure by which a small economy can expand the range of goods it can (potentially) produce, is by selling on the world market. Thus, having a relatively open economy seems to be an important precondition for learning-based growth. Professional training is always considered as an indirect means of learning by doing.

In Algeria, the professional training system, which started less than about 20 years ago, was largely designed to meet the needs of an economy based on PEs providing agricultural products and assembled manufactured goods with low local value-added and entirely oriented to a highly protected local market. At the moment, the education and training system are not able to build a workforce with high skills that are able to meet the challenges of the Algerian economy which needs to be diversified.

4.5. Underdeveloped banking sector

One of the main roles of the financial system is to ensure that resources get transferred to the most efficient use. Thus, a well-functioning financial system is an important precondition for capital accumulation and hence economic growth as well as for a burgeoning private sector. By contrast, the more frictions there are, the less well can the financial system operate as an intermediary in resource (re-) allocation. Thus, a sound financial system is required to allow firms to enter the market and operate effectively as well as to help restructure failing firms. An important task of the financial sector is to support entry of promising firms and re-allocate resources away from failing or underperforming firms to more promising ones. A well-functioning financial sector operating at arm's length from political and corporate interests is crucial for competition and productivity growth. A large body of literature on financial intermediation shows the crucial role played by the financial sector to improve the economy's savings, investment, productivity, and growth. In this regard, developing the financial sector may improve the level of savings, which will likely raise investment levels and growth. In addition, a performing financial sector contributes to higher growth through better allocation of resources. Well-functioning financial markets will allocate resources to users with the highest return and, through the monitoring of creditor's performance, ensure continued efficient use of productive assets (Jbili *et al.*, 1997).

Until the early 1980s, Algeria pursued an inward-looking economic development strategy emphasizing a key role for the state in economic activity to accelerate economic development and ensure government control over "strategic" sectors. These objectives were to be achieved through direct government investment in key productive sectors, the provision of generous incentives (such as interest rate subsidies) to private investment in priority sectors, and through a complex system of trade and exchange controls designed to protect local industries. The strategy resulted in a buildup of a large public sector.

Accordingly, financial resources were allocated to achieve the planning objectives. Thus, available financial resources were first given to government and PEs and secondly to private sector firms operating in key sectors, which are mostly producing for local market and benefiting from high border protection. The remaining financial resources were allocated to private sector firms with high interest rates. During the period from 1996 to 2000, the public sector absorbed 80 percent of domestic credit (IMF, 2001). In addition, inefficiencies of direct government controls on credit allocation contributed to the buildup of non-performing loans in most banks in Algeria, mainly the development banks. This weak financial system in pre-1980 Algeria did not facilitate private sector investment in activities in which the country had a comparative advantage, affecting the level of economic growth as well as productivity.

Faced with the increasing economic difficulties of the mid-1980s and influenced by the worldwide trend toward financial liberalization and deregulation, Algeria embarked on a wide-ranging structural reform program that included liberalization of its financial system. The objectives behind the financial sector reform were to reduce direct government intervention and strengthen the role of market forces in the allocation of financial resources, improve the capacity of financial institutions to mobilize domestic savings, and promote competition among banks.

Thus, the liberalization of the banking sector (abolishing credit control in 1991, liberalizing interest rates on overdrafts in 1992, and on accounts in credit in 1996) and an expansionary monetary policy (reducing intervention rates of the central bank on the money market and reducing reserve requirements) have led to a substantial reduction in interest rates. Figure 5 shows the development of private sector credit as a share of total domestic credit. The sharp decline in the domestic credit allocated to the private sector corresponds closely to the structural adjustment program.

Figure 5.   Credits to private sector/total domestic credit

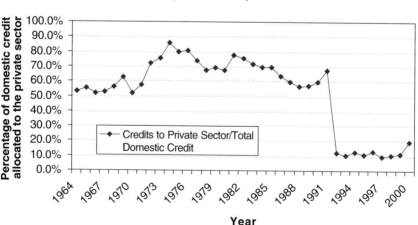

4.6. Inadequate infrastructure

Equally important for economic growth is the quality of infrastructure that allows private entrepreneurs and their employees to operate effectively. De la Fuente (2002) surveyed available evidence and concluded that there are sufficient indications that public infrastructure investment contributes significantly to productivity growth and thereby to economic growth, at least in countries where a saturation point has not been reached. The returns to such investment are probably quite high when infrastructure is scarce and basic networks have not been completed, but fall sharply thereafter. Hence, appropriate infrastructure provision is probably a basic ingredient for growth, even if it does not hold the key to rapid productivity growth in advanced countries, where transportation and communications needs are already adequately served.

For Algeria, there is an urgent need to provide producers, whether they belong to the primary, secondary, or tertiary sectors, with the infrastructure services they need to become or remain competitive at the international level. Thus, and while massive public investment in infrastructure has been happening during the last four decades, the country still suffers from a lack of appropriate infrastructure services. This explains the low level of economic diversification and poor economic and productivity performance observed in the country mainly during the last two decades.

Infrastructure in Algeria is still characterized by public ownership, monopolies, and stifling regulations. The situation is particularly difficult in Algeria because it needs not only to maintain, indeed often to replace, the existing infrastructure, but also to expand it so as to cope with the requirements of more rapid economic growth. During the last decades, inadequate infrastructure in Algeria has paralyzed economic activities owing to traffic bottlenecks, port congestion, and a stalled manufacturing sector as a result of interruptions in energy supply breakdowns on overloaded electricity networks. These are linked to difficulties in complying with international quality standards, longer transit times, and lower productivity.

Furthermore, because of financial constraints and limited resources, the State underinvested in the transport infrastructure. Inadequate resources for its rehabilitation and maintenance were lacking. The resulting deterioration of the infrastructure generates additional costs, and certainly reduces competitiveness. All these factors tend to make Algeria's industries and services less competitive both in local and foreign markets.

5. Conclusion and policy options

The central focus of this paper was to explain the sources of Algeria's economic growth during the past four decades, i.e., since its independence. In doing so, the paper revisits Algeria's economic growth performance to examine the economy's growth path and explain its economic performance over the period 1962–2000. To highlight the sources of economic growth, the paper adopts Solow's accounting exercise to disaggregate overall growth in output into growth in capital, labor, and TFP.

The paper finds that the poor economic growth performance that Algeria experienced during the last four decades is mainly due to poor internal management of the economy and the absence of economic policies in response to external economic shocks. Algeria's slow economic growth performance can be attributed to (i) the country's management of its natural resources; (ii) the country's macroeconomic policies, specifically price deregulation and economic reforms aimed at increasing investment; (iii) structural impediments limiting private sector contributions to the country's economic activities; and (iv) an overall economic environment characterized by a dominant public sector, a weak financial sector, a non-transparent privatization process, and number of other factors that limited the progress of economic reforms.

In addition to the reasons discussed in the paper, other factors played a role as well. Mainly, the recent political context (civil war) and other structural factors continue to block all reform initiatives. What Algeria needs is a focus on supply-side policies to boost the economy's growth capacity. These include measures to improve the competitiveness of existing activities, efforts to attract investment in non-energy sectors so as to diversify the economy. Other complementary supply-side policies may include promoting education and training, and increasing spending in the health sector. Additional economic policy efforts may include accelerating the trade liberalization process and encouraging domestic and foreign investment in export-oriented industries. Moreover, Algeria can aggressively move toward improving its investment climate. Actions under this option can be grouped under three broad headings: (i) deepening of financial markets; (ii) improvements in the judicial and administrative systems governing private and public activities; and (iii) further expansion of privatization. Finally, Algeria can adopt policies intended to accelerate the rate of productivity by adopting an "export push" strategy consisting of three essential elements: (i) accelerating trade liberalization to reduce its anti-export bias; (ii) institutional reforms for trade liberalization; and (iii) targeted investments in trade-related infrastructure.

Acknowledgments

The authors would like to thank Imed Limam, Terry Roe, Magdy Mashaly, Joan Haddock, Jeff Nugent, Hashem Pesaran and two anonymous referees for their comments and useful suggestions. The usual disclaimer applies.

References

Andrés, J. and Hernando, I. (1997), "Does inflation harm economic growth? Evidence for The OECD", Paper presented at the NBER conference on The Costs and Benefits of Achieving Price Stability, February 20–21, 1997, Federal Reserve Bank of New York.

Dasgupta, D., J. Keller and T.G. Srinivasan (2002), "Reform and elusive growth in the Middle East: what has happened in the 1990s", Middle East and North Africa Working Paper Series No. 25, The World Bank, Washington, DC.

De la Fuente, A. (2002), "Does cohesion work? Some general considerations and evidence from Spain", Paper presented at the Conference on Income Convergence and European Regional Policy: Impact, Priorities and Prospects for the EU Candidate Countries, October 10–12, jointly organized by the Bertelsmann Foundation and the World Bank, Barcelona.

Elbadawi, A.I., J.B. Ndulu and N. Ndung's (1996), "Debt overhang and economic growth in Sub-Saharan Africa", Paper presented at the IMF/World Bank conference on External Financing for Low Income Countries, December, Washington.

Gwartney, J., Holcombe, R.G. and Lawson, R.A. (2004), "Institutions and the impact of investment on growth". Memo, Florida State University.

Hall, R.E. and C.I. Jones (1999), "Why do some countries produce so much more output per worker than others?", *Quarterly Journal of Economics*, Vol. 114, pp. 83–116.

Heritage Foundation (2003), *2002 Index of Economic Freedom*, New York: The Heritage Foundation/Wall Street Journal.

IMF (2000), "Algeria: recent economic developments", IMF Staff Country Report No. 00/105, Washington.

IMF (2001), "Algeria: Statistical Appendix", IMF Country Report No. 01/163, Washington.

Jbili, A., K. Enders and V. Treichel (1997), "Financial sector reform in Algeria, Morocco and Tunisia: a preliminary assessment", IMF Working Paper WP/97/81, IMF, Washington, DC.

Keller, J. and M.K. Nabli (2002), "The macroeconomics of labor market outcomes in MENA over the 1990s: how growth has failed to keep pace with a burgeoning labor market", Paper presented at the MDF4, October 2002, Amman.

Lucas, R. (2002), "Making a Miracle", *Econometrica*, Vol. 61(2), pp. 251–272.

Makdisi, S., Z. Fattah, and I. Limam (2007), "Determinants of growth in the MENA countries", Regional Background Paper for the GRP on Explaining Growth in MENA Region.

Mankiw, G., D. Romer and D. Weil (1992), "A contribution to the empirics of economic growth", *Quarterly Journal of Economics*, Vol. 107, pp 407–437.

Nehru, V. and A. Dhareshwar (1994), "New estimates of total factor productivity growth for developing and industrial countries", Policy Research Working Paper No. 1313, the World Bank.

Noth, D.C. (1990), *Institutions, Institutional Change and Economic Performance*, Cambridge: Cambridge University Press.

Otto, G. (1997), "Productivity growth and economic policy in Australia", Research Paper 19, 1996–1997, Parliamentary Library of Australia.

Page, J. and J. Underwood (1996), "Growth, the Maghreb and free trade with the European Union", The Egyptian Center for Economic Studies, Working Paper Series N 07.

Rodrik, D. (editor) (2003), *Search of Prosperity: Analytic Narratives on Economic Growth*, Princeton: Princeton University Press.

Rodrik, D., Subramanian, A. and Trebbi, F. (2002), "Institutions rule: the primacy of institutions over integration and geography in economic development", IMF Working Paper WP/02/189, International Monetary Fund, Washington, DC.

Senhadji, A. (1999), "Sources of economic growth: an extensive growth accounting exercice", IMF Working Paper 99/77, the IMF.

Senhadji, A. (2000), "Sources of Economic Growth: an Extensive Accounting Exercise", IMF Staff Papers Vol. 47(1).

Were, M. (2001), "The impact of external debt on economic growth and private investment in Kenya: an empirical assessment", Paper presented at the wider conference on Debt Relief, August, Helsinki.

World Bank (1994), (The Democratic and Popular Republic of Algeria Country Economic Memorandum: The Transition to a Market Economy), Vol. I (In two volumes), Washington: Country Operations Division.

World Bank (2002), *World Development Indicators*, Washington, DC.

CHAPTER 12

Explaining Growth in an Oil-Dependent Economy: The Case of the United Arab Emirates

Adam B. Elhiraika* and Annas H. Hamed

Abstract

This paper attempts to explain the determinants of economic growth in the United Arab Emirates (UAE) using growth accounting and regression models. The findings indicate the predominance of labour in aggregate growth and a negative contribution by total factor productivity growth (TFPG). In addition to institutional changes and liberal economic policies that encourage re-exports rather than genuine non-oil exports, the evidence on TFPG has been attributed to wide fluctuations in oil price and income that constitute the main omitted variables in TFPG, which is measured as a residual. Econometric results confirm that, unlike the case of countries with diverse resources, natural resource abundance, represented by oil exports, spurs growth in an oil-dependent country such as the UAE. Similarly, changes in oil prices have strong positive effects on economic growth, while all other variables have no important effects, indicating the relatively weak contribution of the non-oil sector. The study discusses policy options for productivity enhancement and for strengthening the trend of increasing genuine exports in recent years as means of achieving true economic diversification and sustainable development.

Keywords: growth, oil-dependent, United Arab Emirates, oil income, non-oil income, development policy

JEL classifications: O11, E22

---

*Corresponding author.

CONTRIBUTIONS TO ECONOMIC ANALYSIS
VOLUME 278   ISSN: 0573-8555
DOI:10.1016/S0573-5555(06)78012-9

1. Introduction

This paper aims at explaining the determinants of growth in the UAE with the objective of highlighting strategies and policies for promoting sustainable development in the country. The search for the determinants of growth has continued to be at the core of economics because of its important policy implications. The allocation and efficient use of resources, income distribution and prospects for sustainable growth are among the main issues of interest in the growth literature. Both fiscal and monetary policy design can benefit from growth analysis.

The UAE is a federation of seven small Gulf emirates that was formed immediately after the withdrawal of Britain from the region in 1971. Before the discovery of oil in Abu Dhabi in 1958 and in Dubai in 1966, economic activity in the seven emirates was dominated by pearling and fishing, which provided employment and income to about 70% of the population (Ghanem, 1992). The rest, 30%, of the population was involved in little agriculture, rural handicraft and herding. There was hardly any kind of industry except for construction of wooden boats and simple handicrafts. The UAE being virtually a desert, its people have been involved in trade since ancient times. Oil wealth has provided the necessary initial conditions for drastic economic and social transformation as well as a rapid increase in population, from 180,000 in 1968 to about 3.7 million in 2002.

In addition to oil, four key factors appear to have contributed to rapid economic growth and increased diversification in the UAE: huge government investment in physical and social infrastructure, a stable macroeconomic environment, availability of capital and absence of restrictions on capital movement together with a high degree of openness and availability of cheap labour from neighbouring Arab countries and the Indian subcontinent.

However, like the other oil-rich small countries in the Middle East and North Africa (MENA) region, the UAE remains heavily dependent on oil income, despite government efforts to encourage private investment in the non-oil sectors. Nevertheless, the UAE economy has been recently classified as the most relatively well-diversified economy in the gulf region (Askari and Jaber, 1999) with an average real GDP growth rate of about 4.5% for the period 1975–2002 compared to a negative average growth for MENA oil-exporting countries during the same period.

It is no surprise that only oil revenue and changes in oil prices appear to have significant effects on the growth of UAE. Unlike the case in countries with a diversified resource base, natural resource abundance induces growth in an oil-dependent country such as the UAE. The study underscores the fact that much of the economic diversification and growth in non-oil income relates to growth in re-exports that have little influence on genuine production of goods and technological progress. Therefore, economic policies and strategies are needed to foster real production and enhance productivity as prerequisites for achieving diversification and sustainable growth.

In the next section, we discuss the performance of the economy during 1975–2002, the period for which data are available. In Section 3, we use a growth accounting framework to estimate the contribution of factor inputs to the overall GDP growth and analyse the findings in a regional context. Also a model of the determinants of UAE growth is specified and estimated and the results discussed in this section. Section 4 gives a detailed analysis of the role of markets, especially the labour and capital markets, in the UAE growth process. Finally, Section 5 concludes with some policy remarks.

2. Performance of the UAE economy

To analyse UAE economic performance during 1975–2002, two distinct sub-periods may be identified. The period from the mid-1970s to the early 1980s was characterized by high growth performance. This was the time when the government directed surpluses from high oil prices into the physical and social infrastructure. The period from around the mid-1980s witnessed significant reduction in economic growth owing to a sharp drop in oil prices. Subsequent government austerity measures were directed largely towards capital expenditures since most of the basic infrastructure projects had been completed by then, while most current expenditure categories have become long-term commitments.

Overall, the performance of the economy fluctuated widely over the period considered though aggregate real GDP rose from US$14.72 billion in 1975 to US$50 billion in 2002 (Table 1). Owing to rapid population growth and immigration, real *per capita* income declined from US$30,161 to US$16,400 during the same period. Economic growth has since the early 1970s relied on both oil and non-oil income, and by 1982 non-oil GDP became more important. The share of crude oil revenue declined from about 70% of GDP in the 1970s to < 40% in the 1990s (Table 2). Despite government efforts to diversify the economy in the face of highly volatile international oil markets and generally declining oil prices and revenues, this trend is mainly a reflection of expansion in the export sector, especially re-exports that amounted to about 30% of the total exports in recent years.

The non-oil GDP originates largely from the services sector with a share of ~ 50% in the last decade. The share of the non-oil goods sector in aggregate GDP has increased, though very slowly, from 21.3% in 1985 to 27% in 2002, reflecting the relatively poor commodity base of the economy. Accordingly, the momentum of economic diversification away from the crude oil sector has been slow despite notable increases in the allocation of capital into the non-oil sector. The bulk of domestic investment in the 1990s and after went to the construction and real estate sector, followed by the transport and communication sector and manufacturing, while the share of oil investments in total domestic investment was almost halved

Table 1.   Some macroeconomic and financial indicators (base = 1990)

Indicator	1975–1985	1986–1990	1991	1992–1995	1996–2000	2001	2002
Real GDP growth (%)	6.85	3.94	–3.11	3.98	3.62	3.6	1.9
Real non-oil GDP (% GDP)	43.5	63.8	54.55	65.61	72.4	70.0	72.0
Real non-oil exports (% of GDP)	11.6	20.4	25.25	37.67	26.0	25.6	23.9
Real non-oil exports (% of total exports)	19.8	36.1	37.34	53.28	61.9	63.5	65.8
Real average GDP *per capita* (US$)	26.6	15.8	18.41	17.40	17.5	17.2	16.4
Gross domestic investment (% GDP)	31.1	23.6	20.7	26.8	27.6	28.8	28.9
Gross domestic saving (% GDP)	39.0	20.5	12.51	21.2	22.7	24.1	21.4
Inflation[a]	2.5	2.5	0	1.94	2.36	2.1	1.3
Real lending rate of interest[b]	7.8	7.21	8.44	5.51	5.31	4.82	3.4
Bank credit to the private sector (% of total)	77.1	81.0	79.8	76.85	83.0	86.9	84.6
Secondary school enrolment ratio	48.0	60.4	69	77	76.0	72.0	74.0

Source: UAE Economic Indicators, 1980, 1989, 1999, Ministry of Planning and the Central Bank's Annual Bulletin (various editions).
[a]Calculated as percentage change in GDP deflator.
[b]Calculated as the difference between nominal fending rate and the rate of inflation.

since the turn of the 1990s (Table 3). The meagre share of manufacturing, the potentially most dynamic sector, in aggregate investment in UAE partly explains why its contribution to GDP is still quite low, at just 14.1% in 2002.

Real GDP growth rates fluctuated widely from one year to another mainly owing to changes in oil prices and revenues (Figure 1). At the same time, with the exception of the First Gulf War period (1984–1988), real non-oil GDP has always maintained positive growth rates. Since the early 1990s, the growth in non-oil income appears to have significantly stabilized aggregate GDP growth. Indeed, growth in the good sectors (agriculture, manufacturing, water and electricity and construction) represented the most stable source of GDP growth in the period considered, followed by growth in the trade and services sectors. This suggests that while the oil sector underpinned the modem economic evolution in the UAE and still dominates overall growth, achieving sustainable growth in the long-run would depend on expansion in other sectors.

While the UAE maintained real GDP growth rate of about 4.5% *per annum* during 1975–2002, the average growth rate was -0.6% for MENA oil-exporting

Table 2. GDP by sector, 1975–2002 (%)

Sector	1975	1980	1985	1990	1995	2000	2001	2002
Agriculture, livestock and fishing	0.8	0.7	1.4	1.6	2.9	3.6	3.5	3.7
Manufacturing	0.9	3.8	9.1	7.7	10.4	13.5	13.9	14.1
Water and electricity	0.5	1.2	2.1	2.0	2.1	2.0	1.93	2.0
Construction	10.9	8.8	8.7	7.7	8.7	6.6	6.9	6.9
Total non-oil commodity sector	*13.1*	*14.5*	*21.3*	*19.1*	*24.0*	*25.7*	*26.2*	*26.7*
Oil and mining	*66.8*	*63.5*	*44.1*	*46.3*	*30.9*	*34.0*	*30.0*	*28.0*
Trade	*8.2*	*8.2*	*8.5*	*9.0*	*11.7*	*8.7*	*9.0*	*9.4*
Transport, storage and communication	3.2	3.3	4.1	5.0	6.7	6.7	7.7	7.8
Finance and insurance	1.6	1.9	5.1	4.1	5.6	5.8	6.6	6.9
Real estate and business services	4.0	3.6	5.1	5.5	10.0	7.5	7.8	7.8
Other services	1.0	0.7	1.6	2.0	1.6	2.1	3.3	3.6
Government services	3.4	5.4	10.8	10.4	10.6	10.5	10.6	11.1
Domestic (household) services	0.1	0.2	0.4	0.4	0.8	0.6	0.8	0.8
Less imputed bank services	−1.4	−1.3	−1.0	−1.6	−2.0	−1.6	−2.0	−2.1
Total services sector	*20.1*	*22.0*	*34.6*	*34.7*	*45.1.*	*40.3*	*43.8*	*45.3*
Gross domestic product	100	100	100	100	100	100	100	100
Total non-oil sector	*33.2*	*36.5*	*55.9*	*53.7*	*69.1*	*66.0*	*70.0*	*72.0*

Source: Development indicators in the UAE (1999, 2003), Ministry of Planning, Abu Dhabi, UAE. Italicized figures represent main economic sectors (total non-oil sector; oil and mining sector; and total services sector) which add up to 100%.

Table 3. Gross domestic investment by sector (%)

Economic Sector	1975–1989	1990–1999[a]	2000	2001	2002
Petroleum	35.78	17.3	13.0	12.8	13.1
Transport, storage and communication	11.36	16.2	17.0	17.9	16.7
Construction and real estate	11.92	20.0	24.6	21.4	21.2
Manufacturing (non-oil)	15.71	15.0	16.7	16.0	16.8
Electricity and water	6.21	10.8	8.0	8.9	8.0
Government services	9.9	9.8	7.0	8.1	8.5
Others	9.12	11.2	13.7	14.9	15.7

Source: UAE Economic Indicators, 1980, 1989, 1999, 2003, Ministry of Planning, UAE.
[a]Excluding 1991.

countries and 1.2% for all MENA countries. Many observers (e.g. Elhiraika and Hamed, 2001) argue that relatively better economic performance in the UAE was spurred by increased domestic investment associated with rapid expansion in foreign trade; a stable macroeconomic environment; liberal financial, exchange rate and trade policies; increased investment in human capital; easy availability of skilled labour from neighbouring countries; and access to Middle Eastern and African product markets.

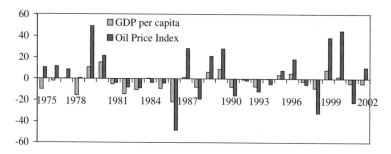

Figure 1. Growth in real GDP per capita and the oil price index (%)

2.1. Domestic investment

Gross domestic investment declined from 34.1% of GDP in the 1970s to 25.6% in the 1980s before rising to 29% by 2002. The UAE average investment rate for the whole period is well above the average rate of 26% for the oil-rich MENA countries and 25% for the entire MENA region. Although public investment continues to dominate, the share of private investment has risen remarkably, from 6.6% of GDP in 1975–1985 to 12% in the 1990s. Meanwhile, the share of petroleum investment in aggregate investment declined from 36% in 1975–1989 to 13% in the 2000s. While public investment is concentrated on infrastructure and services sectors, most of the private investment is in the services and real estate sectors. In explaining the private investment behaviour in the UAE, Elhiraika and Hamed (2001, p. 13) found that "in the long-run, GDP growth[1] has the largest stimulating influence, followed by bank credit to the private sector and a human capital development variable. The real lending rate and government investments are found to have strong but adverse effects on private investment. In the short-run, GDP growth, bank credit and investment in human capital still have positive but weak effects on private investment behaviour, whereas the lending rate and government investment variables retain their significant negative effects".

The finding of a crowding-out effect of public investment on private investment is consistent with the argument of Hakura (2004) that large government size in Gulf Cooperation Council (GCC) countries adversely affects the incentive to accumulate capital per worker and appears to have stifled private sector growth and impeded the diversification of production. The public and private sectors compete with each other in terms of areas of investment rather than sources of finance. Expansion of industrial zones that provide a variety of

---

[1] As Elhiraika and Hamed (2001) note, there can be two-way causation between growth and investment. Therefore, this result was obtained after accounting for endogeneity using the two-stage least squares method.

facilities and services at attractive prices is believed to have encouraged both domestic and foreign private investment. Outside industrial zones, foreign firms are allowed to operate with local UAE participation of at least 51% and company law may vary across emirates. In the zones, both domestic and foreign firms operate under the same company law that has been harmonized across the emirates. In 2004, Jebel Ali, the largest free zone in the UAE, hosted 850 manufacturing, trade and other firms, 200 of which were owned by the UAE nationals.[2]

2.2. Domestic savings

The growth of domestic investment is aided by the easy availability of funds with internationally competitive and positive real interest rates. In the 1980s, Gross Domestic Savings (GDS) fell dramatically from record high levels in the 1970s before rising again in recent years. Recent increases in GDS rates were largely due to increases in private savings, whereas the government sustained current fiscal deficits since the start of the 1990s. The average UAE aggregate saving rate of 33% during 1975–2002 is greater than that of 20% for all MENA countries, but lower than the oil-rich MENA countries' saving rate of 39%. This observation, together with the fact that Gross Domestic Investment rates in the UAE were higher than in the other MENA oil-exporting countries, suggests that the UAE has managed either to make a more productive use of its financial resources or to attract more foreign capital compared to these countries.

2.3. Export growth

As mentioned previously, good economic performance in the UAE, in comparison to other countries in the region, coincided with sharp rises in non-oil exports. However, increases in non-oil exports are mainly due to re-exports that made up 30% of the total exports between 1982 and 2002. Thus, the UAE became the third largest re-export centre in the world, after Singapore and Hong Kong. Whereas the trend of total non-oil exports suggests that the UAE is experiencing an export-led growth phenomenon, the dominance of re-exports points to an important caveat in this trend. With huge investments directed to the re-export sector, the domestic production base of the country remains weak, constraining opportunities for technology transfer and productivity enhancement. Meanwhile, the re-export sector is expected to face fierce competition from the free-trade zones that are rapidly developing in the region, especially in Oman that has a relative advantage in terms of having seaports that are closer to major sea routes. Therefore, sustainable growth in the non-oil export sector

---

[2] For further information see Jebel Ali Free Zone's website: www.freeznoneuate.com/Jebel_fze.htm

would require increased domestic production of export goods rather than re-exports.

2.4. Financial development

Saving and investment performance have been associated with a notable increase in the level of financial development in terms of a high ratio of broad money to GDP, increasing share of bank credit to the private sector in total credit, positive real interest rates and an unusually high ratio of time, saving and investment deposits in total deposits. This signifies the easy availability of credit to finance investment in the country. The development and role of financial markets and institutions in the UAE is discussed in detail in Section 4.

2.5. Human capital development

Increased investment in human capital had led to notable increases in the primary and secondary school enrolment ratios, from < 40% in the 1970s to > 80% in the 2000s. Besides the increased education of the local labour force, educated foreign labour is easily accessible given the relatively high wages paid in the UAE compared to other labour surplus countries in the Middle East and Asia. Immigrant labour accounts for about 70% of the labour force in the country and immigrants are generally better educated than the local population. The IMF (2003) argues that the abundant supply of expatriate workers at internationally competitive wages has been an important source of growth for the non-oil sector of the UAE. Nevertheless, since expatriate workers remit much of their earnings to their countries of origin, their contribution to growth would, other things being equal, be lower than that of local workers. Though important, empirical investigation of the question of how much growth can be created by foreign[3] labour is beyond the scope of this paper.

2.6. Macroeconomic stability

In spite of high fluctuations in oil price and revenue that lead to similar, though smaller fluctuations in real GDP growth, the UAE economy remained remarkably stable in terms of inflation rates and the exchange rate. Since 1981, the UAE dirham has been fully pegged to the US$ at the rate of 3.67 and the inflation rate varied around an average of 2.5% over the period considered. It is believed that, because oil is priced in US dollars and because the UAE has huge investments in the US, the benefits from the peg in terms of economic stability and reduced macroeconomic uncertainty is greater than the cost arising from inability to use exchange rate policy to promote domestic investment and

---

[3] It is worth noting that high export-oriented and high-growth countries such as Singapore and Hong Kong also rely significantly on foreign labour.

international competitiveness. There are, however, no hard statistics to support or negate this argument.

Since the turn of the 1990s, the consolidated budget (including the federal government and emirates' governments) has experienced sustained deficits. But, as Hamed and Elhiraika (2001) argue, the UAE government relies mainly on monetary policy tools, particularly the link between the dirham and the US dollar, to maintain macroeconomic stability, and that the governments of the dominant emirates finance their budget deficits by drawing down their own abundant overseas assets. This helps them to avoid domestic borrowing that can crowd out private sector activities and create macroeconomic instability.

The structure and financing of the budget deficit raises two important questions in the context of long-run growth. The first question relates to fiscal sustainability in the absence of taxes and the second question relates to the potential impact of cuts in government expenditure on growth. Unfortunately, we have insufficient data, especially on accumulated domestic and foreign investment[4] by the various emirates, to answer these questions. To the extent that deficit financing does not exceed the income generated by public assets, the government would be able to maintain fiscal stability. Otherwise, there will be a need for significant adjustment of government expenditure and increases in government revenue. While such moves may adversely affect economic growth in the short-to-medium term, they are paramount for achieving fiscal sustainability, which is in turn a prerequisite for attaining sustainable growth in the long-run.

3. UAE growth in regional perspectives

3.1. Growth accounting framework

In this section, we analyze the determinants of economic growth using the growth accounting framework by decomposing aggregate GDP growth into labour, capital and technical progress. The decomposition is based on the standard neoclassical production function that assumes competitive factor markets, constant returns to scale and neutral technical progress (see Solow, 1956). Accordingly, total output growth can be explained by input growth and improvement of productive efficiency. That is

$$\frac{\dot{Y}}{Y} = \frac{\dot{A}}{A} + \alpha \frac{\dot{K}}{K} + (1 - \alpha) \frac{\dot{L}}{L} \tag{1}$$

where the dotted variables denote the growth rates of output (Y), capital (K) and labour (L). The rate of change of the constant (A) is a measure of total factor productivity growth (TFPG) and is obtained as a residual. TFPG is viewed as

---

[4] The only available data relates to federal government-owned foreign assets, which have been generally increasing throughout the period considered.

Table 4.   *UAE sources of growth in regional and international comparisons*

Country	Period	Growth	Capital	Labour	TFPG
UAE	1975–2002	0.047	0.015	0.052	–0.020
Algeria[a]	1960–1997	0.031	0.034	0.006	–0.009
Egypt	1960–1997	0.057	0.035	0.011	0.011
Kuwait[a]	1960–1997	0.022	–0.015	0.056	–0.018
Venezuela[a]	1990–1997	0.028	0.012	0.023	–0.006
MENA countries	1980–2000	–0.07	0.99	–0.06	–1.00

Source: Development Indicators in the UAE (various issues), Ministry of Planning, Abu Dhabi.
[a]Makdisi and Limam (2000); Hakura (2004).

that part of GDP growth that is not explained by growth in factor inputs and is therefore attributable to technical progress. However, as we explain below, this variable may well reflect the effects of many factors that are not accounted for in the model. This fact explains why, as Barro (1999, p. 119) notes, the usefulness of the growth accounting framework, as a preliminary step for the analysis of fundamental determinants of factor growth, depends on the condition that these factors are substantially independent from those that matter for technological change. α is the elasticity of output with respect to capital, which is equal to the capital-income share.

In addition to physical capital and labour, numerous studies (e.g. Hahn and Kim, 2000) include human capital, usually measured by average years of schooling of the adult population. Because such measures are not available for the UAE for the entire period under review, it is not possible to include a human development variable in the GDP decomposition. The results of the output growth rate's decomposition[5] for the UAE are presented in Table 4 along with the decomposition of GDP growth rates for some comparable countries (the latter from Makdisi and Limam (2000)).

For the UAE, labour contribution amounted to 110% of the overall average GDP growth rate, whereas capital contribution was 32% and contribution by TFPG was −42%. The results clearly indicate the overwhelming predominance of labour over capital and that on average TFPG was negative. This finding is consistent with the results for oil-dependent countries such as Kuwait and Venezuela. In fact, all the five MENA oil-dependent countries included in the sample used by Makdisi and Limam (2000) recorded negative TFPG. But, for the entire sample of 92 developing countries, Makdisi and Limam (2000) find evidence of predominance of capital contribution over that of labour and TFPG.

---

[5]The analysis here is based on real output data obtained from the 2000 and 2003 editions of the International Financial Statistics of the IMF and physical capital and labour data taken from various issues of the Economic Development Indicators (Ministry of Planning). For alternative methods of estimating the growth accounting model see Bisat *et al.* (1997) and Hakura (2004).

Using a different data set, econometric estimates by Bisat *et al.,* (1997) also indicate that TFPG is negatively related to aggregate GDP growth in the UAE. However, they confirm that on average TFPG has a positive contribution to non-oil GDP growth in Saudi Arabia and the UAE, and that the contribution of TFPG to oil GDP growth was negative. Bisat *et al.,* (1997, p. 24) argue that the negative average TFPG rates obtained for the total GDP of oil-exporting countries is misleading since it mainly reflects fluctuations in growth induced by wide changes in oil prices and revenues that constitute the main omitted variables. In other words, changes in GDP growth that are not accounted for by labour and capital inputs are by definition attributed to TFPG.

But, TFPG is dominated by changes in oil prices and revenues, given the high share of oil output in total GDP. This is a measurement problem that exists even if TFPG has no causal relationship with these changes. In fact, should it be possible to isolate the oil price effect, the true production efficiency in oil-exporting countries is likely to be greater than the measured one. Unfortunately, we do not have enough data for the UAE to decompose labour and capital by the oil and non-oil sectors. This decomposition is especially relevant in view of observed relationship between changes in oil prices and measured TFPG. Aside from measurement problems, low TFPG in the UAE may be attributed to the fact that trade openness and liberal economic policies in this case promote re-exports rather than genuine exports based on production of goods.

Indeed, productivity increases have not been an important source of growth in some Arab countries owing to economic policies and external shocks that favoured investments that were often not conducive to improvements in total factor productivity (TFP) (Bisat *et al.,* 1997). Declining investment rates in some countries then compounded the negative trend of productivity growth. In the UAE, however, domestic investment increased since the turn of the 1990s following a sharp decline in the 1980s, although huge price and subsidy distortions (discussed further below) remained important and may be blamed for inducing biases in private investment decisions in favour of housing, services and re-exports.

The finding regarding the contribution of labour to total output growth is in contrast with the Labour Report (Ministry of Labour, 2000) that asserts that the labour market is dominated by foreign labour that is largely unskilled and has low productivity. The results of this study suggest that labour seems to be adequate for doing the jobs they are supposed to do in view of their overwhelmingly high contribution to GDP growth. But, the labour report is perhaps correct as regards the lack of skills needed to increase the productivity of capital, and this partly explains the poor TFPG rate in the UAE.

The abundance of relatively cheap foreign labour is another incentive for private investors to continue to favour labour-intensive investments and re-exports at the expense of genuine capital-intensive investment. Meanwhile, because of price-fixing policies and subsidies, public capital is likely to be inefficiently used. Price-fixing and subsidies relate mainly to housing and land, local farm production and energy cost. For instance, UAE citizens have access to low-cost farm and real estate loans and receive above market wages in government sector (see Section 4 for further discussion). While most of the direct and indirect subsidies, such as artificially low electricity cost,[6] go to UAE nationals, these subsidies affect the relative cost of inputs and are likely to encourage low-return investment as well as the use of unskilled labour by domestic firms and households. Obviously, policies need to be introduced to eliminate price discrimination and increase factor productivity to ensure long-run competitiveness. The importance of education and training in this respect cannot be overstated. A well-trained labour force that is complementary to capital is particularly needed in a labour-scarce country like the UAE, where promoting sustainable growth might require more capital-intensive investments.

3.2. Econometric model of the determinants of UAE growth

3.2.1. Specification of the model

The literature on growth proposes a great number of explanatory variables (see Barro, 1991; Gregorio and Guidotti, 1995). Besides theory, our choice of variables in this study is guided by the specific economic conditions and environment of the UAE as well as by data availability. The dependent variable is real GDP *per capita* growth. The independent variables are as follows.

Although issues of causality between investment and growth may be theoretically debatable, empirical research points out to strong long-run relationship between the two variables. Empirical evidence indicates that capital accumulation, represented by gross domestic investment as a ratio of GDP, often induces faster output growth (see e.g. Batina, 1998).

Growth in a country's terms of trade means increased net exports and aggregate output. The opposite may also be true. Therefore the terms of trade variable can take either sign. Because of lack of data, this variable is represented by changes in the oil price index (ΔOPI), which should be a good proxy as oil represents more than 50% of UAE exports.

Natural resource abundance as the literature suggests is supposed to have an adverse impact on GDP growth owing mainly to the "Dutch disease" (see Sacks and Warner, 1997). High natural resource price and revenues attract factors of production from other sectors that decline as the abundant resource sector expands. More importantly, high natural resource prices often lead to an over-valued exchange rate, which in turn hurts the export sector in general and the exports of other sectors in particular. This added to wasteful use of resources induced by the natural resource abundance and lack of urge for proper resource

---

[6] For example, in 2003, expatriate households were charged DH 0.15/KW of electricity, whereas nationals paid DH 0.05. The same price discrimination also applied to domestic and foreign companies outside free zones.

management can impact negatively on growth. Natural resource abundance is represented in the model by oil exports as a percentage of GDP (XOIL). We have also included the non-oil exports-GDP (XNOIL) rate in the model to assess the impact of economic diversification on growth. Moreover, the sum of exports and imports as a percent of GDP was used to test whether trade openness stimulates growth by encouraging competition and international technology transfer.

Changes in the income of trading partners are envisaged to have a direct impact on growth in a country that is heavily dependent on foreign trade. However, given the nature of demand for UAE exports, GDP growth in the UAE may not be significantly responsive to changes in the incomes of its trading partners. That is the income elasticity of demand for oil, the main UAE export commodity, is believed to be low such that changes in the incomes of its trading partners have little effect on exports and income.

A great deal of theoretical and empirical literature underscores the importance of financial development in economic growth, but several transmission mechanisms have been identified and controversy exists in the literature as to how to measure financial development[7] (see Demirguc-Kunt and Levine, 1996; Levine and Zervos, 1996). Two measures of financial development are adopted in this study. These are the M2/GDP ratio and bank credit to the private sector (BCPS) as a ratio of total credit. Both measures are postulated to have positive coefficients on growth.

Human capital, accumulated through education, has long been acknowledged as an important factor in facilitating economic growth. In most regressions this variable turns out with a positive coefficient (Barro, 1991). Investment in human capital enhances technological progress and raises labour productivity. This is expected to stimulate growth directly as well as indirectly by augmenting the productivity of capital. Barro and Lee (2001) developed an educational attainment census method to construct estimates of human capital that are superior to enrolment ratios. However, owing to unavailability of these estimates, we have used the secondary school enrolment ratio (SSER) as a traditional measure of human capital.

Macroeconomic stability "sends important signals to the private sector about the direction of economic policies and the credibility of the authorities' commitment to manage the economy efficiently. Such stability, by facilitating long-term planning and investment decisions, encourages saving and capital accumulation by the private sector" (Hadjimichael and Ghura, 1995). The most frequently used proxies for macroeconomic stability are variability of the

---

[7] It should also be noted that empirical studies of the relationship between financial and real development include cross-country studies that lump together data from countries with different levels of financial and/or real development as well as country-specific studies, which often use different time frames and model specification rendering comparisons across countries difficult.

inflation rate and of the fiscal deficit/GDP ratio. Since budget deficits are a relatively recent phenomenon in the country, we have used the standard deviation of inflation to account for the possible influence of macroeconomic instability and uncertainty in UAE growth. Measures of macroeconomic instability are expected to have no significant deleterious impact as the UAE economy was very stable during the period considered.

The effects of government consumption and deficits on growth depend on the level of consumption (GCON) and how the deficits (DEF) are financed. Generally, government spending is believed to induce growth. But, through tax distortions and adverse effects on saving, high levels of government consumption and deficit in particular may frustrate growth (Barro, 1991). Accordingly, the coefficients of these variables can take either sign. There is no income or profit tax (aside from taxes on the profits of foreign financial institutions operating in the country) in the UAE, and as mentioned previously deficits are financed mainly from external assets with no direct effect on the exchange rate and/or private saving. Therefore, the coefficients of these variables can take either sign.

3.2.2. Model estimation and discussion of results

The model was estimated using data from various issues of the International Financial Statistics of the IMF, the Annual Reports of UAE Central Bank and the Economic Development Indicators published by the Ministry of Finance, UAE. Prior to estimation, we have investigated the time-series properties of all the variables of the model using the most commonly used tests: an augmented Dickey–Fuller (ADF) and Phillips–Perron (PP) tests. The latter non-parametric test is known to have more power than the parametric ADF. But the power of the two tests decreases in the presence of structural breaks in the series, in which case the test may fail to reject the null hypothesis of unit root when the series is actually stationary (see Enders, 1995).

The two tests confirm that all the variables[8] of the model are stationary at the 5% level or better with all normalized variables, such as the investment/GDP and the broad money/GDP ratios, being entered after taking the first difference (Table 5). Since the stationarity tests reject the null hypothesis of unit root, it is indicative that there was no significant structural change in the series.

Since all variables are stationary, a dynamic form of the model was estimated using ordinary least squares (OLS) technique and a general to specific estimation strategy. Owing to high correlation among trade variables, each of them was entered separately. Likewise, oil price and exports were entered each at a time. In view of possible endogenity of domestic investment, we estimated the model using two-stage least squares (2SLS) technique with domestic investment entered

---

[8] The only exception is the trading partners' GDP *per capita* growth and the M2-GDP variables that are only stationary at the 10% level according to the ADF test, but at the 1% level according to the PP test.

Table 5.   Unit root tests and structural change

Variable	ADF-test	PP test
GDP *per capita* growth rate	−4.51	−4.75
Trading partners' GDP *per capita* growth	−2.63	−3.75
ΔM2–GDP (%)	−2.83	−3.92
Inflation rate	−5.80	−4.10
ΔGross domestic investment (% of GDP)	−4.43	−4.46
ΔOil export (XOIL) in % of GDP	−4.44	−4.43
ΔNon-oil export in % of GDP (XNOIL)	−3.50	−3.88
ΔOil price index (ΔOPI) (%)	−5.98	−6.00
ΔSSER	−3.70	−3.88
ΔGovernment deficit (% of GDP)	−4.88	−6.01
ΔGovernment consumption (% of GDP)	−5.57	−4.69

with various sets of explanatory variables including trade openness, growth in the income of trading partners, standard deviation of inflation, financial deepening[9], human developments and government consumption and fiscal deficit.

Generally, the coefficients of all explanatory variables had the expected signs, but only two of them were statistically significant: natural resource abundance, as represented by changes in the oil revenue/GDP ratio, and the terms of trade variable, as represented by changes in oil prices (equations (1) and (2) of Table 6). All other variables were found to have no significant impact on UAE growth and as equation (3), for example, suggests the estimated 2SLS model is statistically weak. In line with early discussion, these results raise the question of why the non-oil sector and related variables appear to have no important effect on UAE growth so far. To shed light on this question, we concentrate here on the implications of the statistically robust results of the model.

The results for equations (1) and (2) are generally strong in terms of R^2 and the *F*-statistics. The constant term has always turned out with a negative coefficient, which is consistent with the earlier finding of a negative average TFPG rate. Moreover, two dummies, one for the First Gulf War (1984–1988) and the other for the Second Gulf War (1991) always had negative, but insignificant effects. The lag dependent variable always had the right positive and significant coefficient.

Natural resource abundance (XOIL) produced the most interesting result. As mentioned previously, the literature postulates a negative relationship between natural resource abundance and growth. However, the case of the UAE, and perhaps that of all oil-dependent Gulf States, is clearly different. Before the discovery of oil, economic activity was extremely limited owing to the virtually

---

[9] Represented by the broad money to GDP ratio and bank credit to the private sector as a ratio of total credit.

Table 6. Econometric results

Variable	Equation (1)	Equation (2)	Equation (3) (2SLS)[a]
Constant	−0.104 (0.091)	−3.49 (2.01)[b]	−0.951 (-0.40)
Lagged dependent variable	0.190 (1.85)[b]	0.26 (1.84)[b]	–
Change in oil export (XOIL) in % of GDP	0.96 (5.89)[c]	–	–
Change in oil price index (ΔOPI) (%)	–	0.22 (5.44)[c]	–
Change in non-oil export in % of GDP (ΔXNOIL)	–	0.295 (0.63)	–
ΔM2-GDP (%)	–	–	−0.59 (−1.44)
Standard deviation of inflation rate	–	–	0.012 (0.18)
ΔGross domestic investment (% of GDP)	–	–	0.86 (1.50)
ΔSSER	–	–	0.20 (0.36)
R^2	0.65		0.02
F-statistic	18.6		0.40
LM test (F-Form)	1.16 [0.33]	1.26 [0.277]	

Notes: Dependent variable is real GDP *per capita* growth rate; *t*-values within () brackets; LM test is the Lagrange Multiplier test for error autocorrelation with critical values within [ ] brackets.
[a]Instruments consisted of lagged values of dependent and explanatory variables.
[b]Significance at the 55% level.
[c]Significance at the 1% level.

"absolute" scarcity of other resources. There were no developed economic sectors to be adversely affected by increased investment and production in the oil sector. In fact, initial overall growth conditions relied on the growth of this sector, which stimulated other sectors by raising aggregate demand and by providing the funds needed for increased investment in infrastructure and other non-oil activities.

At the same time, the UAE currency is pegged to the US dollar and the exchange rate policy is largely neutral as regards its relative effect on different economic sectors. For example, a weak dollar and hence weak dirham may boost oil as well as non-oil exports and vice versa. At the same time, the exchange rate peg also helps to create a stable macroeconomic environment that is conducive to private investment and growth. As explained before, the exchange rate policy is justified on the ground that, oil, the largest export commodity, is priced in terms of US dollars. The UAE would not be able to maintain the peg without the huge foreign reserves accumulated from sales of the abundant crude oil. In short, whereas the abundance of a natural resource such as oil may be a curse in a country with diverse resources, it is definitely a blessing for a country with little other resources.

Changes in the oil price index (as a proxy for terms of trade) have a highly statistically significant effect on UAE growth. Oil represents about 50% of GDP and about 50% of total exports over the entire period considered, while exports

accounted for about 70% of GDP. Therefore, growth in the UAE is predominantly export-led and oil prices play a key role. International oil markets
exogenously determine oil prices. Because of OPEC's (Organization of Petroleum Exporting Countries) policies and agreements that fix production quotas
and the nature of competition in the oil market, changes in the oil price have an
immediate effect on oil GDP since individual countries may not be able to adjust
quantities in such a way as to offset the price effect. Thus, increases in oil prices
or the terms of trade will normally have a robust positive impact on GDP
growth.

The insignificant coefficient of the standard deviation of inflation is a
testimony to the stability of the economy and the absence of adverse growth
effects owing to economic uncertainty. The findings of positive but weak
coefficients for gross domestic investment and non-oil exports seem to reflect the
fact that domestic investment is largely in the construction and services sectors,
while non-oil exports are dominated by re-exports rather than genuine
goods output. However, the contribution of the non-oil goods sector to domestic output and exports has been rising in recent years. Therefore, the non-oil
sector is likely to play a more important role in the future should this trend be
sustained.

The finding of no significant role for financial deepening, and by implication
monetary policy, is also conceivable since the UAE economy is capital abundant
and investment and growth in the country are limited by the availability of
profitable investment opportunities rather than the availability of capital (see
Farzin, 1993). It is also not surprising that government consumption and deficits
appear to have no important effect on growth in view of the nature of these
variables as discussed previously.

To sum up, econometric evidence confirms the heavy dependence of the UAE
economy on oil exports and income. Therefore, more and concerted efforts need
to be done to accelerate economic diversification and achieve sustainable non-
oil-based growth in the future.

4. Markets and institutions

In this section, we briefly discuss the role of key markets and institutions in the
UAE growth process, focusing on the labour and capital markets that present
the greatest policy challenges and require well-designed institutional interventions. We also discuss the role of institutions[10] in terms of macroeconomic
environment and investment climate.

---

[10] Owing to lack of information, the behaviour of agents–namely firms and households–is not discussed here.

4.1. Labour market

Economic progress engendered rapid population growth and significant changes in the structure of the UAE labour market, which is dominated by immigrant labour. The immigrant population rose from 63.9% of total population in 1975 to 75.6% in 1995 before declining to about 70% in 2002. At the same time, the share of foreign labour increased from 85% in 1975 to 90.9% in 1995 and then decreased to about 87% in 2002. The rate of UAE women participation[11] in the labour force decreased from 11.3% in 1975 to 10.1% in 1995. This is probably due to the fact that many women used to participate in traditional economic activities that have disappeared with the advent of modern activities that require education. However, with increased female education, the participation rate of UAE women in the labour force rose to 26.5% by 2002 compared to 76.6% for males. The average rate of local UAE population participation in the labour force of 60.4% as estimated by the Ministry of Planning[12] in 2002 is quite low by international standards.

The labour market is segmented along different lines with limited labour mobility between them owing to wage rigidities, skills differences and institutional and cultural factors. In the public sector, UAE nationals are more highly paid than expatriates with the same qualifications and who perform the same jobs. For example, using a 1997 survey data from the Emirate of Abu Dhabi, Al-Awad and Elhiraika (2002) find that the income difference between citizens and foreigners is 62% in the case of skilled males and 55% in the case of unskilled men. For skilled and unskilled women, the respective difference is 81% and 55%. Moreover, women are consistently less paid than their male counterparts, irrespective of skills and nationality: the average income of a man is higher than that of a woman by 54% in the case of citizens and by 104% in the case of immigrants. This contrasts sharply with the distribution of skills, which is relatively higher among women (both local and immigrants). In addition to the nature of jobs that are normally preferred by women, gender income inequality in the UAE is attributable to labour regulation. Men are entitled to a variety of fringe benefits, such as housing support, to which women are not entitled. Al-Awad and Elhiraika (2002) conclude that gender is the most important factor behind income inequality in the UAE, followed by skill level and nationality.

Relatively high government wages together with job security, social status and other benefits, make the government the most attractive employer for UAE nationals. The private sector relies on foreign labour that is less well paid and works for fixed contracts. Foreign workers account for 99% of labour in the private sector (Ministry of Labour, 2000). On average, the level of education is

---

[11] This rate refers to the number of working UAE women as a percentage of economically active UAE women population (aged 15 years and above) or UAE women labour force.
[12] See Ministry of Planning "UAE in Figures 2002", Abu Dhabi, UAE.

higher among immigrants compared to nationals, but still the overall average education level is low reflecting the dominance of unskilled labour. This fact is also attributable to the nature of investment that is dominated by labour-intensive projects in the services, transportation and other sectors. In terms of gender and owing largely to social factors, women participation in the labour force is very low and because female mobility is very restricted, they are on average paid far less than men are.

Labour market problems have aggravated in recent years. First, with the government unable to provide enough employment to national entrants, there is a growing problem of unemployment among them. This may be considered as transitional or voluntary unemployment because UAE nationals prefer to wait for a government job rather than taking low-paid and demanding private sector jobs. Therefore, government policy reform is needed to remove the unrealistically high government wages for nationals that lead to such unemployment. In Saudi Arabia, for instance, the reforms consisted of "an array of measures affecting the quantity (quotas) and price (wage subsidies to private sector, government wage restraint and fees and charges on foreign labour) as well as the quality (education and training) of labour" (Sassanpour *et al.*, 1997, p. 26). However, employment quotas and subsidies cannot provide the long-term solution and an effective labour market policy should be based on removal of distortions created by government wage and employment polices besides increasing the market ability to match labour skills with employers' requirements in the private sector.

The absence of clear labour market policies as regards labour compensation in the face of continuous excess supply of labour from neighbouring countries created incentives for investors to favour labour-intensive projects. Government subsidies in terms of low-cost public services are often blamed for encouraging the supply and use of relatively cheap and low-educated foreign labour. Until the early 2000s, in addition to tax-free wages and salaries, these subsidies included free health services to expatriate workers and their families. However, many of the subsidies have been cut recently. Labour market reforms are required to reduce discrepancy between public and private sector wages and encourage more nationals to participate in the private sector; to encourage recruitment and retention of skilled labour; the development of labour skills through training and to induce increased women participation, given the clear domination of women in the country's tertiary institutions and the low current rate of women participation in the labour force.

In line with these arguments, the 2000 Labour Report of The Ministry of Labour proposes that the UAE government should attempt to develop a model of growth similar to that of Singapore. The hallmark of the Singaporean model is that the country managed in less than 15 years to make a drastic move away from low-skill labour-intensive industries to high-skill high-tech industries. Singapore deliberately implemented strategies that made labour relatively expensive such that businesses began to favour capital-intensive investment that eventually spurred rapid technology transfer and adoption, creativity and innovation and faster technical progress. The Government of Singapore invested heavily on education and training to ensure that industry's demand for skilled labour is met. Many of the elements of the model of Singapore may be replicated by UAE, especially in view of relative abundance of capital in the country and its proximity to the Middle East and African markets including the oil-rich GCC countries. Like Singapore, the UAE has a relatively favourable business environment, a strong financial sector and a modern physical infrastructure. However, it remains to be seen if the UAE could effectively implement human resource development strategies similar to those that underpinned market-oriented reforms in Singapore and at the same time attract high-tech investments.

4.2. Financial markets and institutions

The financial system of the UAE is a bank-based system. There are 21 national banks with 310 branches and 26 foreign banks with 112 branches spread throughout the country. This extensive network of banking services contributed to a high degree of financial deepening. Currently, the ratio of quasi money to GDP is about 45% and M2/GDP ratio was about 67% in 2002. These ratios reflect the ability of banks to mobilize sizeable savings that are often far greater than the domestic demand for credit. Consequently, large amounts of deposits are invested abroad. Nonetheless, financial deepening has enhanced the availability of capital to private domestic investment.

In general, banks in the UAE are well capitalized, and the Central Bank regulatory framework meets the international standards. However, until 2000 the country lacked formal capital markets. Owing to the absence of formal markets, investors used the over-the-counter (OTC) market to trade shares. Since the OTC was fragmented and not well regulated, some market participants subjected it to harmful speculations and manipulations. These manipulations inflated share prices, in some cases prices went up 10 times, in a way that was not consistent with companies' performance or their expected future earnings. Such high share prices enticed many ill-informed investors to invest a great deal of their wealth in stocks, and even some borrowed to buy stocks. Suddenly, the bubble burst and many lost a great part of their investments, while others defaulted on their bank loans. As a result, the public has lost confidence in stocks and this has brought the initial public offerings (IPOs) to a halt. This highlights the need for effective regulatory institutions and government support to create a regulated and official stock market.

Following the approval of a law regulating the issuance and exchange of securities in 2000, two stock exchanges have been launched in Dubai and Abu Dhabi. The operations of these exchanges are still limited with the combined value of traded shares of DH 3.87 billion by the end of 2002. This value accounts for < 1% of the total financial assets in the country. It is necessary for the country to develop its capital markets, because in the future these markets will be relied upon for the mobilization of resources and equity financing for the private sector.

4.3. Investment climate

We analyse the investment climate in the UAE in terms of infrastructure, the macroeconomic environment including monetary, fiscal and external policies, beside the laws that are relevant to investment decisions. Irrespective of the efficiency questions concerning provision of public services, as discussed earlier, the UAE has a modern physical and communication infrastructure that puts it on par with developed countries. In general, public investment in infrastructure creates an environment conducive for private sector activity, which can be relied upon to achieve sustainable economic growth in the long-run. In addition, public investment in roads, ports, airports, electricity and water utilities, education and training of work force raises productivity and increases economic efficiency.

The most important feature of UAE monetary policy is that it is essentially targeted at maintaining the stability of the currency by pegging the dirham to the US dollar at a fixed exchange rate of 3.67 AED/$. This exchange rate regime has been adopted since 1981 with great success owing to the huge foreign reserves the country holds. In addition to maintaining the stability of the currency, the policy of linking the dirham to the dollar has also contributed to a low inflation rate. However, the exchange rate policy can have a deleterious effect on growth depending on how import and export demand respond to changes in major currencies relative to the dollar and the size of the UAE trade outside the dollar area.

Fiscal policy has played an active role in developing the economy, transferring wealth and promoting and supporting the non-oil sector. In the absence of income or consumption taxes in the UAE, fiscal performance of the country is largely dependent on oil revenue and income generated from foreign assets. Because not all oil revenues feed directly into current government revenues and owing to rapid population increases, the government's growing wage bill and increasing maintenance costs, the economy has experienced budget deficits since the early 1990s. These deficits have become structural in nature and largely financed by drawing down foreign assets and the earnings they generate. This method of financing the deficit is difficult to sustain in the long run. Therefore, instead of deficit financing, fiscal policy should focus on structural adjustment including widening the non-oil revenue base, privatizing public enterprises, rationalizing government expenditure and reassessing subsidies and incentive programs.

The UAE maintains a long tradition of liberal foreign trade. There are no capital controls or restrictions on foreign trade as is the case in many developing countries. The highest custom tax is 4%. The external sector of the country is solid. Since the first oil boom in 1973–1974 the country has recorded a continual external account surplus, which enabled it to accumulate substantial foreign reserves. In addition to the financing of budget deficits, these reserves act as a cushion that protects the economy from exogenous shocks.

Well-designed laws are important for creating a climate conducive for investment and the smooth functioning of markets. The UAE government seeks to establish a legal framework to cover all aspects of business enterprises in the country. The most important laws in this framework are the federal company law, the commercial agency law and the intellectual rights protection law. In general, the legal framework favours local investors over foreign investors. This can be clearly seen in the following provisions of the company law (see Hamed, 2001). First, the proportion of national ownership of companies established in the UAE must not be lower than 51%. Second, branch offices of foreign companies must have a national sponsor, unless the foreign company establishes its branch office based on an agreement with the federal government. Finally, the law forbids foreigners from owning shares in public joint stock companies directly, but allows ownership through mutual funds that are offered by commercial banks.

However, the UAE as a federation allows considerable variations in company law across emirates. In some cases, for example Abu Dhabi company law, there is discrimination even against citizens of other emirates. As mentioned earlier, company law is more harmonized across emirates regarding free zones. The harmonization process should be extended to cover the laws regulating business outside the free zones.

Overall, with the creation of the free zones, the UAE seems to have created a relatively facilitative business environment that is conducive to local and foreign investors. The main features of this environment are the creation of world-class industrial facilities and business support services as well as the updating of commercial laws and regulations to meet international standards and ensure effective protection for investors. For example, the Jebel Ali Free Zone has become one of the largest industrial complexes in the world, providing a wide range of options to investors including a 100% ownership of investment. Since 1995, the UAE has become a member of the World Trade Organization and this will have a direct impact on the nature and efficiency of investments that have to compete internationally. It is also important to note that favourable tax laws and political stability make the investment climate in the UAE attractive.

5. Conclusion and policy implications

The objective of this paper was to explain the determinants of growth in the UAE as an oil-dependent economy. Like the case of other oil-dependent countries in the region, overall GDP performance in the UAE fluctuated widely over the period 1975–2002. However, the UAE seems to have fared better than most of these countries in terms of a relatively high and positive average growth rate during this period. The UAE economy has been very stable, remarkably open and has the highest share of non-oil income in total GDP. Since the early 1990s, non-oil exports and income have generally exceeded their oil counterparts. However, non-oil exports are dominated by re-exports, reflecting the narrow domestic production base and continued heavy reliance on oil revenues. Achieving sustainable growth in the long run requires greater investment in the production of genuine export goods and increased production efficiency in various sectors.

In analysing GDP growth by source, we found labour to have the most important contribution, followed by capital, while TFP had a negative average contribution. It has been argued that the negative TFPG is perhaps a reflection of the quality of domestic investment, which is dominated by public investment and low productivity private investment in the services and re-export sectors. In addition, TFPG, being measured as a residual might reflect the effect of omitted variables; specifically huge changes in oil prices that tend to dominate changes in growth factors. Unfortunately, owing to data limitations we were not able to isolate the oil price effect within the growth accounting framework that provided preliminary analysis of the UAE growth in this study.

Econometric results indicate that unlike the case of countries with diverse resources, natural resource abundance spurs growth in an oil-dependent economy such as the UAE. Changes in terms of trade, represented by changes in oil prices, are directly related to growth. These findings confirm the heavy dependence of the UAE economy on the oil sector. Increased non-oil investment and exports in recent years appear to have positive but still weak influence on growth. It is important that these trends be accelerated to promote sustainable growth. In this context, the study draws the following main policy recommendations:

1. Institutional reform is called for to address labour market distortions that create an over supply of labour in the public sector and raise the demand for low-paid, low-educated labour in the private sector. Thus, market segmentation by skill, nationality or public versus private sectors should be abolished and subsidies and incentives rationalized. In view of the rapid expansion of tertiary education, relative scarcity of labour and the abundance of capital, the UAE may well emulate the model of Singapore that has successfully moved from low-skill, labour-intensive industries to high-skill, capital-intensive industries. Investment in human capital should continue to focus on improving necessary skills to augment capital investment.

2. To reduce exposure to exogenous shocks, efforts to diversify the economy ought to be broadened by encouraging increased domestic, especially private investment in genuine goods production and expanding output markets regionally and internationally. This will reduce reliance on crude oil exports and re-exports that provide only limited room for productivity improvement.

3. The domestic financial system should be widened in such a way as to be able to finance increased real domestic investment. In particular, the development

of a well-functioning equity market should be seen as an opportunity for encouraging the return of capital to the country, broader participation of domestic investors and inducement of foreign investors who bring in new technology.

4. Public deficits ought to be addressed in a framework that takes into account future fiscal sustainability as a prerequisite for achieving sustainable growth in the long run. Fiscal policy should focus on structural adjustments that include widening the non-oil revenue base, privatization of public enterprises, rationalization of government expenditure and reassessing subsidies and incentive programs.

Acknowledgments

The authors would like to acknowledge financial support from the Economic Research Form (ERF) for Arab Countries, Iran and Turkey, and express their gratitude to the editors of this book and two anonymous referees for their valuable comments.

References

Al-Awad, M. and A. Elhiraika (2002), "Gender, skills, nationality and income inequality in the United Arab Emirate", *Journal of Social Affairs*, Vol. 19(76), pp. 314–328.

Askari, H. and M. Jaber (1999), "Oil-exporting countries of the Persian Gulf: what happened to all that money?", *Journal of Energy Finance and Development*, Vol. 4, pp. 185–218.

Barro, R. (1991), "Economic growth in a cross-section of countries", *Quarterly Journal of Economics*, Vol. 106(2), pp. 407–433.

Barro, R. (1999), "Notes on growth accounting", *Journal of Economic Growth*, Vol. 4(2), pp. 119–137.

Barro, R.J. and J.W. Lee (2001), "International data on educational attainment: updates and implications", *Oxford Economic Papers*, Vol. 53(3), pp. 541–563.

Batina, R. (1998), "On the long-run effects of public capital and disaggregated public capital on aggregate output", *International Tax and Public Finance*, Vol. 5(3), pp. 263–281.

Bisat, A., M. El-Erian and T. Helbing (1997), "Growth investment and saving in the Arab countries", IMF Working Paper WP/97/85.

Demirguc-Kunt, A. and R. Levine (1996), "Stock market development and financial intermediaries: stylized facts", *The World Bank Economic Review*, Vol. 10(2), pp. 291–321.

Elhiraika, A. and Hamed, A. (2001), "Private investment and private sector development in the UAE: empirical and policy analysis", Paper presented at the ERF Annual Conference, October 2001, Amman, Jordan.

Enders, W. (1995), *Applied Econometric Time Series*, New York: Wiley.

Farzin, Y.H. (1993), "Importance of foreign investment for the long-run economic development of the United Arab Emirates", *World Development*, Vol. 12(4), pp. 509–521.

Ghanem, S.M. (1992), *Industrialization in the United Arab Emirates*, New Castle Upon Tyne, UK: Averbury.

Gregorio, J. and P. Guidotti (1995), "Financial development and economic growth", *World Development*, Vol. 23(3), pp. 433–448.

Hadjimichael, M. and Ghura, D. (1995), "Public policies and private savings and investment in Sub-Saharan Africa: an empirical investigation", IMF Working Paper 95/19.

Hahn, C. H. and Kim, J. (2000), "Sources of East Asian growth: some evidence from cross-country studies", Paper prepared fro the Global Development Project Explaining Growth initiated by the World Bank.

Hakura, D. (2004), "Growth in the Middle East and North Africa", IMF Working Paper No. 04/56.

Hamed, A. (2001), "Public and private investment in Abu Dhabi", in: F. Al-Faris, editor, *The Economy of Abu Dhabi*, A. Crown Prince Court, Abu Dhabi: Research and Studies Division Publications.

Hamed, A. and A. Elhiraika (2001), "The budget institutions and procedures in the UAE", Paper prepared for the ERF project on Budgetary Processes in MENA countries, coordinated by Hadi Esfahani.

IMF (2003), *United Arab Emirates: selected issues and statistical appendix*, Washington, DC, USA: IMF.

Levine, R. and S. Zervos (1996), "Stock market development and long-run growth", *The World Bank Economic Review*, Vol. 10(2), pp. 323–339.

Makdisi, S. and Limam, I. (2000), "Determinants of growth in the MENA countries", Paper presented at ERF workshop 6–7 April, 2001, Cairo.

Ministry of Labour (2000), *The labour report: moving from cheap unskilled labour to skilled labour and advance technology*, Abu Dhabi, UAE: Ministry of Labour, (in Arabic).

Sachs, J. and A. Warner (1997), "Natural resource abundance and economic growth", Harvard Institute for International Development Working Paper, pp. 1–150.

Sassanpour, C., Joharji, G., Kireyev, A. and Petri, M. (1997), Labour market challenges and policies in the Gulf cooperation council countries. In: A. Jibili, V. Galbis and A. Bisat, editors, *"Financial systems and reforms in the Gulf cooperation council countries,"* Washington, DC: IMF, 1997, pp. 25–38.

Solow, R. (1956), "A contribution to the theory of economic growth", *Quarterly Journal of Economics*, Vol. 70(1), pp. 65–94.

CHAPTER 13

Institutions, Household Decisions, and Economic Growth in Egypt

Ragui Assaad

Abstract

I argue in this paper that the Egyptian government's longstanding policy to guarantee employment in the government for upper secondary and university graduates, combined with educational policies that strongly favor these levels of education, has had a highly distorting impact on the production and deployment of human capital in the Egyptian economy. By trapping significant portions of existing human capital in unproductive government employment and inducing households to invest in the wrong kind of human capital, this combination of policies in ultimately responsible for the low productivity of human capital in the Egyptian economy.

Keywords: human capital, household decisions, institutions, social norms, gender, returns to schooling, Egypt

JEL classifications: O12, J24, I21, J45, H52

1. Introduction

Macroeconomic analyses of growth in Egypt indicate that labor contributes very little to growth, and that human capital, and in particular female human capital, contributes little to increases in total factor productivity (Kheir-El-Din and Moursi, 2006). These puzzling results come at a time when the role of human capital in generating growth is being increasingly stressed in the international literature and when investment in female human capital, internationally, is deemed to be one of the activities with the highest social returns (cf. Schultz, 1995). One of the main objectives of this paper is to shed light on these seemingly

CONTRIBUTIONS TO ECONOMIC ANALYSIS
VOLUME 278   ISSN: 0573-8555
DOI:10.1016/S0573-8555(06)78013-0

puzzling results by analyzing the microeconomics of the production and deployment of human capital in the Egyptian economy, with a particular emphasis on the institutional contexts in which these decisions are made.

Making productive use of human resources is particularly critical at this stage of Egypt's development as the country enters into its "demographic window of opportunity." This is the phase in the demographic transition when the ratio of the working age to the dependent population rises, providing at least a potential for more rapid growth, through a reduction in the dependency ratio and opportunities to deepen investments in both human and physical capital. For this potential to be realized, institutional impediments to the efficient production and deployment of human capital must be reduced. Moreover, because women constitute at least one-half of the working age population, achieving this potential will in part depend on the extent to which they are able to participate in productive employment.

The main argument of the paper is that the longstanding policy of the Egyptian government to guarantee employment in the government for upper secondary and university graduates has distorted household decisions as to the level and type of human capital to acquire and has resulted in the entrapment of significant portions of the human capital in unproductive government employment. With the distorted signals they receive from the labor market, the educational decisions of households are strongly shaped by the desire to ensure access to lifetime employment in the government, an objective that might well be at odds with realizing the productivity benefits of education. Accordingly, they invest heavily in forms of education – such as technical secondary and higher technical institute education – that have very low returns in the private sector. Faced with strong demand for such education from the population, the government supplies it, at the expense of being able to guarantee basic education of decent quality to all those who are eligible for it. It is easy to see how this combination of educational and hiring policies, when applied over a long period of time, results in the distortion of households' human capital decisions and the misallocation of human capital in unproductive activities, ultimately leading to the observed low productivity of human capital in the economy.

In the case of women, the situation is further compounded by social norms defining what constitutes appropriate female employment. These norms translate into significant barriers to entry for women into the private sector, and a strong preference for the more egalitarian and family-friendly government employment among educated women. Norms that restrict women's employment to a limited range of labor market segments defined by occupations, types of workplaces, and locations, result in overcrowding in these segments and depressed wages. There is also considerable evidence that suggests that the private sector in Egypt, in stark contrast to the public sector, is highly inhospitable to married women. Working women's careers are thus artificially truncated at marriage unless they are able to obtain employment in the public sector.

In Section 2, I examine the growth implications of the demographic transition in Egypt. In Section 3, I examine the institutional setting within which household decisions on human capital investments are made, with a particular focus on government policies on education and public sector hiring. Section 4 examines how a move away from excessive reliance on public sector employment is hampered by social norms about what constitutes appropriate employment for women. Section 5 concludes the paper.

2. Growth implications of the demographic transition

Salehi-Isfahani (2006) identifies three main decisions households make that have direct impact on economic growth: the decision to save, to accumulate human capital, and to procreate. He also discusses in some detail the time allocation decision by which the household determines how much time and effort to allocate to market work, home production, and leisure. In this section, I focus on the changing patterns of procreation in Egypt in the recent past and their implications for future economic growth. In subsequent sections, I address the decision to accumulate human capital and to allocate time between market and home work.

The literature in household economics has clearly demonstrated that parental decisions about child quantity (fertility) cannot be dissociated from decisions about child quality (human capital investments) (Becker, 1991). Moreover, decisions about education are clearly dependent on the returns to such education, which is closely related to opportunities for, and constraints on, labor market participation. For the sake of expositional clarity however, I will tackle each of these areas sequentially, making sure to make the necessary linkages when appropriate.

Fertility rates have declined significantly in Egypt in recent years. As shown in Table 1, the national total fertility rate (TFR) declined from a high of 6.7 in

Table 1. Egypt: TFR 15–49

Year	Urban	Rural	National
1946–1947	–	–	6.3
1959–1960	–	–	6.7
1975–1976	4.6	6.1	5.5
1988[1]	3.6	5.6	4.5
1992[1]	2.9	4.9	3.9
1995[1]	3.0	4.2	3.6
2000[1]	3.1	3.9	3.5
2005[1]	2.7	3.4	3.1

Source: For 1946–1947 to 1975–1976, CAPMAS, Panel on Egypt of the Committee on Population and Demography (1982, p.17). For 1988–2005, El-Zanaty and Way (2006), *Egypt Demographic and Health Survey 2005*.
[1] Rates are for the 36 months period preceding the survey

1959–1960 to 3.6 children per woman in 1995. Fertility decline slowed significantly in the subsequent decade, especially in urban areas (Table 1).

Fertility declines were driven in part by rapid urbanization in the 1960s and the 1970s. Since the mid-1970s, urbanization has slowed significantly. The proportion of the population living in urban areas went from 38 percent in 1960 to 44 percent in 1976, only to stabilize at that level until 1996. Although fertility has continued to decline in rural areas from 5.4 births per woman in 1988 to 3.9 in 2000, the decline has stalled in urban areas from 1992 to 2000 at about 3 births per woman (El-Zanaty and Way, 2006). From 2000 to 2005, the decline in fertility appears to have resumed in both urban and rural areas. Another driver of fertility decline was the decline in the age at which women marry. In 2005, the median age at first marriage among women aged 25–29 years was 21.3, about 1.5 years higher than what it was among women aged 45–49 years (El-Zanaty and Way, 2006, p. 93). This delay in marriage reflects the general increase in educational attainment and a general change in attitudes about early marriage (Singerman and Ibrahim, 2003).

Perhaps the most important driver of fertility decline in Egypt was the substantial increase in survival rates among infants and children in the past three decades (Table 2). Infant and child mortality rates began declining slowly in the 1970s, but the decline accelerated significantly in the 1980s as widespread use of oral rehydration therapy significantly reduced deaths from diarrheal diseases (Miller and Hirschhorn, 1995). With some lag, the increased chances of survival of children translated into fertility decline, as parents increasingly adopted modern family planning practices. Contraceptive use has increased from 24 percent in 1980 to 59 percent in 2005 (El-Zanaty and Way, 2006).

As a result of these developments, Egypt is now at the early stage of an important phase in its demographic transition referred to by some as "the demographic window of opportunity" (Barlow, 1994; Bloom and Williamson, 1998). According to the proponents of this approach, the implications of the recent

Table 2.   **Egypt: infant and child mortality** *(number of deaths per thousand)*

Mid-point	Infant Mortality	Under-five Mortality
1967	141	243
1972	146	238
1976	124	203
1980	108	157
1983	98	140
1986	73	102
1988	74	103
1990	62	85
1993	66	84
1998	44	54
2003	33	41

Source: El-Zanaty and Way (2006), *Egypt Demographic and Health Survey 2005.*

Figure 1.   Evolution of the age structure in Egypt (1950–2050)

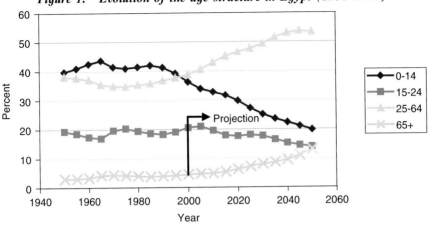

Source: UN Population Division (2003).

fertility declines for the age structure of the population are even more important than its impact on population size. Population growth attributable to a fall in infant and child mortality that is not immediately matched by lower fertility has an immediate negative effect on economic growth by increasing the number of dependents relative to producers. Once fertility starts declining, however, there can potentially be a delayed positive impact on economic growth, as the share of the economically active population begins to grow two decades later.[1]

The impact of the demographic transition on the age structure of the Egyptian population can be clearly ascertained from Figure 1. The proportion of children from 0 to 14 years rose rapidly in the 1960s. It stabilized in the 1980s after a small decline in the 1970s. However, by the 1990s it began to decline steadily and is expected to continue to do so through 2025. The absolute number of those under 15 is expected to stabilize by 2010 and then begin declining by 2015. This suggests that even by sustaining the share of national resources devoted to basic education at present levels, there is now an opportunity to significantly increase educational spending per child, and thus significantly improve the quality of education. This sort of human capital deepening applies to both public resources devoted to education as well as to private resources under household control.

The proportion of those in the prime working age, those between the ages of 25 and 54 years, began increasing in 1975 and will continue to increase steadily through 2025. To the extent that a stable or growing proportion of people in this

---

[1] See also Williamson and Yousef (2002) and Tunali (1996) for a discussion of this phenomenon in the context of the MENA region.

age group become economically active, this trend has the potential of significantly increasing the number of workers and savers *per capita* and in turn the
per-capita rate of economic growth, subject to labor productivity and savings
rates remaining constant or rising.

At the early stages, the increase in the number of adults in their prime working
ages is accompanied by an increase in the numbers of those who are 15 to 24
years, those who constitute the bulk of new entrants to the labor market. For
Egypt, such an increase occurred briefly in the 1970s and resumed in the 1990s,
both periods of severe pressure on the labor market and rising rates of youth
unemployment. Projections indicate that the proportion of those in the 15–24
years age group will begin declining starting in 2005, relieving some of the acute
labor supply pressure. Eventually, the number of older dependents will rise
sufficiently to reduce the number of workers *per capita*, but that is still a relatively
distant prospect for Egypt. The decline in the proportion of school-age children
in the population, which has already begun, provides the country with an immediate opportunity to greatly enhance the quality of human capital investments.

3. Institutional context and investments in educational human capital

In a paper in this volume, Pissarides argues that if we are to understand growth
and development, we need to understand the creation and deployment of human
capital (Pissarides and Véganzonès-Varoudakis, 2007, p. 140). This is precisely
what I attempt to do in this section for the case of Egypt. Since the early 1950s,
the Egyptian government has been investing strongly in expanding access to
education. The effort was meant to substantially increase enrollment rates while
at the same time ensuring access to the rapidly growing number of children. The
evidence also suggests that parents are making significant investments in the
education of their children, which primarily take the form of private tutoring
and enrollment in supplemental evening classes. Despite impressive growth in
the number of graduates at all education levels, the question remains as to why
Egypt has not reaped a significant growth reward for its educational investments. The answer lies in two different areas. First, demographic pressures on
the schooling system forced educational authorities to sacrifice quality to increase quantity. As demographic pressures begin to let up, there is now an
opportunity to refocus efforts on educational quality. Second, by providing the
wrong signals, the institutional setting in the labor market (essentially the public
employment guarantee) has encouraged investment in essentially obsolete human capital and has entrapped much of that human capital in unproductive
employment in the government.

3.1. Expenditures on education and school enrollment

Egypt's rising expenditures in education have done a great deal to expand access
and increase enrollment rates at all educational levels. However, these positive

results are limited by their comparatively small economic impact. The fact that Egypt has increased educational expenditure so hugely while not reaping enormous returns on this investment indicates that there may be some misallocation of funds or lack of attention to quality in pre-university or higher education. Exploration of expenditures per student over a period of 20 years reveal some significant flaws in the way Egypt spends money on education. First, there is a significant discrepancy in spending per student between pre-university and higher education. In 2003, per student expenditures in higher education was up to four times as much as spending at the pre-university level. Second, the spending per student appears to increase with rising enrollment and decrease with lower enrollment, suggesting that overall spending varies more than proportionately with enrollment.

Over the past 20 years, the government made special efforts to substantially increase school enrollments while accommodating the substantial increase in the pre-university-age population. From 1980 to 2002, the number of school-age students has grown by close to 115 percent, with the overall expenditures increasing by an astonishing 320 percent in real terms. Despite continued enrollment pressures, Egypt has increased its *per-capita* spending on primary, preparatory, and secondary students by 95 percent.

Unlike growth rates in pre-university students, which have been fairly steady, university and higher institution enrollments have varied considerably during 1980–2002. After a slow decline in the late 1980s, enrollments in universities rose sharply beginning in 1992. Despite the period of decline, post-secondary enrollments had increased by 133 percent by 2002. *Per capita* student spending in higher education institutions varied enormously over this time period, declining when the government limited enrollment in the second half of the 1980s and early 1990s, and increasing when enrollments grew again thereafter. Per student spending rates were actually fairly similar in 2002 to what they had been in 1980, having increased by only 11 percent (Figure 2).

It thus appears that funding for higher education in Egypt has varied more than proportionally with enrollment. The policy of equalizing per student expenditure at the university and pre-university levels by limiting university enrollment and decreasing university expenditures was fairly short-lived. It soon gave way to rapid increases in enrollment and a growing gap in per student funding between higher and pre-university education in the 1990s.

These growth rates are somewhat deceptive; indeed, years of escalating education expenditure should have resulted in economic growth in Egypt as its human capital pool grew and improved in quality. The problem lies partly in the misallocation of both public and private spending on types of education that do not create the sort of workforce Egypt requires. While it is clear that Egypt is steadily making pre-university education a greater priority in its budget, there is still an enormous gap between higher education and pre-university expenditures per student. The Egypt Human Development Report of 1998/99 argues that there is still substantial misallocation of educational resources despite increasing

**Figure 2.   Real per-student spending and evolution of number of students enrolled,
(pre-university and higher education) during 1980–2003**

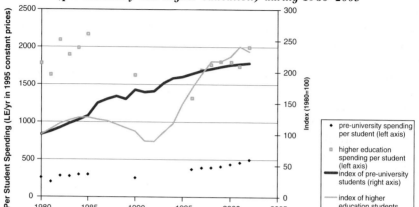

Sources: CAPMAS, *Egyptian Statistical Yearbooks* (various years) (number of student, all years);
UNDP (2000) (educational expenditure: 1990/91 and 1996/97); Devarajan *et al.*, (1996) (educational
expenditure: 1980–1985).

expenditures (UNDP, 2000, pp. 77–78). While figures from the *Egyptian Statistical Yearbook* make it difficult to differentiate between secondary, preparatory, and primary spending, UNDP assessments note that resources at the pre-university level are biased toward the secondary level. Enrollments are far higher at the primary level, but it receives similar funding at the secondary level of education. By no means should one assume that the cost of primary education is comparable to secondary or higher education; however, Egypt's lack of success at these lower levels of education denote the potential need for refocusing or reallocating funds toward these levels.

In an attempt to supplement public educational expenditures that, despite steady increases, do not adequately prepare Egyptians for the job market, parents have significantly increased their own spending on education. Since over 98 percent of Egyptian children are in public schools, this private spending usually takes the form of spending on private tutors or evening support groups for their children, which are often led by the children's own school teacher. These personal investments are common across different regions and even levels of income. Although it is quite difficult to obtain historical data on spending for private lessons, data from the Egypt Labor Market Survey of 1998 suggest that about one-half of primary school children and two-thirds of preparatory and secondary school children participated in some kind of private lessons in the year prior to the survey, with the majority taking the more expensive private lessons (Elbadawy *et al.*, 2004). On average, the parents of a child who took private tutoring spent LE 350 per year on such lessons (ELMS, 1998). UNDP estimates that approximately LE 7 billion is spent on tutoring per year. This cost of private tutoring is only somewhat less than the average public expenditure per student (LE 393 in 1998), and negates the purported right of "free education" available in Egypt. The burden is particularly heavy on poorer families, who pay nearly 10 percent of their annual income in tutoring services (UNDP, 2000, pp. 84–85).

Teachers can earn more from private tutoring than they can from their public school salaries, creating an incentive to focus their time and efforts more heavily on individual instruction. This certainly plays a role in the low quality of education offered at public institutions. To a certain extent, this is a self-perpetuating circle of demand for private tutoring and the low quality of education; the supply of teachers willing to spend more time in private lessons will not decrease until their public salaries are increased. The end result is that tutoring has become a substitute for basic education because of the low-quality instruction offered in schools (UNDP, 2000, pp. 84–85).

Such individual family investments have become necessary because of the inadequacy of much of Egypt's pre-university and post-secondary education. While educational expenditure is rising, Egypt's Human Development Report rightly notes that it is not enough to focus on the acquisition of credentials, but that productive skills must increasingly become the focus of the education system (UNDP, 2000, p. 1). Increased expenditure on education has not been the solution in Egypt because of skewed demand from students seeking degrees guaranteeing public employment rather than market-based skills. The obsolete nature of the abilities acquired in Egypt's educational system inhibit Egyptians from pursuing problem-solving skills that the private sector can use and benefit from. Many students are encouraged to pursue commercial degrees, in which they are taught clerical skills that are of little use to the private sector. In the past, the demand for the more marketable analytical and problem-solving skills has not been overwhelming because of the safety net of public service. This policy, over 40 years, has altered the demand for education in such a way that many available degrees do little to improve students' productive skills. The increasing expenditure on education needs to be focused more directly on skills that match the needs of the economy as Egypt gradually moves away from its government employment guarantee.

3.2. Role of the state as a dominant employer of educated workers

The guarantee of public employment – part of an extensive nationalization drive in 1961 – has played an enormous role in shaping the demand for and the quality of Egyptian education at all levels. The length and impact of the policy must be understood before an adequate assessment of educational reform can be accomplished. Begun as a guarantee to publicly employ all university graduates, it was extended to vocational secondary school and technical institute (2-year post-secondary institutions) graduates and the policy was formalized in Law No.

14 of 1964. It was later made permanent in Law No. 85 of 1973 (Assaad, 1997). Combined with the abolition of fees for higher education institutions in 1963, the employment guarantee for graduates provided a major boost to the demand for education. The employment guarantee greatly enhanced the private benefits of university education and the abolition of fees significantly lowered private costs (Richards, 1992, pp. 8–9).

Since the policy was instituted in the early 1960s, the Ministry of Manpower has maintained a registry of applicants to public sector jobs where graduates are listed by year of graduation and type of degree. While graduates are removed from the registry as a matter of course if they obtain a public sector job, many do not give up their position in the queue if they get a private job, thus reserving their right to a public sector job when their turn comes up. By law, university graduates must wait at least 2 years and secondary school and technical institute graduates 3 years after graduation to apply to the Ministry of Manpower for a government job.[2] By 1984, the waiting period between graduation and appointment had been extended to $3^{1/2}$ years for university graduates and 4 years for vocational secondary and technical institute graduates and, by 1987, to 5 and 6 years, respectively (Handoussa, 1992). Although the policy is still on the books and the Ministry continues to receive applications from graduates, hiring through the centralized manpower allocation system of the Ministry of Manpower has been suspended in the early 1990s, but has not been formally abolished. As of 2004, the last cohorts of graduates to have been offered appointments in its entirety through the centralized manpower allocation system was the 1984 cohort of university graduates and the 1983 cohort of vocational secondary and technical institute graduates. Until 1978, graduates could either be placed in the government or in State-owned enterprises (SOEs), but since then the manpower allocation scheme has stopped applying to SOEs, which have been allowed to control their own hiring directly. Despite the suspension of he centralized manpower allocation system, graduates continued to be hired into the civil service. The Ministry of Education, whose hiring has always been independent of the centralized system continued to hire at a rapid pace and individual government agencies and ministries were also hiring graduates directly through a series of competitions and special arrangements.

The graduate employment guarantee has had major implications for the size and composition of the public sector workforce in Egypt. As a result of the graduate employment guarantee scheme, Egypt has one of the highest proportions of total employment in the civil service in the world. The proportion of the civil service in total employment stood at 24 percent of total employment and 39

---

[2] The waiting period was designed to allow male graduates to complete their military service. With the exception of the period from 1967 to 1973, when conscripts could serve indefinitely, the duration of military service is normally 1 year longer for secondary and technical institute graduates than for university graduates.

percent of non-agricultural employment in 1998, up from 19 percent and 32 percent, respectively in 1988. Despite the formal suspension of the graduate guarantee scheme, government employment continued to grow at 4.8 percent per year in the 1990s, twice the rate of overall employment growth (Assaad, 2002). However, even that rate of growth was significantly below the 7.5–8 percent growth rates logged in the late 1970s and early 1980s (see Handoussa, 1992; Assaad, 1997).

This surprisingly rapid increase in government employment during a period of structural adjustments and budget cuts requires some further explanation. The trend has to be seen against the backdrop of a long-term policy to guarantee employment for all university and vocational secondary school graduates that, although suspended during the relevant decade, was not abolished. Thus, the failure to slow the growth of government employment may have been the result of the very rapid growth in the ranks of those who were until recently eligible for the government employment guarantee, that is those with upper secondary and post-secondary education. Even at sharply lower rates of hiring among these "graduates," the rapid growth of their ranks could be responsible for the continued expansion of government payrolls. Another reason for the more rapid than expected expansion of government payrolls is the changing behavior of *existing* civil servants. As government jobs became more difficult to obtain for new entrants, existing female civil servants were increasingly more likely to hold on to their jobs longer rather than leaving at marriage to start a family. This trend is clearly apparent from the age–employment profiles shown in Figure 3, where there is a clear shift rightward in the age–employment profile of female government workers. By reducing the rate of exits from government employment, this trend contributed to the faster than expected expansion in the 1990s.

3.3. Effects of the graduate employment guarantee on human capital acquisition and rates of return to schooling

Years of promising a public job to anyone who obtains a secondary school certificate has skewed both public and private education spending in Egypt toward the upper secondary and university levels, at the detriment of basic education. A comparison between Egypt and Turkey is quite instructive in this regard. Both countries have achieved an average of about 6 years of schooling for their population 12 years and older, but the distribution of that schooling over the different levels of education looks very different. As shown in Table 3, Egypt has not only a much higher proportion of its population than Turkey that is still illiterate or literate without formal schooling, but also a much higher proportion that has higher secondary and university education. Turkey, in contrast has achieved low rates of illiteracy by investing heavily in elementary education. Egypt's educational resources in comparison to Turkey's are therefore heavily skewed toward the secondary and university levels.

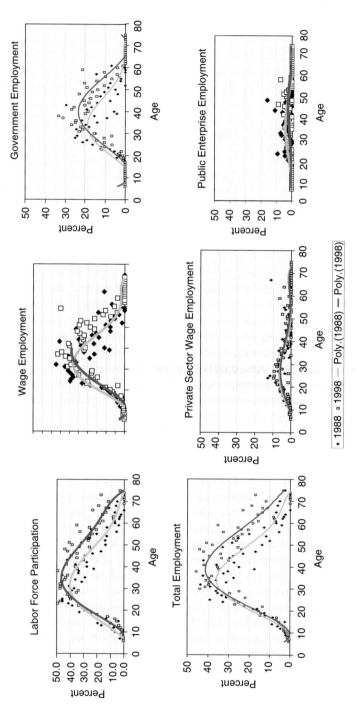

Figure 3.   Labor force participation and employment ratios by type of employment and age for women in urban areas

[1988 □ 1998 — Poly.(1988) — Poly.(1998)]

Source: LFSS, 1988 and ELMS, 1998

Note: The denominator for all ratios shown is the population of the relevant age group. The black and white symbols on the figures indicate mean participation rates by age in 1988 and 1998, respectively. The gray and black solid lines are a fifth-order polynomial fit through these points, for 1988 and 1998

Table 3. *Education of non-institutional civilian population 12 years old and older, 1998 (in percentage)*

	Total		Male		Female	
	Turkey	Egypt	Turkey	Egypt	Turkey	Egypt
Illiterate	14.3	31.9	6.0	20.9	22.3	42.9
Literate without any diploma	5.0	8.7	5.3	10.7	4.8	6.6
Elementary school	51.7	16.2	53.0	18.3	50.4	14.1
Middle school	11.9	13.0	14.9	14.5	9.0	11.4
General secondary school	9.8	4.6	11.3	5.3	8.3	4.0
Vocational secondary school	2.9	14.7	3.7	16.8	2.0	12.6
Universities and other higher educational institutuions	4.5	11.0	5.9	13.6	3.2	8.3
Total	100.0	100.0	100.0	100.0	100.0	100.0

Note: Illiteracy rates from these studies differ from those offered in UNDP's Egypt Human Development Report (UNDP 2000), which give higher numbers of illiteracy (36.4 percent for males and 61.2 percent for females in 1998, and 35 percent and 58 percent in 2000 and 2001, respectively). The studies were conducted in different years (1995 for UNDP and 1998 for the ELMS), and used different age levels (12 years and above and 15 years and above, respectively). The variances as well as variations in the size and origins of the sample contribute to the different results.
Source: HLFS, 1998 for Turkey and ELMS, 1998 for Egypt.

By making this comparison, I am not suggesting that Egypt must reduce its absolute investment in secondary or tertiary education, nor that Turkey has discovered the best possible equation in the allocation of education resources. However, as the results in these charts demonstrate, Egypt has been allocating a significant share of its education resources to the secondary and higher education levels before achieving universal basic education. This misallocation in spending could be redressed by introducing means testing and greater cost recovery at the university level, especially considering the vast difference in per student spending between university students and primary students. Minimization of personal costs and the guarantee of employment have driven the demand for secondary and tertiary education in Egypt to laudable but economically unrealistic levels. The enormous demand for secondary and higher education has biased funding toward these educational levels to the detriment of basic education, while poorly serving the needs of the economy. The evolution of the number and composition of graduates at the secondary and tertiary levels over the past 30 years reveals a fairly erratic process of educational expansion. Table 4 shows the evolution of the number of graduates in various specializations by level of education over the past 40 years according to official government data. The data reveal the rapid growth in the number of of secondary and university education in the 1970s as the public employment guarantee grew more alluring. Most of the expansion in secondary education was in the technical secondary branch, which grew at nearly 10 percent *per annum*. The equally rapid growth in the number of university graduates was more skewed toward humanities and social sciences because it is easier for universities to absorb students

Table 4. *Number of graduates from the formal schooling system, based on number of students who passed general examinations*

Specialization	Number of Graduates					Average Annual Growth Rate (Percent)				
	1973–1974	1981–1982	1990/1991	1995/1996	2000–2001	1973/1974 to 1981/1982	1981/1982 to 1990/1991	1990/1991 to 1995/1996	1995/1996 to 2000/2001	1990/1991 to 2000/2001
All university	37,574	86,841	108,276	126,353	248,451	10.5	2.5	3.1	13.5	8.3
Health sciences	4683	8,340	6,675	5,938	14,539	7.2	-2.5	-2.3	17.9	7.8
Agriculture	5313	6,318	5,845	2,856	4,354	2.2	-0.9	-14.3	8.4	-2.9
Engineering	3910	5,813	5,806	5,226	10,653	5.0	0.0	-2.1	14.2	6.1
Sciences	1543	3,699	4,460	3,869	5,289	10.9	2.1	-2.8	6.3	1.7
Other science-related fields	570	5,943	4,219	4,800	12,787	29.3	-3.8	2.6	19.6	11.1
All sciences	16,019	30,113	27,005	22,689	47,622	7.9	-1.2	-3.5	14.8	5.7
Commerce	7549	20,502	22,378	30,694	47,586	12.5	1.0	6.3	8.8	7.5
Law	2533	8,588	14,258	12,657	23,089	15.3	5.6	-2.4	12.0	4.8
Education	2694	10,717	14,990	26,645	44,875	17.3	3.7	11.5	10.4	11.0
Other humanities and social sciences	8779	16,921	29,645	33,668	85,279	8.2	6.2	2.5	18.6	10.6
All humanities and social sciences	21,555	56,728	81,271	103,664	200,829	12.1	4.0	4.9	13.2	9.0
All higher technical institutes	6998	16,836	35,112	22,506	30,154	11.0	8.2	-8.9	5.9	-1.5
Commercial	4424	12,838	21,911	12,364	13,370	13.3	5.9	-11.4	1.6	-4.9
Industrial	2574	3,998	13,201	10,142	16,784	5.5	13.3	-5.3	10.1	2.4
All technical secondary	82,264	179,585	281,912	547,831	509,750	9.8	5.0	13.3	-1.4	5.9
Agricultural	9317	17,918	35,339	62,884	50,084	8.2	7.5	11.5	-4.6	3.5
Commercial	47,517	111,169	114,234	247,321	219,469	10.6	0.3	15.4	-2.4	6.5
Industrial	25,430	50,498	132,339	237,626	240,197	8.6	10.7	11.7	0.2	6.0
General and Azhari secondary	124,258	171,627	176,946	310,803	377,622	4.0	0.3	11.3	3.9	7.6
All secondary	206,522	351,212	458,858	858,634	887,372	6.6	3.0	12.5	0.7	6.6
General and Azhari preparatory	274,113	431,125	631,811	952,772	1,288,994	5.7	4.2	8.2	6.0	7.1
General and Azhari primary	399,565	582,534	984,181	1,259,201	1,377,455	4.7	5.8	4.9	1.8	3.4

Sources:

(1) *Statistical Year Book of the Arab Republic of Egypt*, 1995–2002 (Cairo, June 2003) for 1998–1999 and 2000–2001 figures.
(2) *Statistical Year Book of the Arab Republic of Egypt*, 1990–1995 (Cairo, July 1996) for 1990/1991 figures.
(3) *Statistical Year Book of the Arab Republic of Egypt*, 1952–1986 (Cairo, June 1987) for 1981–1982 figures.
(4) *Statistical Year Book of the Arab Republic of Egypt*, 1952–1978 (Cairo, July 1979) for 1973–1974 figures.

in these departments. In the presence of the employment guarantee for technical secondary and university graduates, this explosive growth fueled a tremendous expansion of government employment in that decade, which in turn was made possible by the flow of oil and oil-related revenues into government coffers (see El-Issawy, 1983; Handoussa, 1992).

Alarmed by the rapid growth in the number of secondary and university graduates, educational authorities appear to have applied the brakes on educational expansion in the 1980s. The government's attempt to slow down the increase in the number of university graduates in the 1980s and early 1990s began by controlling the intake into general secondary schools and directing the growing number of degree seekers to technical secondary education. As a result of this policy, the share of enrollment in general secondary schools declined steadily from a high of 60 percent in 1965/66 to a low of 31 percent in 1995/96 (Antoninis, 2002). The decline in general secondary enrollment resulted in an eventual decline in university graduates in the late 1980s and early 1990s (see Figure 2). The decline was particularly sharp in the science-related fields, which contracted in absolute terms.

The first half of the 1990s witnessed a tremendous acceleration of technical secondary education in all branches, but continued slow growth of university education. In particular, the industrial branch of technical secondary education grew rapidly in the first half of the 1990s, possibly as a result of a belief on the part of education officials that industrial skills would be in more demand in the private sector. This pattern was entirely reversed in the second half, as the number of technical secondary graduates shrunk in absolute terms and the number of university graduates exploded at a rate of 13.5 percent *per annum*. A similarly erratic pattern can be seen in the evolution of the number of graduates from higher technical institutes. These 2-year post-secondary institutions, whose graduates were also covered by public employment guarantee, grew rapidly in the 1970s and 1980s, but then contracted sharply in the first half of the 1990s, only to recover somewhat in the second half.

The explosive, if somewhat erratic growth of technical secondary education is in large part driven by the promise of government employment and the higher returns of such employment on these educational investments. In Table 5 below, we reproduce results on rates of return to schooling in Egypt in 1988 and 1998 for various levels and types of schooling in the private and public sectors presented in Zhang (2003). Zhang estimated a series of wage equations by sex and sector for data derived from the Egypt Labor Force Sample Survey 1988 and the Egypt Labor Market Survey of 1998. These equations are corrected for selectivity into the non-agricultural wage labor force and into the public and private sectors using the Heckman two-stage method.

The most striking result is that rates of return for males to all levels of schooling in the private sector are falling. While there is a positive return for each consecutive year of schooling, with university educations offering the highest return at above 10 percent each year, the overall return in the private

Ragui Assaad

Table 5. *Incremental Mincerian returns to education per year of schooling, Egypt (1988, 1998), non-agricultural wage workers*

Year	Read and Write vs. Illiterate (percent)	Primary vs. Illiterate (percent)	Vocational Secondary vs. Primary (percent)	Post-secondary vs. Vocational Secondary (percent)	University vs. Vocational Secondary (percent)	Years of Schooling (percent)
Males						
Government						
1988	6.9	6.4	9.7	9.1	11.7	9.0
1998	9.1	6.3	9.5	12.5	14.0	9.2
Non-government						
1988	4.4	2.8	5.1	7.8	12.4	5.3
1998	4.9	2.2	4.3	7.3	11.0	4.4
Females						
Government						
1988	7.3	0.1	24.4	7.8	11.6	10.5
1998	10.4	7.9	19.7	17.6	14.4	13.3
Non-government						
1988	16.4	8.9	8.5	−2.0	14.7	9.6
1998	4.3	9.5	3.3	15.6	18.3	9.4

Source: Zhang (2003).

sector for each year of education decreased from 1988 to 1998 (from 5.3 percent to 4.4 percent). There is not a great appreciation of even primary education in the private sector; the rates of return to primary schooling and vocational secondary schools are quite low. These results suggest that the government's policy to restrict university education in the 1980s and then reverse that trend in the 1990s initially reduced the surplus of graduates at that level (giving them higher returns) and then returned to a surplus (decreasing the rates of return). However, rates of return to schooling are lower or even negative for higher technical institute graduates whose numbers were also rising rapidly in the 1980s.

In all cases except university levels in 1988, rates of return to education in the public sector are higher than in the private sector. In addition, from 1988 to 1998, all rates of return increased for government work, while all private sector rates of return declined. This suggests public sector employment still looms large in the motivations of students to pursue secondary and higher education. The rapid expansion in the number of university graduates since 1995 is likely to have significantly increased their supply to the labor market and to have further reduced the premium they are able to receive for their education outside the government sector.

The graduate employment guarantee generated an artificial incentive to achieve the lowest educational threshold to qualify for the guarantee. That minimum threshold is the technical secondary degree, which, despite its name, is not very vocational or technical in nature. A significant proportion of vocational secondary graduates are in fact in the "commercial" branch, which essentially imparts bureaucratic and clerical skills, which are in little demand in the private sector (Antoninis, 2002). With the suspension of the graduate employment guarantee and the relative slowdown of government hiring, there was a serious glut of graduates at that level of education in the late 1990s (Assaad, 2002). The government has since curtailed enrollment in technical secondary schools and expanded it significantly at the university level. It remains to be seen what effect this will have on the returns to university education.

What is readily apparent, however, is that Egypt's attempts to control access to various levels of education and steer students toward the government's institution of choice has not had the desired impact on reducing graduate unemployment rates or increasing rates of return to education outside the government. At the university, higher institute, and secondary level, the issue is not how many students to have at each level, but the quality of the education they are receiving.

3.4. "Entrapment" of graduates in the public sector

The public employment guarantee for graduates has skewed demand for higher education while doing little to add to economic growth. An unfortunate consequence of this decades-old policy is that much of Egypt's educated human capital is trapped in the public sector, particularly in the civil service component of the public sector, thus contributing little to raising productivity in the rest of the economy. The guarantee of employment offers little incentive to seek out skills more marketable in the private sector. In the long-term, the promise of lifetime employment with benefits does not encourage transfer between the sectors. Although this is beginning to change as the growth of the government bureaucracy begins to slow, it will take a while before the stock of educational human capital shifts to the private sector.

As shown in Table 6, nearly 60 percent of employed males and 80 percent of employed females with secondary education or above worked in the public sector in 1988, compared to 21 percent of employed males and 2 percent of employed females with a lesser education level.[3] Although one would expect the public sector workforce to be more educated, these lopsided numbers suggest that the education system in Egypt is effectively geared toward meeting the demands of the bureaucracy. Although there have been efforts to move away from this dominant pattern in recent years, progress has been slow. The proportion of employed graduates working in the public sector was still 52 percent and 63 percent for males and females, respectively. Young graduates, in particular, were finding it increasingly difficult to get these public sector jobs.

---

[3] The vast majority (77 percent) of educated workers in the public sector are in the civil service component of that sector.

Ragui Assaad

Table 6. *Proportion of employed working in the public sector by education and age*

Education	Age	LFSS (1988)			ELMS (1998)		
		Urban	Rural	Total	Urban	Rural	Total
Males							
Below secondary	15–34	14.1	8.0	10.1	11.2	8.0	9.1
	35–64	41.2	22.9	30.1	32.1	29.4	30.4
	All	29.8	15.8	20.9	24.1	20.1	21.4
Secondary and above	15–34	47.7	53.9	50.3	33.4	32.9	33.1
	35–64	72.9	88.3	76.7	69.4	75.1	71.5
	All	59.2	63.1	60.6	53.0	49.8	51.6
All	15–34	29.8	19.4	23.8	24.2	18.1	20.6
	35–64	52.3	29.5	40.3	51.2	41.4	46.0
	All	41.7	24.2	32.0	39.8	30.0	34.3
No. of observations		3245	3000	6245	3341	1861	5202
Females							
Below secondary	15-34	12.2	0.8	2.4	4.0	1.0	1.4
	35-64	9.5	0.4	2.0	9.7	0.8	2.5
	All	10.7	0.6	2.2	7.7	0.9	2.0
Secondary and above	15-34	75.9	72.5	74.9	54.4	34.7	44.3
	35-64	91.5	92.3	91.6	90.1	76.6	87.0
	All	81.1	75.8	79.9	74.1	45.4	62.9
	15-34	54.6	8.4	22.2	38.9	9.2	16.6
	35-64	47.9	2.8	15.2	57.2	7.9	25.0
	All	51.8	5.9	19.1	49.7	8.6	20.9
No. of observations		1157	2173	3330	1572	1507	3079

Source: LFSS, 1988; ELMS, 1998.

Whereas 50 percent of male graduates in the age group of 15– 34 years was working in public sector in 1988, this proportion was down to 33 percent in 1998. Among young female graduates, the share in the public sector dropped equally fast from 75 to 44 percent. Older educated workers continued to be highly concentrated in the public sector, in both 1988 and 1998, however. For older educated females over 35, public sector work is nearly the only option. Those who are unable to get public sector work simply drop out of the labor market after marriage, since private sector employment is deemed incompatible with the domestic responsibilities of married women in Egypt.

4. Gender norms and barriers to entry for women in the private sector

The institutional norms that entrap human capital in public sector employment are all the more limiting in the case of women. In addition to the demand for the security of public sector employment, norms that define what is appropriate female employment often prevent women from taking up employment in the private sector. These norms define appropriate gender roles regarding women's participation in the public sphere. Women are expected to assume the primary responsibility for the domestic sphere and to prioritize that responsibility over their professional careers outside the home. Women's safety from male harassment or molestation is often so highly prized as to place severe constraints on how far they can travel to go to work, how late they can remain outside their homes, and what kind of workplace is appropriate. These norms not only shape what women and their families perceive as an acceptable form of involvement in the labor market, but they also determine employers' perceptions of female workers. For instance, the general tendency for women to stop working at marriage to devote themselves completely to domestic responsibilities discourages employers from investing in their training. Women are therefore often relegated to jobs that require little training and that can tolerate high levels of job turnover.

Folbre (1996, p. 128), among others, has described development as involving the gradual transition of economic activities from the household economy to the market economy. Being at the interface of this divide between the household and the market, women see a significant change in their roles as development proceeds. As fertility declines and the focus of economic activity shifts away from the family farm and the family enterprise, women have sought greater participation in paid work. Rising educational attainment among women further reinforces these trends, leading to a significant association between educational attainment and work outside the home. These powerful forces are partially counteracted by the strong social norms discussed above that are much slower to change.

Historically, government policies have had a major role in changing gender norms about women's employment outside the home. In fact, the graduate employment guarantee mentioned above, by applying equally to male and female graduates, has resulted in large numbers of women joining the public sector workforce. Consequently, employment outside the home is now part of the normal expectations of young women who achieve a secondary level of education. This is clearly apparent when one examines the pattern of female labor force participation by educational attainment, where there is a sudden and large increase at the secondary education level, the point at which graduates become eligible for the employment guarantee (see Assaad, 2002). Besides making paid employment the norm for educated females, the employment guarantee scheme has also helped shape what is deemed female-appropriate employment. Public sector work is strongly preferred by female workers, not only because it pays better than the private sector, but also because it has other important characteristics that make it gender-appropriate.[4] These characteristics include generous

---

[4] The government does not discriminate along gender lines on pay, whereas there is a large unexplained wage gap between male and female workers in the private sector, giving females in the public sector a significant pay advantage over their private sector counterparts (Assaad, 1997).

medical and retirement benefits, relatively short work hours (six hours a day, six days per week is the public sector norm in Egypt), low effort requirement, transportation provided by the employer in many instances, and the presence of a large number of other women in the workplace, providing a measure of sexual safety. With the inevitable slowdown in public sector employment, its role in "normalizing" female employment outside the home might see a significant reversal. Although a relatively small proportion of Egyptian women work for pay in the private sector, few remain in that sector after marriage and many would rather queue for years for a public sector job rather than take one in the private sector.

4.1. Female participation in the Egyptian labor market in the 1990s

A closer look at the evolution of female participation from 1988 to 1998 reveals that participation among older, married females was increasing in urban areas, but the increase can be attributed entirely to female government employees (who make up the bulk of female wage employees) holding on to their increasingly valuable public sector jobs. As shown in Figure 3, the employment ratio in the government for urban females has shifted noticeably to the right, not only indicating that older women were staying longer on government payrolls, but also that young women had reduced, or at least delayed, access to government employment. Employment in public enterprises, in contrast, was falling in all age groups, but the decline was the largest among younger females. The situation in rural areas (Figure 4) is less clear given the relatively limited role of wage employment among females, but it suggests that government employment continued to increase among prime working-age females there as well.

Reduced access to public sector employment for young women was not being counteracted by increased access in the private sector. In fact, although private sector wage employment was primarily the domain of young women in their twenties and early thirties, access to it had not increased from 1988 to 1998. Employment ratios in that type of employment remained virtually unchanged for urban women and declined slightly in rural areas. There seems therefore to be some support for Moghadam's contention that structural adjustment is crowding women out of the Egyptian labor market by reducing access to public employment without affecting the barriers to entry that women face in the private sector (Moghadam, 1998, pp. 109–112).

The problem is not one of general lack of dynamism in the private sector. Wage employment in the private non-agricultural sector was the second-fastest growing segment of the labor market after government. It grew at an average of 4.3 percent per year from 1988 to 1998, a rate that is 72 percent higher than the 2.5 percent overall employment growth rate in that period. However, the growth of employment in that sector was much more rapid for males (4.7 percent per year) than for females (1.6 percent per year), despite the fact that overall female employment growth was more rapid than that of males. Given the almost certain

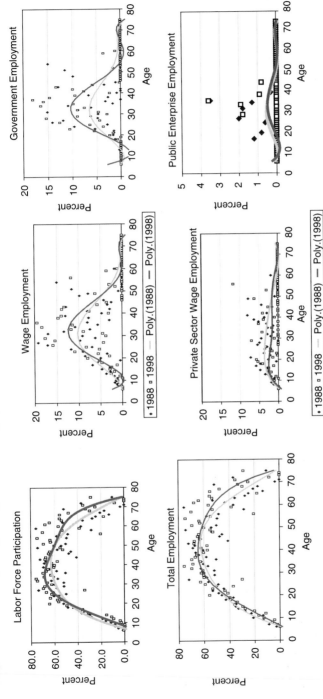

Figure. 4. Labor force participation and employment ratios by type of employment and age for women in rural areas

Source: LFSS, 1988 and ELMS, 1998

Note: The denominator for all ratios shown is the population of the relevant age group. The black and white symbols on the figures indicate mean participation rates by age in 1988 and 1998, respectively. The gray and black solid lines are a fifth- order polynomial fit through these points for 1988 and 1998 prospects of a slowdown in the growth of public sector employment in Egypt, the barriers to female employment in the private sector may lead to continued high unemployment rates for women and a possible reversal in the growth of female labor force participation observed in recent years. Thus, it appears that the growth of the female labor force in Egypt in the foreseeable future will be more constrained by factors related to labor demand and labor market structure than to labor supply.

4.2. Barriers to private sector employment for women

Women's paid employment in the private sector is one area in which the prevalent social norms interact with government policies in powerful ways. The availability of government employment for female graduates has done a lot to attenuate strong social norms that discourage women's employment outside the home. In 1998, nearly 32 percent of Egyptian women with secondary education or above (the group that is eligible for the public employment guarantee) worked for pay, compared to <3 percent of those who have less than a secondary education. Government employment has therefore "normalized" working for educated women in Egypt. Although most of them work for the public sector, their involvement in private sector wage employment is also significantly higher than their less-educated counterparts. What government employment has also done, however, is define what is a gender-appropriate job in Egypt. If private sector work does not fit into that category, it is virtually closed to women, both because employers do not consider them worthy candidates for such jobs and because the women and their families do not consider it suitable employment.

Some have argued that excessive regulation, and in particular female-specific mandates, such as paid and unpaid maternity leave and childcare provisions, discourage private employers from hiring women (see discussion in Moghadam, 1998, p. 119). This argument appears to be somewhat exaggerated, however, given that the Egyptian government has been very lax about enforcing its own labor laws in recent years. A comparison of survey data from 1988 and 1998 shows that only 15 percent of new jobs obtained by women in the non-agricultural private sector in Egypt were protected by a legal employment contract (Assaad, 2002). One can safely assume that jobs that are not protected by a contract will not provide all the female-specific benefits that the law stipulates.

The main reason Egyptian employers are reluctant to hire women has to do with the widespread perception that women have a low attachment to the workforce. This perception manifests itself in several ways, including a sense that female workers have a high turnover rate, which makes them poor prospects for training, that they have high absenteeism rates, and that they are unwilling to work the long hours that the private sector in Egypt requires. Such low commitment to the workforce is a direct outcome of social norms that make the home women's primary domain of responsibility. Although this applies to both married and unmarried women, the situation for married women is compounded to an extent that private sector wage work is seen as totally incompatible with marriage, leading to a virtual certainty of quitting such work at marriage.

While I do not have direct evidence on the reluctance of private sector employers to hire female workers, gender wage differentials are fully consistent with such a hypothesis. The much lower wages that female employees receive in the private sector, after correcting for productivity-related characteristics, suggest that low rates of wage employment among females are not simply due to supply constraints (Assaad, 1997). In fact, female labor supplies studies indicate that female participation in paid work is quite responsive to wages (Assaad and El-Hamidi, 2002). Low female wages are most likely due to barriers to entry that force female workers to crowd into limited segments of the labor market, depressing their wages in these segments. These barriers are undoubtedly due to employer perceptions about the suitability, reliability, and productivity of female labor; perceptions that are themselves shaped by the predominant gender norms in the society.

Besides employers' reluctance to hire them, women face other sorts of constraints in the private labor market. Women tend to prefer working in relatively large establishments with many other female workers in them because of the protection against sexual harassment that the presence of other women provides. Unfortunately, the share of such large establishments in the Egyptian private sector is rather small. In 1998, nearly 48 percent of all private non-agricultural wageworkers in Egypt worked in establishments of less than 5 workers, and only 20 percent were in establishments of 30 or more workers.

Women are also more geographically constrained than men. Their place of residence is generally determined by either parents or husbands, so that they cannot adjust where they live to where the jobs are (Moghadam, 1998, pp. 118–119). Moreover, they are less able to commute long distances to work because of time constraints and safety concerns. A comparison of commuting times in 1988 and 1998 for men working in the private sector in Egypt shows that men were having to commute significantly more to get to private sector jobs. Women's inability to make such commutes limits them to jobs that are locally available, and therefore is likely to be an important entry barrier to women in the private sector (Assaad and Arntz, 2005).

To conclude, gender norms about the primacy of women's reproductive role and the sexual division of labor constrain women's geographical mobility. Women tend to be disproportionately concentrated in the public sector, partly because public sector jobs tend to be more compatible with women's household responsibilities than paid employment in the private sector, and partly because public sector employers are less able to discriminate against women.

5. Conclusions

The demographic transition presents Egypt with a window of opportunity to significantly raise economic growth over the near future. A number of policy actions will be necessary to capitalize on this opportunity. The first set of actions relates to the educational field, where the government must at least maintain the share of national resources devoted to education at present levels to allow for a significant increase in resources per child. Part of improving the quality of education is to increase its relevance to the needs of an increasingly market-oriented economy. Furthermore, improvements in the quality of education will provide additional incentives for households to increase their own human capital investments. A second set of actions relates to maintaining or increasing labor force participation rates among adults so that the changing age structure actually results in an increase in the economically active population. This appears to be occurring in Egypt, as female participation rates are on the rise (Assaad, 2002). However, the inevitable contraction of the public employment option without a concurrent improvement in opportunities in the private sector could jeopardize this trend. Finally, policies are necessary to ensure a sufficiently dynamic economic system so that productivity levels continue to rise, or at least do not fall, as more people join the work force.

In assessing the micro-determinants of economic growth in Egypt, I emphasized the way in which household decisions are shaped and constrained by strong institutional forces deriving from government policy and gender norms. In the fertility realm, I discussed how declining fertility levels in recent years can contribute to economic growth if the additional human resources that are being made available by a growing share of the working-age population can be used effectively and if the declining number of children can be used as an opportunity to deepen investments in productive human capital. Both potentialities are present in Egypt, but their realization will depend on developments in the arenas of human capital accumulation and the labor market.

Investments in human capital have been strongly shaped by the longstanding, albeit officially suspended, policy of guaranteeing public employment for all technical secondary school, post–secondary, and university graduates. This policy has resulted in an overinvestment in the threshold level of education that can make a graduate eligible for the guarantee, namely technical secondary degrees. As a result, there is a large surplus of graduates at that level, leading to negative rates of return on the human capital investment in the private sector and to high unemployment rates among members of this group. The situation is similar for graduates from 2-year post-secondary institutions, but quite different for university graduates. Until the mid-1990s the government had followed a deliberate policy to limit the number admitted to that stage of education by means of controlling entry requirements in the predominantly public university education system. As a result, rates of return to university education have been relatively high and rose significantly until the mid-1990s. Since then, however, the government reversed its policy and significantly increased the number of university graduates. The labor market impact of this change has not yet been detected in the available data.

Overall, however, Egypt has historically neglected basic education relative to secondary and tertiary education, but has made efforts to close the gap in recent years. The challenge now that demographic pressures on the education system are subsiding is to focus resources on improving the quality of education, both at the basic level as well as for vocational secondary schools.

Another consequence of the graduate employment guarantee is the trapping of a large portion of Egypt's educational human capital in the civil service, where its contribution to economic growth is dubious at best. The employment guarantee scheme has therefore not only had an impact on the sorts of human capital investments that were made, but has also starved the private sector of the human capital it needs.

With regard to labor force participation, the employment guarantee, which is applied equally to male and female graduates, has made it the norm for women to work outside the home once they achieve the secondary level of education. As a result, female participation in paid work rises sharply once this level of education is reached. With the slowdown in government hiring in recent years, the expectation of work remains, judging from the high number of female graduates seeking paid employment. However, the opportunities to work are becoming increasingly limited owing to the presence of significant barriers to female employment in the private sector. Unless these barriers can be reduced in the near future, the gains achieved from significant increases in female participation in the labor market are liable to be reversed.

Acknowledgments

The author would like to thank two anonymous referees for their excellent comments and suggestions and Jessica Soto and Loren DeJonge for their able research assistance.

References

Antoninis, M. (2002), "An empirical investigation of the effects of the expansion of technical secondary education on the Egyptian Labor Market. A tale of two data sets", forthcoming at the Sixth Annual ERF Conference, January 15–17, 2002, Cairo, Egypt.

Assaad, R. (1997), "The effects of public sector hiring and compensation policies on the Egyptian Labor Market", *The World Bank Economic Review*, Vol. 11(1), pp. 85–118.

Assaad, R. (editor), (2002), "The transformation of the Egyptian Labor Market: 1988–1998", *The Labor Market in a Reforming Economy*, Cairo: American University Press.

Assaad, R. and M. Arntz (2005), "Constrained geographical mobility and gendered labor market outcomes under structural adjustment: evidence from Egypt", *World Development*, Vol. 33(3), 431–454.

Assaad, R. and F. El-Hamidi (2002), "Female labor supply in Egypt: participation and hours of work", forthcoming in: I. Sirageldin, editor, *Population Challenges in the Middle East and North Africa: Towards the 21st Century*, London: I.B. Tauris.

Barlow, R. (1994), "Population growth and economic growth: some more correlations", *Population and Development Review*, Vol. 20(1), pp. 153–165.

Becker, G.S. (1991), *A Treatise on the Family*, second edition, Cambridge, MA: Harvard University Press.

Bloom, D. and J.G. Williamson (1998), "Demographic transition and economic miracles in emerging Asia", *The World Bank Economic Review*, Vol. 12(3), pp. 419–455.

CAPMAS (various years), *Egyptian Statistical Yearbook*, Cairo: Central Agency for Public Mobilization and Statistics.

Devarajan, S., V. Swaroop and H.-F. Zou (1996), "Public expenditures data – 1975–1985 for 69 countries: composition of public expenditure and economic growth", *Journal of Monetary Economics*, Vol. 37(1996), pp. 313–344.

ELMS (1998), *Egypt Labor Market Survey 1998*, Cairo, Egypt: Economic Research Forum.

Elbadawy, A., R. Assaad, D. Ahlburg and D. Levison (2004), "Private and group tutoring in Egypt: where is the gender inequality?", Paper presented at the ERF 11th Annual Conference, December 14–16, 2004, Beirut, Lebanon.

El-Issawy, I. (1983), "Labour force, employment and unemployment", The Technical Papers of the ILO/UNDP comprehensive employment strategy mission to Egypt, No. 4. International Labour Office (ILO), Geneva.

El-Zanaty, F. and A. Way (2006), *Egypt Demographic and Health Survey 2005*, Cairo, Egypt: Ministry of Health and Population, National Population Council, El-Zanaty and Associates, and ORC Macro.

Folbre, N. (1996), "Engendering economics: new perspectives on women, work, and demographic change", in: M. Bruno and B. Pleskovic, editors, *Annual World Bank Conference on Development Economics 1995*, Washington, DC: The World Bank.

Handoussa, H. (1992), "The burden of public sector employment and remuneration: the case of Egypt", in: W. Van Ginneken, editor, *Government and its Employees: Case Studies of Developing Countries*, Aldershot, Hants, England: Avebury.

HLFS (1998), *Household Labor Force Survey 1998*, Ankara, Turkey: State Institute of Statistics.

Kheir-El-Din, H. and T. Moursi (2006), "Sources of economic growth and technical progress in Egypt: an aggregate perspective", chapter 7 in: J. Nugent and H. Pesaran, editors, *Explaining Growth in the Middle East, Contribution to Economic Analysis*, Amsterdam: Elsevier.

LFSS (1988), *October 1988 Round of the Labor Force Sample Survey*, Cairo, Egypt: Central Agency for Public Mobilization and Statistics.

Miller, P. and N. Hirschhorn (1995), "The effect of a national control of diarrheal diseases program on mortality: the case of Egypt", *Social Science And Medicine*, Vol. 40(10), pp. S1–S30.

Moghadam, V. (1998), *Women, Work and Economic Reform in the Middle East and North Africa*, Boulder, London: Lynne Rienner Publishers.

Panel on Egypt, Committee on Population and Demography (1982), *The Estimation of Recent Trends in Fertility and Mortality in Egypt*, Committee on Population and Demography, Report No. 9, Washington, DC: National Academy Press.

Pissarides, C. and M.A. Véganzonès-Varoudakis (2007), "Labor markets and economic growth in the MENA region", chapter 5 in: J. Nugent and H. Pesaran, editors, *Explaining Growth in the Middle East, Contribution to Economic Analysis*, Amsterdam: Elsevier.

Richards, A. (1992), "Higher education in egypt", Policy Research Working Paper No. 862. The World Bank.

Salehi-Isfahani, D. (2006), "Microeconomics of growth in MENA- the role of households", chapter 6 in: J. Nugent and H. Pesaran, editors, *Explaining Growth in the Middle East, Contribution to Economic Analysis*, Amsterdam: Elsevier.

Schultz, T.P. (editor) (1995), *Investment in Women's Human Capital*, Chicago: Chicago University Press.

Singerman, D. and B. Ibrahim (2003), "The cost of marriage in Egypt: a hidden variable in the new Arab demography", in: N. Hopkins, editor, *The New Arab Family, Cairo Papers in Social Science,* Vol. 24 (1–2) pp. 80–116.

Tunali, I. (1996). "Labor market implications of the demographic window of opportunity", *The Forum*, Vol. 3(2), ERF: Cairo.

UNDP (2000), *Egypt Human Development Report (1998/1999)*, Cairo: Institute of National Planning and UNDP.

UN Population Division (2003), World populations prospects: 2002 revision population database, *http://esa.un.org/unpp/index.asp?panel=2*.

Williamson, J. and T. Yousef (2002), "Demographic transitions and economic performance in the Middle East and North Africa", in: I. Sirageldin, editor, *Population Challenges in the Middle East and North Africa: Towards the 21st Century*, London: I.B. Tauris, forthcoming.

Zhang, H. (2003), "Sample selection bias and returns to education in Egyptian Labor Market, 1988 and 1998", Paper completed for partial fulfillment of Masters in Urban Planning degree program requirements, Humphrey Institute of Public Affairs, Minneapolis, MN.

Notes on the Authors

Ragui Assaad is regional director for West Asia and North Africa at the Population Council. He has over 20 years of research experience on gender, poverty, and labor market and is an expert on statistical and econometric modeling using household survey and census data. Before joining the Population Council, Assaad served as professor of planning and public affairs at the Humphrey Institute of Public Affairs at the University of Minnesota. Assaad has a PhD in City and Regional Planning from Cornell University. He also holds a B.Sc. in physics and an M.Sc. in mechanical engineering from Stanford University.

Mohamed Z. Bechri is currently senior economist with the Central Bank in Abu Dhabi. He holds a PhD in Economics from the University of Southern California. He taught economics at the University of Tunisia and worked at the African Department of the International Monetary Fund in Washington. His main field of interest is Development Economics, New Institutional Economics and Political Economy.

Mohamed Abdelbasset Chemingui is a research scientist at the Techno-economics Division of the Kuwaiti Institute for Scientific Research (KISR). Before joining KISR, he has worked as associate researcher with the University of Montpellier and as research assistant and economist at the OECD Development Center (1998 and 2000). He has a PhD in economics from the University of Montpellier (France) in 2000. He was awarded a first place with a medal prize for his study on income distribution in Tunisia under the Second Global Awards Competition organized by the Global Development Network in Rio de Janeiro in December 2001, and the best policy oriented paper in trade topic during the ERF 12th annual conference held in Cairo 2005. His research interest has been in partial and general equilibrium modeling, macroeconomics, international trade, and regional integration, labor market and poverty analysis, growth and productivity changes, and agricultural and environmental economics. He has worked on projects sponsored by World Bank, ESCWA, European Commission, ETF, IDRC, ERF, GDN, IFPRI, UNIDO, API, and other national agencies in the capacity of Project Leader/Principal Investigator/Consultant.

Adam B. Elhiraika holds a PhD in Economics from the University of Glasgow (1991) and a Masters degree in Economics from the University of Kent at Canterbury. He taught Economics at Gezira University (Sudan), Fort Hare University (South Africa) the University of Swaziland (Swaziland), and the United Arab Emirates University. He served as Economist at the Islamic Development Bank (Saudi Arabia) before joining the United Nations Economic Commission for Africa as Economic Affairs Officer in 2004. His main areas of specialization are macroeconomics and finance with special interest in Islamic finance. He has several publications in internationally refereed journals and books.

Moataz Mostafa El-Said is a technical assistance advisor with the Poverty and Social Impact Analysis (PSIA) group at the Fiscal Affairs Department of the International Monetary Fund (IMF), where he works on the distributional implications of the IMF program policies in low-income countries. Prior to joining the IMF, he worked at the Trade and Macroeconomics division and the Development Strategy and Governance Division of the International Food Policy Research Institute (IFPRI). He has a PhD in Economics from the George Washington University.

Hasan Ersel received his PhD in Economics from the Ankara University in 1971, where he was a faculty member until 1983. He served at the Capital Markets Board as senior research officer and at the Central Bank of Turkey as the head of the research department before becoming its vice governor. He worked for the Yapi Kredi Bank as senior vice president and later as a member of its board of directors. He is on the board of trustees of the Turkish Economic Policy Research Foundation (TEPAV) and a research fellow of the ERF. Presently, he teaches at the Sabanci University.

Hadi Salehi Esfahani is a professor of Economics at the University of Illinois at Urbana-Champaign. He has also worked for the World Bank as a visiting staff economist and a consultant. He received a B.Sc. in engineering from Tehran University and a PhD in economics from the University of California at Berkeley. His theoretical and empirical research focuses on the role of politics and governance institutions in the formation of fiscal, trade, and regulatory policies and their outcomes. He serves as a research fellow of the ERF and as executive secretary for the Middle East Economic Association.

Zeki Fattah holds PhD in Economics from Oxford University. He is a consultant in Middle Eastern economies, and advises member governments in the region in economic development. He is an advisor in the Economic Research Forum for the Arab Countries, Iran, and Turkey in Cairo. He directed the United Nations Economic Development Program and the Economic Analysis Program, Sectoral Issues Program, and Science and Technology Program for the Middle East in the Economic and Social Commission for Western Asia (UNESCWA)) from 1981 to 2003. He lectures on economic development in the Institute of Money and Finance at the American University in Beirut.

Anas H. Hamed holds a PhD in Economics from Arizona State University (1992). He served as deputy general manager, Khartoum Stock Exchange (Sudan). He taught Economics at Grambling State University, and the United Arab Emirates University. He served as economist at Abu Dhabi Fund for Development (UAE) before joining Social Security Investment Authority (Sudan) as an assistant general commissioner, Research and Information. His main areas of specialization are International Economics and Finance with special interest in Financial Markets and Institutions. He published in internationally refereed journals.

Ahmad R. Jalali-Naini is a member of the Department of Economics at the Institute for Management and Planning Studies in Tehran, Iran, where he served as a chairman during 1998–2004. He has taught graduate macroeconomics and monetary theory/finance.

His research interests and works cover economic growth, monetary and exchange rate policies, and business cycles, particularly in the MENA countries. He has also served as the director of Financial Markets in Energy at the International Institute for Energy Studies and the director of Foreign Exchange Studies at the Institute for Monetary and Banking Research, the Central Bank of Iran. He has a PhD in Economics from the University of Kent, a master's in Public Administration from New York University, and an MA in economics from University of Southern California. He is currently a visiting researcher at the Petroleum Market Analysis Department, OPEC, in Vienna.

Magda Kandil is a senior economist at the IMF Institute. Prior to her Fund career, she was professor and department chair at the University of Wisconsin-Milwuakee. Her publications include 66 articles (as author or co-author) in international professional journals, five chapters in books, six book reviews, nine IMF working papers, and numerous other working papers. In 2000, she was ranked 344th among the top 500 economists in the world based on quality and quantity of published papers during 1994–1998 using BAUWENS. She is a research fellow of the Economic Research Forum for the Arab Countries, Iran, and Turkey.

Hanaa Kheir-El-Din is an Egyptian national. She received a B.Com. (Economics) from Cairo University, Egypt and a PhD in Economics from the Massachusetts Institute of Technology (M.I.T), USA. She has been appointed since 1978 as a professor of Economics at the faculty of Economics and Political Science, Cairo University where she held the positions of director of the Center for Economic and Financial Research and Studies (1985–1991) and of the chairperson of the Department of Economics (1990–1996). She has been a member of the Board of the United Nations University (1994–1998). She has acted as a consultant to various national, regional, and international organizations including the Egyptian Ministries of Agriculture, Economy and Foreign Trade, Finance, International Cooperation and Planning, the UN/ESCWA and the World Bank. She is currently a member of the Egyptian Shura Council (Egyptian Senate) and the executive director and director of Research of the Egyptian Center of Economic Studies (ECES). Her areas of research include: trade policy, industrial policy, macro-economic modeling, growth and equity, poverty assessment, and targeting for poverty alleviation.

Imed Limam is a Tunisian national holding a PhD degree in Economics from the University of Southern California. He held the position of Economist and then Deputy Director General of the Arab Planning Institute (API) during the period 1992–2005. In September 2005, he joined the Arab Fund for Economic and Social Development as a senior economist. He has a special interest in development economics in general and applied economics, and econometric modeling in particular, areas where he has published regionally and internationally. He was the co-editor of the Journal of Development and Economic Policies since its foundation until 2005. He is also member of numerous international professional associations and advisory committees.

Samir Makdisi is a professor of Economics and the director of the Institute of Financial Economics, American University of Beirut and currently member of the board of the Global Development Network; formerly deputy president of the American University of Beirut (1993–1998), Chairman of the board of the Economics Research Forum for the Arab Countries, Iran, and Turkey (1993–2001) and Minister of Economy and Trade,

Republic of Lebanon (1992); has been a guest lecturer at major universities in the US, Europe and Asia; the author of several books and numerous scholarly papers in academic and professional journals; holds a PhD in Economics from Columbia University and is the recipient of the American University of Beirut Medal for distinguished service to the university.

Tarek Abdelfattah Moursi is a professor at the Department of Economics, Faculty of Economics and Political Science, Cairo University. His primary fields of interest include economic development, economy-wide planning and poverty targeting with specific emphasis on the Egyptian economy. Apart from serving with the Egyptian Ministry of Economy and Economic Cooperation and with the American University in Cairo, he has also provided consultation to various national institutions and international organizations including the Egyptian Ministries of Agriculture and of Planning, the (Egyptian) Cabinet Information and Decision Support Centre (IDSC), the Food and Agriculture Organization (FAO) and the Ford Foundation.

Sonia Naccache is lecturer of economics at the University of Tunisia. Her research focus is on the Political Economy of Trade and Financial Sector Reforms in developing countries.

Jeffrey B. Nugent is a professor of Economics at the University of Southern California. He earlier taught at UCLA, was a research fellow at Yale University, and served as economic affairs officer at the United Nations Economoic and Social Commission for Western Asia. He specializes in development economics, and is the author of over 150 journal articles and book chapters and the author or co-author of six books. While he has worked on agriculture, trade, income inequality, foreign investment and macroeconomics, in recent years, much of his work has focused on institutional issues. He is on the editorial boards of several journals, on the boards of directors of several associations and currently serves as president of the Middle East Economic Association.

Kıvılcım Metin Özcan received her PhD in Economics from Oxford University in 1992. She joined Bilkent University, where she is presently associate professor. She is currently working on sources of growth, on macroeconomic models of inflation, budget deficit, and financial markets. Her works have been published in journals including *Oxford Bulletin of Economics and Statistics, European Journal of Operational Research, Journal of Business and Economics Statistic, Empirical Economics, Applied Financial Economics, Canadian Journal of Development Studies, Multinational Finance Journal,* and *Substance Use and Misuse.* She has also published a book titled *The Analysis of Inflation: The Case of Turkey (CMB, 1995).*

Ümit Özlale received his PhD in Economics from Boston College in 2001. After working in Bilkent University as an assistant professor from 2001 to 2006, he recently joined TOBB Economics and Technology University as an associate professor. In addition, he is affiliated with Economic Policy Research Institute and has been serving as a project advisor for the Central Bank of the Republic of Turkey. He is currently working on optimal monetary policy and exchange rate dynamics. He has several publications in journals including Journal of Economic Dynamics and Control, Scottish Journal of Political Economy and Applied Economics.

Hashem Pesaran is a professor of Economics at the University of Cambridge and USC, and a professorial fellow of Trinity College, Cambridge. Previously he has been the head of the Economic Research Department of the Central Bank of Iran, the Under-Secretary of the Ministry of Education, Iran, professor of economics at University of California at Los Angeles, and a vice president at the Tudor Investment Corporation. Dr Pesaran is the founding editor of the *Journal of Applied Econometrics* and has served as a director on the Board of Acorn Investment Trust. He is honorary president of Cambridge Econometrics. He has held visiting positions at Harvard University, UCLA, University of Pennsylvania, and the University of Southern California. He has over 150 journal publications in the various areas of econometrics, empirical finance and macroeconomics, and the Iranian economy. He is the author of several books and edited volumes, and is a co-developer of the econometric software package *Microfit*, published by Oxford University Press. He is a fellow of the Econometric Society, a fellow of British Academy and a recipient of one of the Royal Economic Society Prizes for the best article in the *Economic Journal*.

Christopher A. Pissarides is professor of Economics, London School of Economics. He has written extensively on the economics of labor markets. His book *Equilibrium Unemployment Theory* is a standard reference in the economics of unemployment. He is a fellow of the British Academy and the Econometric Society and Council member, European Economic Association and the Econometric Society. He is a research fellow of CEPR and IZA, a non-national senior associate, Economic Research Forum for the Arab Countries, Iran and Turkey and a member of the Cyprus Monetary Policy Committee. In 2005 he received, with Dale Mortensen, the IZA Prize in Labor Economics.

Djavad Salehi-Isfahani graduated with a PhD in Economics from Harvard University in 1977. He is currently professor of Economics at Virginia Polytechnic Institute and State University in Blacksburg, Virginia. He has taught at the University of Pennsylvania, 1977–1984, and was visiting faculty at the University of Oxford (1991–1992). He is a research fellow and member of the board of trustees of the Economic Research Forum based in Cairo. His research has been in population economics, energy economics, and the economics of the Middle East. His current research is in human resources and the economics of the family in Iran and the Middle East. He has coauthored, with Jacques Cremer, the World Oil Market, 1991, and edited Labor and Human Capital in the Middle East, 2001. His articles have appeared in *Economic Journal, Journal of Development Economics, and Economic Development and Cultural Change*, among others.

Çağrı Sarıkaya, who was born in 1979, took his B.Sc. and M.Sc. degrees from the Economics Department of the Middle East Technical University in 2001 and 2004, respectively. He has been working in the Central Bank of the Republic of Turkey since 2001 and he is currently working as an assistant economist in the Structural Analysis Division of the Research and Monetary Policy Department. His major research interests are the real side of the economy, growth and macroeconometrics.

Marie Ange Véganzonès-Varoudakis is a research fellow at the Centre National de la Recherche Scientifique (*CNRS*), France, associated with the Centre d'Etudes et de Recherches sur le Développement International (*CERDI*). She has held assignments with the

World Bank, the Organization of Economic Cooperation and Development (*OECD*), the French Ministry of Economy, and the United Nations. She has published a book on Argentinean economic history, and several articles in academic journals on economic policy, economic growth, governance, foreign direct investment, exchange rate misalignment, productivity and technical efficiency, with focus on countries in the Middle East, Latin America, and South Asia.

Subject Index